Impact of New Technology on Next-Generation Leadership

Alka Agnihotri
Galgotias University, India

Renu Agarwal
UTS Business School, Australia

Alka Maurya
Amity University, Noida, India

Manasi Sinha
Galgotias University, India

Balamurugan Balusamy
Shiv Nadar Institution of Eminence, India

A volume in the Advances in Business Strategy and Competitive Advantage (ABSCA) Book Series

Published in the United States of America by
IGI Global
Business Science Reference (an imprint of IGI Global)
701 E. Chocolate Avenue
Hershey PA, USA 17033
Tel: 717-533-8845
Fax: 717-533-8661
E-mail: cust@igi-global.com
Web site: http://www.igi-global.com

Copyright © 2024 by IGI Global. All rights reserved. No part of this publication may be reproduced, stored or distributed in any form or by any means, electronic or mechanical, including photocopying, without written permission from the publisher. Product or company names used in this set are for identification purposes only. Inclusion of the names of the products or companies does not indicate a claim of ownership by IGI Global of the trademark or registered trademark.
                    Library of Congress Cataloging-in-Publication Data

CIP Pending

Impact of New Technology on Next-Generation Leadership
Alka Agnihotri, Renu Agarwal, Alka Maurya, Manasi Sinha, Balamurugan Balusamy
2024 Business Science Reference

ISBN: 979-8-3693-1946-8
eISBN: 979-8-3693-1947-5

This book is published in the IGI Global book series Advances in Business Strategy and Competitive Advantage (ABSCA) (ISSN: 2327-3429; eISSN: 2327-3437)

British Cataloguing in Publication Data
A Cataloguing in Publication record for this book is available from the British Library.

All work contributed to this book is new, previously-unpublished material. The views expressed in this book are those of the authors, but not necessarily of the publisher.

For electronic access to this publication, please contact: eresources@igi-global.com.

Advances in Business Strategy and Competitive Advantage (ABSCA) Book Series

Patricia Ordóñez de Pablos
Universidad de Oviedo, Spain

ISSN:2327-3429
EISSN:2327-3437

Mission

Business entities are constantly seeking new ways through which to gain advantage over their competitors and strengthen their position within the business environment. With competition at an all-time high due to technological advancements allowing for competition on a global scale, firms continue to seek new ways through which to improve and strengthen their business processes, procedures, and profitability.

The **Advances in Business Strategy and Competitive Advantage (ABSCA) Book Series** is a timely series responding to the high demand for state-of-the-art research on how business strategies are created, implemented and re-designed to meet the demands of globalized competitive markets. With a focus on local and global challenges, business opportunities and the needs of society, the **ABSCA** encourages scientific discourse on doing business and managing information technologies for the creation of sustainable competitive advantage.

Coverage

- Strategic Management
- Outsourcing
- Entrepreneurship & Innovation
- Competitive Strategy
- Economies of Scale
- Small and Medium Enterprises
- Balanced Scorecard
- Adaptive Enterprise
- Globalization
- Joint Ventures

IGI Global is currently accepting manuscripts for publication within this series. To submit a proposal for a volume in this series, please contact our Acquisition Editors at Acquisitions@igi-global.com or visit: http://www.igi-global.com/publish/.

The Advances in Business Strategy and Competitive Advantage (ABSCA) Book Series (ISSN 2327-3429) is published by IGI Global, 701 E. Chocolate Avenue, Hershey, PA 17033-1240, USA, www.igi-global.com. This series is composed of titles available for purchase individually; each title is edited to be contextually exclusive from any other title within the series. For pricing and ordering information please visit http://www.igi-global.com/book-series/advances-business-strategy-competitive-advantage/73672. Postmaster: Send all address changes to above address. Copyright © 2024 IGI Global. All rights, including translation in other languages reserved by the publisher. No part of this series may be reproduced or used in any form or by any means – graphics, electronic, or mechanical, including photocopying, recording, taping, or information and retrieval systems – without written permission from the publisher, except for non commercial, educational use, including classroom teaching purposes. The views expressed in this series are those of the authors, but not necessarily of IGI Global.

Titles in this Series

For a list of additional titles in this series, please visit: http://www.igi-global.com/book-series/advances-business-strategy-competitive-advantage/73672

Economics and Environmental Responsibility in the Global Beverage Industry
Cristina Raluca Gh. Popescu (University of Bucharest, Romania & The Bucharest University of Economic Studies, Romania) Javier Martínez-Falcó (University of Alicante, Spain & University of Stellenbosch, South Africa) Bartolomé Marco-Lajara (University of Alicante, Spain) Eduardo Sánchez-García (University of Alicante, Spain) and Luis A. Millán-Tudela (University of Alicante, Spain)
Business Science Reference • copyright 2024 • 439pp • H/C (ISBN: 9798369321492) • US $285.00 (our price)

Building Organizational Resilience With Neuroleadership
Shefali Saluja (Chitkara Business School, Chitkara University, India) Jyoti Kukreja (Jagannath International Management School, India) and Sandhir Sharma (Chitkara Business School, Chitkara University, India)
Business Science Reference • copyright 2024 • 352pp • H/C (ISBN: 9798369317853) • US $275.00 (our price)

Business Continuity Management and Resilience Theories, Models, and Processes
José Carlos Rouco (Universidade Lusófona, Portugal) and Paula Cristina Nunes Figueiredo (Universidade Lusófona, Portugal)
Business Science Reference • copyright 2024 • 333pp • H/C (ISBN: 9798369316580) • US $290.00 (our price)

Applying Business Intelligence and Innovation to Entrepreneurship
Kannapat Kankaew (International College, Burapha University, Thailand) Parinya Nakpathom (International College, Burapha University, Thailand) Alhuda Chnitpphattana (International College, Burapha University, Thailand) Krittipat Pitchayadejanant (International College, Burapha University, Thailand) and Siwaporn Kunnapapdeelert (Faculty of Logistics and Transportation Management, Panyapiwat Institute of Management, Thailand)
Business Science Reference • copyright 2024 • 346pp • H/C (ISBN: 9798369318461) • US $275.00 (our price)

Fostering Innovation in Venture Capital and Startup Ecosystems
Renuka Sharma (Chitkara Business School, Chitkara University, Punjab, India) Kiran Mehta (Chitkara Business School, Chitkara University, Punjab, India) and Poshan Yu (Soochow University, China & Australian Studies Centre, Shanghai University, China)
Business Science Reference • copyright 2024 • 430pp • H/C (ISBN: 9798369313268) • US $270.00 (our price)

Entrepreneurship and Creativity in the Metaverse
Shivani Inder (Chitkara Business School, Chitkara University, India) Byoung-chul Min (Chung-Ang University, South Korea) and Sandhir Sharma (Chitkara Business School, Chitkara University, India)
Business Science Reference • copyright 2024 • 301pp • H/C (ISBN: 9798369317341) • US $275.00 (our price)

701 East Chocolate Avenue, Hershey, PA 17033, USA
Tel: 717-533-8845 x100 • Fax: 717-533-8661
E-Mail: cust@igi-global.com • www.igi-global.com

Table of Contents

Preface xiv

Chapter 1
Emerging Technology: Present and Future Generation Leadership 1
    Tarana Afrin Chandel, Integral University, India

Chapter 2
Transformative Strategies: Shaping Digital Culture and Employee Attitudes Towards Digital
Transformation 29
    Saurabh Sugha, Birla Institute of Technology and Science, Pilani, India
    Mohammad Faraz Naim, Birla Institute of Technology and Science, Pilani, India
    JiaLal Koundal, Suresh Gyan Vihar University, India

Chapter 3
Navigating Crisis Situations: The Role of Digital Resilience in Effective Leadership and
Organizational Continuity 51
    Prachee Mittal Tandon, GNIT College of Management, India

Chapter 4
Leadership and Technology Integration in India: A Systematic Literature Review 76
    K. H. Pavitra, Galgotias University, India
    Alka Agnihotri, Galgotias University, India
    Bindu Tiwari, Kings College, Nepal

Chapter 5
Understanding the Role of Digital Leadership on the Digital Transformation in the Time of
COVID-19 and Beyond 91
    Mübeyyen Tepe Küçükoğlu, Trakya University, Turkey

Chapter 6
Masterminds and Machines: Harnessing AI in Strategic Leadership 107
    Geetha Manoharan, SR University, India
    Sunitha Purushottam Ashtikar, SR University, India
    C. V. Guru Rao, SR University, India
    Sundarapandiyan Natarajan, Adithya Institute of Technology, India
    M. Nivedha, Robert Gordon University, UK

Chapter 7
Rise of Clone-Leadership in the Shadow of Artificial Intelligence 120
    Amanpreet Singh Chopra, Chitkara Business School, Chitkara University, Punjab, India
    Sridhar Manohar, Chitkara Business School, Chitkara University, Punjab, India

Chapter 8
AI-Enhanced Leadership Decision Support System Using ChatGPT for Ethical Learning 137
    Balamurugan M., Dayananda Sagar College of Engineering, India
    Raghu N., Jain University, India
    Dayananda L. N., Jyothy Institute of Technology, India
    Sarat Kumar Sahoo, Parala Maharaja Engineering College, India
    Smitha Ankanahalli Shankaregowda, BGS Institute of Technology, India
    Niranjan Kannanugo, Powerschool, India
    Deepthi M., College of Engineering, University of Visveshwaraya, India
    Vinod Kumar M., Don Basco College, India

Chapter 9
AR/VR and Robotics and Their Role in Leadership 162
    Preethi D., Vel Tech Rangarajan Dr. Sagunthala R&D Institute of Science and Technology, India
    Valarmathi R. S., Vel Tech Rangarajan Dr. Sagunthala R&D Institute of Science and Technology, India
    Aanandha Saravanan K., Vel Tech Rangarajan Dr. Sagunthala R&D Institute of Science and Technology, India

Chapter 10
Blockchain and Its Role in Leadership 179
    Nivodhini M. K., KSR College of Engineering, India
    Vadivel S., KSR College of Engineering, India
    Vasuki P., KSR College of Engineering, India
    Banupriya S., KSR College of Engineering, India

Chapter 11
Blockchain as a Service: Empowering Enterprise HRM Leadership for the Future 206
    Moushami Panda, GIET University, India
    Smruti Rekha Sahoo, GIET University, India
    Saumendra Das, GIET University, India
    Jyotikanta Panda, GIET University, India
    Mariofanna Milanova, University of Arkansas, USA

Chapter 12
A Bibliographic Study on Challenges and Management Issues in Leadership and Technology
Integration 230
    Nitish Kumar Minz, K.R. Mangalam University, India
    Richa Nangia, Sushant University, India
    Alka Agnihotri, Galgotias University, India

Chapter 13
Megatrends in Leadership and Technology Across Industries 250
    Vaishnavi Gadi, SVKM'S NMIMS, Mumbai, India
    Pathik Govani, SVKM's NMIMS, Mumbai, India

Chapter 14
Future Mega Trends in Leadership and Technology 275
    Poornima Tyagi, Noida Institute of Engineering and Technology, India
    Divya Sahu, Noida Institute of Engineering and Technology, India
    Renuka Sharma, SGT University, India

Compilation of References 299

About the Contributors 329

Index 335

Detailed Table of Contents

Preface xiv

Chapter 1
Emerging Technology: Present and Future Generation Leadership 1
    Tarana Afrin Chandel, Integral University, India

COVID-19 had a great impact on our lives and work. These impacts have forced us to explore new innovations and technologies for better social life and economic developments. Adaption of technologies are increasing exponentially thus changing the life of people towards thinking, learning, education, communication, reshaping the social and economic developments. We can clearly say that technology developments and social development are co-related to each other and influence each other. Advancement and utility of technologies are having impact on human beings, thus showing progress for future generation. Diverse and challenging workforce should be incorporated with latest technologies to become the future leader. In this chapter, the author discusses the evolutional changes in organizational approach, leading towards training, development and leadership, impact of technologies in different sectors towards leadership, achievements and participation of African Union in G20 turning to G21, marking a bench mark, making India a current leader at International level.

Chapter 2
Transformative Strategies: Shaping Digital Culture and Employee Attitudes Towards Digital Transformation.. 29
    Saurabh Sugha, Birla Institute of Technology and Science, Pilani, India
    Mohammad Faraz Naim, Birla Institute of Technology and Science, Pilani, India
    JiaLal Koundal, Suresh Gyan Vihar University, India

The purpose of this chapter is to identify the relationship between digital transformation leadership in shaping digital culture and employee attitude and contrasting strategical approach in startups and mature organizations. Based on a review of extant literature, this study develops a theoretical rationale behind developing a conceptual framework to organizations specific digital transformation strategies. There is a different strategical approach that a digital transformation leadership needs to address while implementing any technological initiatives as organizational ability to rapidly adapt to the new innovative transformed solution is very critical in shaping company growth trajectory. A conceptual framework of digital transformation through digital culture and employee attitude requires the empirical validation of the suggested conceptual framework. Organizations should focus on enhancing digital skills of employees and digital culture to foster adoption of new technologies.

Chapter 3
Navigating Crisis Situations: The Role of Digital Resilience in Effective Leadership and
Organizational Continuity 51
 Prachee Mittal Tandon, GNIT College of Management, India

Navigating modern crises requires digital resilience, a fusion of technology, leadership, and adaptability. This chapter explores its pivotal role, emphasizing robust tech infrastructure, crisis communication, cyber security, and leadership skills. Resilient leadership with ethical considerations and employee well-being are crucial. Measurable metrics assess digital resilience effectiveness, and strategies like predictive analytics and AI enhance crisis preparation. Globalization challenges demand nuanced approaches, and leaders drive cultural shifts toward adaptability. Social media's role in crisis communication is analyzed, and long-term planning ensures sustainable digital resilience. Embracing these principles ensures organizational survival, growth, and adaptability in the digital age.

Chapter 4
Leadership and Technology Integration in India: A Systematic Literature Review 76
 K. H. Pavitra, Galgotias University, India
 Alka Agnihotri, Galgotias University, India
 Bindu Tiwari, Kings College, Nepal

Leadership has a critical role to play in the adoption of the transformational technology of artificial intelligence (AI). As India leads the AI revolution, this study aims to understand the role of leadership in AI adoption, the necessary competencies required for leaders to be successful in the current era of AI, and the most frequently occurring themes in AI and leadership in India, in the last decade. A systematic literature review (SLR) was conducted in Scopus, on studies published in a period of ten years from 2013 to 2023. Findings show that the role of leadership in AI adoption is of paramount importance. The theories identified by researchers to infer different facets of AI and leadership research are elaborated. The mental and emotional competencies needed for leaders are emphasized for successfully navigating the AI era. Practical implications for leaders in organizations are discussed. This is the first study to review research conducted between 2013 and 2023 which links leadership and AI in Indian organizations.

Chapter 5
Understanding the Role of Digital Leadership on the Digital Transformation in the Time of
COVID-19 and Beyond 91
 Mübeyyen Tepe Küçükoğlu, Trakya University, Turkey

The importance of strong DL skills comes to the front in the rapid adaptation of organizations. DL plays the role of a critical success factor on the way to the strategic visions that organizations want to achieve from their current situation. For this reason, the scope of DL should be understood correctly by organizations and employees. In this direction, this study aims to present a conceptual structure and at the same time exploratory results by addressing the concept of DL with all its dimensions. This study consists of two parts. The first part has a conceptual structure that examines the definition of DL, and emphasizes the basic skills and characteristics that a digital leader should have. In the second part, studies carried out during and after the COVID-19 outbreak will be examined, with the intention of guiding both organizations and academics.

Chapter 6
Masterminds and Machines: Harnessing AI in Strategic Leadership 107
    Geetha Manoharan, SR University, India
    Sunitha Purushottam Ashtikar, SR University, India
    C. V. Guru Rao, SR University, India
    Sundarapandiyan Natarajan, Adithya Institute of Technology, India
    M. Nivedha, Robert Gordon University, UK

Artificial intelligence is a vital tool for any organization and is quickly growing in all business streams. AI is leading commercial decision-making in all areas. Digital technology has created free time for many chores, but now AI determines commercial variables. Advancements have caused exponential growth in almost every firm. Businesses that conduct repeated operations require a long time to accomplish other jobs, yet labor hours or other factors cannot be avoided. Business growth is driven by predictive analytics, natural language processing, etc. AI-based predictive analytics employs data mining, machine learning, and statistical algorithms to examine previous data to forecast future trends. The NLP may use different algorithms to identify problem statement patterns and concerns. Proactive problem-solving is its key attribute. Businesses that employ AI solutions will always have higher productivity in several industries. This chapter will teach how AI can improve company leadership.

Chapter 7
Rise of Clone-Leadership in the Shadow of Artificial Intelligence 120
    Amanpreet Singh Chopra, Chitkara Business School, Chitkara University, Punjab, India
    Sridhar Manohar, Chitkara Business School, Chitkara University, Punjab, India

AI could take different pathways for development. This chapter emphasises the issues regarding strategic approach that the next generation business leaders need to adopt to coexist with these technological transformations. These development pathways could be the ones where the dependency on an AI-driven support system drains out the leadership abilities, intellect, and creativity of future leaders, resulting in the emergence of 'Clone Leadership'. Or, will they lead to a best-case scenario in which AI is regulated and emerge as a stakeholder in the business ecosystem, resulting in growth and prosperity? The chapter deliberates upon the decision-making approach that business leaders would be adopting in AI dominated business environment, especially with respect to governance, morality, and ethical behavior. Finally, the chapter analyzes the efforts being made to develop ethical, transparent, and accountable principles and guidelines to manage responsible AI.

Chapter 8
AI-Enhanced Leadership Decision Support System Using ChatGPT for Ethical Learning 137
    Balamurugan M., Dayananda Sagar College of Engineering, India
    Raghu N., Jain University, India
    Dayananda L. N., Jyothy Institute of Technology, India
    Sarat Kumar Sahoo, Parala Maharaja Engineering College, India
    Smitha Ankanahalli Shankaregowda, BGS Institute of Technology, India
    Niranjan Kannanugo, Powerschool, India
    Deepthi M., College of Engineering, University of Visveshwaraya, India
    Vinod Kumar M., Don Basco College, India

Open AI's ChatGPT-3—"Chat Generative Pre-Trained Transformer"—has been increasingly popular among academic institutions. Practitioners that attempt to determine the sincerity of student work have highlighted worries about the employment of an AI-driven chatbot. The educators can use artificial intelligence tools like ChatGPT to help youngsters who already have admirable qualities thrive in the classroom, according to the proposed approach. These students are adept at communicating with the ChatGPT application and have the knowledge and abilities to use it positively. Genuine evaluation and character development are aided by leadership as a basic strategy and facilitator. Using ChatGPT and other AI techniques, educators can leverage this to build engaging learning environments for their hard-working moral fiber-developing students. The importance of establishing stronger character, encouraging more good psychological outcomes like flow states, helping students meet their psychological needs, and creating opportunities for them to receive support as they adjust and gain self-assurance are explored.

Chapter 9
AR/VR and Robotics and Their Role in Leadership.. 162
    Preethi D., Vel Tech Rangarajan Dr. Sagunthala R&D Institute of Science and Technology, India
    Valarmathi R. S., Vel Tech Rangarajan Dr. Sagunthala R&D Institute of Science and Technology, India
    Aanandha Saravanan K., Vel Tech Rangarajan Dr. Sagunthala R&D Institute of Science and Technology, India

Augmented reality (AR) and virtual reality (VR) are immersive technologies that can significantly impact leadership in various ways. AR and VR can create realistic simulations for leadership training programs such as decision-making, communication, conflict resolution, and other leadership skills in immersive virtual environments. AR can overlay real-time data and analytics onto physical spaces, helping leaders make informed decisions. VR can provide virtual boardrooms or data environments for in-depth analysis and planning. Leaders can use VR to simulate different scenarios and test the impact of various decisions, allowing them to develop better strategies and contingency plans.

Chapter 10
Blockchain and Its Role in Leadership 179
    Nivodhini M. K., KSR College of Engineering, India
    Vadivel S., KSR College of Engineering, India
    Vasuki P., KSR College of Engineering, India
    Banupriya S., KSR College of Engineering, India

Blockchain technology revolutionizes leadership through transparency, accountability, and decentralization. By providing an immutable ledger, it enhances transparency, fostering trust. Its decentralized nature ensures accountability, empowering individuals and challenging traditional hierarchies. Secure data management safeguards sensitive information. Automation streamlines processes, fostering collaboration. Tokenization creates incentive mechanisms. Overall, blockchain empowers leaders to navigate modern complexities with transparent, accountable, and decentralized approaches.

Chapter 11
Blockchain as a Service: Empowering Enterprise HRM Leadership for the Future 206
    Moushami Panda, GIET University, India
    Smruti Rekha Sahoo, GIET University, India
    Saumendra Das, GIET University, India
    Jyotikanta Panda, GIET University, India
    Mariofanna Milanova, University of Arkansas, USA

As organizations continue in the evolving landscape of the digital, leaders of human resource management (HRM) face unprecedented challenges and opportunities. Blockchain technology has emerged as a disruptive force, offering innovative solutions to longstanding HRM issues. This explores the potential of blockchain as a service (BaaS) in transforming enterprise HRM practices, enhancing security, efficiency, and transparency while paving the way for future leaders where HRM in enterprises will be empowering. Blockchain technology, renowned for its decentralized, secure, and transparent nature, offers a scalable, cost-effective way for organizations to harness the power of blockchain without the complexities of building and maintaining their blockchain infrastructure. This study explores the transformative potential and impact of blockchain as a service (BaaS) on HRM practices within enterprises with adaptive and proven case studies by investigating the advantages, challenges, and prospects of implementing BaaS solutions to harness and empower enterprise HRM leaders for the future.

Chapter 12
A Bibliographic Study on Challenges and Management Issues in Leadership and Technology Integration.. 230
    Nitish Kumar Minz, K.R. Mangalam University, India
    Richa Nangia, Sushant University, India
    Alka Agnihotri, Galgotias University, India

This comprehensive bibliometric research delves into global interdisciplinary studies, exploring leadership, technology integration, finance, and sustainability. Investigating diverse topics, including total quality management challenges in Malaysian SMEs, geopolitical influences on eService adoption, and leadership dynamics in culturally diverse tech projects, the narrative extends to broader domains such as financial literacy, UK construction post COVID-19, and sustainable practices in contaminated campus areas. The review evaluates senior IT leadership's impact, virtual clinic lessons post COVID-19, global business knowledge management challenges, and safety data ecosystems using analytics, synthesizing insights from 54 papers. Concluding with a bibliometric analysis, the research provides a panoramic view of evolving research trends from 1989 to 2023, enhancing understanding across disciplines.

Chapter 13
Megatrends in Leadership and Technology Across Industries 250
    Vaishnavi Gadi, SVKM'S NMIMS, Mumbai, India
    Pathik Govani, SVKM's NMIMS, Mumbai, India

The chapter explores the concept of megatrends in leadership and technology, emphasizing their growing importance in shaping organizations. It explores the interconnectedness of leadership styles and technological advancements, integrating change management to highlight the need to adapt to these megatrends for sustained success. It analyzes the transformative shifts in leadership at various organizational levels, from the C-suite executives to operational and management roles, including empathetic, purpose-driven, and collaborative leadership, and the rise of data-driven decision-making, agile leadership, and adaptability in various functions such as sales and marketing, human resources, operations and finance. It also discusses the impact of technological advancements across sectors like FMCG, pharma, manufacturing, IT, and Edtech, examining the impact of AI, ML, blockchain technology, IoT, automation, and virtual reality applications. Challenges related to data privacy and other technological innovations are also highlighted.

Chapter 14
Future Mega Trends in Leadership and Technology 275
    Poornima Tyagi, Noida Institute of Engineering and Technology, India
    Divya Sahu, Noida Institute of Engineering and Technology, India
    Renuka Sharma, SGT University, India

In the past decade, leadership has evolved significantly due to the integration of machine learning and AI in the business environment. These advancements have enabled leaders to make well-informed decisions based on real-time data, enhancing their collaborative, innovative, and efficient capabilities. The strategic integration of these technologies has revolutionized leadership decision-making, enabling data-driven decisions, improved security, and transparency. Next-generation leadership, focusing on managing change and demonstrating resilience, is crucial for the 21st century leadership landscape. Agile leaders can quickly adapt to novel circumstances, while self-aware leaders can identify strengths and limitations.

Compilation of References 299

About the Contributors 329

Index 335

Preface

In today's rapidly evolving technological landscape, the intersection of innovation and leadership has become a focal point for scholars and practitioners alike. The fast changing landscape of leadership shows a new dynamic data and technology driven perspective, we, the editors of the book *Impact of New Technology on Next-Generation Leadership*, contemplated on bringing out the deep insights in this context. It is our utmost delight to present this comprehensive reference book that delves into analysis, meta analysis, synthesis and antithesis of interaction of technology and leadership. This book is a step forward in the direction towards uncovering the latest in the field of technology and its application for leadership. As emerging technologies such as robots, artificial intelligence, the Internet of Things, and machine learning continue to advance at an exponential pace, the traditional paradigms of leadership are being challenged like never before.

The *Impact of New Technology on Next-Generation Leadership*, edited by Alka Agnihotri, Renu Agarwal, Alka Maurya, Manasi Sinha, and Balamurugan Balusamy, delves into this transformative shift in leadership dynamics. This edited reference book explores how these technological advancements are reshaping the way leaders connect, automate, and augment various aspects of organizational life.

This book unfolds informative and insightful experience for readers. It retains the essence of the leadership and technology interface. Readers will gain profound insights into the opportunities and challenges associated with integrating technology into leadership. The read has been planned to be made more interesting by incorporating real-world case studies, cutting-edge research findings, and practical recommendations.

The book aims not only to equip the readers with the knowledge, tools and techniques required to understand the new scenarios of leadership and technology but also fosters ethical discussions, presents real-world case studies and examples. It promotes interdisciplinary perspectives and meta analysis. The book also aims to foster interdisciplinary collaboration among different stakeholders. Through this book we ultimately aspire to contribute not only to better understanding of present and future leadership landscape and the opportunities and the challenges therein but also to the brighter future of leadership and technology interface.

At its core, this book underscores the imperative for leaders to embrace novel technological tools in order to anticipate shifts in the business environment, foster organizational agility, and navigate the complexities of the digital age. Through insightful analyses and practical recommendations, it equips next-generation managers and leaders with the knowledge and skills needed to thrive amidst rapid technological disruption.

Incorporating insights from AI, machine learning, augmented reality, virtual reality, blockchain technology, and more, this monograph provides a comprehensive examination of the evolving relationship

Preface

between technology and leadership. From strategic trends to practical applications, it offers a roadmap for leaders to navigate the uncertain terrain of the future workplace.

Moreover, this book transcends academia, offering valuable insights for practitioners across various industries. Through in-depth case studies and theoretical frameworks, it bridges the gap between theory and practice, catering to a diverse audience ranging from management students to seasoned professionals.

As the pace of technological innovation shows no signs of slowing down, the need for continuous learning and adaptation has never been more pressing. The Impact of New Technology on Next-Generation Leadership serves as a timely resource for leaders seeking to stay ahead of the curve and harness the full potential of emerging technologies.

We, the editors, are confident that this book will serve as a valuable guide for navigating the complexities of modern leadership in an increasingly digital world. We extend our gratitude to the contributing authors. We sincerely hope that the book proves to be an invaluable resource for all students, researchers, teachers and professionals who seek to understand and practice leadership with technical edge and they find it both informative and inspiring.

ORGANIZATION OF THE BOOK

Chapter 1: "Emerging Technology Present and Future Generation Leadership" by Tarana Chandel

In the wake of the COVID-19 pandemic, the world has witnessed a profound impact on both society and work. Tarana Chandel delves into this phenomenon, highlighting the rapid adoption of innovative technologies as a response to these changes. This chapter explores the intricate relationship between technological advancements and social development, emphasizing the need for future leaders to adeptly navigate this evolving landscape. From organizational transformations to global leadership benchmarks, Chandel offers a comprehensive analysis of the intersection between technology and leadership.

Chapter 2: "Transformative Strategies: Shaping Digital Culture and Employee Attitudes Towards Digital Transformation" by Saurabh Sugha, Mohammad Faraz Naim, JiaLal Koundal

Sugha, Naim, and Koundal delve into the transformative power of digital transformation leadership, focusing on its influence on organizational culture and employee attitudes. Through a review of existing literature, they develop a conceptual framework for organizations to strategically approach digital transformation initiatives. This chapter emphasizes the critical role of digital skills and culture in driving technological adoption within organizations, offering insights for both startups and mature enterprises.

Chapter 3: "Navigating Crisis Situations: The Role of Digital Resilience in Effective Leadership and Organizational Continuity" by Prachee Mittal Tandon

Prachee Tandon explores the concept of digital resilience in navigating modern crises, highlighting its fusion of technology, leadership, and adaptability. From robust tech infrastructure to crisis communication strategies, Tandon emphasizes the importance of resilient leadership amidst globalization challenges. This chapter provides actionable strategies for leaders to ensure organizational survival and growth in the face of digital disruptions.

Chapter 4: "Leadership and Technology Integration in India: A Systematic Literature Review" by K. H. Pavitra, Alka Agnihotri, Bindu Tiwari

Pavitra, Agnihotri, and Tiwari delve into the evolving role of leadership in the adoption of transformative technologies, particularly artificial intelligence (AI), in India. Through a systematic literature review, they uncover the critical competencies required for leaders to navigate the AI era successfully. This chapter offers practical implications for leaders in Indian organizations, shedding light on the intersection of leadership and AI research in the Indian context.

Chapter 5: "Understanding the Role of Digital Leadership on the Digital Transformation in the Time of COVID-19 and Beyond" by Mübeyyen Tepe Küçükoğlu

Küçükoğlu examines the significance of digital leadership in facilitating organizational adaptation amidst the COVID-19 pandemic and beyond. This chapter presents a conceptual framework for understanding digital leadership, emphasizing the essential skills and characteristics required for digital leaders. Through exploratory results, Küçükoğlu provides guidance for organizations and academics in navigating the digital landscape effectively.

Chapter 6: "Masterminds and Machines: Harnessing AI in Strategic Leadership" by Geetha Manoharan, Sunitha Ashtikar, C. V. Guru Rao, Sundarapandiyan Natarajan, M. Nivedha

Geetha Manoharan and colleagues delve into the transformative potential of Artificial Intelligence (AI) in strategic leadership. The chapter emphasizes how AI has become indispensable across various business domains, driving commercial decision-making and operational efficiencies. Through predictive analytics and natural language processing, AI enables proactive problem-solving and enhances productivity. By leveraging AI-based solutions, organizations can gain a competitive edge and improve leadership decision-making processes.

Chapter 7: "Rise of Clone-Leadership in the Shadow of Artificial Intelligence" by Amanpreet Chopra, Sridhar Manohar

Amanpreet Chopra and Sridhar Manohar explore the potential pathways of development for Artificial Intelligence (AI) and its implications for future business leaders. This chapter delves into the concept of "Clone Leadership," where AI-driven support systems may overshadow human leadership abilities. The authors analyze decision-making approaches in AI-dominated environments, emphasizing the need for ethical and accountable leadership practices. Through this exploration, the chapter aims to guide leaders in navigating the complexities of AI integration responsibly.

Preface

Chapter 8: "AI-Enhanced Leadership Decision Support System Using ChatGPT for Ethical Learning" by Balamurugan M., Raghu N., Dayananda L. N., Sarat Sahoo, Smitha Ankanahalli Shankaregowda, Niranjan Kannanugo, Deepthi M., Vinod Kumar M.

Balamurugan M and colleagues introduce an innovative approach to leadership development using OpenAI's ChatGPT-3. This chapter highlights the potential of AI-driven chatbots in facilitating ethical learning and character development among students. By leveraging AI tools like ChatGPT, educators can create engaging learning environments and foster moral fiber development in students. The chapter underscores the importance of integrating AI techniques in education to promote genuine evaluation and character building.

Chapter 9: "AR/VR and Robotics and Their Role in Leadership" by Preethi D., Valarmathi R. S., Aanandha Saravanan K.

Preethi D and colleagues explore the transformative impact of Augmented Reality (AR), Virtual Reality (VR), and Robotics on leadership development. This chapter highlights how immersive technologies can enhance leadership training programs, decision-making processes, and communication skills. By overlaying real-time data and creating virtual environments, AR and VR empower leaders to make informed decisions and simulate various scenarios. The authors emphasize the potential of these technologies to revolutionize leadership practices across industries.

Chapter 10: "Blockchain and Its Role in Leadership," by Nivodhini M. K., Vadivel S., Vasuki P., Banupriya S.

Nivodhini M K, Vadivel S, Vasuki P and Banupriya S delve into the transformative potential of blockchain technology in leadership. This chapter explores how blockchain enhances transparency, accountability, and decentralization, revolutionizing traditional leadership approaches. By providing an immutable ledger and streamlining processes through automation, blockchain empowers leaders to navigate modern complexities effectively. The chapter emphasizes the role of blockchain in fostering trust, enhancing data management, and creating incentive mechanisms, ultimately empowering leaders to drive organizational success.

Chapter 11: "Blockchain as a Service Empowering Enterprise HRM Leadership for the Future" by Moushami Panda, Smruti Sahoo, Saumendra Das, Jyotikanta Panda, Mariofanna Milanova

Moushami Panda and colleagues examine the potential of Blockchain as a Service (BaaS) in transforming enterprise Human Resource Management (HRM) practices. This chapter highlights how blockchain technology offers innovative solutions to longstanding HRM challenges, including security, efficiency, and transparency. By leveraging BaaS solutions, organizations can empower HRM leaders to adapt to the evolving digital landscape and drive future success. Through adaptive case studies and insights, the chapter provides a comprehensive overview of the transformative impact of blockchain on HRM leadership.

Chapter 12: "A Bibliographic Study on Challenges and Management Issues in Leadership and Technology Integration" by Nitish Minz, Richa Nangia, Alka Agnihotri

Nitish Minz, Richa Nangia and Alka Agnihotri conduct a bibliometric research study exploring global interdisciplinary studies on leadership and technology integration. This chapter provides insights into diverse topics, including Total Quality Management challenges, geopolitical influences, and leadership dynamics in culturally diverse contexts. By synthesizing insights from 54 papers, the authors offer a panoramic view of evolving research trends from 1989 to 2023. The chapter aims to enhance understanding across disciplines and inform future research directions in leadership and technology integration.

Chapter 13: "Megatrends in Leadership and Technology Across Industries" by Vaishnavi Gadi, Pathik Govani

Vaishnavi Gadi and Pathik Govani explore the concept of megatrends in leadership and technology, emphasizing their growing importance in shaping organizations. This chapter analyzes transformative shifts in leadership styles and technological advancements across various sectors, including FMCG, pharma, manufacturing, IT, and Edtech. By examining the impact of AI, ML, blockchain, and automation, the authors provide insights into the challenges and opportunities faced by leaders in adapting to these megatrends for sustained success.

Chapter 14: "Future Mega Trends in Leadership and Technology" by Poornima Tyagi, Divya Sahu, Renuka Sharma

Poornima Tyagi, Divya Sahu and Renuka Sharma explore the future mega trends in leadership and technology, focusing on the evolving role of machine learning and AI in the business environment. This chapter highlights how advancements in AI have enabled leaders to make data-driven decisions and enhance organizational efficiency. By emphasizing the importance of next-generation leadership qualities such as agility and resilience, the authors offer insights into navigating the complexities of the 21st-century leadership landscape. Through a strategic integration of technology, leaders can drive innovation and adaptability, ensuring organizational success in the digital era.

As editors, we believe that each chapter in this edited reference book offers valuable insights into the evolving relationship between technology and leadership. From exploring the impact of emerging technologies on future leadership paradigms to examining the role of blockchain and AI in transforming organizational practices, this book provides a comprehensive overview of the challenges and opportunities faced by leaders in the digital age. We extend our gratitude to all the contributing authors for their scholarly contributions and hope that readers will find this book informative and inspiring.

IN CONCLUSION

As editors of this edited reference book, we have embarked on a journey to explore the dynamic interplay between technology and leadership in the modern era. Through the diverse perspectives

Preface

presented in each chapter, we have witnessed the transformative power of emerging technologies such as artificial intelligence, blockchain, augmented reality, and virtual reality on leadership practices across industries.

From understanding the role of digital resilience in navigating crises to harnessing the potential of AI in strategic decision-making, each chapter offers valuable insights and practical recommendations for leaders striving to thrive in an increasingly digital world. We have delved into topics ranging from digital culture and employee attitudes to the ethical implications of AI-driven leadership, providing readers with a holistic understanding of the challenges and opportunities that lie ahead.

As we conclude this preface, we are reminded of the importance of continuous learning and adaptation in the face of technological disruption. The journey towards effective leadership in the digital age is ongoing, and this book serves as a beacon of knowledge and inspiration for leaders and scholars alike. We hope that readers will find this collection of chapters informative, thought-provoking, and ultimately, empowering as they navigate the complexities of leadership in the 21st century.

With sincere appreciation to all the contributing authors for their scholarly contributions and to our readers for their interest in exploring the intersection of technology and leadership.

Alka Agnihotri
Galgotias University, India

Renu Agarwal
UTS Business School, Australia

Alka Maurya
Amity University, Noida, India

Manasi Sinha
Galgotias University, India

Balamurugan Balusamy
Shiv Nadar Institution of Eminence, India

Chapter 1
Emerging Technology:
Present and Future Generation Leadership

Tarana Afrin Chandel
https://orcid.org/0000-0002-8605-6018
Integral University, India

ABSTRACT

COVID-19 had a great impact on our lives and work. These impacts have forced us to explore new innovations and technologies for better social life and economic developments. Adaption of technologies are increasing exponentially thus changing the life of people towards thinking, learning, education, communication, reshaping the social and economic developments. We can clearly say that technology developments and social development are co-related to each other and influence each other. Advancement and utility of technologies are having impact on human beings, thus showing progress for future generation. Diverse and challenging workforce should be incorporated with latest technologies to become the future leader. In this chapter, the author discusses the evolutional changes in organizational approach, leading towards training, development and leadership, impact of technologies in different sectors towards leadership, achievements and participation of African Union in G20 turning to G21, marking a bench mark, making India a current leader at International level.

1. INTRODUCTION

In current scenario, the educational professionals are adapting the emerging technologies as the predominant factor in training and development (Lonnie Morris,2017; Ladyshewsky, R, 2008). Previously researches were restricted to integration of innovation towards training and developments. However, importance was given in the field of business i.e. sales/marketing and technology (Webber, C. F., 2003). Training and developments has always been a driving source towards organizational growth (Boyce, L. A., 2008; Cercone, K. (2008); Ladyshewsky, (2008)). Initially, the organization needs to frame out their strategies, work on it and provide training in leadership development in order to decline failure in their areas (Beer, Finnstrom, & Schrader, 2016). Apart of it, organization should strive for maximum alignment between trending technologies with their outcomes. Strong and effective alignment has shown 70% gain

DOI: 10.4018/979-8-3693-1946-8.ch001

in developing leaders (Colfax, Santosa, & Diego, 2009). Organization has started taking advantages of technologies for better skilled based requirements and focussing the impact of technology learning as a door key towards leadership developments. In current scenario, organizational technical advancement has re-explored how to raise crow funding (free fundraiser), access transportation sharing network and secure transportation accommodation i.e. peer to peer (P2P) accommodation market (McCafferty, 2016). The very challenging hindrance of technology gap towards leadership is the human factor. Developing clear and crystal objectives, utilizing relevant strategies, efficient placement and regular evaluations are the organizational challenges for scrambling both i.e. managing trending technologies and growing leadership need.

An interesting study was conducted by Hilde Hetland, A. Skogstad, J. Hetland, and A. Mikkelsen back in 2011 (Haryo Suryosumarto, 2023), which analysed the link between leadership styles and learning climate. It offers valuable insights into the kind of leadership needed to drive innovation, creativity, and growth in today's fast-paced business landscape. Another study was carried out, whose titled was ***Leadership and Learning Climate in a Work Setting"*** (Haryo Suryosumarto, 2023), examining 1061 employees from Norwegian Postal services. The study showed that effect of two style of leadership i.e. *transformational leadership*, which is proactive and engaging, and *passive-avoidant leadership*, which is often described as *'absentee' leadership* — on various aspects of the learning climate; including autonomy, guidelines, team style, opportunities to develop, and time. The former leadership has positive influence on the learning environment, leaving positive impact on employees and guidelines, developing their autonomy opportunity in building a strong team. While, absentee leadership has negative impact on employees with time and guidelines. These findings are momentous for commercial leaders and entrepreneurs. In contemporary business surroundings, an uninterrupted learning and innovations are the keys parameters for staying competitive in the market, thus the role of leadership is becoming crucial.

Proactive Leadership: Proactive leaders take initiative and anticipate future challenges and opportunities. They are forward-thinking and strategic in their decision-making. Here are some characteristics of proactive leadership (Dragan Kesic, 2023):

a. **Visionary Perspective**: Proactive leaders have a clear vision for the future and proactively work towards it.
b. **Planning and Preparation**: They invest time planning, setting goals, and developing strategies.
c. **Risk Management**: Proactive leaders identify potential risks and take measures to mitigate them.
d. **Continuous Learning**: They promote a culture of learning and adaptation to keep up with the times.
e. **Empowerment:** Proactive leaders empower their teams, fostering innovation and creativity.

Leadership can be discovered and categorised by 4 different approaches (Future Learn). These are absent, reactive, deliberate and strategic.

i. **Absent leadership approach**: Absent leaders are considered as Silent killers of commercial transformation efforts (Haryo Suryosumarto, 2023). 'Absentee' leadership, also often referred to as laissez-faire leadership, is a form of leadership where the leader is largely uninvolved, disengaged, and neglects their responsibilities. Passive-avoidant or 'absentee' leadership can hamper the development of a productive learning environment. Absentee leadership often flies under the radar as it is characterized by inaction rather than negative action. Absentee' leaders tend to be passive, failing to provide guidance, feedback, or support to their team. Absentee leaders do not interfere with daily operations or employee autonomy, their lack of presence and engagement often results in a lack of direction, decreased morale, and lower productivity within the team.

ii. **Reactive leadership approach:** Reactive leaders respond to situations as they arise and make decisions based on immediate needs. While this strategy may be successful in some circumstances, it may not be suitable for long-term success. Here are some characteristics of reactive leadership:
   a. **Short-Term Focus**: Reactive leaders prioritize solving immediate problems over long-term planning.
   b. **Fire-fighting Mentality**: They may address crises constantly without addressing root causes.
   c. **Lack of Strategy**: Reactive leaders may lack a clear strategy, making it challenging to achieve sustainable growth.
   d. **Stress and Bur**nout: Constantly reacting to issues can lead to stress and burnout for leaders and their teams.
   e. **Missed Opportunities**: Opportunities for innovation and growth may be missed due to a lack of proactive thinking.

According to Dragan Kesic, both proactive and reactive leadership have their own place in leadership, but understanding when to employ each approach is crucial (Dragan Kesic, 2023). Effective leaders often blend elements of both styles to navigate the complex challenges of the modern business world.

iii. **Deliberate leadership approach**: Deliberate leadership approach to leadership development involves intentional efforts to identify and nurture potential leaders within the organisation. Managers and departments may take the initiative to provide development opportunities for their team members, but the approach may not be unified or standardised across the organisation. Deliberate leaders make it clear where they stand and share the logic behind their arguments. They are willing to take the time to form and deliver a clear message. They aren't so excited by a new idea that they forget to bring others into the loop and up to speed when something might change. There are three major approaches or theories toward this leadership. Firstly; the traits or psychological approach, secondly; the situational or contingency approach and thirdly; the behavioural approach.

iv. **Strategic leadership approach**: The strategic approach to leadership development is considered as gold standard in organisational commitment to investing in future leaders. In organisations following this approach, leadership development is a core part of the business strategy. The development of leaders is seen as a long-term investment, with clear goals, systematic processes, and integration with the organisation's vision and values. Strategic organisations actively identify high-potential individuals, create personalised development plans, and provide on-going support, feedback, and coaching. They also establish leadership pipelines, succession plans, and promote a culture of continuous learning and growth. Strategic leadership development ensures a robust talent pool, agility in adapting to change, and the ability to drive innovation.

Strategic leadership development requires a proactive and comprehensive approach. Organisations adopting this approach prioritise the identification, assessment, and development of future leaders. They invest in leadership programs, executive coaching, mentoring, and other developmental opportunities that align with organisational goals.

2. APPROACHES FOR LEADERSHIP DEVELOPMENT

According to Wilson learning *"The motive of a leader is to engage other in accomplishing their full energies in creating values and success"* (Jack J. Corcker). The above statement has some pivotal elements which is the heart of leadership views given bellows.

i. **Engaging others**: The key difference between a leader and a common man contributor is to achieve of objectives by engaging other. To succeed in achieving the goals, leaders not only give directions but also motivate and support their talents toward their thrilling vision.
ii. **Accomplishing their full energies**: A true leader creates passion that ignites to peak commitment; employees are geared up and ready to bestow all their creativity, ability and learning to the organization with full enthusiasm. In return the employees receive success and achieve professional benefits.
iii. **Creating values and success**: Efficient leader knows how to survive and progress. All the frameworkers, owners, employees and customers should obtain values from the organization. An efficient leader always make everyone focus on their growth values; making the growth of individuals as well as origination also.

Leaders who have the above mentioned qualities have integrated the essence and form of effectual leadership. **Essence** is the qualities that give identity to leaders while **Form** is what a leader says and do it. Effective leaders always think what to do if they are empowered as a leader and which type of leaders they want to be. The principles and self-awareness of the values are two important key factors in the individuals for becoming a leader (Daniel Goleman, 1995). This depends on the leadership character. An integrated leadership model is shown in figure 1.

Figure 1. An integrated leadership model

Leadership character is the root, or essence, of all effectual leadership. Leader's character is categorised into three mail parts i.e. personal leader character, social leader character and organizational leader character. Firstly, personal leadership character has the quality of steadfast and adversity quotient, Secondly, social leadership character has the quality of having respect and regards to others, being empathic and compassionate and giving values to individual difference of opinion and lastly, organizational leadership character has the quality of willingness to do everything whenever required and satisfy the customers accordingly rather than one's own personal. Efficient leaders always maintain balance in the three characters mentioned above.

Simply having leadership character is not sufficient for becoming an effective leader. Until and unless the leader's root is nourished by the skills and technologies required implementing on those values and principles, a leader face failure in producing the necessary results for achieving success. The skills of a leader for effective leadership are Visionary, Facilitator, Contributors and Strategist. These skills are correlated to each other. Thus an effective leader has the ability in maintaining balance among all skills and integrating these skills with all leadership character.

2.1 Why a Techno-Leader?

We are aware that only 10% people are leaders inborn while organizational report says that 77% of people lack in leadership (30 Lynne Pratt, 2023). We are surprise to see this data. No matters how we look into it, especially when 83% of businessman accept that it is essential to develop leaders at every stage in an industry. More than 86% person believes that business leaders expect others to lead them on social problems, affecting them at larger rate than public leaders (30 Lynne Pratt, 2023). For investment purpose, customers and investor require good business leaders and this is a true fact.

The utility of technology along with digital transformation is the path for businessman in leading their company. Emerging technologies are changing the work style, connecting people globally and expanding their business. Technical leaders are good or not, this can be judged on global platform. Their implementation of innovative technologies and change in their work style are influencing their business and attracting globally. Such companies with techno-leaders are raised up with larger visibility.

Now we come to the difference between techno-leaders and business leaders. The real and basic difference is that a techno-leader focuses on technology for solving the problems, promotes inventions through golden opportunities and touches the sky with its innovative driving, rather than depending upon market availability.

According to author **Tarana A Chandel**, **"Technology is an integrated tool for developing a future leader"**

Techno-leader's shaping people, process and technology (SK Panda, 2016) is shown in figure 2.

3. INFLUENCE OF EMERGING TECHNOLOGIES

Emerging technologies has its own impact for future generation. As a current leader it is necessary to have information about the applications of the trending technologies and how to drive it in the field of Entrepreneurship, Agriculture, Education, Administration and many other sectors to enhance economic growth, efficiency, competitiveness, satisfy customer requirements and become a future leader at international level.

Figure 2. Techno-leader's shaping people, process and technology

3.1 Impact of Technology in Education Towards Leadership

An Educational leadership also called as teacher leadership refers to quality educational organizational approach that brings everyone under an umbrella making simple and conventional goals and values. In other words it is linked with transformational leadership style that spotlight positive change and growth and inspire students to utilize their full potential for combined benefits to all. Usually principals and directors of colleges emerge as leaders due to following reasons

- Showing commitments to set values to subordinates and their students
- Uniting each & every one and uplifting others
- Having good connections among theirs teaching and nonteaching staff, students and their parents
- Embracing difference in views by valuing their thoughts, ideas and opinion
- Become a problem solver and willing to make amendments for the benefits of staff and students
- Appreciate team work by inspiring positive work-style
- Exchange thoughts and have potential to conquer challenges

3.1.1 Technologies Transforming the Education Sector

Technology is rapidly expanding in every corner of our life style i.e. from swapping intelligence by speaking and communicating to education, marketing, occupation and in our daily routine (T.A Chandel, 2022). The major part is influenced by education in schools and colleges (Jaskaran S., 2021). Smart teaching and learning environments are conducted by Information Communications Technology (ICT), along with innovatory techniques such as Internet of Things (IoTs) and Artificial Intelligence (AI), helping us in achieving quality education, thus fulfilling SDG-4, which is part of the 2030 Agenda, i.e. Parris Agreement on sustainability development goals (T.A. Chandel, 2020). This 2030 Agenda has 17 sustainability development goals (Zeeshan, K et al, 2022; Américas, E., 2016; Thang, S. M, 2011).

The concept of smart learning-teaching having the goal of providing excellent education (SDG- 4) can be obtained at broad spectrum. According to the report of National Home Education Research in America, 1.6 million children or more are taking education from home. Internet of Things (IoT) based education are transforming the education system into new learning-teaching environment. Smart classes involve latest technology devices such as projectors, PC systems, cameras, interactive learning sessions such as games puzzle quizzes, white boards and technology with feedback sessions for sustainable education system (Rajpara S., 2020).

Thus schools or colleges or universities having the facilities of ICT such as virtual learning classrooms, self-learning management system, & and sustainable resource management system (SRMS) are referred as smart school/ smart university as shown in figure 3. (Chandel, T.A., 2023). The utility of technologies in the field of education are becoming important worldwide. Internet of things (IoTs), artificial intelligent (AI), machine learning (ML), and deep learning (DL) are different technologies often used for education. Utility of these latest technologies are progressing towards

Figure 3. Smart teaching-learning environment

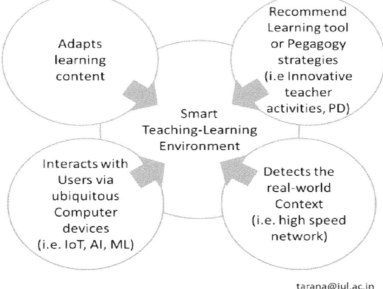

Figure 4. Transformation of school in world class learning center

smart education system. Figure 4. Shows, how technology can transform school into world class learning center by using it.

3.1.2 Importance of Educational Leadership

Educational leadership is essential due to the fact that it enables colleges and universities to conquer challenges by guiding them an innovative path to deliver knowledgeable classroom experiences to the students. Recent example of leadership in education is the way school, colleges and universities countered during the outbreak of the COVID-19 pandemic. It is because International Society of Technology in Education (ISTE) promoted technology in education sector. Only technology driven system in education, can promote students towards innovative learning. During COVID-19 pandemic, student's efficient learning at their residence was possible only because of enhanced technology. In addition, latest online education tool such as Google meet, Zoom and many learning management systems helped students to learn more effectively from home (Chandel, T.A., 2023). Online teaching has inclined the ingress towards internet from 17% (2015) to 34.45% (2017) (Jaskaran S., 2021). Approach towards internet is twice now. During pandemic efficient leaders addressed the challenges caused by public health crises. They focussed on addressing the requirements of students or making education more available to poor students with learning challenges. Some of the real time leaders in education are as follows (School of education, 2023)

- S. Khan, founder and CEO of Khan Academy. He launched a non-profitable organization with the objective of serving free of cost education in developing countries.
- Dr. Maria Montessori in 1907, proved leadership by introducing collaborative play and hands-on learning in classroom. This experimental learning method made students learn and understand deeper in their schoolwork and it enhanced social interaction among the students.

3.1.3 Strategies for Effective Educational Leadership

To become an efficient leader in education sector, one should have strong technical & socializing skills, and a habit of comprehending teaching and learning environment. Strategies to become an efficient leader in education sector (Denny, C.A., 2023) are as follows:

- Clarity in vision is necessary for focussing the goals and giving directions. Educational leaders should be specific towards their priorities, challenges and communicating it properly and effectively to the stakeholders.
- An educational leader should upgrade the culture of collaboration, innovation and respect among each other in their opinion. This is possible by conducting professional development programs (PDP) for faculties and staff members, providing smart classroom for student's engagements (T.A. chandel, 2023)
- Technology plays crucial role in education. Educational leaders should adopt technologies in improving pedagogy, training, administrative procedures and making correspondence faster.
- An educational leader should invest fund on conferences, workshop, and PDP and allowing their faculties and staff members to enhance their qualifications.

3.1.3 Careers in Educational Leadership

Leadership in education sector can have teaching as well as administrative roles. Some of the high profile careers in education sector leadership are as follows

- **Directors**: An executive who operates the entire college/ university.
- **District Basic Education Officer**: A leader of schools at district level whose responsibility is to appoint principals, manages finance & accounts and monitor performance of schools as well as teachers.
- **Department head**: A leader who manages departmental activities along with teachers and technical staffs.
- **Principal:** A leader of schools/ polytechnic who also look after teacher and staffs and manages all going activities in the school/ polytechnic

"An educational leader is a role model for others who collaborate with their colleagues on challenging opportunities".

For edification across the world, India has led top position institutions to attain a global space. According to Phil Baty (Chief Global Affairs officer, T.H.E, London), Indian institutions are participating in the global grading for uplift teaching and learning at international level (Manash P.G. & Hemali C., 2023). India's position in global ranking is on top three institutions ranked by World University Ranking with an outcome of 44.9 (i.e. approx. 50 points) in 2020 (S. Priyanka, 2023). Position of IIT Bombay is in between top 150 varsities, achieving the ever-top position of 147. ***Improvements in quality teaching and learning methods have made India a present and future leader in an education sector globally.***

3.2 Impact of Technology in Energy Sector Toward leadership

Investigating energy transition investment opportunities of India, reveals a successful perspective for our nation. The 4th International Conference & Exhibition on 'Atmanirbhar Bharat for Clean Energy Transition was organized by Somesh Kumar, EY India Power & Utilities Leader on 19 Oct 2023. A report titled "Global champions for advancing renewable energy innovation and manufacturing" quotes that ***India is prepared to affirm itself as a global leader in RE innovation and manufacturing*** (S.Kumar (EY),2023). This statement was jointly stated by Ernst & Young Global Limited (EY) and Confederation of Indian Industry (CII), based on the analysis of different facets of business and policy support. This is a potential statement for enhancing manufacturing of RE in India over future decades. Thus providing support to global investors in tracking and identifying investments throughout the business. The energy transition investment monitor is shown in figure 5. Furthermore India is in position to fascinate considerable numbers of investments in RE sectors such as in (EY,2023)

- Solar PV Manufacturing Projects
- Advanced Chemistry Cell Battery Manufacturing Projects
- Supply Chain Resilience

India has great potential to improve the supply-chain resilience globally for RE innovations and critical elements. ***India is ranking itself as a global winner in RE services, trading, innovations and manufacturing.*** India is also able to handles challenges in affordability, competitiveness,, policies, climatic and environment issues and infrastructures developments. The various polices measures for transition towards RE are as follows

- Adoption of harmonized Green Energy Open Access Regulations
- Long-term predictability regarding Open Access Charges
- Efficient imposition of Renewable Purchase Obligations (RPO) and Energy Storage Obligations (ESO)

3.2.1 Necessity for Technology Transformation in Energy Sector

Energy sector has always been slow in adopting digital technologies due to some or other reasons. The basic reason were investment of high cost in new energy sector and the complexity of the present infrastructure. However, with rapid increase in energy demand and an international pressure for reducing carbon emission following the 2030 agenda of sustainability development goals i.e Affordable and Green Energy (SDG-7) and Global Warming and Climate Change (SDG-13), energy sector is pressurized to find solutions in improving electricity generation and its efficiency.

Emerging Technology

Figure 5. Energy transition investment monitor

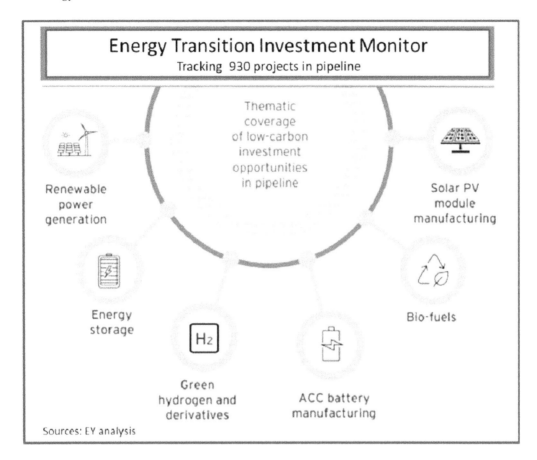

As international investment in harnessing green energy has become top priorities in power sector, therefore technology transformation in energy sector is most required than ever. Now energy sector is progressing day by day. New technologies are introduced to address the challenges in an industry. The top most technologies used in energy sector are (Sarahrudge, 2023; Michał Krzysztof, 2023) as follows

- **Internet of Things (IoT):** It is sensor based device connected to internet (Chandel, 2023. It connects many devices to provide business via real time data for optimizing working operations and enhancing efficiency. It can monitor energy transition, track the performances of energy generation and distribution; optimize energy demand in electricity generation. Today, IoT sensors are becoming censorious element for prognosticative maintenance, allowing fault detection in the equipment's before problem arises. The real time data collected by sensors are helping the organization for smart decision in the maintenance department and enhance the energy efficiency without any hurdles, establishing reliable and continuous energy supply. Thus with IoT technology, balance energy consumption with adequate resources can be achieved.
- **Artificial Intelligence (AI) and Machine Learning (ML):** By using actual data obtained from sensors, AL and ML can support energy entrepreneurs to optimize their business operations, improve efficiency with reduced cost. This is because; AL is revolutionizing and remodelling the

energy sector by allowing predictive analysis in maintenance and optimizing energy demand and consumption. AI algorithm are also analysing energy harnessing and distribution to decline waste and enhance the output, thus saving time and money. In the current scenario, it is very important as energy transition focus on integrated non-conventional energy sources such as solar, wind, hydo, geothermal. Thus machine learning platform was developed by Enel to forecast solar and wind energy power generation so that entrepreneurs can manage their energy resources in best ways. In other words digital technologies can easily and successfully predict and optimize output of RE sources. General Electric (GE) scientists were the first to used Artificial Intelligence and Machine Learning to decline wind turbine installation and logistic cost. ***New state-of-the-art Artificial Intelligence (AI)/Machine Learning (ML) technology developed by GE scientists recognized with a prestigious Manufacturing Leadership Award (MLA) by the National Association of Manufacturers on 4 April 2022*** (NISKAYUNA, NY, 2022). **Bharat petroleum** is also using AI to prevent from various failures, thus improving its efficiency in oil and gas exploration (Michał Krzysztof, 2023). For enhancing drill efficiency with reduced cost, the industry has developed an AI platform for analysing seismic data and forecasting the fossil fuels where it is likely to be found. Another industry is *Tesla*, using ML algorithm to forecast enegy demand and optimize energy distribution and its storage.

It is observed that AI and ML tools are supporting industries in declining green gas emission and contributing towards sustainable future. As per World Economic Forum, utility of both these technologies can increase energy efficiency upto 20% and declining energy consumption by 10% (Michał Krzysztof, 2023). Thus we can say confidently that AI and ML are two crucial tools with which a company can face challenges in fast growing energy sector and can be competitive in energy market globally.

- **Blockchain**: It is providing energy access to all equally. It is a secured and distributed technology. It used for supply chain management system and energy marketing, developing a transparent and secured system for energy transaction tracking. *WePower* and *Green Energy lab* has set up their start-ups related to energy are based on block chain (Michał Krzysztof, 2023).. This platform is making easy for energy producers in selling energy to consumer directly. Due to transparency and security in block chain supply, it is known for its impenetrable records of energy transaction and its billing. Block chain supply technology is being used globally. Examples are *LO3 or Power Ledger* (Michał Krzysztof, 2023). They authorize their consumer to procure and sell renewable energy in local area directly, thus building more resilient and sustainable energy grid. Bloch chain technology has potential to develop transparent, secure and effective energy system, thus it can be used in the transformation of energy sector. McKinsey reported that block chain can save energy and boost up the energy business upto $500 billion till 2030 (Michał Krzysztof, 2023).
- **Cloud Computing**: By applying this technology in energy sector, industries streamlined their data, analyzed it and reduced the electricity cost. In other words, we can say that cloud computing manages energy transition globally and ensure sustainable developments. Duke Energy Corporation utilized cloud computing to maximize its wind turbine (Michał Krzysztof, 2023) while General Electric has used cloud based predictive maintenance to brush-up the reliability in its power generation system (Michał Krzysztof, 2023).

Emerging Technology

- **Renewable energy sources**: The most popular RE sources include Solar, wind, hydro and geothermal. These energy sources are more sustainable with minimal carbon footprint as compared to conventional fossil fuels. These energies sources are easily affordable and are accessible to small and large scale enterprenuership.
- **Battery technology**: The energy storage system are utilised to store conventional and non-conventional energies in order to maintain and provide constant supply of electricity. The energy can be stored during off-peak times and utilize it at peak demand times.
- **Smart grid technology (SGT)** : The conception of remodelled grid along with electric power network is dependent on digital technology (Chandel,T.A., 2023). It is a modern electric grid. It utilises sensors, automation, digitally controlled appliance and many other technologies to enhance the reliability and efficiency. It also involve an intelligent monitoring system providing bidirectional information of energy generation/transmission, distribution to customer (Chandel,T.A., 2023). Smart grid also allows the distribution division to monitor the electricity demand and supply in real time. In other words we can say that smart grid operate more effectively, making affordable electric tariff with less effect on environment (European Smart Grids Technology Platform, 2006; M.Y.Yasin,, 2020, M.A Mallick, 2021).These technologies help in declining the wastage of electricity and green gas emission, also prevent power outages

3.3 Entrepreneurship Developments

Entrepreneurship development is a procedure of supporting an individual and organization to develop learning, understanding and skills for start-ups. This process also involves trainings, mentoring/ supervising, fundraising and other resources for successful business. The motive of green entrepreneurship (Chandel. T.A, 2022) development is to develop an clean and green atmosphere where individual or group of peoples having resources may turn their ideas into realistic business.

Digital innovations are driving entrepreneurs toward entrepreneurship development since decades. Continuous application of technologies has shown drastic change. With the arrival of Artificial Intelligence, Internet of Things and Cloud Computing, entrepreneurs can access new resources and abilities. The growing tradition of entrepreneurships in our nation has shown good result in economic development. The escalating opportunities for entrepreneur is to establish their business, open new market and become a boss. Another aspect of entrepreneurship is to become financially independent. A strong entrepreneurial approach among the youth of our nation is helping India in becoming developed nation. Some facts towards the growing tradition of entrepreneurship in India (Jaro Education, 2023) are mentioned below

- In favour of entrepreneurs, Government has made policies for beginning their start-ups
- Increased financial growth in India
- Talented youth are in search for beginning their start-up. This culture has certainly boosted Indian economy.

3.3.1 Impact of Technology on Entrepreneurship Development

Technology has great impact on entrepreneurship development. Four areas where technology has great impact (Holger Arians, 2023; Muslim Ameer, 2023; Usman zaheer, 2023) are as follows:

- **E-Commerce**: E-commerce has exponential growth over last decade. Entrepreneurs can grow their business online on social media platform, work globally, and optimise their working operations. E-commerce provides businessman to launch their business within an affordable capital and gets opportunity to expand their business along with data-driven opportunities at internet cost and benefits of competitive market. Moreover the entrepreneurs have flexible and responsive market shifting conditions. E-commerce has shown a great resource for endless success and a path to reach their client globally.

In current scenarios shopping via e-commerce has increased to $4.8 trillion globally (Jaro Education, 2023). This sale includes both i.e. industry to industry (I2I) sale and industry to customer (I2C) sale. Online sales are growing continuously. By the end of 2026, most of the retail sales will be online. Small businessman should move toward web stores. From e-commerce website platform builders, one can easy list their product, handle the shipments and take their payment of the product easily. The following names mentioned are the best e-commerce platforms (Harry Guinness, 2023; Alexandra Sheehan, 2023)

- **Shopify**: This platform is made for all type of businesses where you can start

your business, run and expand your business. Shopify traders can view all the activities from back office. Trades can optimize online store, grow their business by selling their product on social media. When you product gets a brand name, shopify will enhance your selling possibilities. It is trusted by biggest brands and has world highest converting checkout via online with shop pay, while point of sale (POS) makes it simple and easy to serve consumer in person, synchronizing orders to consumers', dashboard of shopify website is shown in figure 6.

Shopify e-commerce has following features

- Manage inventory
- Generate product description
- Handle international currencies
- Capture hesitant buyer
- Fulfil orders on move
- Evolve your store

- **Square**: This platform is for small business. It permits traders to join online and sales in-store through square payment. It powers your entire business in retail sale. Drawback of this platform is that it doesn't have integrated channel, basically for square payment users only. Dashboard of Square website is shown in figure 7.
- **Ecwid by Lightspeed**: It is a website store where businessman can set up their Ecwid store for selling their products across a world, social media, and marketplaces.
- **BigCommerce**: This platform is used by enterprise-level industries examples are Shopify and Wix. It provides solution, web hosting, customized stores along with tool for selling globally howevers traders fell lack of flexibility and simplicity. The dashboard of BigCommerce website is shown in figure 8.

Emerging Technology

Figure 6. Dashboard of shopify website

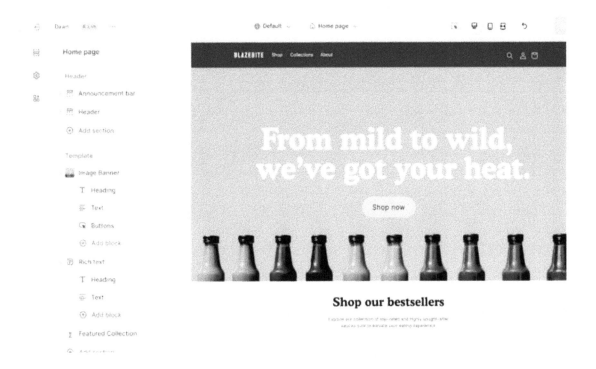

Figure 7. Dashboard of Square website

Figure 8. Dashboard of BigCommerce website

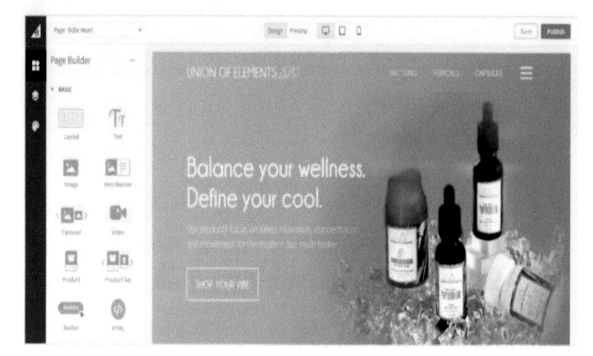

- **WooCommerce**: This platform is utilized for creating online e-commerce shop. With this software, anyone can develop their own website into a complete operating online store having all e-commerce features. It is an open-source e-commerce platform for blogging platform wordpress. This is a free and flexible platform, amplified by worldwide community. One can also design an advance version of websites with the inclusion of shipping securities, customized themes along with other standard features. The dashboard of WooCommerce is shown in figure .This is a free and flexible platform, amplified by worldwide community. One can also design an advance version of websites with the inclusion of shipping securities, customized themes along with other standard features. The dashboard of WooCommerce is shown in figure 9.
- **Wix**: It is a free, user-friendly website building platform and powerful search engine optimization (SEO) tool. It has its own customized tamplates. It require registration of web hosting domain name. One can design its own website for free. This platform begins from initial website builder to advance business solutions. This patform accepts payment online; track the orders and helps in managing your orders from numerous channels. It has its own features. Low stock alarm or inventory management system is missing. For getting inventory management, a trader has to use third part app via social media, the dashboard of Wix is shown in Figure 10.
- **Open Cart**: Open cart is free platform with an open source. This platform helps in creating and managing many stores which shows sales and their repeated consumers as shown in figure. It does not have any integrated sale challenges. Dashboard of Open Cart website is shown in figure 11.
- **Volution**: It was launched in 1999, one of the oldest platform. It is a user-friendly wibesite creator. This platform is for small scale business. One can create its business home page and product page, can add 30 payment gateways. It does not have any free plans, never allow selling of digital

Emerging Technology

Figure 9. Dashboard of WooCommerce website

Figure 10. Dashboard of Wix website

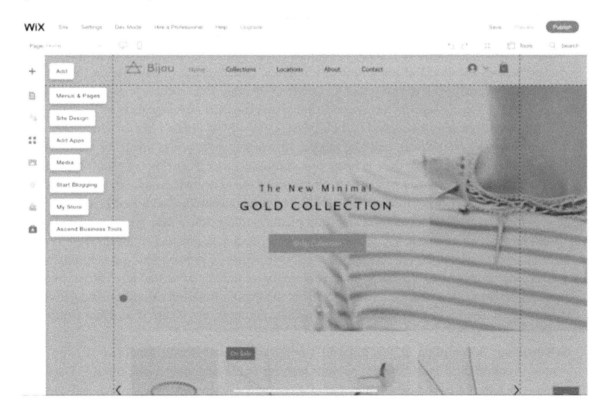

Figure 11. Dashboard of Open Cart website

products, no free Secure Sockets Layer (SSL) security. Limited plans for sale volumes and product listing. Plan charge begins at $31.50. The dashboard of Volution website is shown in Figure 12.
- **Digital Marketing Platform**: A platform such as WhatsApp, Facebook, Instagram and twitter has changed communication and connections with others. The influence of business on social media has changes everything. It is a good tool for sales and showing great success in digital era (Muslim Ameer, 2023). These platforms have become a market place, virtual hangouts spots and all in one. In 2023 there were approximately 3.02 billion users globally on digital platform (Jaro Education, 2023). This platform helps in building market values, networking and involving consumers. It is a cost effective platform, easily interact with consumers and get reviews of their products and gratitude them, thus enhancing business and making a brand of their product in the market. It is essential for entrepreneur's to move along with emerging technology with best practices to stay long in the market. Thus social media is a best platform to maximize their business potential.
- **Cloud Hosted**: To establish an online store that is accessible in public, hosting solution is must. Hosting stores give all the information on the server, which is visible to all users on internet. If you feel scared about the third party, your store can be secured by paying addition fees to solution provider. Example of such cloud hosted platform is Shopify. Building cloud hosted e-commerce platform provides hassle free server with all update automatically. Apart, it provides freedom to spotlight your business.
- **Self-hosting:** Self-hosting is also known as non-hosting e-commerce platform. It is an open source, required third party for hosting your website but is customized and control. Third part requires charges for providing services. Good servicing fee structures are very high and with low

Emerging Technology

Figure 12. Dashboard of Volution website

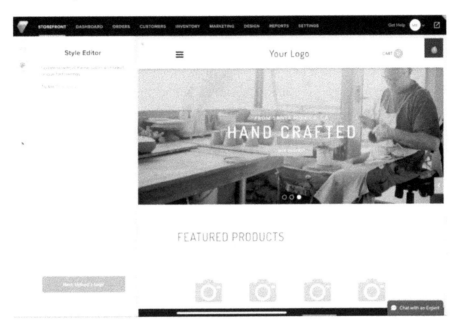

price structure doesn't have much customer support facilities. One can switch the server, modify their codes and build their customised online store.

For self-hosting e-commerce platform, traders have to manage their own server space or have to take rent for server space. Server space on rent becomes complex in managing website, self-responsible for website updating, maintenance and problem fixing. It also demands large internet resources.

- **Expanded Connectivity and communication**: To enhance your business, it is essential to connect with the customer. In previous decades, collaboration meant conducting meeting in conference hall. Days are far behind when business were not on front foot in visualise. Today, this problem has a solution with the help of real time innovators such as Zoom, Google Meet and Microsoft team. Meeting can be scheduled face-to-face, virtually. Meeting on zoom made all feel as if they all are in same room having official chit-chat. Microsoft team provide blended chat meeting, file/document sharing, coordinating projects. These tools have revolutionized team dynamics with possibility of remote work. This credit goes to social media. Products in real time are linked with consumers.

3.3.2 Impact of Technology in Entrepreneurship Toward Leadership

Since decades, involvement of digital technology was on progress for harmonizing the trending demand for techno-solution. The fast growing techno-innovation has found a drastic change in business dynamics forces, significantly remodelling the business through techno-solutions. The developed techno-pattern has raised the potential of advanced emerging technology, thereby changing entrepreneurial work activities (Elia et al., 2020). Major roles are played by ICT in uplifting and making a road-map for incorporating novel inventions for entrepreneurial achievements and activities (Ben-Oni Ardelean, 2023). The intersection of digital technology and entrepreneurship has transformed a business into a new species of entrepreneurs launching new operations and projects. Developed entrepreneurs have changed the scenario of business market.

New era business roadmap, consist of convergence of artificial intelligence and secured cloud computing. These tools enable the teams to collaborate with each other more effectively rather than previous working environment, empowering industries to enter new market globally. Now let us analyse how emerging technology influences businesses and develop entrepreneurs as a techno-leaders. Impact of emerging technology toward present leaders (Holger Arians, 2023) and entrepreneurship developments is as follows

- **Manage projects and employees:** Days are left behind when decisions were kept pending due to unavailability of managers/ executive authorities. With the access of software on multiple devices such as tablet, laptop, mobiles, leaders can manage conducting meetings and make effective decision online/virtually.
- **Embrace Diversity:** Language is the biggest challenge for industries while expanding their business overseas. Talents and developed market remain unexploited due to difference in english ascent and proficiency. But due to the availability of translating tools/software, business can be explored, establishing it branch office globally.
- **Flexibility to the Employees:** In the fast going working environment, many industries offer same package benefits to their employee. But the work style of the employees becomes a key differentiator for their loyalties. As all the departments in modern business are decentralized it is not necessary for different team members to stay back in the office. Various software share real time date and maintains strong collaboration with different departments working on same projects. Thus, employees have the flexibility to work in comfort zone outside office i.e. work while staying with their families at homes or outstation, thereby increasing work productivity.
- **Data-driven Decision Making (DDDM):** For business, it is critical to take decision on external factors. Data fulfil many roles. Data analysis is important for decision making and achieving a competitive edge of their business in the market (Muslim Ameer, 2023). Businessman should consult data analytics as key tool for their business opportunities. It serves as benchmark to the present existence, allows understanding the impact of decisions taken for your business. Data are concrete and logical and are always correct in making decisions. If process of data collection and interpretation are synchronized, then decision made on data can never be wrong (Tim Stobierski, 2023). Data may reflect some specific pattern or suggestions for your business outcome.

Data driven decision making means that on the basis of the facts found on research, strategies are framed to achieve their goals. In this process analysis is done on the real time data collected by marketing research, sketching the layout for the benefit of the business or organization (Devan Grant, 2023). Data-driven decision-making, function the same way as heart does in human body. Decision making with no real ground facts may cause tremendous harm to business and consumers also.

- **Artificial intelligence (AI):** The evolution of artificial intelligence is changing the landscape of entrepreneurship. Most important is that the technology is making simpler and easier to examine big data. Entrepreneurs can immediately comprehend big data with the utility of AI-powered ana-

Emerging Technology

lytics solution, enabling them in making decision faster and better. With the help of AI-powered assistants, entrepreneurs can launch new products and provide better services to the customers rather than previous (Muslim Ameer, 2023).. Chatbots can provide 24/7 personalised consumer assistance in upraising both product and service (Muslim Ameer, 2023).s.

- **Cloud computing (CC):** Cloud computing is another tool for entrepreneurs. Entrepreneurs switching towards cloud computing have the benefits of enhanced adaptability, reduced cost and efficient data security. One can use the software along with data information from any place; collaborate with their teams immediately, speeding up their procedures by storing them in the cloud.

Previously entrepreneurs used to invest large capital on their infrastructure, estimating future requirements and ensuring proper significant investments. This burden is eliminated by cloud computing, permitting business to scale up their store, network, and real time resources with computing efficiency.

Entrepreneurs can do remote work and check their employee updates. CC is flexible and reliable, uplifts performance and increase efficiency and reduces IT costs. It also helps in improving innovations, permitting organizations to attain faster market values. In this modern world, cloud computing has made access of data fast, and can handle crucial business application from any location with internet connect ions globally. Today business has squeezed up in air with a single laptop or tablet with specific software application.

4. 2023 G20 NEW DELHI SUMMIT

The 2023 G20 New Delhi Summit was the eighteenth meeting of G20 (Group of Twenty). The symbolic representation design of G20 Submit is shown in figure 13.

Figure 13. Symbolic representation design of G20 Submit 2023

It was held in Bharat Mandapam, an International Exhibition-Convention Centre, Pragati Maidan, New Delhi on 9–10 September 2023 under the theme 'Vasudhaiva Kutumbakam or **"One Earth · One Family · One Future"**. The concept of Vasudhaiva Kutumbakam originates from Hitopadesha, termed from Sanskrit scripture the Maha Upanishad. Vasudhaiva Kutumbakam has its own significance i.e. "The world is one family". In other words it emphasizes global unity. 2023 G20 New Delhi summit focus toward earth under single umbrella for future growth as shown in figure 14. It was the first G20 summit held in India.

G20 India has put forth six agenda priorities for the G20 dialogue in 2023:

- Green Development, Climate Finance & LiFE
- Accelerated, Inclusive & Resilient Growth
- Accelerating progress on SDGs
- Technological Transformation & Digital Public Infrastructure
- Multilateral Institutions for the 21st century
- Women-led development

On 26 August 2023, Honourable Prime Minister Modi expressed optimism about the G20 countries' evolving agenda under India's presidency, shifting toward a human-centric development approach that aligns with the concerns of the Global South, including addressing climate change, debt restructuring through the G20's Common Framework for Debt, and a strategy for regulation of global crypto currencies.

Indian Prime Minister Mr. Narendra Modi welcomed the African Union to take a seat as a permanent member at the start of the G20 summit in New Delhi, marking the first expansion of in a group of 20 major economies, in 1999.

The invitation of African Union in G20 by India had made the biggest achievement of its G20 presidency till now. The participation of African Union in G20 has turned to G21, marking a bench mark, making India a current leader at International level.

Figure 14. Vasudhaiva Kutumbakam or "One Earth, One Family, One Future", G20 Summit

RESULTS

The statistical analysis done shows organizational success hinges on effective leadership capable of steering its workers to endeavour toward common goals. With this view, it is imperative to facilitate leadership development training programs to equip, would-be leaders with the requisite skills to sustain and improve their competencies, analyse situations, prepare a plan of action, and influence the manner in which activities are conducted in a work unit (Baron, I., Agustina, H., 2017). To measure the effectiveness of leadership skills training being applied at the corporate level, the facts and figures surrounding the impact of organizational or corporate leadership training programs are explored. The result of Leadership Training Statistics for 2024: Data, Insights & Predictions (Imed Bouchrika, 2014) are highlighted below:

i. **State of Leadership Training**: Statistic data in Table 1, shows that companies are increasing their budget on leadership training programs.
ii. **Benefits of Leadership Training:** After undergoing leadership training, participants were found to have a 25% increase in learning and 20% in overall job performance (Lacerenza, et. al., 2017). This signals that a lot of programs are centered not only on leadership theories and practices but also on how they can be applied to the office setting.
iii. **A Modern Approach to Effective Leadership Training**: Leadership training has to evolve to account for technology's entry into business as well as the preferences and behaviours of today's leaders (Deloitte, 2019). Research suggests that innovating on traditional techniques has contributed to a 9% improvement in organizational growth, profit, productivity, and transformation (Towards Maturity, 2019).

Table 1. Global investment in leadership training program

Year	Training Budget ($)
2010	271.7
2015	355.6
2018	366.2
2019	370.7
2020	169.4 *

*Showing training budget during COVID-19

Table 2. Performance improvement due to leadership training

Year	Performance in %age
Leadership Behaviour	28
Learning	25
Organizational Outcomes	25
Overall job performance	20
Subordinate outcomes	8

Table 3. Leadership style change in 21th century

Training Approach	Leadership Style Change %age
New Technology	75
The pace of change in workspace	66
A change in employee demographic and expectations	57
Changing custom expectation	53

CONCLUSION

Technologies play an important role in entrepreneurship developments. In current scenarios, multinational companies are awakened by the facts that social media and networking platforms will play major tools for future success, as these tools encourage new inventions and collaboration globally. Small to medium scale trades are also climbing high on board as technology has more benefits with affordable amount.

The impact of technology towards leadership is considerable and beneficial. Important and challenging to all the leaders is to choose right technology at right time and implement it in right direction along with reduced human efforts. Technology has not only changed the working and operating style but it has also produced new leadership style. Leaders now adapt new inventions and utilize technology to lead their teams and work. We expect to see even bigger technology transformation in influencing business towards techno-leadership.

Several studies have proven leadership training's effectiveness in producing not just strong leaders, but also stewards of positive outcomes (Lacerenza, et. al., 2017; Mandachian, et al., 2016; Baron & Agustina, 2017). The program's benefits include significant increases in learning, leadership behaviors, and organizational outcomes. It also contributes to a slight increase in subordinate outcomes (Lacerenza, et. al., 2017)..

It is important to note that technology and its advanced solutions have penetrated the global business sphere, so creating a leadership training program that resolves the aforesaid concerns, alone, won't be enough to produce the desired results. Leadership development organizations understand the evolving requirements of leadership in the modern setting. These organizations emphasize the development of tech-savviness, the ability to discern ideal solutions through analytics, and the creation of a collaborative environment among leaders and teams. By partnering with leadership training organizations, businesses can ensure comprehensive and tailored leadership programs that address the specific needs of the digital age and foster effective leadership practices in a rapidly evolving business landscape.

REFERENCES

Ameer, M. (2023). *The Impact Of Technology On Entrepreneurship - 5 Ways To Leverage It.* https://www.linkedin.com/pulse/impact-technology-entrepreneurship-5-ways-leverage-muslim-ameer/

Américas, E. (2016). *Sustainable Development Goals (SDGs): Our history and close relationship.* https://www.enelamericas.com/en/investors/a202107-sustainable-developmentgoals-sdgs-our-history-and-close-relationship.html

Arians, H. (2023). The impact of technology on leadership. *The People Development Magzine.* https://peopledevelopmentmagazine.com/2023/04/07/impact-of-technology/

Baron, I., & Agustina, H. (2017). The Effectiveness of Leadership Management Training. *Polish Journal of Management Studies, 16*(2), 7–15. doi:10.17512/pjms.2017.16.2.01

Beer, M., Finnstrom, M., & Schrader, D. (2016). Why leadership training fails - and what to do about it. *Harvard Business Review, 94*(10), 50–57.

Ben-Oni Ardelean. (2021). *Role of Technological Knowledge and Entrepreneurial Orientation on Entrepreneurial Success: A Mediating Role of Psychological Capital Front.* https://www.frontiersin.org/articles/10.3389/fpsyg.2021.814733/full doi:10.3389/fpsyg.2021.814733

Bouchrika, I. (2024). 24 Leadership Training. https://research.com/careers/leadership-training-statistics

Boyce, L. A., LaVoie, N., Streeter, L. A., Lochbaum, K. E., & Psotka, J. (2008). Technology as a tool for leadership development: Effectiveness of automated web-based systems in facilitating tacit knowledge acquisition. *Military Psychology, 20*(4), 271–288. doi:10.1080/08995600802345220

Cercone, K. (2008). Characteristics of adult learners with implications for online learning design. *AACE Journal, 16*(2), 137–159.

Chandel, T. A. (2022). *Green and Sustainable Infrastructure in India, ebook Achieving the Sustainable Development Goals Through Infrastructure Development.* doi:10.4018/979-8-3693-0794-6.ch006

Chandel, T. A. (2023). *Hybrid Energy Storage Systems for Renewable Energy Integration and Application.* doi:10.4018/978-1-6684-8816-4.ch011

Colfax, R. S., Santosa, A. T., & Diego, J. (2009). Virtual leadership A green possibility in critical times but can it really work. *Journal of International Business Research, 8*(2), 133–139.

Deloitte. (2019). *The Deloitte Global Millennial Survey 2019.* Retrieved from https://www2.deloitte.com/global/en/pages/about-deloitte/articles/millennialsurvey.html

Denny, C. A. (2023). The role of leadership in shaping the future of education. *Academy of Educational Leadership Journal, 27*(1), 1-2. www.bantamdell.com

Elia, G., Margherita, A., & Passiante, G. (2020). Digital entrepreneurship ecosystem: How digital technologies and collective intelligence are reshaping the entrepreneurial process. *Technological Forecasting and Social Change, 150,* 119791. doi:10.1016/j.techfore.2019.119791

European Smart Grids Technology Platform. (2006). *European Commission Directorate-General for Research Information and Communication Unit FutureLearn: How do organisations approach leadership development?* https://www.futurelearn.com/info/courses/designing-and-implementing-a-leadership-development-strategy/0/steps/380052#:~:text=Deliberate%20leadership%20development%20involves%20intentional,or%20standardised%20across%20the%20organisation

Goleman, D. (1995). Emotional Intelligence. Bantam.

Grant, D. (2023). *What is Data-Driven Decision Making? (And Why It's So Important)*. https://www.driveresearch.com/market-research-company-blog/data-driven-decision-making-ddm/

Guinness, H. (2023). *The 6 best eCommerce website building platforms for online stores in 2024*. https://zapier.com/blog/best-ecommerce-shopping-cart-software/

Jaskaran Singh Saluja. (2021). *Indian infrastructure in sustainable development: Need of the hour*. The Daily Guardian. https://thedailyguardian.com/indian-infrastructure-in-sustainable-development-need-of-the-hour/

Kesic, D. (2023). *Proactive vs. Reactive Leadership: Navigating the Path to Success*. https://www.linkedin.com/pulse/proactive-vs-reactive-leadership-navigating-path-success-dragan-kesic/

Krzysztof, M. (2023). *Top 5 Digital Technologies Transforming the Energy Sector*. https://codete.com/blog/top-5-digital-technologies-transforming-the-energy-sector

Kumar, S. (2023). *Unleashing India's renewable energy potential: a global manufacturing hub*. https://www.ey.com/en_in/energy-resources/unleashing-india-s-renewable-energy-potential-a-global-manufacturing-hub#:~:text=India's%20renewable%20energy%20sector%20boasts,for%20its%20sustainable%20energy%20future

Lacerenza, C., Reyes, D., Marlow, S., Joseph, D., & Salas, E. (2017). Leadership Training Design, Delivery, and Implementation: A Meta-Analysis. *The Journal of Applied Psychology, 102*(12), 1686–1707. doi:10.1037/apl0000241 PMID:28749153

Ladyshewsky, R., Geoghegan, I., Jones, S., & Oliver, B. (2008). A virtual academic leadership program using a blend of technologies. *International Journal of Learning, 14*(12), 53–62. doi:10.18848/1447-9494/CGP/v14i12/45535

Ladyshewsky, R., Geoghegan, I., Jones, S., & Oliver, B. (2008). A virtual academic leadership program using a blend of technologies. *International Journal of Learning, 14*(12), 53–62. doi:10.18848/1447-9494/CGP/v14i12/45535

Mallick, M. A., Chandel, T. A., & Yasin, M. Y. (2021). *Performance Analysis of Rooftop Grid Connected Solar Photovoltaic System*. https://stm.bookpi.org/AAER-V13/article/view/1173 doi:10.9734/bpi/aaer/v13/9364D

Mandachian, M., Hussein, N., Noordin, F., & Taherdoost, H. (2016). Leadership Effectiveness Measurement and Its Effect on Organization Outcomes. *Procedia Engineering, 181*, 1043–1047. doi:10.1016/j.proeng.2017.02.505

MaturityT. (2019, February). *The Transformation Journey*. Retrieved from https://emeraldworks.com/research-and-reports/strategy/the-transformation-journey#downloadReportForm

McCafferty, D. (2016, October 18). Delaying a digital transformation is bad business. *CIO Insight*, 1. Retrieved from http://eds.a.ebscohost.com.ezproxy.umuc.edu/eds/detail/detail?sid=9413cc58-0b27-406f-9d18-8cca931b71a6@sessionmgr4010&vid=1&hid=4203&bdata=JnNpdGU9ZWRzLWxpdmUmc2NvcGU9c2l0ZQ==#AN=118921693&db=heh

Morris. (2017) *The Impact of Emerging Technology on Leadership Development.* doi:10.4018/978-1-5225-2399-4.ch034

Panda, S. K. (2016). *A Leader's Role in Shaping People, Process & Technology, VP Global Service Operations.* https://www.linkedin.com/pulse/leaders-role-shaping-people-process-technology-sk-panda/

Patil, D. Y. (2023). *Understand the Impact of Technology on Entrepreneurship Development in 2023.* Jaro Education. https://www.jaroeducation.com/blog/understand-the-impact-of-technology-on-entrepreneurship-development-in-2023/

Pratt, L. (2023). *What is Technological Leadership and What Does it Mean for Your Business?* https://future-business.org/what-is-technological-leadership-and-what-does-it-mean-for-your-business/

Rajpara, S. (2020). *6 Internet of Things Benefits in the Education Sector.* https://justtotaltech.com/internet-of-things-benefits/

Sarahrudge. (2023). *Technologies used in the energy sector.* https://energy-oil-gas.com/news/top-5-technologies-used-in-energy-sector/

Saxena, S. (2023). *Lead school.* https://leadschool.in/blog/what-technology-is-used-in-schools/

School of Education. (2023). https://soeonline.american.edu/blog/educational-leadership/

Sheehan, A. (2023). *11 Best Ecommerce Platforms for Your Business in 2024.* https://www.shopify.com/blog/best-ecommerce-platforms

Srivastava, P. (2023). Indian institutes are keen to participate in Worlds Rankings to have a global visibility. *Times of India.* https://timesofindia.indiatimes.com/education/news/indian-institutes-are-keen-to-participate-in-world-rankings-to-have-a-global-visibility/articleshow/98471868.cms

Stobierski, T. (2023). *The advantages of data-driven decision-making.* Harvard Business School. https://online.hbs.edu/blog/post/data-driven-decision-making

Suryosumarto, H. (2023). *Absentee Leadership is The Silent Killer of Corporate Transformation Efforts.* https://www.linkedin.com/pulse/absentee-leadership-silent-killer-corporate-efforts-suryosumarto/

Thang, S. M., Hall, C., Murugaiah, P., & Azman, H. (2011). Creating and maintaining online communities of practice in Malaysian smart schools: Challenging realities. *Educational Action Research*, *19*(1), 87–105. doi:10.1080/09650792.2011.547724

Usman. (2023). *Role of Technology in Modern Entrepreneurship.* https://www.linkedin.com/pulse/role-technology-modern-entrepreneurship-usman-zaheer/

Webber, C. F. (2003). Technology-mediated leadership development networks. *Journal of Educational Administration*, *41*(2), 201–218. doi:10.1108/09578230310464693

Wilson Learning. (n.d.). https://global.wilsonlearning.com/resources/balance-essence-form/

Yasin, M. Y., Chande, T. A., & Mallick, M. A. (2020). Performance of Rooftop Grid Connected Solar Photovoltaic System. *International Journal of Recent Technology and Engineering, 9*(1).

Zeeshan, K., Hämäläinen, T., & Neittaanmäki, P. (2022). *Internet of things for sustainable smart education: An overview. Sustainability, 14, 4293*. doi:10.3390/su14074293

Chapter 2
Transformative Strategies:
Shaping Digital Culture and Employee Attitudes Towards Digital Transformation

Saurabh Sugha
Birla Institute of Technology and Science, Pilani, India

Mohammad Faraz Naim
Birla Institute of Technology and Science, Pilani, India

JiaLal Koundal
Suresh Gyan Vihar University, India

ABSTRACT

The purpose of this chapter is to identify the relationship between digital transformation leadership in shaping digital culture and employee attitude and contrasting strategical approach in startups and mature organizations. Based on a review of extant literature, this study develops a theoretical rationale behind developing a conceptual framework to organizations specific digital transformation strategies. There is a different strategical approach that a digital transformation leadership needs to address while implementing any technological initiatives as organizational ability to rapidly adapt to the new innovative transformed solution is very critical in shaping company growth trajectory. A conceptual framework of digital transformation through digital culture and employee attitude requires the empirical validation of the suggested conceptual framework. Organizations should focus on enhancing digital skills of employees and digital culture to foster adoption of new technologies.

1. INTRODUCTION

Internal business innovation for any company depends on creative thinking of the management, customer service, competitive intelligence, design thinking, process improvement and lean management. Companies need to work for continuous business model innovation based on the customer ever changing demands to maintain their competitive advantage (Shaughnessy, 2018). This path becomes challenging

DOI: 10.4018/979-8-3693-1946-8.ch002

not only for a startup but also for a mature organization. Creating a strong decision support system is quintessential for an organization to drive sustainable business growth. A strong digital command center which provides data reliability and predictive actionable insights helps the Leadership in making fast and informed decisions. For Industry 4.0 digital connectivity is now shifted to intuitive visibility, transparency, predictive capacity, and adaptability. Variations in technological adoption and utilization are evident across industries; for instance, the automotive sector incorporates augmented reality and collaborative robotics, whereas industrial manufacturing predominantly relies on self-learning systems. (Terhoeven et al., 2022). A company can create an ecosystem of not just a physical product, but also ecosystem of digital services through Internet of things (IOT) and processes through big data (Matzler et al., 2018). Three tiers of digitalization, each presenting distinct business prospects for accruing incremental value can be used like delivery of digitalized products and services via IoT and smart devices, facilitated by big data utilization, engenders digital productization and process enhancement. The digital metamorphosis therefore within entrepreneurial enterprises, catalyzed by information exchange within their operational milieu, exemplifies digital transformation. (Matzler et al., 2018). Various hierarchical factors must be considered when formulating an efficacious digital transformation strategy. These factors include individual levels (motivation), group levels (employee skills), and organizational levels (resources) that are influenced by contextual variables which can significantly affect the effectiveness of digital initiatives within the organization. (Trenerry et al., 2021). Therefore, the paradigm for organizational integration entails the simultaneous amalgamation of four fundamental components like intellectual integration, characterized by a shared knowledge base; operational integration, achieved through standardized technological infrastructure; emotional Integration, fostered by a common purpose and identity; and social integration, reinforced by collective bonds of performance. (Myung, 2016).

2. LITERATURE REVIEW

The digital transformation comprises three foundational elements that demand the diligent attention of digital transformation leaders: firstly, the refinement of customer experience, this involves the meticulous analysis and segmentation of customers, augmentation of revenue streams via digitally fortified sales techniques such as predictive marketing, and the optimization of customer interactions across multiple touchpoints through seamless cross-channel coherence and self-service capabilities. Secondly, operational enhancement which necessitates a thorough overhaul facilitated by digitalization of processes, empowerment of the workforce, and rigorous performance monitoring. Lastly, reconfiguration of business models to embrace the imperatives of digital globalization and the integration of digital modifications into existing business frameworks. (El Hilali et al., 2019). There exist five tiers of IT-facilitated digital transformation within business operations: business scope redefinition, business network redesign, business process overhaul, internal integration, and localized exploitation each with set of potential benefits for organizations. (Steiber& Alänge, 2021). A successful innovation has 3 benchmarking features, user desirability, business viability and technology feasibility each of them are interconnected with centrally held through Innovation (Brown 2009). There exist primarily six developmental stages in the process of digitalization: Computerization, Connectivity, Visibility, Transparency, Predictive Capacity, and Adaptability. One should expect latency at different levels of actions undertaken while conducting digital transformation while taking actions, making decision, analyzing data, and capturing insights. (Schuh et al., 2017)

For a new startup, the Lean Startup methodology provides a framework to innovate more effectively, reduce risk, and increase the likelihood of building successful, sustainable businesses. It emphasizes a customer-centric and data-driven approach to entrepreneurship, enabling organizations to iterate quickly and adapt to changing market dynamics. Design thinking and lean startup methodologies operate synergistically to facilitate the development of successful enterprises. The choice between employing a design thinking or lean startup approach depends on the specific circumstances of each case. (Müller et al., 2012)

Transformation leaders should strategically consider six corporate transformation levers when designing the digital transformation strategy encompassing growth trajectory, organizational culture, attitudes of personnel, business operations, and metrics for assessing digital progress. Additionally, there exist five dimensions of growth—customer, geography, product, capability, and culture. (Cohan et al., 2020). Business should progress through various stages of the lean startup methodology, starting from the ideation phase and proceeding to experimental design and testing of any new business concept. (Bocken et al., 2020)

Designing any new Digital transformation tool employee segregation within an organization into innovators, early adopters, early majority, late majority, laggards etc. Digital Business Transformation is an experience-based holistic framework were understanding misconceptions, considering readiness for transformation, implementation by overcoming DBT challenges and transforming is done through period feedback loop on learning. (Evans et al., 2022)

The role of a Digital Transformation Leader is multifold from creating tools while optimizing cost, improving digital skills, maintaining data hygiene, accurate data driven actionable insights, increasing new system adoptability. Digital Transformation system should have one source of truth with a single partner onboarding window and an accurate master data management system which will be sacrosanct for developing highly accurate innovative predictive models for deriving business action-

Figure 1. Process model for lean startup (Authors' elaboration based on Müller et al., 2012)

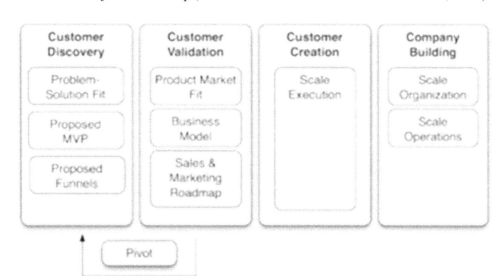

Figure 2. Business model develop through lean startup (Author's elaboration based on Bocken et al., 2020)

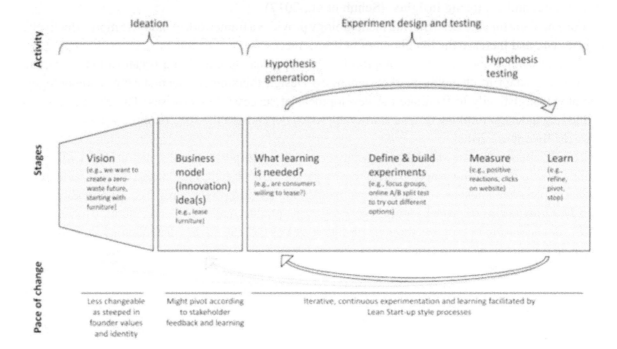

able insights. Leader should also play an important role in identifying novel value proposition, revising novel customer relationship, and performing customer segmentation through upgraded delivery channels (Gupta et al., 2022).

3. CHALLENGES

Making the internal and external stakeholders adapt to the new innovative business transformation and imbibe to changing organization digital culture. Corporate adaptation process often suffers from action latency, decision latency, analysis latency and insights latency. Having motivated, skilled, and trained employees who can facilitate digital transformation of the company and imbibe various important aspects of business innovation. Employee Motivation, Mental and Physical health, attraction, retention, learning skill and maintenance, technology attitude and behavior, job performance/innovation of the employee at work is equally important while designing a robust DBT system (Parker et al., 2022)

The leader must consistently assess the risks inherent in digital transformation endeavors, including those pertaining to mobility, suboptimal technical support, or dispersed team structures. It is imperative for the leader to engage proactively with diverse stakeholders to effectively mitigate these risks and alleviate employee stress. (Bregenzer et al.,2021)

Organization needs to design smart digital solutions to improve customer experience enhance operational processes and renovate business model any customer facing any modern app for a company should follow rapid experimentation through idea generation and aggressive design pro-

Transformative Strategies

Figure 3. Corporate adaptation process (Authors' elaboration based on Schuh et al., 2017)

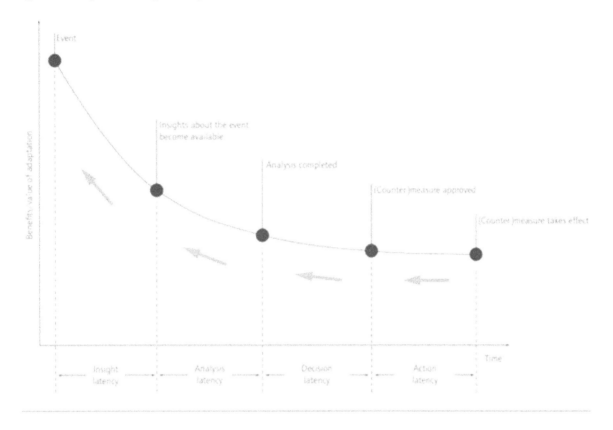

totyping followed by test and validation in a control feedback loop. While creating Work Design for a new Digital Transformation project company should use design thinking, lean philosophy, and growth hacking framework for integrating with Digital Marketing Techniques, Data Analysis and Coding and Automation (Bohnsack et al.,2019). Merging the best of both innovation strategies leads to the "Lean design thinking" model which is more promising and has better success rate (Müller et al., 2012). Identifying the right fitment based on organization digital maturity remains a challenge.

Improving the data quality of an organization incurs a substantial expenditure. This endeavor involves assessing and addressing multiple dimensions of data quality, including accuracy, reliability, timeliness, and relevance, in the development of a robust Master Data Management (MDM) system for integration with the decision support system. The categorization of information quality can be delineated as either context-independent or context-dependent. The presence of low-quality data incurs both direct and indirect costs, encompassing expenses related to verification, re-entry, compensation, reputational damage, erroneous decisions, and sunk investments. Significantly, substantial efforts are necessitated to enhance data quality, involving activities such as training, monitoring, deployment, analysis, and rectification. (Haug et al.,2011)

4. RESEARCH GAPS

Understanding how entrepreneurial ecosystems and clusters impact entrepreneurial outcomes and interactions among economic activities, actors, and elements to foster startup growth and sustainability remains a challenge. Correia et al. (2021). Also, while implementing artificial intelligence (AI) mediated transformative strategies will vary within different kinds of organization setups one can argue that there is a tradeoff between various variables impacting digital transformation. Further, a transformative leader needs to weigh various employee performance, employee motivation and digitalization metrics to increase adoption within an organization. Digital transformative leadership needs to provide impetus to employee motivation and digital culture in context of startup and matured organization remains unexplored areas in the leadership research. Relationship between entrepreneurial passion and work engagement in diverse knowledge work settings, highlighting its importance for both entrepreneurs and employees, and role of entrepreneurial passion in enhancing well-being and autonomy in knowledge work. (Toth et al. 2021). Understanding what aspects management should cover in digital transformation, emphasizing the need for a comprehensive, validated framework that addresses various dimensions and action fields for successful AI strategy implementation. (Bumann et al. 2019). A specific requirement necessary for successful and sustainable adoption of Industry 5.0 in Small and Medium Enterprises (SMEs) (Cramner 2021) thus becomes very essential. Through this book chapter, we wish to provide a conceptual model which digital transformation leaders can use to navigate the complexities of implementing A.I.-mediated transformative strategies, fostering entrepreneurial ecosystems, enhancing employee motivation, enhancing digital culture, and ensuring successful adoption of Industry 5.0 in Small, Medium and Large Enterprises for sustainable growth and innovation.

5. CHAPTER OBJECTIVES

In this chapter, we wish to explore the relationship between Digital Transformative Leadership driving an optimized varied business function through an Industry 4.0 Technologies like a Dealer Management System, Master Data Management, AI assistance and other Digital Transformation Tools while adopting various parameters of organization's Digital Culture to successfully manage profitability of self, and its relationship with upstream and downstream partners. We analyze how a strong Technology mix will help in addressing business challenges of maintaining optimum channel inventory in the market, control supply chain at various hubs across the territory, monitor product level month of stocks, provide stock replenishment norm, address demand volatility and trigger stock outs. Identifying key metrics digitalization scores, product fill rates for maintaining channel hygiene and manage partners loyalty programs in Consumer Durable Sector which is impacted by seasonality, climatic factors, and demand volatility during festive occasions and environmental factors like temperature fluctuation impacted the air conditioner sales, humidity impacting the washing machine etc.

6. RESEARCH METHODOLOGY

Ensuring the validity and reliability of study conclusions requires a robust research methodology. This study extensively reviewed literature to synthesize theoretical frameworks on digital transformative leadership in a tech-driven world. To identify the relevant research articles, we identified keywords which are relevant to our research frameworks like "Digital Transformation Leadership", "Digital Agility", "Employee Attitude", "Digital Transformation". We used to google scholar, Scopus and web off science for finding research articles relevant to the study. Journal of Business Strategy, Applied Psychology and Strategy & Leadership were the key journal sources which provided us knowhow of concepts and framework. To identify relationship between the variables a composite search was done keeping two-three variables' combinations and searching over google scholar for identifying research article having share linkage.

The research methodology for studying Digital Transformative Leadership and its impact on decision-making for Digital Transformation involved identifying a framework to guide the investigation, focusing on understanding the dynamics of leadership in the context of digital transformation and the variables influencing decision-making processes. This framework was developed through an extensive literature review, where various existing frameworks and theories related to digital transformation and leadership were explored and analyzed.

Following the literature review, the proposed framework was validated based on the findings and insights gathered from the existing literature. This validation process ensured that the framework was grounded in established theories and concepts, providing a solid foundation for the subsequent analysis. The validation also helped refine the framework to ensure its applicability to the specific context of digital transformative leadership and decision-making. Overall, this research methodology combined theoretical analysis with practical insights, leveraging existing literature to develop a comprehensive understanding of digital transformative leadership and its impact on decision-making, while also providing actionable guidance for organizational leaders and managers in driving successful A.I. mediated digital transformations.

Table 1. Composite search keywords list

Digital agility (DA), Employee attitude (EA)
Digital culture (DC), Digital agility (DA)
Digital culture (DC), Digital transformation (DT)
Digital culture (DC), Employee attitude (EA)
Digital transformation (DT), Digital agility (DA)
Digital transformational leadership (DTL), Digital agility (DA)
Digital transformational leadership (DTL), Digital agility (DA), Digital transformation (DT)

7. CONCEPTUAL FRAMEWORK AND PROPOSITIONS

Figure 4. Conceptual framework

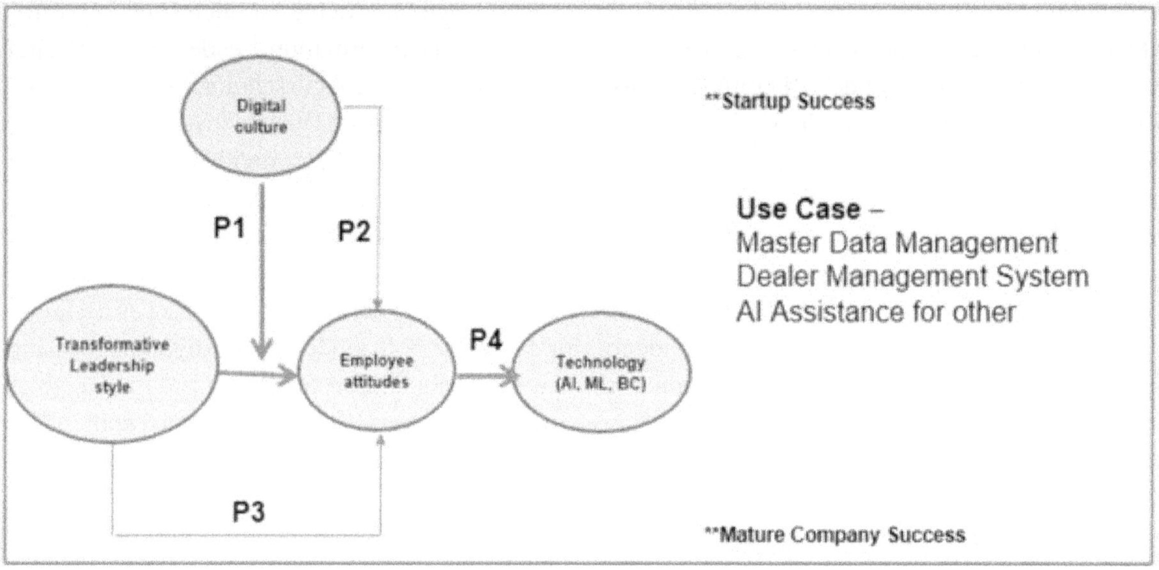

Diffusion of Innovation Theory (DOI), Self-Determination Theory (SDT), and Technology Adoption Mode (TAM)

Leaders can use Diffusion of Innovation Theory (DOI) by categorizing employees based on their prowess and inclination to Technology adaptation. A robust change model, vital for guiding technological innovation, involves iterative modifications and presentations of innovations tailored to meet the diverse needs of adopters across various levels. Emphasis is placed on effective communication channels and fostering peer networks throughout the adoption process. The digital transformation leader must adhere to the Self-Determination Theory (SDT) when discerning the competence, relatedness, and autonomy needs of employees. This approach fosters intrinsic motivation among employees, facilitating their adaptation to the evolving digital transformation landscape. (Jabagi et al., 2019)

The Technology Adoption Model (TAM) defines users' perceptions of a technology's usefulness and ease of use strongly influence their intention to adopt and use it. By assessing perceived usefulness and ease of use, TAM helps researchers and practitioners anticipate user acceptance and design interventions to enhance technology adoption. The model can be useful for digital transformation leaders to access the perceived usefulness of transformation initiative by the employees.

Digital Business Transformation Framework (DBT) and Agile Innovation

Digital Business Transformation is a complex, iterative process involving the identification of misconceptions, comprehension of transformative domains, assessment of readiness for transformation, resolu-

Figure 5. Diffusion of innovation model process (Authors' elaboration based on Miller, 2015)

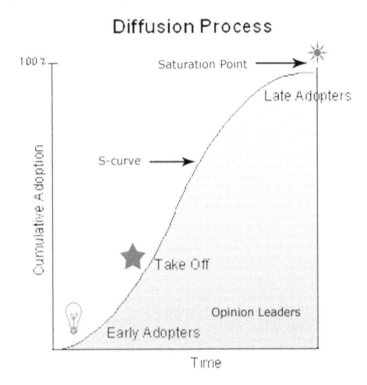

tion of implementation challenges, continual examination of the underlying mechanisms and rationales, and the execution of transformative initiatives within the organizational framework. (Evans et al.,2022)

The integration of business development methodologies such as design thinking and lean startup enhances success probabilities by fostering agile innovation. An optimal amalgamation of these approaches generates distinctive value propositions for the organization. (Lichtenthaler et al., 2020)

A spectrum of intervention strategies, encompassing human-centric, policy-centric, design-centric, and training-centric approaches, serves to facilitate the alignment of high-level organizational digital objectives with individual-level goals. These strategies entail the identification of key technologies and the enhancement of work designs to foster improved digital transformation. The selection of appropriate strategies by digital transformation leaders hinges upon the existing digital culture within the organization. (WorldParker et al., 2022)

7.1 Digital Transformational Leadership and Employee Attitude

The influential role of external business environments, including factors such as specialization, market dynamics, public policy, and societal trends, significantly impacts the generation of innovative outcomes. Leaders should conscientiously consider these factors when formulating their digital transformation strategies. Studies have elucidated multiple facets of consumer value sought during brand interactions. (Cockburn et al., 2018). Preparing Workplaces for Digital Transformation individual group and organizational factors needs to be accessed. Individually -Technology acceptance and adoption, perception and attitude, skills and training, workplace resilience and adaptability, work-related stress and well-being all

Figure 6. Work design as a key to achieving benefits of digital technologies (Authors' elaboration based on WorldParker et al., 2022)

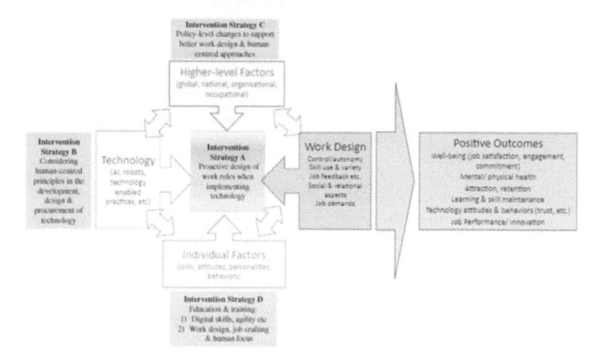

need to be accounted for. At group level - Team communication and collaboration, workplace relationship and team management, Team resilience and adaptability are important factors while designing Digital Transformation tools. At Organization level Leadership and culture play important roles in transforming (Trenerry et al., 2021)

The decision support model offers insights into the level of employee acceptance regarding the adoption of new digital performance changes. A digital transformation leader must adeptly discern the phase at which existing employees reside when introducing such changes. Employee energy levels may fluctuate from shock to denial during the initial phase, transitioning towards realization, understanding, and acceptance during subsequent testing phases, culminating in final integration. (Eickemeyer et al., 2021)

Conducting emotional intensity profiling of employees is imperative during the monitoring of digital transformation adoption. Positive emotional intensity fosters adoption, whereas negative emotional intensity hampers it. Evaluating pre- and post-activity stimuli related to digital transformation can elucidate its impact and the process of innovation diffusion. (Wortha et al., 2019)

Thus, from the above literature, we posit that:

P1: Digital transformational leadership employee attitude has a positive relationship with employee attitudes

Transformative Strategies

Figure 7. Decision support model for dealing with employee during digital transformation (Authors' elaboration based on Eickemeyer et al., 2021)

7.2 Employee Attitude and Digital Culture

The positive attitude of employee towards technology adoption and digital transformations has a significant impact on shaping the digital culture of the organizations There exist five facets of digital maturity contingent upon a company's level of digital transformation (Fahimi et al., 2023). These facets encompass "Strategy," "Organization," "Personnel," "Technology," and "Data." Leaders are tasked with delineating the demarcations among digitization, digitalization strategy, and preparedness for digitalization, aligning them with an organization's digital acumen and the adaptive capacities of its workforce to navigate the evolving digital terrain. (Aslanova et al., 2020). A Leader should define his boundaries depending on the level of organization maturity, either a startup or mature company.

Categorizing the employees' adoptions with a selected few exhibiting receptiveness and incorporate the innovation into their lives. As these early adopters disseminate information, the acceptance of the innovation gradually expands, eventually reaching a critical mass. Over time, the innovation diffuses throughout the populace until saturation occurs. This diffusion process delineates adopters into categories such as innovators (technology enthusiasts), early adopters (visionaries), early majority (pragmatists), late majority (conservatives), laggards (skeptics), and non-adopters. (Kaminski et al., 2011).

Thus, from the above literature, we posit that:

P2: Employee attitudes have a positive relationship with digital culture

Figure 8. Defining boundaries (Authors' elaboration based on Aslanova et al., 2020)

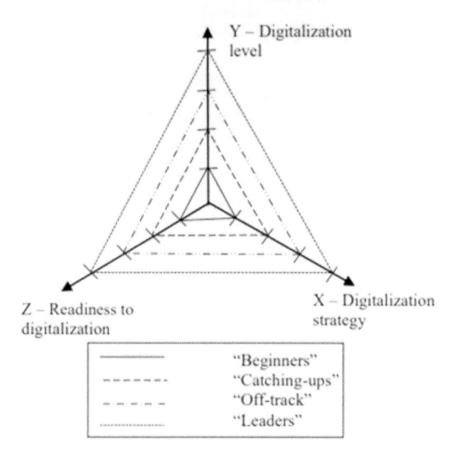

Figure 9. Diffusion of Innovation percentage (Authors' elaboration based on Kaminski et al., 2011)

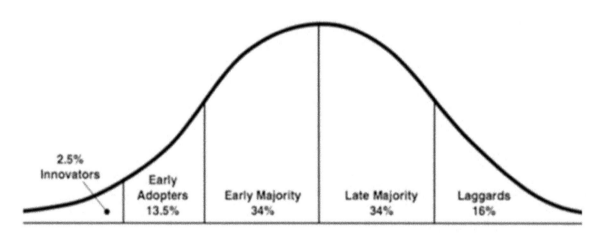

7.3 Digital Culture and Transformative Strategies

The paramount importance of data quality within organizational frameworks necessitates rigorous procedures for unstructured data refinement through Extract, Transform, Load (ETL) processes prior to integration. Integral to data governance initiatives, the establishment of Data marts mandates meticulous steps such as ontology engineering, semantic reasoning, data profiling, archiving, and delivery. Establishing a resilient Master Data framework is a foundational prerequisite upon which all Digital Transformation endeavors are predicated. Within a pristine dataset encompassing sales, service, product, and supply chain management, predictive and prescriptive analytics can efficaciously operate. Therefore, the systematic development of MDM warrants a delineated approach, structured across three distinct stages: initiation, progression, and termination. These steps facilitate data refinement conducive to the extraction of actionable insights for management through the application of Artificial Intelligence (AI) and Machine Learning (ML) atop sanitized datasets. An imperative task within the company entails the development of multi-domain data integration ontologies tailored to various departments, aimed at establishing a digital command center capable of seamlessly amalgamating disparate systems across multiple sectors into a unified Master Data Management (MDM) framework. (Fitzpatrick et al.,2012). MDM (Master Data Management) data can be classified into categories such as Product, Customer, Supplier, Location, and Vendor Data. The establishment of MDM encompasses four primary phases: Enrichment (comprising cleaning, transformation, and integration), Matching (entailing threshold value determination, identification of best, average, and worst matches), Merging (which can be either automatic or manual), and governance (encompassing validation processes and policy and rule implementation).(Kaur et al.,2021) . Ataccama, an integration tool utilized for Data Quality Optimization and Decision Making, is renowned for its Consistency, facilitating the provision of dependable data to users and applications at significantly reduced AI systems leverage deep learning and fuzzy logic methodologies to establish an effective feedback mechanism for assessing employees' propensity towards embracing digital transformation. (Eickemeyer et al., 2021) for capturing the emotional intensity of an employee.

Data reconciliation is imperative for the rectification of legacy data, while repeated classification, validation, and repositioning serve to enhance data-driven predictive capabilities and facilitate the derivation of inferential insights. These processes are essential for the development and maintenance of Customer Relationship Management (CRM) utilities, enabling the capture of sales pipelines, identification of business opportunities, management of accounts, and incorporation of product prices and allowances within the system. (Hansen et al., 2021). Depending on corporate objectives resource and financial prowess a suite of technological facilitators, such as artificial intelligence and big data, catalyzes digital transformation, thereby influencing workplace dynamics through the provision of instantaneous decision-making capabilities within employee domains. The construction of a resilient decision support system necessitates the integration of diverse digital frameworks into a unified software platform, fostering optimal proactive change management. (Eickemeyer et al., 2021). A leader should maintain vigilance regarding the frequency of communication directed towards stakeholders (employees within the organization). While infrequent communication may result in reduced uptake of digital transformation initiatives, increased communication frequency can induce digital stress, consequently leading to diminished adoption of digital transformation activities. (Steele et al.,2020)

Thus, from the above literature, we posit that:

P 3: Digital Culture has a positive relationship with adoption of transformative strategies

8. DISCUSSION

Business Model Canvas (BMC) framework based on 9 building blocks an effective digital transformation leader can micromanage, cocreate and redesign an effective digital command center for his organization. A robust dealer management system should use diffusion of organization innovation framework by (Steiber et al., 2021) where we modify a both internal (Desirability, Feasibility, First Trial, implementation, Sustaining) and external context of dealer management system. Digital process reengineering and developing a holistic digital command center through Flow Agile framework where one must divide each department as a single module of digital transformation has to be considered (Shaughnessy et al., 2018). 5 levels of it enabled business transformation with the varying degree of impact on business involving localized exploration, internal integration business process redesign, business network redesign and business scope redesign (Steiber et al.,2021). Process models for lean startup were customer discovery, customer validation, customer creation, company building where main pillars were given. Design Thinking model given by (Thoring & Muller 2011) used steps like Understand, Observe, point of view, ideation, prototyping and testing of a digital transformation system.

The efficacy of artificial intelligence (AI) assistance within a company is contingent upon a diverse array of tools. The complexity of these tools fluctuates based on the company's level of business maturity and brand outreach. A Leader shall design his strategy keeping in mind the challenges of cost optimization, resource availability and desired outcomes and benefits. AI assistive tool is specific for specific business use cases, facilitating the optimization of operational efficiency within enterprises.

Figure 10. BMC model (Authors' elaboration based on Feher, 2019)

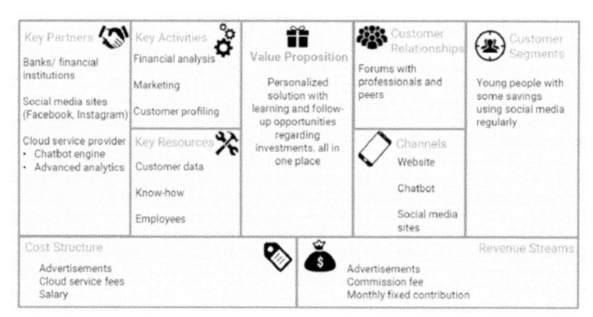

There are various sets of business-wide use cases for AI which were identified from the literature reviews for all business functions whose implementation in startup or mature organization can vary is based on Complexity of Business and desired impact. The impact score can vary from company to company, its priorities, nature of business operations and industry. Transformational Leader can prioritize this AI assistance based on transformation requirements and organizational needs.

The role of Master Data Management (MDM) is crucial for building AI solutions as it ensures the integrity, consistency, and quality of data, which is fundamental for AI algorithms to generate accurate insights and make informed decisions. MDM enables organizations to effectively manage and govern their data assets, providing a single, trusted view of data across the enterprise. This enhances the reliability and efficiency of AI models by ensuring they are trained on high-quality data. Additionally, MDM facilitates data integration and interoperability, enabling seamless data flow between different systems and applications, which is essential for AI tools to function optimally. Therefore, integrating MDM into AI initiatives is essential for maximizing the effectiveness and impact of AI solutions across various business functions and maturity levels, from startups to mature organizations.

9. THEORETICAL IMPLICATIONS

Paper extends the knowledge and aggregates various models and variables that can help leaders to facilitate digital transformation in startup and mature organization. It also elaborates the differentiation between design thinking and lean startup as a best fit for any organization. It contributes to our understanding of organizational behavior in the context of digital transformation. The paper also highlights the importance of leadership, culture, and structure in facilitating successful adaptation to technological changes. The emphasis on internal business innovation and continuous adaptation to customer demands adds to our understanding of how organizations can remain competitive in dynamic environments. It underscores the role of creativity, customer-centricity, and agility in driving innovation. Diffusion of Innovations theory, emphasizing the role of individual, group, and organizational factors in shaping technology adoption. Theoretical model emphasis leaders to continuously evolve their business models, leverage digital technologies, and align with industry-specific trends to maintain a competitive advantage. companies can create value by integrating digital components into their offerings and processes, thereby shaping broader industry ecosystems. It highlights the importance of integrating digital technologies such as AI, machine learning, IoT, and big data analytics into various functional areas of organizations. This integration is crucial for enhancing productivity, efficiency, and competitiveness in today's rapidly evolving business landscape. Employee motivation and inculcating digital culture is essential for navigating the complexities of technological change and ensuring successful adoption across all levels of the organization.

10. MANAGERIAL IMPLICATIONS

This paper provides digital transformation leaders a guide to implement digital Transformation and AI assistance mix with respect to resource available, digital maturity of company and regularly monitor the innovation diffusion. Digital Transformation leaders need to leverage technologies like AI and machine learning to gain insights into customer needs and preferences by implementing systems that facilitate real time actionable insights for maintaining a competitive advantage. This study provides the potential of digital technologies to enhance productivity, promote a culture of innovation, adaptability, and continuous learning to navigate the complexities of digital transformation successfully. Various factors such as employee skills, motivation, cost implications, and available resources when implementing digital transformation initiatives. Balancing these variables is crucial for ensuring successful adoption and integration of new technologies. Encouraging internal business innovation through creative thinking, customer service, competitive intelligence, design thinking, process improvement, and lean management is vital. Additionally, establishing strong decision support systems that provide reliable data and predictive actionable insights can facilitate faster and more informed decision-making.

In Indian Consumer Durable Sector, Marketing, Sales, Service and Retail Operation are heavily focused upon use AI assistance mix to connect to the customer at each step of journey. The customer touchpoints are impacted and influenced by these AI assists to generate repeated purchases and increase Brand's mind share. This assists not only create customer perception about company being tech savvy but also gives the company unique competitive advantage against the competitors. Health assist and Care+ are focused on employee wellbeing and tracking mental health to create wellness programs for the employees and improve their digital skills and adoptions.

11. LIMITATION AND FUTURE SCOPE

Empirical studies on leadership's role in digital transformation are scarce (Larjovuori et al. 2018). Various disciplines offer diverse perspectives on leadership, encompassing technology, ethics, and individual needs, yet the impact of digitalization on leadership remains largely unexplored, which we address in the subsequent subsection focusing on Information Systems (IS). (Gierlich-Joas et al. 2020). Longitudinal studies could provide valuable insights into the evolving nature of leadership in response to digitalization and its long-term effects on organizational performance. Furthermore, the existing literature often focuses on specific aspects of leadership in digital transformation, such as strategic decision-making or change management, without fully exploring the multifaceted nature of leadership in the digital era. This limited scope may overlook important dimensions of leadership that could significantly influence the success of digital initiatives.

Future technologies that need to be explored in Digital Transformation space are Collaborative robotics, Self-learning systems, Driverless transport system. Augment Reality and Exoskeletons etc. Few of these technologies have practical application in the automotive and manufacturing industries but these technologies are making their way slow rather steady in other sectors like Consumer Durable. Industry wide need assessment can be evaluated further. Also, Digital Stress components like Availability, Approval Anxiety, Fear of Missing Out, Connection Overload need to be explored to identify inhibitors to a positive organization digital transformation change. More quantitative research that systematically examines the relationship between leadership behaviors, digital technologies, and organizational outcomes is needed to provide a more comprehensive understanding of the role of leadership in digital transformation.

12. CONCLUSION

This study highlights the nexus of business sustainability, user preference, and technological feasibility resides innovation. (Müller et al., 2012). The customer life cycle encompasses phases of acquisition, activation, retention, and referral. It is imperative that digital strategies are synchronized to optimize each stage of the customer acquisition journey. The resource allocation and time investment required for each phase are contingent upon the specific focus of the digital transformation leadership. (Bohnsack et al., 2019) Organization digital maturity is evaluated through 5 key components Strategy, organization culture, people, technologies, and data. More robust and well embedded all the components in the organization are more digitally mature and organization is. (Aslanov et al., 2020). Maturity level of innovations towards commercialization is calculated through various set of innovation indicators like Innovation potential indicator, market potential indicator, innovation management indicator, innovation readiness indicator, innovator capacity indicator, innovator ability indicator and Innovator environment indicator to identify whether an organization is Market Ready, Tech Ready, Business ready or exploring. Metrics such as the net promoter score, which facilitates an organization's assessment of its social influence, organizations can also employ the calculation of a digitization score to engage with their clientele.

Indicators of innovation potential can function as a robust metric for assessing the efficacy of a Digital transformation endeavor, while innovator capacity indicators gauge the environmental conditions and the capability to embrace innovation. (Desruelle et al., 2017). Ultimately, this research advocates the future technologies like cloud computing and integrated AI assistance for facilitating the rapid integration of diverse digital processes and applications, thereby enabling efficient monitoring, management, scheduling, visualization, and resource adjustment. (Zhou et al.,2019). As digital transformation leader one should find the right technological mix to cater to organization while equally accessing the digital maturity of the company.

REFERENCES

Aaldering, L. J., & Song, C. H. (2021). Of leaders and laggards-Towards digitalization of the process industries. *Technovation*, *105*, 102211. doi:10.1016/j.technovation.2020.102211

Al-Ali, A. G., Phaal, R., & Sull, D. (2020). Deep learning framework for measuring the digital strategy of companies from earnings calls. arXiv preprint arXiv:2010.12418 doi:10.18653/v1/2020.coling-main.80

Aslanova, I. V., & Kulichkina, A. I. (2020, May). *Digital maturity: Definition and model. In 2nd International Scientific and Practical Conference*. Atlantis Press. https://www.atlantis-press.com/proceedings/mtde-20/125939845

Bocken, N., & Snihur, Y. (2020). Lean Startup and the business model: Experimenting for novelty and impact. *Long Range Planning*, *53*(4), 101953. doi:10.1016/j.lrp.2019.101953

Bohnsack, R., & Liesner, M. M. (2019). What the hack? A growth hacking taxonomy and practical applications for firms. *Business Horizons*, *62*(6), 799–818. doi:10.1016/j.bushor.2019.09.001

Bregenzer, A., & Jimenez, P. (2021). Risk factors and leadership in a digitalized working world and their effects on employees' stress and resources: Web-based questionnaire study. *Journal of Medical Internet Research, 23*(3), e24906. doi:10.2196/24906 PMID:33709933

Bumann, J., & Peter, M. (2019). Action fields of digital transformation–a review and comparative analysis of digital transformation maturity models and frameworks. *Digitalisierung und andere Innovationsformen im Management, 2*(November), 13-40. https://www.researchgate.net/publication/337167323_Action_Fields_of_Digital_Transformation_-_A_Review_and_Comparative_Analysis_of_Digital_Transformation_Maturity_Models_and_Frameworks

Chang, K. (2020). Artificial intelligence in personnel management: The development of APM model. *The Bottom Line (New York, N.Y.), 33*(4), 377–388. doi:10.1108/BL-08-2020-0055

Cockburn, I. M., Henderson, R., & Stern, S. (2018). *The impact of artificial intelligence on innovation* (Vol. 24449). National Bureau of Economic Research. https://www.degruyter.com/document/doi/10.7208/9780226613475-006/pdf?licenseType=restricted

Cohan, P. S. (2020). *Goliath Strikes Back: How Traditional Retailers Are Winning Back Customers from Ecommerce Startups*. Apress. doi:10.1007/978-1-4842-6519-2

Correia, M. J., & Matos, F. (2021). The impact of artificial intelligence on innovation management: A literature review. *The impact of artificial intelligence on innovation management: A literature review*, 222-230., https://repositorio.iscte-iul.pt/handle/10071/25484

Cramner, I. (2021). *Digital Maturity in the Public Sector and Citizens' Sentiment Towards Authorities: A study within the initiative Academy of Lifelong Learning, in partnership with RISE and Google.* https://www.diva-portal.org/smash/record.jsf?pid=diva2%3A1591257&dswid=8216

Davis, F. D. (1989). Technology acceptance model: TAM. *Information Seeking Behavior and Technology Adoption, 205*, 219. https://quod.lib.umich.edu/b/busadwp/images/b/1/4/b1409190.0001.001.pdf

Desruelle, P., & Nepelski, D. (2017). The 'Innovation Radar': A New Policy Tool to Support Innovation Management. https://papers.ssrn.com/sol3/papers.cfm?abstract_id=2944104

Eickemeyer, S. C., Busch, J., Liu, C. T., & Lippke, S. (2021). Acting instead of reacting—Ensuring employee retention during successful introduction of i4. 0. *Applied System Innovation, 4*(4), 97. doi:10.3390/asi4040097

El Hilali, W., & El Manouar, A. (2019, March). Towards a sustainable world through a SMART digital transformation. In *Proceedings of the 2nd International Conference on Networking* (pp. 1–8). Information Systems & Security. doi:10.1145/3320326.3320364

Evans, N., Miklosik, A., Bosua, R., & Qureshi, A. M. A. (2022). Digital business transformation: An experience-based holistic framework. *IEEE Access : Practical Innovations, Open Solutions, 10*, 121930–121939. doi:10.1109/ACCESS.2022.3221984

Fahmi, T. A., Tjakraatmadja, J. H., & Ginting, H. (2023). An empirical study of emerging digital culture and digital attitudes in an established company. *Journal of Industrial Engineering and Management, 16*(2), 342–362. doi:10.3926/jiem.5976

Fazeli, Z., Shukla, P., & Perks, K. (2020). Digital buying behavior: The role of regulatory fit and self-construal in online luxury goods purchase intentions. *Psychology and Marketing*, *37*(1), 15–26. doi:10.1002/mar.21276

Fehér, P., & Varga, K. (2019, August). Identifying digital investing services using design thinking methodology. In *2019 13th International Conference on Software, Knowledge, Information Management and Applications (SKIMA)* (pp. 1-8). IEEE. https://ieeexplore.ieee.org/abstract/document/8982477

Fitzpatrick, D., Coallier, F., & Ratté, S. (2012). A holistic approach for the architecture and design of an ontology-based data integration capability in product master data management. In *Product Lifecycle Management. Towards Knowledge-Rich Enterprises: IFIP WG 5.1 International Conference, PLM 2012, Montreal, QC, Canada, July 9-11, 2012, Revised Selected Papers 9* (pp. 559-568). Springer Berlin Heidelberg. https://link.springer.com/chapter/10.1007/978-3-642-35758-9_50

Gierlich-Joas, M., Hess, T., & Neuburger, R. (2020). More self-organization, more control—or even both? Inverse transparency as a digital leadership concept. *Business Research, 13*(3), 921-947. https://link.springer.com/article/10.1007/s40685-020-00130-0

Gupta, G., & Bose, I. (2022). Digital transformation in entrepreneurial firms through information exchange with operating environment. *Information & Management*, *59*(3), 103243. doi:10.1016/j.im.2019.103243

Hansen, L. H., van Son, R., Weiser, A., & Kjems, E. (2021). Addressing the elephant in the underground: An argument for the integration of heterogeneous data sources for reconciliation of subsurface utility data. *The International Archives of the Photogrammetry, Remote Sensing and Spatial Information Sciences*, 43–48. doi:10.5194/isprs-archives-XLVI-4-W4-2021-43-2021

Haug, A., Zachariassen, F., & Van Liempd, D. (2011). The costs of poor data quality. *Journal of Industrial Engineering and Management*, *4*(2), 168–193. doi:10.3926/jiem.2011.v4n2.p168-193

Heinemann, J., Platzen, O., & Schiefer, C. (2019). Successful Navigation through digital transformation using an innovation radar. *Future Telco: Successful Positioning of Network Operators in the Digital Age*, 155-164. https://link.springer.com/chapter/10.1007/978-3-319-77724-5_13

Huang, Y., Benford, S., Li, B., Price, D., & Blake, H. (2023). Feasibility and Acceptability of an Internet of Things–Enabled Sedentary Behavior Intervention: Mixed Methods Study. *Journal of Medical Internet Research*, *25*, e43502. doi:10.2196/43502 PMID:36848183

Huang, Z. (2022, June). Design and Development of University Information System Based on MDM-A Case Study of the Service Satisfaction Evaluation System. In *Proceedings of the 2022 3rd International Conference on Internet and E-Business* (pp. 153-160). https://dl.acm.org/doi/abs/10.1145/3545897.3545920?casa_token=vg2gB0W1NF4AAAAA:iMZQ_Ci9_O9xfjVutyVuW2tUpZcq-hsy3yYOQYpilSt-4QmcCRaelcxKCl-3dXOt59H8OdWSa-Vg

Jabagi, N., Croteau, A. M., Audebrand, L. K., & Marsan, J. (2019). Gig-workers' motivation: Thinking beyond carrots and sticks. *Journal of Managerial Psychology*, *34*(4), 192–213. doi:10.1108/JMP-06-2018-0255

Jamal, A., Quadri, M. P., & Rafeeq, M. (2023). Data Quality Optimization for Decision Making Using Ataccama Toolkit: A Sustainable Perspective. *International Journal on Recent and Innovation Trends in Computing and Communication, 11*(8), 217–228. doi:10.17762/ijritcc.v11i8.7947

Kaminski, J. (2011). Diffusion of innovation theory. *Canadian Journal of Nursing Informatics, 6*(2), 1–6. https://cjni.net/journal/?p=1444

Kaur, D., & Singh, D. (2021). Critical Data Consolidation in MDM to Develop the Unified Version of Truth. *International Journal of Advanced Computer Science and Applications, 12*(12). Advance online publication. doi:10.14569/IJACSA.2021.0121242

Kohli, R., & Melville, N. P. (2019). Digital innovation: A review and synthesis. *Information Systems Journal, 29*(1), 200–223. doi:10.1111/isj.12193

Koilada, D. K. (2019, June). Value-based digital transformation: innovating customer experiences. In *2019 IEEE Technology & Engineering Management Conference (TEMSCON)* (pp. 1-5). IEEE https://ieeexplore.ieee.org/abstract/document/8813559

Larjovuori, R. L., Bordi, L., & Heikkilä-Tammi, K. (2018, October). Leadership in the digital business transformation. In *Proceedings of the 22nd international academic mindtrek conference* (pp. 212-221)., https://dl.acm.org/doi/abs/10.1145/3275116.3275122?casa_token=CCrOz8KYG6MAAAAA:m_SN-6c4UbBID7wBqbO4SOtaEbMNDtTIHRTsHSlCpl9p_m1Cbwj339_mmUKp6ltVTjNKZSYNII4WF

Lawanot, W., Inoue, M., Yokemura, T., Mongkolnam, P., & Nukoolkit, C. (2019, January). Daily stress and mood recognition system using deep learning and fuzzy clustering for promoting better well-being. In *2019 IEEE International Conference on Consumer Electronics (ICCE)* (pp. 1-6). IEEE https://ieeexplore.ieee.org/abstract/document/8661932/

LeCun, Y., Bottou, L., Bengio, Y., & Haffner, P. (1998). Gradient-based learning applied to document recognition. *Proceedings of the IEEE, 86*(11), 2278–2324. doi:10.1109/5.726791

Li, M., Lv, T., Chen, J., Cui, L., Lu, Y., Florencio, D., . . . Wei, F. (2023, June). Trocr: Transformer-based optical character recognition with pre-trained models. In *Proceedings of the AAAI Conference on Artificial Intelligence* (Vol. 37, No. 11, pp. 13094-13102). https://ojs.aaai.org/index.php/AAAI/article/view/26538

Lichtenthaler, U. (2020). Agile innovation: The complementarity of design thinking and lean startup. *International Journal of Service Science, Management, Engineering, and Technology, 11*(1), 157–167. https://www.igi-global.com/article/agile-innovation/240619. doi:10.4018/IJSSMET.2020010110

Mammadli, E., & Klivak, V. (2020). Measuring the effect of the Digitalization. *SSRN, 3524823*. https://papers.ssrn.com/sol3/papers.cfm?abstract_id=3524823

Matzler, K., Friedrich von den Eichen, S., Anschober, M., & Kohler, T. (2018). The crusade of digital disruption. *The Journal of Business Strategy, 39*(6), 13–20. doi:10.1108/JBS-12-2017-0187

Miller, R. L. (2015). Rogers' innovation diffusion theory (1962, 1995). In *Information seeking behavior and technology adoption: Theories and trends* (pp. 261-274). IGI Global. https://www.igi-global.com/chapter/rogers-innovation-diffusion-theory-1962-1995/127136

Müller, R. M., & Thoring, K. (2012). Design thinking vs. lean startup: A comparison of two user-driven innovation strategies. *Leading Through Design, 151*, 91-106. https://d1wqtxts1xzle7.cloudfront.net/43840251/Leading_Innovation_through_Design_Procee20160317-10435-1rg9nmt.pdf?1458268120=&response-content-disposition=inline%3B+filename%3DLeading_Innovation_through_Design_Procee.pdf&Expires=1712061945&Signature=GxYZa~QlBBf-IlO7wvCAMFOFeT8Chjmx1BhOY3wHOgnAgx6KZpX1zs2dFzaY1AEO9lOUzHV9NOJBh1zPtINrg~AWpSlsKLi8We-wtXsdIE3D9-FiSjOjv0cn78NGH8dxhicR6iTjoczHFstcA7QRDm62dp8fR6dKAP~m0RsDS-98~I0wgpjajU~8zLxSbX0uQFtnJ-BHmsqiXN0XtZqpENM6Mb3ZUOxjqEFw9xAq9GbErQtYF2ZS~v5ULIADMw3t2UitzlNusntD1QGFzAF6FJnIBMl~wHCE9APIosrw-neTK9Dv0OhThkc-nvHVvGu-TyDYLOICpvUmfFaMm~u16qtw__&Key-Pair-Id=APKAJLOHF5GGSLRBV4ZA#page=181

Myung, S. (2016). Master data management in PLM for the enterprise scope. In *Product Lifecycle Management in the Era of Internet of Things: 12th IFIP WG 5.1 International Conference, PLM 2015, Doha, Qatar, October 19-21, 2015, Revised Selected Papers 12* (pp. 771-779). Springer International Publishing. https://link.springer.com/chapter/10.1007/978-3-319-33111-9_70

Nosratabadi, S., Atobishi, T., & Hegedűs, S. (2023). Social sustainability of digital transformation: Empirical evidence from EU-27 countries. *Administrative Sciences, 13*(5), 126. doi:10.3390/admsci13050126

Parker, S. K., & Grote, G. (2022). Automation, algorithms, and beyond: Why work design matters more than ever in a digital world. *Applied Psychology, 71*(4), 1171–1204. doi:10.1111/apps.12241

Pisoni, G. (2021). Going digital: Case study of an Italian insurance company. *The Journal of Business Strategy, 42*(2), 106–115. doi:10.1108/JBS-11-2019-0225

Schuh, G., Anderl, R., Gausemeier, J., ten Hompel, M., & Wahlster, W. (2017). Industrie 4.0 maturity index. *Managing the digital transformation of companies, 61*. https://fundacioperlaindustria.org/wp-content/uploads/2021/07/2020.acatech_STUDIE_Maturity_Index.Update.pdf

Shaughnessy, H. (2018). Creating digital transformation: Strategies and steps. *Strategy and Leadership, 46*(2), 19–25. doi:10.1108/SL-12-2017-0126

Steele, R. G., Hall, J. A., & Christofferson, J. L. (2020). Conceptualizing digital stress in adolescents and young adults: Toward the development of an empirically based model. *Clinical Child and Family Psychology Review, 23*(1), 15–26. doi:10.1007/s10567-019-00300-5 PMID:31392451

Steiber, A. (2020). Corporate-startup Collaboration: Its Diffusion to and within the Firm. *Triple Helix (Heidelberg), 7*(2-3), 250–276. doi:10.1163/21971927-bja10005

Steiber, A., & Alänge, S. (2021). Corporate-startup collaboration: Effects on large firms' business transformation. *European Journal of Innovation Management, 24*(2), 235–257. doi:10.1108/EJIM-10-2019-0312

Terhoeven, J., Tegtmeier, P., & Wischniewski, S. (2022). Human-centred work design in times of digital change–work conditions, level of digitization and recent trends for object-related tasks. *Procedia CIRP, 107*, 302–307. doi:10.1016/j.procir.2022.04.049

Toth, I., Heinänen, S., & Puumalainen, K. (2021). Passionate and engaged? Passion for inventing and work engagement in different knowledge work contexts. *International Journal of Entrepreneurial Behaviour & Research, 27*(9), 1–25. doi:10.1108/IJEBR-09-2020-0632

Trenerry, B., Chng, S., Wang, Y., Suhaila, Z. S., Lim, S. S., Lu, H. Y., & Oh, P. H. (2021). Preparing workplaces for digital transformation: An integrative review and framework of multi-level factors. *Frontiers in Psychology*, *12*, 620766. doi:10.3389/fpsyg.2021.620766 PMID:33833714

Wortha, F., Azevedo, R., Taub, M., & Narciss, S. (2019). Multiple negative emotions during learning with digital learning environments–Evidence on their detrimental effect on learning from two methodological approaches. *Frontiers in Psychology*, *10*, 479184. doi:10.3389/fpsyg.2019.02678 PMID:31849780

Wu, G. Z., & You, D. M. (2021). Will enterprise digital transformation affect diversification strategy? arXiv preprint arXiv:2112.06605. https://arxiv.org/abs/2112.06605

Zhou, N., Esparza, S. G., & Garshol, L. M. (2019). A Semantic Schema for Data Quality Management in a Multi-Tenant Data Platform. arXiv preprint arXiv:1908.10754 https://arxiv.org/abs/1908.10754

Chapter 3
Navigating Crisis Situations:
The Role of Digital Resilience in Effective Leadership and Organizational Continuity

Prachee Mittal Tandon
https://orcid.org/0009-0006-0499-9757
GNIT College of Management, India

ABSTRACT

Navigating modern crises requires digital resilience, a fusion of technology, leadership, and adaptability. This chapter explores its pivotal role, emphasizing robust tech infrastructure, crisis communication, cyber security, and leadership skills. Resilient leadership with ethical considerations and employee well-being are crucial. Measurable metrics assess digital resilience effectiveness, and strategies like predictive analytics and AI enhance crisis preparation. Globalization challenges demand nuanced approaches, and leaders drive cultural shifts toward adaptability. Social media's role in crisis communication is analyzed, and long-term planning ensures sustainable digital resilience. Embracing these principles ensures organizational survival, growth, and adaptability in the digital age.

INTRODUCTION

In an era marked by unprecedented technological advancements, organizations find themselves navigating a landscape fraught with unforeseen challenges and disruptions. Crises, whether arising from cyber threats, global pandemics, or natural disasters, have become inevitable facets of the contemporary business environment. Effective leadership in these tumultuous times demands not only resilience but a profound understanding of the transformative power of digital tools and strategies.

The intersection of leadership, crisis management, and digital resilience has emerged as a critical domain that defines organizational survival and growth. Anticipating change speed, adapting to it, as well as crisis recovery — are not a privilege today but an imperative need. This book, "Navigating Crisis Situations: This study namely titled "The Role of Digital Resilience in Effective Leadership and Organization Continuity" aims at deciphering this intersection and provide guidance on how

DOI: 10.4018/979-8-3693-1946-8.ch003

leaders can leverage digital resilience to see their organizations over storms and even better off than before.

The Digital Imperative: Digital resilience, at its core, is a proactive response to the evolving challenges of the digital age. It represents an organization's capacity to endure disruptions, innovate in the face of adversity, and ultimately thrive amidst uncertainty. As the digital landscape continues to shape and redefine business paradigms, leaders are compelled to reassess their strategies, incorporating digital tools not only as enablers but as integral components of crisis preparedness and response.

The Components of Leadership in Crisis: Effective leadership in crisis situations transcends traditional paradigms. It requires a strategic amalgamation of technological readiness, crisis communication prowess, and a resilient organizational culture. A robust technological infrastructure ensures the availability and security of critical data, while crisis communication strategies leverage digital channels to disseminate timely and transparent information, fostering trust. Leaders must possess the agility to make informed decisions amidst chaos, strategic foresight, and the ability to communicate empathetically with stakeholders.

Defining the Scope: This book chapter embarks on a comprehensive exploration of the multifaceted nature of digital resilience and its central role in the continuum of effective leadership and organizational continuity. From delving into case studies that illuminate real-world applications of digital resilience strategies to dissecting the ethical and legal considerations in the digital realm, our journey encompasses the holistic spectrum of challenges and opportunities faced by leaders in times of crisis.

The Significance of Case Studies: Real-world scenarios serve as our guiding beacons, offering tangible examples of leaders who have successfully navigated crises through the prism of digital resilience. Whether in response to a cyber security breach, a global pandemic, or a sudden economic downturn, these case studies illuminate the transformative impact of digital resilience on leadership practices and organizational outcomes.

An Invitation to Explore: As we navigate through the pages of this book chapter, we extend an invitation to leaders, scholars, and practitioners alike to delve into the intricacies of digital resilience. By unraveling its principles, analyzing its practical applications, and envisioning its future trajectories, we aim to equip readers with actionable insights that transcend theoretical frameworks, providing a roadmap for effective leadership in an era defined by uncertainty and rapid technological evolution.

In the subsequent sections, we delve into the core components of digital resilience, exploring its ethical dimensions, the transformative role of innovative strategies, and the global implications of leadership in crisis situations. This journey is not just an exploration; it is an essential guide for leaders forging ahead in a landscape where digital resilience is not just an option but a strategic imperative.

Introduction to Digital Resilience

Digital resilience refers to an organization's ability to adapt, recover, and thrive in the face of digital disruptions, crises, or unexpected challenges. It involves strategically leveraging digital tools, technologies, and strategies to withstand and recover from disruptions to digital infrastructure, data breaches, cyberattacks, and other forms of technological crises.

Key components of digital resilience include:

1. **Technological Infrastructure:** A robust and secure technological foundation, including reliable data storage, backup systems, and disaster recovery plans, is crucial for digital resilience. This

ensures that an organization's critical digital assets remain accessible and secure during and after a crisis.
2. **Crisis Communication Strategies:** Digital resilience involves effective communication strategies that leverage digital channels. Transparent and timely communication through platforms such as social media, email, and messaging apps is essential for maintaining trust with stakeholders during crises.
3. **Cyber security Measures:** Protection against cyber threats is integral to digital resilience. Robust cyber security measures, including firewalls, encryption, and threat detection systems, help safeguard an organization's digital infrastructure and sensitive data.
4. **Leadership Skills for Crisis Management:** Leadership plays a pivotal role in digital resilience. Leaders need to possess agile decision-making skills, strategic planning abilities, and effective communication skills to navigate crises. They must foster a culture of adaptability and innovation within their teams.
5. **Innovative Strategies:** Forward-thinking organizations employ innovative strategies to enhance digital resilience. This may involve the use of predictive analytics to identify potential threats, scenario planning for crisis simulation, and the adoption of emerging technologies like artificial intelligence for proactive crisis management.
6. **Ethical Considerations:** Digital resilience also encompasses ethical considerations in the use of technology. This includes ensuring data privacy, compliance with legal and regulatory frameworks, and making ethical decisions in the face of complex digital dilemmas.
7. **Employee Well-being:** Recognizing that organizational resilience is interconnected with the well-being of its workforce, digital resilience considers the impact of crises on employee mental health and well-being. Organizations that prioritize the support and well-being of their employees are better positioned to weather crises.

Digital resilience is not only about bouncing back from disruptions but also about using these challenges as opportunities for growth, adaptation, and innovation. It requires a proactive and strategic approach to digital challenges, ensuring that an organization remains agile and adaptable in an ever-changing digital landscape.

Ethical Dimensions of Digital Resilience

The ethical dimensions of digital resilience are critical considerations that organizations must address in their strategies to navigate crises and disruptions. Here are key ethical dimensions associated with digital resilience:

1. **Data Privacy and Protection:**
    - *Ethical Consideration:* Organizations must uphold individuals' rights to privacy and ensure the responsible collection, storage, and processing of data.
    - *Challenges:* Balancing the need for data-driven decision-making with respect for individual privacy rights can be challenging. Transparent data practices and robust cybersecurity measures are essential.
2. **Transparency in Communication:**
    - *Ethical Consideration:* Transparent communication during crises is crucial for building and maintaining trust with stakeholders.

- *Challenges:* Organizations may face dilemmas when balancing transparency with the need to protect sensitive information. Ethical communication involves providing accurate and timely information while avoiding unnecessary panic.

3. **Informed Consent in Technology Use:**
    - *Ethical Consideration:* Organizations should seek informed consent when implementing technologies that may impact individuals, especially in crisis situations.
    - *Challenges:* Rapid adoption of technologies during crises may lead to challenges in obtaining explicit consent. Organizations must communicate the purpose and implications of technology use clearly.
4. **Equitable Access to Technology:**
    - *Ethical Consideration:* Ensuring that all individuals have equal access to technology resources during crises is essential to avoid exacerbating existing inequalities.
    - *Challenges:* Disparities in access to technology may widen during crises, raising ethical concerns. Organizations must consider inclusive strategies to address these disparities.
5. **Digital Inclusion and Accessibility:**
    - *Ethical Consideration:* Organizations should ensure that digital resilience strategies are inclusive and accessible to individuals with diverse abilities and backgrounds.
    - *Challenges:* The rapid digitization of services during crises may inadvertently exclude individuals who face challenges in accessing digital platforms.
6. **Responsibility in Artificial Intelligence (AI):**
    - *Ethical Consideration:* Organizations leveraging AI for decision-making during crises must ensure responsible and unbiased use.
    - *Challenges:* Bias in AI algorithms and the potential for unintended consequences raise ethical concerns. Organizations must implement fairness and transparency measures in AI systems.
7. **Security and Protection of Critical Infrastructure:**
    - *Ethical Consideration:* Safeguarding critical digital infrastructure is an ethical imperative to protect the well-being of individuals and communities.
    - *Challenges:* Balancing security measures with the potential for overreach and surveillance requires ethical decision-making. Organizations must prioritize security without compromising civil liberties.
8. **Crisis Communication and Misinformation:**
    - *Ethical Consideration:* Organizations must combat misinformation ethically, ensuring that communication is accurate and reliable during crises.
    - *Challenges:* The fast-paced nature of crises may lead to challenges in verifying information. Ethical communication involves efforts to clarify and correct misinformation promptly.
9. **Accountability and Learning from Crises:**
    - *Ethical Consideration:* Organizations should be accountable for their actions during crises and should use these experiences to learn and improve.
    - *Challenges:* Acknowledging mistakes and learning from crises may be challenging. Ethical leadership involves taking responsibility for actions and committing to continuous improvement.
10. **Global Collaboration and Ethical Leadership:**
    - *Ethical Consideration:* Ethical leadership involves fostering global collaboration to address digital resilience challenges collectively.

- *Challenges:* Ethical leadership in a global context requires navigating diverse cultural norms and legal frameworks. Organizations must respect and incorporate varied perspectives in their strategies.

Addressing these ethical dimensions ensures that digital resilience strategies are not only effective but also aligned with principles of fairness, transparency, and respect for individuals' rights. Organizations that prioritize ethical considerations in their digital resilience initiatives are better positioned to build and maintain trust in times of crises.

Digital Resilience

Digital resilience plays a central role in the continuum of effective leadership and organizational continuity by serving as a strategic and adaptive framework that enables organizations to navigate disruptions, ensure operational continuity, and foster sustained growth. Here's an exploration of how digital resilience functions at different stages of this continuum:

1. **Preparedness and Proactive Leadership:**
    - *Role of Digital Resilience:* Digital resilience involves proactive measures to prepare for potential disruptions, such as cybersecurity threats, technological failures, or unforeseen crises. Leaders, equipped with a resilient mindset, anticipate challenges, implement robust technological infrastructures, and establish crisis communication strategies in advance.
    - *Impact on Leadership:* Leaders who prioritize digital resilience demonstrate a forward-thinking approach. They instill a culture of preparedness within the organization, positioning it to respond effectively to unforeseen challenges.
2. **Crisis Response and Decision-Making:**
    - *Role of Digital Resilience:* When a crisis strikes, digital resilience empowers leaders to make agile and informed decisions. This includes leveraging technology for real-time data analysis, utilizing crisis communication channels for transparent updates, and deploying cybersecurity measures to mitigate threats.
    - *Impact on Leadership:* Leaders adept in digital resilience respond swiftly and decisively to crises, maintaining open lines of communication, ensuring data integrity, and minimizing disruptions. Their ability to navigate these challenges reflects the strength of their digital resilience strategies.
3. **Organizational Adaptability and Innovation:**
    - *Role of Digital Resilience:* Digital resilience fosters organizational adaptability by encouraging innovation in response to disruptions. Leaders leverage technological advancements, such as artificial intelligence or data analytics, to identify new opportunities, optimize processes, and drive innovation during periods of uncertainty.
    - *Impact on Leadership:* Leaders promoting digital resilience inspire a culture of innovation, encouraging teams to view disruptions as catalysts for positive change. This adaptability ensures that the organization not only recovers but evolves and thrives in the post-crisis landscape.
4. **Continuous Improvement and Learning:**

- *Role of Digital Resilience:* After a crisis has been managed, digital resilience supports a culture of continuous improvement. Organizations assess their responses, identify areas for enhancement, and refine their digital strategies for future resilience.
- *Impact on Leadership:* Leaders committed to digital resilience embrace a learning mindset. They lead post-crisis evaluations, incorporating lessons learned into strategic planning. This commitment ensures that the organization becomes more resilient with each experience.

5. **Sustainable Growth and Future-Proofing:**
   - *Role of Digital Resilience:* Digital resilience is not just about overcoming immediate challenges; it involves future-proofing the organization against emerging threats. Leaders implement strategies that consider long-term sustainability, anticipate technological trends, and position the organization for ongoing growth.
   - *Impact on Leadership:* Forward-thinking leaders integrate digital resilience into the organization's strategic vision. They make decisions with a long-term perspective, ensuring that the organization remains adaptive and competitive in an ever-changing digital landscape.

Digital resilience serves as the linchpin in the continuum of effective leadership and organizational continuity. It equips leaders to proactively prepare for disruptions, respond decisively during crises, foster adaptability and innovation, continuously learn and improve, and position the organization for sustainable growth. By embracing digital resilience, leaders not only navigate challenges but also transform disruptions into opportunities for organizational evolution and success.

Recent trends and Emerging Technologies in Digital Resilience

Recent traits and emerging technology in virtual resilience are unexpectedly transforming the panorama of organizational continuity and disaster control. As cyber threats become increasingly sophisticated and ubiquitous, agencies should adopt superior strategies and leverage modern technology to protect their virtual infrastructure and ensure operational stability. Recent literature examines key tendencies and emerging era in virtual resilience, highlighting their impact on powerful management and organizational continuity.

1. AI Threat Detection and Response

AI-pushed danger detection and response technology have become fundamental to enhancing digital resilience. According to a latest study via Williams and Green (2021), using synthetic intelligence (AI) and machine getting to know (ML) algorithms enables businesses to hit upon and reply to cyber threats in real time. These technologies can analyze massive amounts of facts to perceive patterns and anomalies, supplying leaders with actionable insights and enhancing reaction instances.

2. Zero Trust Architecture

The adoption of zero consider structure (ZTA) is a growing fashion in virtual resilience, as noted by using Patel and Zhao (2022). This technique assumes that no person or tool is inherently trustworthy and requires continuous verification of identities and permissions. ZTA enhances protection via proscribing get entry to sensitive records and resources, thereby minimizing the risk of statistics breaches and insider threats.

3. Quantum-Safe Cryptography

As quantum computing advances, the capacity for breaking conventional encryption strategies becomes a problem. Smith and Brown (2023) talk the emergence of quantum-secure cryptography, which aims to secure data in opposition to capacity quantum attacks. Organizations are more and more exploring and adopting those encryption strategies to future-evidence their records protection techniques.

4. Blockchain Technology for Data Integrity

Blockchain technology is gaining traction as a means of making sure records integrity and agree with in digital transactions. In their paper, Johnson and Lee (2021) spotlight how blockchain's decentralized and immutable ledger may be leveraged to beautify transparency and safety in deliver chain management, monetary services, and healthcare.

5. Dynamic Cybersecurity Policies and Automation

The shift in the direction of dynamic cybersecurity rules, supported by means of automation, is transforming virtual resilience strategies. According to investigate via Kim and Singh (2020), non-stop tracking and automated reaction structures permit companies to evolve to evolving threats quickly. These policies incorporate adaptive controls that alter in real-time based totally at the chance landscape.

6. Cloud-Native Security

The growing reliance on cloud-based totally solutions necessitates a focus on cloud-local safety practices. Chen and Wilson (2022) emphasize the significance of securing cloud infrastructure thru identification and get right of entry to control (IAM), records encryption, and steady APIs. Cloud-local security aligns with the scalability and flexibility of cloud environments, ensuring sturdy safety in opposition to threats.

7. Threat Intelligence Platforms and Collaboration:

The rise of risk intelligence systems and collaborative networks is a latest trend in virtual resilience. Research by using Thompson and Garcia (2021) highlights how these structures facilitate the sharing of risk records and first-class practices amongst businesses. Collaborative networks decorate situational recognition and permit a greater proactive approach to cyber defense.

8. Digital Twin Technology for Risk Assessment:

Digital dual generation, which creates virtual replicas of physical structures, is being applied to chance assessment and disaster control. Lee and Martinez (2023) talk how virtual twins can model and simulate various eventualities, permitting groups to assess ability risks and broaden more powerful resilience strategies.

Recent trends and emerging technology in digital resilience present new possibilities and challenges for corporations and leaders. By adopting AI-pushed threat detection, 0 trust structure, quantum-safe cryptography, blockchain, dynamic cybersecurity regulations, cloud-native protection, threat intelligence structures, and virtual twin era, groups can enhance their digital resilience and improve organizational continuity. These improvements empower leaders to navigate complicated disaster situations with agility and foresight, in the end contributing to a greater secure and sustainable virtual future.

Components of Leadership in Crisis

Leadership in a crisis requires a unique set of skills and qualities to navigate challenges, inspire confidence, and guide organizations through uncertainty. The components of leadership in a crisis encompass a range of characteristics and actions that effective leaders demonstrate during turbulent times. Here's a detailed description of each component:

1. **Calm and Composed Presence:**
    - **Description:** In the midst of a crisis, leaders need to maintain a calm and composed presence. This involves controlling personal emotions, projecting confidence, and providing a sense of stability to the team and stakeholders.
    - **Detail:** Leaders who remain composed inspire confidence and reduce anxiety among team members. This presence is not a display of indifference but a strategic demonstration of resilience and focus, reassuring others that challenges are being addressed with a clear head.
2. **Decisiveness:**
    - **Description:** Decisiveness is the ability to make timely and effective decisions, even when faced with incomplete information. In a crisis, quick decisions are often necessary to manage the situation and mitigate potential damage.
    - **Detail:** Leaders must weigh available information, assess risks, and make decisions that align with the organization's values and goals. While perfection may be elusive, decisive actions demonstrate leadership and prevent indecision from exacerbating the crisis.
3. **Effective Communication:**
    - **Description:** Communication is critical during a crisis. Leaders must articulate the situation transparently, share relevant information, and provide guidance to team members and stakeholders.
    - **Detail:** Effective communication involves both clarity and empathy. Leaders should convey a clear understanding of the crisis, the organization's response, and any necessary actions. Empathetic communication demonstrates understanding and fosters a sense of unity during challenging times.
4. **Strategic Thinking:**
    - **Description:** Strategic thinking involves the ability to analyze the crisis context, anticipate potential outcomes, and formulate plans that align with the organization's long-term objectives.
    - **Detail:** Leaders must go beyond immediate problem-solving and consider the broader implications of their decisions. This component involves understanding how actions taken during a crisis impact the organization's future and positioning it for resilience and growth.

5. **Adaptability:**
    - **Description:** Adaptability is the capacity to adjust to changing circumstances and unexpected developments. In a crisis, situations evolve rapidly, and leaders need to be flexible in their approaches.
    - **Detail:** Leaders who demonstrate adaptability are open to new information, willing to adjust strategies as needed, and agile in responding to emerging challenges. This component enables leaders to navigate uncertainty with resilience.
6. **Empathy and Emotional Intelligence:**
    - **Description:** Empathy involves understanding and sharing the feelings of others, while emotional intelligence is the ability to recognize and manage one's own emotions and those of others.
    - **Detail:** Leaders who express empathy and emotional intelligence during a crisis create a supportive environment. Acknowledging the emotional impact of the crisis on individuals fosters trust and builds stronger connections within the team.
7. **Collaboration and Team Building:**
    - **Description:** Collaboration is the ability to work effectively with others, fostering teamwork and unity. Team building involves creating a cohesive and resilient team that can collectively address challenges.
    - **Detail:** Leaders must encourage collaboration, ensuring that team members share information, support one another, and work towards common goals. Building a cohesive team enhances the organization's collective ability to overcome crisis-related obstacles.
8. **Resilience:**
    - **Description:** Resilience is the capacity to bounce back from adversity and maintain effectiveness in the face of challenges. In a crisis, leaders must demonstrate personal and organizational resilience.
    - **Detail:** Resilient leaders model perseverance and determination. They inspire resilience in their teams by emphasizing the importance of learning from challenges, adapting strategies, and maintaining a forward-looking mindset.
9. **Ethical Decision-Making:**
    - **Description:** Ethical decision-making involves considering moral principles and values when making choices, especially in challenging situations where ethical dilemmas may arise.
    - **Detail:** Leaders must uphold ethical standards, making decisions that align with the organization's values and ethical principles. Transparency and fairness are crucial elements of ethical decision-making during a crisis.
10. **Preparedness and Risk Management:**
    - **Description:** Preparedness involves anticipating potential crises and having plans and resources in place to respond effectively. Risk management is the systematic identification, assessment, and mitigation of potential risks.
    - **Detail:** Leaders who prioritize preparedness and risk management are proactive in their approach to crises. They invest in contingency planning, scenario analysis, and risk mitigation strategies to minimize the impact of potential disruptions.
11. **Visionary Leadership:**
    - **Description:** Visionary leadership involves providing a compelling vision for the future and inspiring others to work towards shared goals, even in challenging circumstances.

- **Detail:** Leaders who offer a clear vision during a crisis instill hope and purpose. Communicating a vision for recovery and growth motivates the team to overcome obstacles and move toward a positive future.

Effective leadership during a crisis involves a combination of personal qualities, strategic thinking, and interpersonal skills. Leaders who embody these components can guide their organizations through uncertainty, inspire confidence, and foster resilience, ultimately contributing to the continuity and long-term success of the organization.

Impact of new technology on leadership and crisis situations

Technological crises gift unique challenges for leaders, who have to navigate a swiftly changing panorama even as safeguarding their agencies in opposition to diverse virtual threats. Such crises can arise from various assets, along with cybersecurity breaches, system screw ups, deliver chain disruptions, and statistics loss. As corporations turn out to be an increasing number of dependent on digital structures, leaders have to increase techniques to manipulate and mitigate the dangers related to technological crises. Here are a number of the key management challenges and potential strategies to deal with them:

1.Rapid Decision-Making and Agility

Challenge: In the face of technological crises, leaders must make quick choices to include the state of affairs and save you further harm.

Approach: Developing agile selection-making frameworks permits leaders to reply quickly and correctly. Leaders must empower their groups to take initiative and make selections primarily based on predefined crisis protocols.

2. Ensuring Business Continuity

Challenge: Technological crises can disrupt everyday operations and effect enterprise continuity.

Approach: Leaders have to set up comprehensive commercial enterprise continuity plans that account for various digital threats. This consists of having backup systems, records redundancy, and clear recovery techniques in region.

3. Awareness and Preparedness of Cybersecurity

Challenge: The constantly evolving nature of cyber threats requires constant vigilance.

Approach: Priortizing cybersecurity cognizance and education across their businesses

4. Crisis Communication and Transparency

Challenge: Effective verbal exchange for the duration of technological crises is essential to preserve stakeholder consider and control reputational hazard.

Navigating Crisis Situations

Approach: Leaders should establish clear verbal exchange protocols and designate spokespersons for crisis conditions. Transparent and clear communication can help manage public notion and reassure stakeholders.

5. Ethical Decision-Making

Challenge: Leaders face ethical dilemmas when balancing the dynamic needs of disaster management with lengthy-term effects.

Approach: Ethical selection-making frameworks ought to manual leaders in navigating complicated conditions. Leaders must weigh the capability impact on personnel, clients, and society whilst making crucial selections.

6. Resilient Supply Chains and Ecosystems

Challenge: Supply chain disruptions because of technological crises may have some distance-achieving consequences on operations and international change.

Approach: Leaders ought to paintings with providers and partners to construct resilient deliver chains. Diversifying providers, making an investment in superior tracking technology, and fostering collaboration can mitigate dangers.

7. Emotional Intelligence and Crisis Leadership

Challenge: Technological crises create high-stress environment employee morale and productiveness.

Approach: Leaders need to exhibit emotional intelligence and offer support to their groups. This consists of being empathetic, communicating in reality, and supporting personnel manage stress.

8. Innovation and Adaptation

Challenge: Technological crises can reveal vulnerabilities and prompt the need for innovation and model.

Approach: Leaders have to view crises as opportunities to innovate and improve approaches. Encouraging innovative hassle-solving and experimenting with new technology can power lengthy-term resilience.

Technological crises gift multifaceted demanding situations for leaders, requiring a combination of short choice-making, clean verbal exchange, and moral concerns. By adopting a proactive approach and specializing in resilience, preparedness, and non-stop analyzing, leaders can navigate the ones crises efficiently and emerge stronger. The potential to adapt, innovate, and foster a lifestyle of safety and transparency is vital for overcoming the annoying conditions posed via way of technological disruptions.

The Changing Landscape of Industry Management in the Clever Digital Era

Behie et al. Examine how technological improvements including the Internet of Things (IoT), synthetic intelligence (AI), and statistics analytics are remodeling industry management and reshaping the management landscape. Leaders have to adapt to the requirements of Industry by means of developing a deep know-how of these technologies and integrating them into organizational strategies. Leaders need to showcase agility and a ahead-searching attitude to successfully navigate the smart digital generation. The paper highlights the importance of fostering a way of life of innovation and continuous studying to stay in advance of the curve and leverage generation for aggressive benefit.

1. The Digital Course to Business Resilience

Close et al. Talk how digital transformation enhances enterprise resilience by way of enabling groups to reply speedy to crises and adapt to converting environments. The paper emphasizes the position of virtual equipment and records-driven decision-making in improving agility and versatility. Leaders who include virtual transformation can better expect risks, streamline operations, and keep continuity for the duration of disruptions. By investing in digital infrastructure and fostering a virtual-first mind-set, leaders can make stronger their enterprise's resilience to crises and function themselves for lengthy-term fulfillment.

2. The Cyber-Resilience of Financial Institutions

Dupont (2019) explores the annoying conditions that financial institutions face within the realm of cyber threats and the importance of virtual resilience. The paper highlights the need for leaders in the monetary region to expand strong cybersecurity techniques and invest in technology that guard critical records and systems. Effective leadership in this context entails balancing the demands of regulatory compliance, consumer accept as true with, and innovation. Leaders have to proactively manipulate cyber dangers and construct resilience via fostering a subculture of cybersecurity cognizance across the organization.

3. Strategies and Mechanisms for Constructing Virtual Resilience of Box Delivery Structures in Disaster Conditions

Gao et al. (2023) cognizance on digital resilience in the container transport industry, examining strategies and mechanisms to protect digital platforms during crises. The paper highlights the significance of resilient virtual infrastructure and the combination of superior technology inclusive of blockchain and AI for risk management and decision-making. Leaders in the transport enterprise should prioritize statistics safety and hold efficient operations despite disruptions. Building virtual resilience guarantees the continuity of worldwide supply chains and supports international exchange even in instances of disaster.

4. Conceptualizing Digital Resilience for AI-Based Information Systems

Schemmer et al. Look into the concept of virtual resilience in AI-based information structures, which offers unique challenges and possibilities for management. The paper discusses the want for leaders to recognize the intricacies of AI technology and their effect on organizational resilience. Leaders must navigate moral concerns and manage risks associated with AI adoption while leveraging its ability to enhance performance and innovation. A recognition on sturdy statistics governance, moral AI use, and non-stop development is important for a hit AI integration.

The convergence of management and rising technologies requires a dynamic method to crisis management. The selected papers illustrate how leaders must include virtual transformation, foster innovation, and prioritize digital resilience throughout industries. By expertise and integrating cutting-edge technologies inclusive of AI, blockchain, and IoT, leaders can navigate crises extra efficaciously and secure the destiny fulfillment in their organizations. This holistic method to virtual resilience empowers leaders to assume, mitigate, and reply to technological crises with agility and foresight, making sure continuity and sustainable boom in the contemporary digital generation.

Innovative Strategies for Digital Resilience

Innovative strategies for digital resilience involve forward-thinking approaches to prepare, adapt, and respond to disruptions in the digital landscape. These strategies leverage cutting-edge technologies, creative thinking, and proactive measures to enhance an organization's ability to withstand and recover from digital challenges. Here are innovative strategies for digital resilience:

1. **Predictive Analytics and Threat Intelligence:**
    - **Description:** Utilize predictive analytics and threat intelligence to anticipate and identify potential cyber threats before they manifest.
    - **Benefits:** Proactively identifying and mitigating potential threats enhances cybersecurity measures, preventing or minimizing the impact of cyberattacks.
2. **Blockchain Technology for Data Integrity:**
    - **Description:** Implement blockchain technology to ensure the integrity and security of critical data. Blockchain's decentralized and tamper-resistant nature makes it valuable for maintaining the integrity of digital records.
    - **Benefits:** Enhances data security and trust, particularly in industries where data integrity is paramount, such as finance, healthcare, and supply chain.
3. **Dynamic Cybersecurity Policies:**
    - **Description:** Develop dynamic cybersecurity policies that adapt to changing threat landscapes in real-time. Incorporate machine learning algorithms to continuously analyze and update security protocols.
    - **Benefits:** Improves the agility and responsiveness of cybersecurity measures, allowing for rapid adaptation to emerging threats.
4. **Red Teaming and Simulation Exercises:**
    - **Description:** Conduct red teaming exercises and simulations to simulate real-world cyber threats and test the organization's response capabilities.
    - **Benefits:** Identifies weaknesses in existing systems and response plans, allowing organizations to refine their digital resilience strategies.
5. **Artificial Intelligence (AI) for Anomaly Detection:**
    - **Description:** Implement AI-driven anomaly detection systems that can identify unusual patterns in network behavior, indicating potential security threats.
    - **Benefits:** Enhances the ability to detect and respond to cyber threats in real-time, minimizing the impact of security breaches.
6. **Zero Trust Architecture:**
    - **Description:** Adopt a zero-trust architecture that assumes no implicit trust within the network, requiring verification from anyone trying to access resources.
    - **Benefits:** Enhances security by minimizing the potential damage of insider threats and ensuring continuous verification of users and devices.

7. **Cloud-Based Disaster Recovery:**
    - **Description:** Leverage cloud-based disaster recovery solutions to ensure data availability and business continuity in the event of a system failure or cyberattack.
    - **Benefits:** Facilitates faster recovery times, reduces downtime, and provides scalable and cost-effective solutions for data recovery.
8. **Quantum-Safe Cryptography:**
    - **Description:** Explore quantum-safe cryptographic algorithms to secure sensitive information against potential threats from quantum computers in the future.
    - **Benefits:** Future-proofs data encryption methods, ensuring that sensitive information remains secure even as quantum computing capabilities evolve.
9. **Threat Hunting and Cyber Threat Intelligence Platforms:**
    - **Description:** Employ threat hunting practices and leverage cyber threat intelligence platforms to proactively search for and identify potential threats within the organization's network.
    - **Benefits:** Improves the organization's ability to detect and neutralize threats before they escalate, enhancing overall cybersecurity posture.
10. **Robotic Process Automation (RPA) for Incident Response:**
    - **Description:** Integrate RPA into incident response processes to automate routine tasks, allowing cybersecurity professionals to focus on more complex and strategic aspects of incident management.
    - **Benefits:** Speeds up incident response times, reduces human error, and allows cybersecurity teams to allocate resources more efficiently.
11. **Continuous Employee Training and Awareness:**
    - **Description:** Implement continuous and engaging training programs to educate employees on cybersecurity best practices and create a culture of security awareness.
    - **Benefits:** Strengthens the human firewall, reducing the likelihood of successful social engineering attacks and enhancing overall cybersecurity resilience.
12. **Digital Supply Chain Security:**
    - **Description:** Strengthen the security of the digital supply chain by implementing secure coding practices, conducting security assessments of third-party vendors, and ensuring the integrity of software and firmware.
    - **Benefits:** Reduces the risk of supply chain attacks, ensuring the security and integrity of digital products and services.

Incorporating these innovative strategies into a comprehensive digital resilience framework positions organizations to proactively address digital threats, adapt to evolving challenges, and build a robust defense against potential disruptions. The integration of emerging technologies and dynamic approaches ensures that organizations remain resilient in the face of an ever-changing digital landscape.

Transformative Role of Innovative Strategies

let's delve into the transformative role of the innovative strategies mentioned above and how they contribute to the digital resilience of organizations:

1. **Predictive Analytics and Threat Intelligence:**
    - **Transformative Role:** By leveraging predictive analytics and threat intelligence, organizations transform from reactive to proactive cybersecurity postures. The ability to predict and preemptively address potential threats enhances overall digital resilience. It shifts the focus from responding to incidents to preventing them, significantly reducing the likelihood and impact of cyberattacks.
2. **Blockchain Technology for Data Integrity:**
    - **Transformative Role:** Blockchain transforms data integrity practices by providing a decentralized, tamper-resistant ledger. This technology ensures that data remains unaltered and trustworthy, particularly critical in industries where data integrity is paramount, such as healthcare and finance. The transformative impact is a heightened level of trust in digital transactions and records.
3. **Dynamic Cybersecurity Policies:**
    - **Transformative Role:** The adoption of dynamic cybersecurity policies transforms the traditional static approach. Using machine learning for continuous analysis and adaptation allows organizations to dynamically respond to evolving cyber threats. This agility ensures that security measures are always aligned with the current threat landscape, enhancing the organization's ability to stay ahead of cyber risks.
4. **Red Teaming and Simulation Exercises:**
    - **Transformative Role:** Red teaming and simulations transform crisis preparedness by providing realistic scenarios for testing and refining digital resilience strategies. Organizations evolve from theoretical planning to practical application, identifying weaknesses, and refining their response capabilities. This hands-on approach ensures that the organization is better prepared for real-world cyber threats.
5. **Artificial Intelligence (AI) for Anomaly Detection:**
    - **Transformative Role:** AI-driven anomaly detection transforms security monitoring by automating the identification of unusual patterns in network behavior. This real-time analysis enables swift responses to potential security threats, reducing the detection-to-response time. The transformative impact is a more adaptive and responsive security infrastructure.
6. **Zero Trust Architecture:**
    - **Transformative Role:** Zero Trust Architecture transforms traditional security models by assuming no implicit trust, requiring continuous verification. This approach minimizes the potential damage of insider threats and ensures that trust is never assumed, even within the organization's network. The transformation is a security model built on continuous verification and a fundamental shift in the approach to trust.
7. **Cloud-Based Disaster Recovery:**
    - **Transformative Role:** Cloud-based disaster recovery transforms traditional recovery strategies by providing scalable, cost-effective, and resilient solutions. It shifts organizations from relying on on-premises recovery systems to leveraging the flexibility and accessibility of the cloud. The transformative impact is enhanced business continuity, reduced downtime, and improved recovery capabilities.
8. **Quantum-Safe Cryptography:**
    - **Transformative Role:** Quantum-safe cryptography transforms traditional encryption methods by providing protection against potential threats from quantum computers in the future.

This forward-looking approach ensures that sensitive information remains secure even as quantum computing capabilities evolve. The transformative impact is future-proofing data encryption methods.

9. **Threat Hunting and Cyber Threat Intelligence Platforms:**
   - **Transformative Role:** Threat hunting and cyber threat intelligence platforms transform cybersecurity from a reactive to a proactive stance. These approaches enable organizations to actively search for potential threats within their networks, improving detection capabilities. The transformative impact is a cybersecurity strategy that anticipates and neutralizes threats before they escalate.

10. **Robotic Process Automation (RPA) for Incident Response:**
    - **Transformative Role:** RPA in incident response transforms the efficiency of cybersecurity teams by automating routine tasks. This allows human experts to focus on more complex and strategic aspects of incident management. The transformative impact is accelerated incident response times, reduced human error, and optimized resource allocation.

11. **Continuous Employee Training and Awareness:**
    - **Transformative Role:** Continuous employee training transforms the organization's security culture. By fostering awareness and education, employees become an integral part of the cybersecurity defense. The transformative impact is a more resilient human firewall, reducing the risk of successful social engineering attacks.

12. **Digital Supply Chain Security:**
    - **Transformative Role:** Strengthening digital supply chain security transforms risk management practices. Organizations evolve from a focus on internal security to ensuring the security and integrity of the entire digital supply chain. The transformative impact is a more comprehensive and secure ecosystem for digital products and services.

These innovative strategies transform the traditional paradigms of cybersecurity and digital resilience. They usher in a new era where organizations are not just responding to digital challenges but proactively anticipating and mitigating risks. The transformative impact is a more adaptive, agile, and resilient digital infrastructure that can withstand and thrive in the face of evolving threats.

Global Implications of Leadership in Crisis Situations

Leadership in crisis situations has profound global implications, influencing not only the affected organizations or nations but also shaping the interconnected fabric of the international community. Here's a detailed exploration of the global implications of leadership in crisis situations:

1. **Global Economic Impact:**
   - *Role of Leadership:* Effective crisis leadership can mitigate economic downturns and promote stability. On the global stage, the decisions made by leaders during crises can have ripple effects on economies worldwide.
   - *Implications:* Collaborative and strategic crisis management can contribute to the resilience of the global economy. Conversely, poor leadership or lack of coordination may exacerbate economic challenges and amplify the impact of the crisis.

Navigating Crisis Situations

2. **International Relations and Cooperation:**
   - *Role of Leadership:* Crisis situations often require international cooperation. Leaders must engage in diplomacy, collaboration, and resource-sharing to address global challenges like pandemics, environmental disasters, or geopolitical tensions.
   - *Implications:* Effective crisis leadership fosters trust and collaboration between nations. Conversely, a lack of international cooperation can hinder efforts to address transnational crises, leading to prolonged and intensified challenges.
3. **Global Health and Well-being:**
   - *Role of Leadership:* During health crises, leaders play a pivotal role in coordinating global responses, sharing information, and facilitating the distribution of resources such as vaccines and medical supplies.
   - *Implications:* Strong leadership in the health domain can contribute to the containment and mitigation of pandemics. Conversely, inadequate leadership may result in delayed responses, increased mortality rates, and prolonged global health threats.
4. **Technological Innovation and Security:**
   - *Role of Leadership:* Leaders influence how nations and organizations respond to technological crises, including cybersecurity threats and disruptions in digital infrastructure.
   - *Implications:* Innovative leaders prioritize digital resilience, invest in cybersecurity, and foster technological advancements. In contrast, a lack of technological leadership may lead to vulnerabilities, data breaches, and disruptions with far-reaching consequences.
5. **Environmental Stewardship:**
   - *Role of Leadership:* Leaders guide global efforts to address environmental crises, such as climate change and natural disasters. Decisions on policies, resource management, and international cooperation are central to effective crisis leadership in this domain.
   - *Implications:* Visionary leaders contribute to global environmental sustainability, influencing policies and practices that can mitigate the impact of climate-related crises. Poor leadership may result in inadequate responses to environmental challenges with widespread consequences.
6. **Humanitarian Responses and Refugee Crises:**
   - *Role of Leadership:* Leaders play a key role in responding to humanitarian crises, including conflicts, natural disasters, and refugee situations. Their decisions shape international aid, cooperation, and efforts to address the root causes of displacement.
   - *Implications:* Compassionate and collaborative leadership can contribute to effective humanitarian responses and the resolution of conflicts. Conversely, inadequate leadership may lead to prolonged human suffering, displacement, and strained international relations.
7. **Ethical and Moral Leadership:**
   - *Role of Leadership:* Ethical and moral leadership is crucial during crises, influencing decisions on resource allocation, human rights, and the treatment of vulnerable populations.
   - *Implications:* Ethical leadership contributes to trust and legitimacy, fostering a sense of shared responsibility. Conversely, leadership lacking ethical considerations may lead to human rights abuses, social unrest, and erosion of international norms.
8. **Information and Disinformation Management:**
   - *Role of Leadership:* Leaders influence how information is managed and disseminated during crises. Transparent communication is essential for building trust and countering disinformation.

- *Implications:* Leaders who prioritize accurate and timely information contribute to public trust and effective crisis management. Conversely, leadership failures in information management can lead to confusion, panic, and the spread of misinformation globally.
9. **Crisis Preparedness and Resilience:**
    - *Role of Leadership:* Leaders influence the level of preparedness and resilience of their nations or organizations to face crises. Investments in infrastructure, healthcare systems, and disaster preparedness are critical.
    - *Implications:* Proactive leadership enhances global resilience by setting examples and promoting best practices. Conversely, a lack of preparedness may lead to cascading effects, impacting not only the immediate region but also neighboring nations and the global community.
10. **Social and Cultural Impact:**
    - *Role of Leadership:* Leaders shape the narrative around crises, influencing public perceptions and social cohesion. They must consider cultural nuances and social dynamics in crisis response.
    - *Implications:* Culturally sensitive leadership fosters unity and resilience. In contrast, leadership that neglects cultural considerations may face challenges in garnering public support, leading to social unrest and resistance to crisis measures.

Leadership in crisis situations extends beyond national borders and has far-reaching implications for the global community. Collaborative, ethical, and visionary leadership contributes to international stability, resilience, and the ability to address shared challenges. Conversely, leadership failures can exacerbate crises, strain international relations, and have enduring consequences on a global scale.

Interplay Between Ethical Considerations and Global Implications

In an an increasing number of virtual world, leaders should not most effective navigate the complexities of rising technology however additionally don't forget the wider ethical and worldwide impacts in their choices. This interconnectedness requires a more holistic angle on disaster control and organizational continuity.

ETHICAL CONSIDERATIONS

Data Privacy and Protection

Leaders must prioritize statistics privateness and safety as they leverage emerging technologies together with AI and blockchain. Adhering to international records protection standards and guidelines (e.g., GDPR, CCPA) is vital for maintaining client consideration and heading off criminal repercussions. Behie et al. (2023) emphasize the significance of ensuring ethical statistics practices and transparency, in particular in Industry 4.Zero.

AI and Algorithmic Fairness

The use of AI in selection-making processes can cause biases and discrimination if now not controlled well. Leaders need to ensure that AI systems are fair, obvious, and responsible. Schemmer et al. (2021) spotlight the moral demanding situations of AI-primarily based completely information structures, together with capability biases and absence of explainability.

Cybersecurity and Innovation

With the increasing reliance on virtual infrastructure, leaders must put money into cybersecurity measures that protect vital statistics and structures. Responsible innovation includes balancing the advantages of emerging technology with the dangers they may pose to security and stability. Dupont (2019) stresses the significance of building cyber-resilience in monetary institutions.

Human-Centered Design

Leaders should prioritize human-focused design in era adoption, making sure that digital systems serve the wishes of humans as opposed to replacing them.

GLOBAL IMPLICATIONS

Cross-Border Collaboration

Global crises require global cooperation and collaboration, especially while coping with complicated and interconnected supply chains. Gao et al. (2023) emphasize the need for constructing digital resilience in box shipping platforms to ensure continuity and performance in international alternate.

Standardization and Interoperability

Global virtual resilience necessitates the standardization of protocols and practices across industries and international locations. This ensures interoperability and complements the potential to respond together to crises.

Global Governance and Regulation

The improvement and enforcement of worldwide regulations concerning virtual resilience and emerging technologies are critical to maintaining secure and stable worldwide digital surroundings. Close et al. (2020) propose that virtual transformation can aid worldwide governance efforts in disaster control.

Impact on Developing Nations

The digital divide remains a massive venture for many developing nations, which may also lack the resources and infrastructure to fully gain from rising technologies. Leaders ought to take into account the capability exacerbation of present inequalities and work to make sure equitable get right of entry to virtual tools and resources.

Interconnectedness of Global Crises and Digital Resilience

The interconnected nature of worldwide crises and virtual resilience highlights the need for a extra holistic approach to crisis management. Crises in one part of the sector could have cascading outcomes across industries and areas, emphasizing the importance of digital resilience on a international scale.

Supply Chain Vulnerability

Global deliver chains are especially interconnected, and disruptions in a single location will have ripple consequences internationally. Building virtual resilience into deliver chain control, as highlighted by means of Gao et al. (2023), can help mitigate risks and make certain continuity.

Information Sharing and Collaboration

Leaders should foster records sharing and collaboration throughout borders to address global crises efficiently. Shared risk intelligence and best practices can beautify collective resilience.

Humanitarian and Environmental Considerations

Leaders need to recall the humanitarian and environmental effects of digital transformation. Ethical management entails prioritizing sustainability and the well-being of communities stricken by virtual disruptions.

Strategies to Overcome Global Implications of Leadership in Crisis Situations

Overcoming the global implications of leadership in crisis situations requires strategic and coordinated efforts at national, international, and organizational levels. Here are strategies to address and mitigate the challenges associated with leadership in global crises:

1. **International Collaboration and Cooperation:**
   - *Strategy:* Foster increased collaboration and cooperation among nations and international organizations. Establish and strengthen frameworks for sharing information, resources, and expertise during crises.
   - *Implementation:* Develop and reinforce international agreements and platforms for collaborative crisis response. Encourage the formation of alliances and partnerships that facilitate joint efforts in addressing global challenges.
2. **Transparent Communication and Information Sharing:**
   - *Strategy:* Prioritize transparent communication and information sharing at all levels of leadership. Ensure that accurate and timely information is disseminated to the public and across borders.

Navigating Crisis Situations

- *Implementation:* Establish communication protocols that promote transparency. Utilize technology and social media platforms to disseminate information globally. Collaborate with international organizations to share data and insights.

3. **Investment in Global Health Infrastructure:**
   - *Strategy:* Increase investments in global health infrastructure, including research, healthcare systems, and pandemic preparedness.
   - *Implementation:* Collaborate with international health organizations to strengthen global health systems. Support initiatives that aim to improve healthcare access, vaccine distribution, and disease surveillance worldwide.

4. **International Leadership Development Programs:**
   - *Strategy:* Develop programs that focus on leadership development with an international perspective. These programs should equip leaders with the skills and mindset to address global challenges.
   - *Implementation:* Establish educational and training initiatives that promote cross-cultural leadership competencies. Encourage participation in international forums and conferences to broaden leaders' perspectives.

5. **Global Crisis Response Task Forces:**
   - *Strategy:* Establish international task forces dedicated to crisis response and management. These task forces should be equipped to respond rapidly to emerging global threats.
   - *Implementation:* Create and fund multinational task forces with experts from various fields, ready to deploy in response to crises. Develop standardized protocols for cooperation and coordination among task force members.

6. **Digital Resilience and Cybersecurity Collaboration:**
   - *Strategy:* Strengthen global cybersecurity collaboration to address cyber threats that can have widespread implications.
   - *Implementation:* Foster information-sharing agreements among nations to combat cyber threats collectively. Support international efforts to establish cybersecurity standards and best practices. Collaborate with private sector organizations to enhance global digital resilience.

7. **International Humanitarian Coordination:**
   - *Strategy:* Improve coordination and collaboration in humanitarian efforts during crises. Streamline international aid distribution and response mechanisms.
   - *Implementation:* Enhance coordination between international humanitarian organizations, governments, and non-governmental organizations (NGOs). Establish rapid response teams that can be deployed globally to provide assistance during crises.

8. **Global Environmental Agreements:**
   - *Strategy:* Strengthen and adhere to global environmental agreements to address climate change and other environmental crises.
   - *Implementation:* Advocate for and participate in international agreements and treaties aimed at mitigating climate change. Support research and initiatives that promote sustainable practices globally.

9. **Ethical Leadership Promotion:**
   - *Strategy:* Promote ethical leadership principles and values on a global scale. Encourage leaders to prioritize ethical considerations in decision-making.

- *Implementation:* Support international initiatives that promote ethical leadership. Establish codes of conduct and guidelines for leaders participating in global organizations and forums.
10. **International Crisis Simulation Exercises:**
    - *Strategy:* Conduct international crisis simulation exercises to enhance preparedness and coordination.
    - *Implementation:* Organize regular multinational crisis simulations involving leaders from different countries and sectors. Evaluate and learn from these exercises to improve global crisis response capabilities.
11. **Cultural Sensitivity Training:**
    - *Strategy:* Implement cultural sensitivity training programs for leaders involved in global crisis management.
    - *Implementation:* Integrate cultural competency training into leadership development programs. Provide resources and support for leaders to understand and navigate diverse cultural contexts.
12. **Global Public-Private Partnerships:**
    - *Strategy:* Encourage public-private partnerships at a global level to enhance resources and capabilities in crisis response.
    - *Implementation:* Facilitate collaborations between governments, international organizations, and private sector entities. Leverage the expertise and resources of the private sector in areas such as technology, logistics, and innovation.

By implementing these strategies, leaders can collectively work towards overcoming the challenges associated with global implications of crises. The emphasis is on collaboration, communication, preparedness, and ethical leadership to build a more resilient and interconnected global community.

CONCLUSION

In the labyrinth of global challenges, the nexus between leadership and crisis response resonates with a profound impact that transcends borders and echoes through the interconnected tapestry of our world. The strategies delineated above illuminate a path towards not just mitigating the repercussions of crises but sculpting a future characterized by resilience, collaboration, and ethical fortitude on a truly global scale.

At the heart of these strategies lies the imperative of international collaboration. The complexity of today's challenges demands a collective response that spans continents and unites nations. The call to forge stronger alliances, share resources, and synchronize efforts underscores the recognition that a crisis anywhere is a concern everywhere. The power of collaboration is not merely a diplomatic nicety but a strategic necessity, acknowledging that our destinies are intertwined, and our collective strength lies in unity.

Transparent communication emerges as a linchpin, a force capable of dispelling uncertainty, mitigating misinformation, and fostering a global environment of shared understanding. In an era where information travels at unprecedented speeds, leaders wielding the power of transparent communication become architects of trust, weaving a narrative that transcends borders and resonates with clarity. The impact of open dialogue is not confined to crisis moments alone but permeates the fabric of international relations, building bridges that withstand the test of time.

Ethical leadership emerges as a guiding star in the tumultuous seas of crisis management. As leaders navigate uncharted territories, the moral compass they wield becomes the beacon that guides nations through stormy waters. The transformative power of ethical leadership is not confined to immediate decision-making but extends into the annals of history, shaping the legacy of nations and leaving an indelible mark on the global consciousness.

Preparedness emerges as the armor against the unforeseen, the proactive stance that leaders must adopt to shield their nations from the onslaught of crises. The call to invest in global health infrastructure, cyber security collaboration, and crisis response task forces is a clarion call to fortify our defenses against the unpredictable nature of contemporary challenges. It is an investment not just in the present but a down payment on the future resilience of nations interconnected in the delicate dance of a globalized world.

In the realm of international relations, cultural sensitivity emerges as the bridge that spans diverse landscapes and fosters a harmonious symphony of collaboration. The world is a mosaic of cultures, and leaders who understand and appreciate this diversity are better equipped to navigate the complexities of global crisis response. The impact of cultural sensitivity is not just diplomatic finesse but the forging of bonds that withstand the strains of adversity.

As we contemplate the strategies outlined above, we are confronted with the realization that the stakes are not merely national but planetary. The strategies are not just simple prescriptions but instead they form an overall manifesto of a world that wants to surpass difficulties in order to build a community with diversity in unity, force in cooperation and resilience against odds.

These strategies have the ability to change things not so much because of their execution but because they give birth to a universal ethic to recognize our common weaknesses, appreciate our common personhood, and rallying for this world to prepare better for upcoming disasters. In the crucible of crisis, leadership becomes the crucible where nations are forged anew, and the strategies outlined above become the alchemy that transmutes challenges into opportunities, adversity into resilience, and uncertainty into a shared promise of a better, more connected world for generations to come.

REFERENCES

Acciarini, C., Boccardelli, P., & Vitale, M. (2021). Resilient companies in the time of Covid-19 pandemic: A case study approach. *Journal of Entrepreneurship and Public Policy*, *10*(3), 336–351. doi:10.1108/JEPP-03-2021-0021

Assibi, A. T. (2022). The Role of Enterprise Risk Management in Business Continuity and Resiliency in the Post-COVID-19 Period. *OAlib*, *9*(6), 1–19. doi:10.4236/oalib.1108642

Behie, S. W., Pasman, H. J., Khan, F. I., Shell, K., Alarfaj, A., El-Kady, A. H., & Hernandez, M. (2023). Leadership 4.0: The changing landscape of industry management in the smart digital era. *Process Safety and Environmental Protection*, *172*, 317–328. doi:10.1016/j.psep.2023.02.014

Behie, S. W., Pasman, H. J., Khan, F. I., Shell, K., Alarfaj, A., El-Kady, A. H., & Hernandez, M. (2023). Leadership 4.0: The changing landscape of industry management in the smart digital era. *Process Safety and Environmental Protection*, *172*, 317–328. doi:10.1016/j.psep.2023.02.014

Close, K., Grebe, M., Andersen, P., Khurana, V., Franke, M. R., & Kalthof, R. (2020). The digital path to business resilience. Boston Consulting Group Report.

Corrales-Estrada, A. M., Gómez-Santos, L. L., Bernal-Torres, C. A., & Rodriguez-López, J. E. (2021). Sustainability and resilience organizational capabilities to enhance business continuity management: A literature review. *Sustainability (Basel)*, *13*(15), 8196. doi:10.3390/su13158196

Dubey, R., Bryde, D. J., Dwivedi, Y. K., Graham, G., Foropon, C., & Papadopoulos, T. (2023). Dynamic digital capabilities and supply chain resilience: The role of government effectiveness. *International Journal of Production Economics*, *258*, 108790. doi:10.1016/j.ijpe.2023.108790

Dupont, B. (2019). The Cyber-Resilience of Financial Institutions: A preliminary working paper on significance and applicability of digital resilience. *Global Risk Institute*.

Dupont, B. (2019). The cyber-resilience of financial institutions: Significance and applicability. *Journal of Cybersecurity*, *5*(1), tyz013. doi:10.1093/cybsec/tyz013

Elgazzar, Y., El-Shahawy, R., & Senousy, Y. (2022). The role of digital transformation in enhancing business resilience with pandemic of COVID-19. *Digital transformation technology Proceedings of ITAF*, *2020*, 323–333.

Gao, X., Kong, Y., & Cheng, L. (2023). Strategies and mechanisms for building digital resilience of container shipping platform in crisis situations: A network orchestration perspective. *Ocean and Coastal Management*, *246*, 106887. doi:10.1016/j.ocecoaman.2023.106887

GaoX.YudanK.LuC. (n.d.). Strategies and Mechanisms for Building Digital Resilience of Container Shipping Enterprises Under Crisis Situations: An Orchestration Role Perspective. *Available at* SSRN 4530751. doi:10.2139/ssrn.4530751

Greenwood, L. L., Hess, D., Abraham, Y., & Schneider, J. (2023). Capacity Building for Organizational Resilience: Integrating Standards on Risk, Disruption and Continuity in the Curriculum. *International Journal on Social and Education Sciences*, *5*(2), 327–340. doi:10.46328/ijonses.508

He, Z., Huang, H., Choi, H., & Bilgihan, A. (2023). Building organizational resilience with digital transformation. *Journal of Service Management*, *34*(1), 147–171. doi:10.1108/JOSM-06-2021-0216

Kerr, H. (2016). Organizational resilience. *Quality*, *55*(7), 40–43.

Kohn, V. (2023). *Operationalizing digital resilience–A systematic literature review on opportunities and challenges*. Academic Press.

Nkomo, L., & Kalisz, D. (2023). Establishing organisational resilience through developing a strategic framework for digital transformation. *Digital Transformation and Society*, *2*(4), 403–426. doi:10.1108/DTS-11-2022-0059

Romine, J. D. (2012). *Business Continuity and Resilience Engineering: How Organizations Prepare to Survive Disruptions to Vital Digital Infrastructure* (Doctoral dissertation, The Ohio State University).

Schemmer, M., Heinz, D., Baier, L., Vössing, M., & Kühl, N. (2021, June). Conceptualizing Digital Resilience for AI-based Information Systems. In ECIS.

Sinha, R., & Ola, A. (2021). Enhancing business community disaster resilience. A structured literature review of the role of dynamic capabilities. *Continuity & Resilience Review*, *3*(2), 132–148. doi:10.1108/CRR-03-2021-0009

Suryaningtyas, D., Sudiro, A., Eka, T. A., & Dodi, I. W. (2019). Organizational resilience and organizational performance: Examining the mediating roles of resilient leadership and organizational culture. *Academy of Strategic Management Journal*, *18*(2), 1–7.

Syed, H. A., Schorch, M., Hassan, S. S., Skudelny, S., Grinko, M., & Pipek, V. (2020). *From technology adoption to organizational resilience: A current research perspective*. Academic Press.

Wu, W. N. (2021, July). Organizational Resilience: Examining the Influence of Information Cost and Organizational Capacity on Business Continuity Management. In *International Conference on Human-Computer Interaction* (pp. 444-455). Cham: Springer International Publishing. 10.1007/978-3-030-77750-0_28

Zahari, A. I., Mohamed, N., Said, J., & Yusof, F. (2022). Assessing the mediating effect of leadership capabilities on the relationship between organisational resilience and organisational performance. *International Journal of Social Economics*, *49*(2), 280–295. doi:10.1108/IJSE-06-2021-0358

Chapter 4
Leadership and Technology Integration in India:
A Systematic Literature Review

K. H. Pavitra
Galgotias University, India

Alka Agnihotri
Galgotias University, India

Bindu Tiwari
Kings College, Nepal

ABSTRACT

Leadership has a critical role to play in the adoption of the transformational technology of artificial intelligence (AI). As India leads the AI revolution, this study aims to understand the role of leadership in AI adoption, the necessary competencies required for leaders to be successful in the current era of AI, and the most frequently occurring themes in AI and leadership in India, in the last decade. A systematic literature review (SLR) was conducted in Scopus, on studies published in a period of ten years from 2013 to 2023. Findings show that the role of leadership in AI adoption is of paramount importance. The theories identified by researchers to infer different facets of AI and leadership research are elaborated. The mental and emotional competencies needed for leaders are emphasized for successfully navigating the AI era. Practical implications for leaders in organizations are discussed. This is the first study to review research conducted between 2013 and 2023 which links leadership and AI in Indian organizations.

INTRODUCTION

Artificial intelligence (AI) has become the technological bedrock of worldwide digital transformation, as noted by the national association of software and services companies (NASSCOM) according to

DOI: 10.4018/979-8-3693-1946-8.ch004

Leadership and Technology Integration in India

The Hindu Bureau (2023). Increased implementation of modern-day technologies such as AI, machine learning, and internet of things (IoT) has resulted in considerable shifts in the manner work is performed in organizations (Jain & Ranjan, 2020). More than any other topic today, AI occupies centre stage in boardroom discussions, strategies, and dialogue (Katyal, 2023).

AI is understood as "the machine's ability to keep improving its performance without humans having to explain exactly how to accomplish all the tasks it's given" (Brynjolfsson & McAfee, 2017, p.257). AI is defined as "a set of procedures that authorize computers to accomplish tasks that would otherwise necessitate the cognitive skills that human intelligence fetches." (Kaushal et al., 2023, p.3). AI is defined as "Artificial tools that can automatically accumulate experience (i.e., make sense of objective environments) and constantly learn from past experience to perform cognitive tasks" (Pan & Froese, 2023, p.13). AI is noted to be the "potential of machines to impersonate the capabilities of the human mind" (The Economic Times, 2023a, p.3). AI-based solutions can be implemented across companies for task-automation, strategic decision-making, improved employee-engagement, and better customer-management. Hence, it is observed that organizations can achieve competitive advantage due to implementation of AI (Kar et al., 2021; Schrettenbrunnner, 2020).

It is noted that the adaptation of AI will cause higher economic growth in India (Varma et al., 2023). As per Accenture, AI has the capacity to contribute around 957$ billion, or 15% of current gross value added amount to the economy of India by the year 2035 (Varma et al., 2023). This is corroborated by the fact that popular adherents of AI such as Amazon, Alphabet and Tencent are some of the most well-known stocks worldwide which generate returns (Varma et al., 2023). Multinational technology behemoths such as IBM, Adobe, SAP and Microsoft are creating advanced AI solutions in India for their operations worldwide (Majumdar & Agarwal, 2023). Chief executive officers (CEOs) of these global companies note how India is becoming a pivotal part of AI development, and observe that India has an important part to perform in the future research on the disruptive technology that is AI (Majumdar & Agarwal, 2023). Based on findings of a survey of 200 top level executives in Indian companies, it was noted that 60% of companies appreciate that generative AI will have a considerable impact on their business models (The Economic Times Bureau, 2023). India currently is home to over 100 generative AI startups and fundings accumulated by novel generative AI startups and the acquisition of Indian AI companies by multinational companies headquartered in countries with larger economies are "good validations" (Roy & Lohchab, 2024, p.7) of the burgeoning AI ecosystem in India as per the senior vice president of NASSCOM (Roy & Lohchab, 2024). India today leads the way in AI revolution that is spreading across the world (The Economic Times, 2023b). In 2020, India surpassed countries such as UK, USA and Japan to possess the highest adoption of AI (National Association of Software and Services Companies [NASSCOM], 2021). As per the CEO, Tata Consultancy Services (TCS), India is poised to be at the heart of the generative AI revolution by its ability to develop AI-based solutions in Indian locations, for businesses in India, and businesses worldwide (Krithivasan, 2024). A 2022 report by NASSCOM about India's sector-wise advancement in AI implementation, based on a survey of more than 345 senior-level executives such as CXOs from industries like consumer packaged goods and retail, banking financial services and insurance, industrials and automotive, observed that forceful and determined leadership at companies is needed to quickly execute AI-oriented solutions (NASSCOM, 2022). Regarding the role of leadership in technology adoption in India, it is seen that leaders of the organization, such as CEOs, have historically played an important role in enabling technology implementation across industries, by identifying challenges of technology adoption and formulating solutions for the same (Associated Chambers of Commerce and Industry of India [ASSOCHAM], 2023). As mentioned by Arunabha Ghosh, founder and CEO of Blue Copper Technologies Pvt. Ltd., "As a business leader, I have taken every step to understand the various digital transformation challenges which are or are not directly related to technological concerns or technical barriers. It is imperative that we identify and assess which specific problems affect a business to create a plan to overcome them" (ASSOCHAM, 2023, p.46). As per a study conducted by NASSCOM and Boston Consulting Group (BCG) in February 2024, more than 69% of technology services-based firms in India have put in place AI leadership roles (Roy, 2024). According to staffing firms, many companies including IT services, banking and financial services, and consulting companies, are seeking employees for AI leadership positions such as AI director, vice president for AI, and CAIO (chief AI officer) in India as per Roy (2024). As per a CEO of an AI-based company, establishment of an AI leadership position in a company is important as AI becomes more central to businesses, not just as an enabling factor, but also as a possible disrupting factor in businesses (Roy, 2024). This underscores the importance of leadership in AI implementation in India. Hence, on observing the importance of AI implementation, the part played by leadership in AI implementation in India, and the potential for AI to benefit India, this study aims to understand the role of leadership in enhancing adoption of AI in companies in India. The purpose of the study is to find answers to the following research questions (RQs):

RQ1: What is the role played by leaders in the adoption of AI in an organization?

RQ2: What are the theories used to interpret different aspects of AI and leadership research?

RQ3: What are the necessary competencies required for leaders to be successful in the current era of AI?

Research Methodology

A systematic literature review (SLR) was conducted in the academic database Scopus. Scopus was selected as the database to conduct the article search as it is one of the most popular databases for journals and it covers a wide range of disciplines (Paul et al., 2021). A search was run on Scopus on October 6, 2023 with the search string 'lead* AND "artificial intelligence" OR "AI"'. The search term lead* was used because it was considered necessary to include articles with words which emanate from the root word 'lead' such as 'lead', 'leading', 'leader', and 'leadership'. This search was conducted with search terms being searched in article title, abstract and keywords only. With this search string, 39,515 results were obtained. The time range was selected as 2013 to 2023, as only the last ten years' studies were to be considered. Although the idea of AI was introduced in the 1950s, its implementation did not meet expectations due to restrained processing capabilities and data (Ramamoorthy, 2023). However, 2010 was a turnaround year when there was an abundance of data and development of cloud computing. The year 2010 onwards, proliferation of data has enabled the re-emergence of AI (Ramamoorthy, 2023). Also, the usage of AI was not widely known before 2011 (NASSCOM, 2021). Hence, this study considers a period of ten years from 2013 to 2023. Selection of this time range yielded 29,637 results. The subject areas were selected as "business, management, and accounting", "social sciences", "decision sciences", "economics, econometrics, and finance", and "psychology", as only these areas were considered relevant to our topic. This selection of subject areas yielded 5614 results. Further, the search was limited to the document type of "article", the language of "English", country/territory of "India", and publication stage of "final". This selection yielded 177 results. Within these 177 results, the abstracts of all the articles

Leadership and Technology Integration in India

were screened to ascertain that leadership and AI were the focal areas of study. All papers which did not have leadership and AI as the focal areas of study were excluded. Two studies were included where leadership was not studied as a construct, but insights from senior leaders were collected regarding the implementation and impact of AI at work (Jain & Ranjan, 2020; Malik et al., 2022). After the screening of the abstracts, 14 articles remained, which formed the basis of our review. The process followed for filtering of articles is shown in Figure 1.

Leadership and AI Adoption in Organizations

RQ1 is answered here. Chaudhuri et al. (2022) found that in the manufacturing companies, support of leadership acts as a moderator in the association between AI implementation rationale and AI sustainability of these companies, such that with more leadership support, AI implementation rationale leads to a high level of AI sustainability as compared to less support of leadership. The senior leaders of the company must ensure that their employees do not face problems in the implementation of novel AI-oriented systems (Chaudhuri et al., 2022). Also, Chaudhuri et al. (2022) recommend that the support of leadership should be extended to all levels of employees, and not just some levels.

Figure 1. Flowchart of search criteria for selection and screening of articles (Authors)

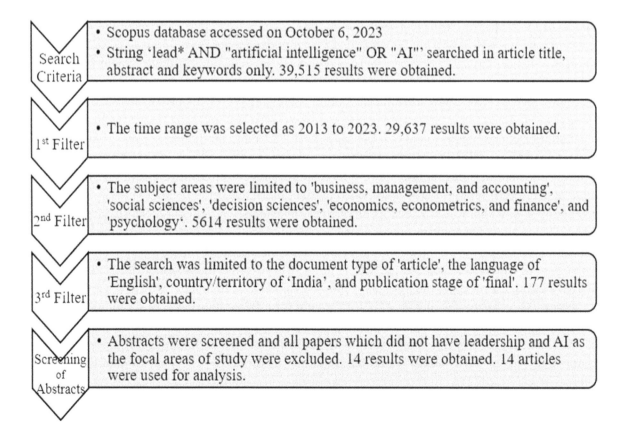

Vrontis et al. (2023) found that motivation by leadership moderates the association between the implementation of generative AI such as ChatGPT and sustainability of business in a manner that with more leadership motivation, a high level of ChatGPT implementation will result in a high level of sustainability of business. Vrontis et al. (2023) noted that the leadership of companies has a pivotal role in motivating and encouraging their employees to adopt these technologies in order to accomplish improved business sustainability. The leaders of the organization may demonstrate instances of successful adoption of ChatGPT or other GPT technologies so that employees understand that companies need to honour their obligations to society and achieve goals directed towards environmental sustainability which will boost their performance in the long run and their competitiveness in the industry (Vrontis et al., 2023).

Malik et al. (2022) conducted interviews with senior managers and leaders including senior HR leader, senior innovation leader and senior leader and they found that use of AI in human resource management (HRM) such as deployment of AI-based bots, personal and digital assistants (for performing various human resource-based tasks which were standard, interactive and communication-oriented involving employees), led to high employee satisfaction, employee commitment, and reduced employee turnover behaviour. So, leaders attest that AI in HRM has benefits for the company (Malik et al., 2022).

Chatterjee et al. (2021) found that support of leadership acts as a moderator in the relationship between perception of usefulness of AI and the intention to implement AI, and in the relationship between perception of ease of usage of AI and the intention to implement AI, in such a manner that with a high level of support from leadership, a perception of greater usefulness of AI may result in a higher adoption of AI, and a perception of greater ease of usage of AI may result in a higher adoption of AI in companies. Thus, Chatterjee et al. (2021) emphasize that only when there is a strong support from leadership, the implementation of any modern technology in an organization will be successful. Leadership has a critical role to play in fostering a favourable environment for the adoption of AI (Chatterjee et al., 2021). Also, in case of implementation of new technologies in the case of ecommerce and cloud computing, the support of leadership played a vital role in usage and success (Chatterjee et al., 2021).

Chatterjee et al. (2022a) found that the support of leadership moderates the association between business-to-business (B2B) relation satisfaction and performance of firm in a such a way that with a high level of support of leadership, more B2B relation satisfaction leads to a better performance of the firm. Here B2B relation satisfaction encompasses the satisfaction level of various stakeholders engaged in a B2B relationship such as employees, managers, and clients. Performance of firm in this study considers the contribution of artificial intelligence-based customer relationship management (AI-CRM) systems to improvement of B2B relation management, and to overall functioning of the firm (Chatterjee et al., 2022a). The support of leadership helps orient the mind-set of employees with the strategy of the company, and helps channel employees' efforts towards adoption of the new AI technologies like an AI-CRM system for a B2B situation. The facilitation provided by the leadership also helps overcoming hesitation of employees to adopt the new AI systems who may not be ready as they not comfortable with the usage of new technologies. Employees may be equipped to use new AI systems by obtaining training facilitated by the leadership of the company (Chatterjee et al., 2022a).

Chatterjee et al. (2022b) found that the support of leadership moderated the link between an employee's intention to use AI-CRM based business model and the actual use of AI-CRM system in such a manner that with strong support of leadership, a high level of intention to use AI-CRM based business model resulted in a high actual use of AI-CRM system.

Chatterjee et al. (2020a) found that the support of leadership was amongst one of the important critical success factors for the successful implementation of AI-CRM technology developed for improved knowledge management, in order to enhance the business process.

Chatterjee et al. (2020b) found that the support of leadership moderated the association between two employee attitudes (utilitarian attitude and hedonistic attitude) and the employee's behavioural intent to use AI-CRM technology, such that with a high level of leadership support, high level of employee attitudes led to increased intent to use AI-CRM technology. Utilitarian attitude refers to the employee's opinion that the system is usable and has practical benefits, and hedonistic attitude explains that the employee derives enjoyment from the usage of technology and finds the technology attractive (Chatterjee et al., 2020b).

Priya et al. (2023) found that the AI implementation in management institutes in India, in the education sector, is highly influenced by leadership support. Priya et al. (2023) found that leadership support has the most important role to play when it comes to the implementation of AI in higher education institutes offering management education in India.

Maity (2019) noted through interviews with 27 HR executives and training professionals belonging to eight companies across industries such as FMCG and oil and natural gas, that AI can itself play the role of a leader: Particularly in the domain of training and development, AI bears the potential to lead the practices of knowledge management in companies such as development and recording of knowledge.

Kar et al. (2021) found that a lack of leadership commitment is a barrier to AI adoption in organizational strategy, and this barrier also influences other barriers such as a lack of employees with experience and expertise in AI, and a lack of job security.

Das (2023) noted that the strategic decision of the individual company in the selection and implementation of AI also depends on the industry leader, so this is another manner in which leadership in industry influences a company's strategic decision of whether or not to implement AI in its business processes.

Hence, the following points which elaborate the relationship between leadership and AI implementation, can be understood from the aforementioned studies:

1. As per interviews of leaders in companies, use of AI in HRM led to positive consequences for organizations such as high satisfaction and low employee turnover (Malik et al., 2022).
2. Leadership support enhances the adoption of AI in management institutes in the education sector in India (Priya et al., 2023).
3. Absence of leadership commitment forms a barrier to the integration of AI in organizational strategy (Kar et al., 2021).
4. Support of leadership and motivation by leadership has a huge role to play in the adoption of AI, as it acts as a moderator in several predictor-criterion relationships related to the implementation of AI (please see table 1).

The word cloud shown in figure 2 generated by Nvivo for RQ1 illustrates the most frequently occurring themes in AI and leadership in India, in the last decade. It is seen from figure 2 that "management", "technology" and "adoption" are highlighted the most in these studies, followed by "leadership" and

Table 1. Role of support of leadership as a moderator in AI and leadership research

Sno.	Independent Variable	Dependent Variable	Moderator	Authors
1	AI implementation rationale	AI sustainability	Support of leadership	Chaudhuri et al. (2022)
2	Implementation of generative AI	Sustainability of business	Motivation by leadership	Vrontis et al. (2023)
3	Perception of usefulness of AI	Intention to implement AI	Support of leadership	Chatterjee et al. (2021)
4	Perception of ease of usage of AI	Intention to implement AI	Support of leadership	Chatterjee et al. (2021)
5	B2B relation satisfaction	Performance of firm (includes contribution of AI)	Support of leadership	Chatterjee et al. (2022a)
6	Employee's intention to use AI-CRM based business model	Actual use of AI-CRM system	Support of leadership	Chatterjee et al. (2022b)
7	Employee's utilitarian attitude	Employee's behavioural intent to use AI-CRM technology	Support of leadership	Chatterjee et al. (2020b)
8	Employee's hedonistic attitude	Employee's behavioural intent to use AI-CRM technology	Support of leadership	Chatterjee et al. (2020b)

"intelligence", among others, followed by "support". Hence, in the papers obtained through a search for the terms "lead*" and "AI" or "artificial intelligence" in the period 2013 to 2023 (along with other search criteria given in the section 'research methodology'), it is seen that the word cloud highlights "adoption" and "support" as some of the recurring themes. This emphasizes the significance of leadership support in the adoption of AI by firms.

The Theories Used to Interpret Different Aspects of AI and Leadership Research

RQ2 is answered here. The resource-based view (RBV) theory as per Chatterjee et al. (2022a) posits that companies develop certain core competencies which enables them to perform better than their competitors. Companies should have the ability to obtain valued, scarce, unparalleled, and non-replaceable resources (e.g. data through deployment of AI) which is the central tenet of RBV theory (Chatterjee et al., 2022a). RBV theory helps in identifying the strategic resources that can be tapped by firms for the achievement of competitive advantage in a sustainable manner (Chatterjee et al., 2022a). The RBV theory emphasizes the skilling of employees at the company which plans to implement AI, so that they can work with new technologies such as AI and unearth opportunities for improvement (Chatterjee et al., 2022b). Hence, the RBV theory contributes to understanding the importance of the implementation of AI in the improved performance of the firm and this may then lead to a sustained competitive advantage for the company (Chatterjee et al., 2022a; Chatterjee et al., 2022b). The achievement of competitive advantage by adoption of modern technologies such as AI as per the RBV theory may be achieved by identification of new opportunities by employees equipped with the knowledge of working with modern technologies. The RBV theory further underscores the importance of leadership support, as it is only through facilitators like leadership support that technological resources such as AI (Chatterjee et al., 2020a; Chatterjee et al., 2020b; Chatterjee et al., 2021; Chatterjee et al., 2022a; Chatterjee et al., 2022b; Chaudhuri et al., 2022; Kar et al., 2021; Malik et al., 2022; Priya et al., 2023; Vrontis et al., 2023) and human resources

Figure 2. Word cloud based on papers selected for analysis (Authors)

(Chatterjee et al., 2022b) can be deployed in the most effective manner, to achieve competitive advantage for the firm.

The status quo bias (SQB) theory as per Chatterjee et al. (2022b) explains the employee's resistance to use new technologies such as AI. Due to disruptive technologies such as AI, the business models of companies are also changing. Companies are now looking for the best ways to deploy AI in their strategy This causes resistance on the part of the employee who is required to work with AI. This resistance may cause problems such as deferrals, budget increases, and also complete failing of the novel technological framework. As per SQB theory, employees will be hesitant to use new technologies until they understand that the change will bring more benefits than risks (Chatterjee et al., 2022b). Aspects like transaction cost, fear of downsizing by the employer, being unable to learn new technologies cause employees to be resistant to change and to continue with status quo. Hence, SQB theory emphasizes the role of leadership support in overcoming the employee's resistance to use new technologies, through leadership interventions in the form of motivation, coaching, training (Chatterjee et al., 2022b).

The Necessary Competencies Required for Leaders to Be Successful in the Current Era of AI

RQ3 is answered here. Jain and Ranjan (2020) conducted a panel discussion with experienced industry leaders and found that while technical knowledge may have a short half-life (sometimes 4-5 years), elementary skills and abilities such as creativity, resourcefulness, fastidious planning through discussion and dissemination of information to all stakeholders, and stringent implementation assume greater importance in the current era of AI.

As per Vaidya et al. (2020), leader agility and leader adaptability are essential if firms aim to be successful in the new business climate. So as to deal with changes, leaders are required to continually adapt to changes in the processes, organizational structure, employees and technologies. This calls for a speedy decision making ability and capability to be flexible as the situation demands. Vaidya et al. (2020) note that leaders who possess mental and emotional competencies, in addition to abilities and skills required by leaders will be able to successfully navigate the disruptive business climate. Leaders with the ability of emotional regulation have a higher likelihood of taking quicker decisions, solve problems, empathize with problems faced by one's subordinates, and handle conflicts among one's team members, in the fast changing business environment brought by the emergence of industry 4.0 and the development of modern advancements such as AI, machine learning.

To summarize, the necessary competencies required for successful leadership in the age of AI are creativity, emotional intelligence, conflict management, rapid decision-making ability, to name a few (Jain & Ranjan, 2020; Vaidya et al., 2020).

CONCLUSION

AI is a transformational technology that has the potential to bring change to nations and economies (NASSCOM, 2021). AI is today adopted across sectors such as agriculture, healthcare, retail, education, manufacturing and governance (NASSCOM, 2021), and is only set to grow. In this context, RQs 1,2, and 3 were examined, and it was found as an answer to RQ1 that leadership has a pivotal role to play in the adoption of AI by companies (Chatterjee et al., 2020a; Chatterjee et al., 2020b; Chatterjee et al., 2021; Chatterjee et al., 2022a; Chatterjee et al., 2022b; Chaudhuri et al., 2022; Das, 2023; Kar et al., 2021; Malik et al., 2022; Priya et al., 2023; Vrontis et al., 2023). Whether a company implements AI or not depends a good deal on the support and motivation of leadership (Chatterjee et al., 2020a; Chatterjee et al., 2020b; Chatterjee et al., 2021; Chatterjee et al., 2022a; Chatterjee et al., 2022b; Chaudhuri et al., 2022; Kar et al., 2021; Malik et al., 2022; Priya et al., 2023; Vrontis et al., 2023). It was found in answer to RQ2 that RBV and SQB theories were used by researchers to infer different aspects of leadership and AI research such as a reluctance of employees to work with new technologies such as AI (Chatterjee et al., 2022b), need for implementation of AI from a strategic point of view (Chatterjee et al., 2022a; Chatterjee et al., 2022b), how AI can be implemented through unearthing of opportunities by technologically skilled employees (Chatterjee et al., 2022a). It was found as an answer to RQ3 that competencies such as creativity, imagination, empathy, emotional intelligence and speedy decision making skills in the fast changing business environment contribute to leadership success in the era of AI (Jain & Ranjan, 2020; Vaidya et al., 2020).

On comparing this study with the SLR of Kaushal et al. (2023), it was seen that while the latter studied the implementation of AI in various functions of HRM in different contexts, the current study deals with leadership and AI, particularly in India, in the time period of 2013 to 2023. This study was not restricted to the functions of HRM in organizations. The current study reviews studies which explore the link between leadership and AI in Indian organizations across functions [such as customer relationship management (CRM)], in the aforementioned time period. On comparing the current study with the SLR of Kabalisa and Altmann (2021), it was found that the latter dealt with exploring the motives for AI implementation by countries and companies in the period 2000 to 2021, and the study found that one of the common motives of countries and companies was to gain the positioning of a leader. The current study reviews studies which explore the importance of leadership in the adoption of AI in Indian companies, in the period of 2013 to 2023. On comparing the current study with the SLR of Bhatt and Muduli (2023), it was found that the latter analysed studies published between 1996 and 2022, and concluded that leadership skills were important for the implementation of AI in the learning and development function of companies. The current study specifically looks at the role of leadership in AI implementation in Indian organizations, across business functions (such as CRM) and even the overall sustainability of business. The current study is not restricted to any one particular function of HRM. On comparing the current study with the SLR of Mer and Virdi (2023), it was found that while the latter dealt with the impact of AI on HRM and the impact of COVID-19 on HRM practices, the former deals with the importance of leadership in AI implementation in India. On comparing the current study with the SLR of Pai et al. (2022), it was found that while the latter focussed on exploring how AI helps companies in their knowledge management practices, the former focuses on examining the link between AI and leadership in the Indian context, including knowledge management. While Pai et al. (2022) suggest a high level of moral and financial responsibility of leaders for implementing a company-wide knowledge management strategy, the current study reviews studies which explore how leadership aids in AI adoption in Indian organizations. In addition, this study also elaborates on successful leadership competencies needed to navigate the current age of AI in Indian organizations, and not solely for knowledge management. On comparing this study with the SLR of Varsha (2023), it was found that while the latter dealt with how business leaders can tackle AI bias in their organizations, this study focuses on the link between AI and leadership in Indian organizations. On comparing this study with the SLR of Tetteh (2023), it was found that while the latter dealt with the themes of leadership and the 4th industrial revolution across many countries in the period from 2016 to 2021, this study focuses on the link between AI and leadership in Indian organizations only, in the period from 2013 to 2023. Also, the SLR of Tetteh (2023) reviews studies on the fourth industrial revolution (which includes AI, robotics, internet of things, 3D printing among others), but the current study reviews studies only on AI. Thus, on comparing the current study with similar SLRs conducted previously, it is seen that this study makes unique contributions to literature as this is the first study to review research linking leadership and AI implementation in Indian companies, conducted in the time period between 2013 and 2023.

Practical Implications

RQ1 highlights the importance of leadership in the application of AI by companies (Chatterjee et al., 2020a; Chatterjee et al., 2020b; Chatterjee et al., 2021; Chatterjee et al., 2022a; Chatterjee et al., 2022b; Chaudhuri et al., 2022; Das, 2023; Kar et al., 2021; Malik et al., 2022; Maity, 2019; Priya et al., 2023; Vrontis et al., 2023). Hence, all efforts made by the organization will be in vain without the support, facilitation, and motivation by the leadership of the organization in AI adoption. Leaders and managers must exhibit commitment towards the amalgamation of AI adoption with their organizational strategy, equip their employees, train them adequately, mentally align them towards the strategy of AI usage (to combat SQB), and counsel them when in crisis, related to AI adoption (Chatterjee et al., 2020a; Chatterjee et al., 2020b; Chatterjee et al., 2021; Chatterjee et al., 2022b; Chaudhuri et al., 2022; Kar et al., 2021; Priya et al., 2023; Vrontis et al., 2023). RQ2 shows that adoption of AI could lead to competitive advantage, as per RBV theory (Chatterjee et al., 2022a) and employees do face resistance while adopting new technologies as per SQB (Chatterjee et al., 2022b), and the implication for leaders/managers here is that patience along with support should be practiced while setting goals related to the implementation of AI by employees, who may need handholding mentally and psychologically, in the initial phases at least. RQ3 shows that even though technology is changing at lightning speed, and new technologies such as AI have gained the spotlight now, people skills and competencies such as emotional intelligence, creativity, conflict management and rapid decision making will always be required by leaders, irrespective of the technology that is developed currently (Jain & Ranjan, 2020; Vaidya et al., 2020).

Limitations and Future Research Directions

In this study, only Scopus database was considered for a search of relevant articles. Hence, there is a narrow focus on articles. For future research in this area, databases such as Web of Science, PsychINFO (Tandon et al., 2021) and articles included in journals listed in Australian Business Deans Council (ABDC) journal quality list can also be considered as Web of Science is believed to be a prominent academic database of peer-reviewed research (Tandon et al., 2021), and ABDC is noted to be more extensive than Scopus database (Pahlevan-Sharif et al., 2019). Also, AI can be studied in detail by seeking specific technologies/applications of AI research in the aforementioned databases such as "natural language processing", "opinion mining" or "face recognition" (Kaushal et al., 2023) to name a few.

REFERENCES

Associated Chambers of Commerce and Industry of India. (2023). *India Leading the Global Digital Transformation Journey*. https://www.assocham.org/uploads/files/Digital%20Transformation.pdf

Bhatt, P., & Muduli, A. (2023). Artificial intelligence in learning and development: A systematic literature review. *European Journal of Training and Development*, 47(7/8), 677–694. doi:10.1108/EJTD-09-2021-0143

Brynjolfsson, E., & McAfee, A. (2017). The business of artificial intelligence. In *HBR at 100* (pp. 257–272). Harvard Business Review Press. (Original work published 2022)

Chatterjee, S., Chaudhuri, R., & Vrontis, D. (2022a). AI and digitalization in relationship management: Impact of adopting AI-embedded CRM system. *Journal of Business Research*, 150, 437–450. doi:10.1016/j.jbusres.2022.06.033

Chatterjee, S., Chaudhuri, R., Vrontis, D., & Jabeen, F. (2022b). Digital transformation of organization using AI-CRM: From microfoundational perspective with leadership support. *Journal of Business Research*, *153*, 46–58. doi:10.1016/j.jbusres.2022.08.019

Chatterjee, S., Ghosh, S. K., & Chaudhuri, R. (2020a). Knowledge management in improving business process: An interpretative framework for successful implementation of AI–CRM–KM system in organizations. *Business Process Management Journal*, *26*(6), 1261–1281. doi:10.1108/BPMJ-05-2019-0183

Chatterjee, S., Nguyen, B., Ghosh, S. K., Bhattacharjee, K. K., & Chaudhuri, S. (2020b). Adoption of artificial intelligence integrated CRM system: An empirical study of Indian organizations. *The Bottom Line (New York, N.Y.)*, *33*(4), 359–375. doi:10.1108/BL-08-2020-0057

Chatterjee, S., Rana, N. P., Dwivedi, Y. K., & Baabdullah, A. M. (2021). Understanding AI adoption in manufacturing and production firms using an integrated TAM-TOE model. *Technological Forecasting and Social Change*, *170*, 120880. doi:10.1016/j.techfore.2021.120880

Chaudhuri, R., Chatterjee, S., Vrontis, D., & Chaudhuri, S. (2022). Innovation in SMEs, AI dynamism, and sustainability: The current situation and way forward. *Sustainability (Basel)*, *14*(19), 12760. doi:10.3390/su141912760

Das, D. (2023). Understanding the choice of human resource and the artificial intelligence: "strategic behavior" and the existence of industry equilibrium. *Journal of Economic Studies (Glasgow, Scotland)*, *50*(2), 234–267. doi:10.1108/JES-06-2021-0305

Jain, A., & Ranjan, S. (2020). Implications of emerging technologies on the future of work. *IIMB Management Review*, *32*(4), 448–454. doi:10.1016/j.iimb.2020.11.004

Kabalisa, R., & Altmann, J. (2021). AI technologies and motives for AI adoption by countries and firms: a systematic literature review. In *Economics of Grids, Clouds, Systems, and Services: 18th International Conference, GECON 2021* (pp. 39-51). Springer International Publishing. 10.1007/978-3-030-92916-9_4

Kar, S., Kar, A. K., & Gupta, M. P. (2021). Modeling drivers and barriers of artificial intelligence adoption: Insights from a strategic management perspective. *International Journal of Intelligent Systems in Accounting Finance & Management*, *28*(4), 217–238. doi:10.1002/isaf.1503

Katyal, S. (2023, December 15). Exploring advances in AI-driven devices. AIding the future. *The Economic Times*, p.3.

Kaushal, N., Kaurav, R. P. S., Sivathanu, B., & Kaushik, N. (2023). Artificial intelligence and HRM: Identifying future research Agenda using systematic literature review and bibliometric analysis. *Management Review Quarterly*, *73*(2), 455–493. doi:10.1007/s11301-021-00249-2

Krithivasan, K. (2024). India will be the global nucleus of generative AI. *The Economic Times*, p.12.

Maity, S. (2019). Identifying opportunities for artificial intelligence in the evolution of training and development practices. *Journal of Management Development*, *38*(8), 651–663. doi:10.1108/JMD-03-2019-0069

Majumdar, R., & Agarwal, S. (2023). In AI, I is for India: Tech majors build cutting edge solutions for the world. *The Economic Times*. https://economictimes.indiatimes.com/tech/technology/in-ai-i-is-for-india-tech-majors-build-cutting-edge-ai-solutions-for-the-world/articleshow/103312655.cms?from=mdr

Malik, A., Budhwar, P., Patel, C., & Srikanth, N. R. (2022). May the bots be with you! Delivering HR cost-effectiveness and individualised employee experiences in an MNE. *International Journal of Human Resource Management*, *33*(6), 1148–1178. doi:10.1080/09585192.2020.1859582

Mer, A., & Virdi, A. S. (2023). Navigating the paradigm shift in HRM practices through the lens of artificial intelligence: a post-pandemic perspective. In P. Tyagi, N. Chilamkurti, S. Grima, K. Sood, & B. Balusamy (Eds.), *The Adoption and Effect of Artificial Intelligence on Human Resources Management* (pp. 123–154). Emerald Publishing Limited. doi:10.1108/978-1-80382-027-920231007

National Association of Software and Services Companies. (2021). *AI gamechangers: Accelerating India with innovation*. https://nasscom.in/ai-gamechangers2021/pdf/AI-Gamechangers0582021.pdf

National Association of Software and Services Companies. (2022). *AI adoption Index: Tracking India's Sectoral Progress on AI Adoption*. https://nasscom.in/knowledge-center/publications/nasscom-ai-adoption-index

Pahlevan-Sharif, S., Mura, P., & Wijesinghe, S. N. (2019). A systematic review of systematic reviews in tourism. *Journal of Hospitality and Tourism Management*, *39*, 158–165. doi:10.1016/j.jhtm.2019.04.001

Pai, R. Y., Shetty, A., Shetty, A. D., Bhandary, R., Shetty, J., Nayak, S., Dinesh, T. K., & D'souza, K. J. (2022). Integrating artificial intelligence for knowledge management systems–synergy among people and technology: A systematic review of the evidence. *Economic Research-. Ekonomska Istrazivanja*, *35*(1), 7043–7065. doi:10.1080/1331677X.2022.2058976

Pan, Y., & Froese, F. J. (2023). An interdisciplinary review of AI and HRM: Challenges and future directions. *Human Resource Management Review*, *33*(1), 100924. doi:10.1016/j.hrmr.2022.100924

Paul, J., Lim, W. M., O'Cass, A., Hao, A. W., & Bresciani, S. (2021). Scientific procedures and rationales for systematic literature reviews (SPAR-4-SLR). *International Journal of Consumer Studies*, *45*(4), 1–16. doi:10.1111/ijcs.12695

Priya, S. S., Jain, V., Priya, M. S., Dixit, S. K., & Joshi, G. (2023). Modelling the factors in the adoption of artificial intelligence in Indian management institutes. *Foresight*, *25*(1), 20–40. doi:10.1108/FS-09-2021-0181

Ramamoorthy, R. (2023, December 15). Past, present, future. AIding the future. *The Economic Times*, 3.

Roy, A. (2024, April 29). Firms rush to recruit chief AI officers amid AI tech frenzy. *The Economic Times*, 16.

Roy & Lohchab. (2024, January 4). Indian GenAI Firms Raised $700m in 3 yrs, says Nasscom. *The Economic Times*, 7.

Schrettenbrunnner, M. B. (2020). Artificial-intelligence-driven management. *IEEE Engineering Management Review*, *48*(2), 15–19. doi:10.1109/EMR.2020.2990933

Tandon, A., Dhir, A., Almugren, I., AlNemer, G. N., & Mäntymäki, M. (2021). Fear of missing out (FoMO) among social media users: A systematic literature review, synthesis and framework for future research. *Internet Research*, *31*(3), 782–821. doi:10.1108/INTR-11-2019-0455

Tetteh, E. N. (2023). Leadership and the fourth industrial revolution: A systematic literature review. *International Social Science Journal*, *73*(250), 939–957. doi:10.1111/issj.12380

The Economic Times. (2023a). Experts speak. AIding the future. *The Economic Times*, 3.

The Economic Times. (2023b). Why AI is not a job-stealing, creativity-killing monster and how to regulate it. *The Economic Times*. https://economictimes.indiatimes.com/opinion/et-commentary/why-ai-is-not-a-job-stealing-creativity-killing-monster-and-how-to-regulate-it/articleshow/104222327.cms?from=mdr

The Economic Times Bureau. (2023). Gen AI could boost India's economy by $1.5t in 7 years. *The Economic Times*, 10.

The Hindu Bureau. (2023). India's AI penetration factor at 3.09, highest among all G20, OECD countries: Nasscom. *The Hindu*. https://www.thehindu.com/business/Industry/indias-ai-penetration-factor-at-309-highest-among-all-g20-oecd-countries-nasscom/article66522647.ece

Vaidya, D. R., Prasad, D. K., & Mangipudi, D. M. R. (2020). Mental and emotional competencies of leader's dealing with disruptive business environment-A conceptual review. *International Journal of Management*, *11*(5).

Varma, A., Dawkins, C., & Chaudhuri, K. (2023). Artificial intelligence and people management: A critical assessment through the ethical lens. *Human Resource Management Review*, *33*(1), 100923. doi:10.1016/j.hrmr.2022.100923

Varsha, P. S. (2023). How can we manage biases in artificial intelligence systems–A systematic literature review. *International Journal of Information Management Data Insights*, *3*(1), 100165.

Vrontis, D., Chaudhuri, R., & Chatterjee, S. (2023). Role of ChatGPT and Skilled Workers for Business Sustainability: Leadership Motivation as the Moderator. *Sustainability (Basel)*, *15*(16), 12196. doi:10.3390/su151612196

KEY TERMS AND DEFINITIONS

Artificial Intelligence: The simulation of human thinking by computers.
Competency: Clusters of knowledge, skills and attitudes required by an individual to be successful at his/her job.
Emotional Intelligence: Awareness and regulation of one's emotions as well as emotions of others for effective interpersonal relationships.
Empathy: Understanding others' emotions and the ability to feel what the other person may be feeling.
Leadership: An individual's ability to influence a group towards attaining a goal.
Leadership Support: The mental and emotional help extended by the supervisors or managers to their subordinates which enables them to overcome their challenges in an organization.

Moderator: A variable that has a notable contributory effect on the primary relationship between the independent variable and the dependent variable.

Systematic Literature Review: Use of systematic, specific and clearly defined protocols to identify and synthesize literature available for a given topic.

Chapter 5
Understanding the Role of Digital Leadership on the Digital Transformation in the Time of COVID-19 and Beyond

Mübeyyen Tepe Küçükoğlu
https://orcid.org/0000-0002-3717-4165
Trakya University, Turkey

ABSTRACT

The importance of strong DL skills comes to the front in the rapid adaptation of organizations. DL plays the role of a critical success factor on the way to the strategic visions that organizations want to achieve from their current situation. For this reason, the scope of DL should be understood correctly by organizations and employees. In this direction, this study aims to present a conceptual structure and at the same time exploratory results by addressing the concept of DL with all its dimensions. This study consists of two parts. The first part has a conceptual structure that examines the definition of DL, and emphasizes the basic skills and characteristics that a digital leader should have. In the second part, studies carried out during and after the COVID-19 outbreak will be examined, with the intention of guiding both organizations and academics.

INTRODUCTION

Developments in information and communication technologies bring organizations closer to digital transformation every day. All organizations have received their share from the accelerated digital transformation with the Covid epidemic. It is obvious that in the Covid epidemic and its aftermath, organizations have faced many opportunities and challenges. This situation sped up a transformation in the existing business processes of the organizations and emphasized the importance of rapid adaptation ability. In today's competitive environment, organizations that adapt easily to digitalization by acting faster and more flexibly are successful. Digitization leads to the transformation of many

DOI: 10.4018/979-8-3693-1946-8.ch005

business processes such as production, logistics, communication, and human resources. Innovative approaches, new collaboration, and communication methods created value in the digitalization process via smart devices (Oberer & Erkollar, 2018). Leadership is a key factor that enables businesses to succeed in the digital transformation process (Promsri, 2019). Leadership, which is considered the third function of management, directing, stands out in many organizational change successes. Digital transformation is emerging as one of them.

Traditional hierarchical leadership theories and models have begun to become dysfunctional because they are not designed for the digital age, and different leadership models that are more suitable for the digital age are needed. One of these leadership types in the digital age is digital leadership (DL) (Malakyan, 2020). DL is a new type of leadership that has become widespread and developed with digital transformation (Ercan Önbıçak & Akkoyun, 2022).

With the spread of remote working models together with the Covid-19 epidemic, the continuous increase in the number of virtual organizations has enabled the effective use of information technologies and management information systems in business processes (Erer, Demirel & Savaş, 2023). Although digitalization is an important issue for the future success of businesses, today's leadership skills are not enough to meet the opportunities and challenges brought by digitalization. Therefore, digital leaders are expected to realize a human-centered vision with the necessary skills and mindset (Hensellek, 2022). What makes a leader the digital leader is not the working area of the business. Supportive leadership style and encouragement of employees to bring their innovative ideas to life also play an important role (Oberer & Erkollar, 2018). According to the results of a survey conducted by Kane and colleagues, (2016), 90% of senior executives stated that a sectoral change will occur with digitalization. However, 56% stated that they were not prepared enough for this situation. They stated that DL is important in directing the business correctly.

The importance of strong DL skills comes to the front in the rapid adaptation of organizations. DL plays the role of a critical success factor on the way to the strategic visions that organizations want to achieve from their current situation. For this reason, the scope of DL should be understood correctly by organizations and employees. In this direction, this study aims to present a conceptual structure and at the same time exploratory results by addressing the concept of DL with all its dimensions.

This study consists of several parts. The first and second parts have a conceptual structure that examines the definition of DL, and emphasizes the basic skills and characteristics that a digital leader should have. The third part emphasizes the importance of DL for digital transformation during and after the Covid-19 outbreak. The fourth part mentions the strategic importance of the successful management of DL. In the fifth part, a content analysis is performed and studies carried out during and after the Covid-19 outbreak will be examined to guide both organizations and academics. The reason for choosing this period is that the digital transformation in organizations has accelerated with the pandemic and this situation has also been reflected in academic studies. In this direction, open-access articles published in the Science Direct database between 2020-2023 are analyzed with descriptive content analysis, and a short-term photograph is taken to reveal the trend in DL area.

Definition of DL

Advances in digital transformation are making new demands on today's leaders (Hensellek, 2022). Organizations in the new digital business world, which is considered as today's modern world; emerge as structures trying to survive in a chaos full of uncertainty, rapid change, and risk (Erer et al., 2023).

Today, with the increasing digitalization, working life changes rapidly and leaves managers with new challenges to overcome and problems to be solved. While dealing with these difficulties, the concept of DL finds its place as a key concept in line with what skills a manager should acquire (Zeike, Bradbury, Lindert &Pfaff, 2019).

It is seen that DL studies have started to take place in the literature (Ercan Önbıçak & Akkoyun, 2022). The subject of DL is a relatively new and emerging field of research (Zeike et al., 2019), and retrospective studies are few. Since it is a fairly new field of study, its popularity among academics is developing and studies in many different fields are published in increasing numbers every day. It has not yet reached the maturity stage, therefore each new study published triggers more studies. Tigre and colleagues (2023), in their research, stated that the number of studies between 2009-11 was more stable, and it has been in an upward trend since 2018. (see Figure 1 below)

Businesses have to adapt to the change in their external environment in the post-modern period. Businesses and organizations that fail to adapt may face being unable to sustain their life cycles (Ercan Önbıçak & Akkoyun, 2022). It has been revealed that the digital leader stands out with her thoughts and skills in the digitalizing world and leads the change, (Çelik Şahin, Avcı & Anık, 2020).

Ordu and Nayır (2021) stated that the definitions of DL in the literature cover the themes of change (transformation, creating a vision), using technology (using digital tools, being able to manage technology), and innovation (thinking differently, innovation culture and focusing on innovation). Below Table 1 shows some DL definitions of various researchers from literature.

Digital leaders undertake the task of facilitating the adaptation of employees to new technologies and applications in businesses (Ercan Önbıçak & Akkoyun, 2022). In some studies, it has been seen that DL is explained only by using technology or having technical knowledge and skills, only adapting to change or just being innovative. However, DL is a comprehensive concept that requires all these competencies to come together (Ordu & Nayır, 2021).

Figure 1. Growth of the number of studies about DL area (Tigre, Curado & Henriques, 2023)

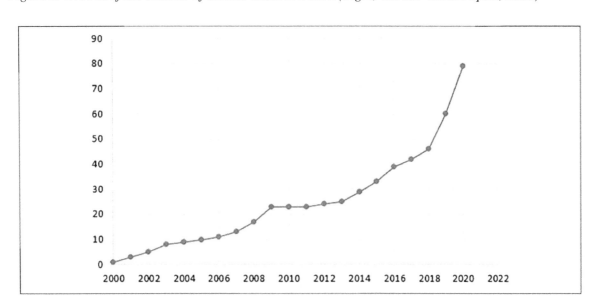

Table 1. Various DL definitions from literature

The leaders' ability to create a clear and meaningful vision for the digitalization process and the capability to execute strategies to actualize it	(Larjovuori, Bordi, Mäkiniemi & Heikkilä-Tammi, 2016)
DL is a complex construct aiming for a customer-centered, digitally enabled, leading-edge business model by transforming the role, skills, and style of the digital leader, realizing a digital organization, including governance, vision, values, structure, culture and decision processes, and adjusting people management, virtual teams, knowledge, and communication and collaboration on the individual level.	(Eberl & Drews, 2021)
DL (leadership 4.0) is a fast, cross-hierarchical, team-oriented, and cooperative approach, with a strong focus on innovation	(Oberer & Erkollar, 2018)
DL is an ethical and agile mindset that quickly responds to changes and learns from them, fostering a trust-based culture that values people and its diversity, coaching them to collabo-rate and thrive in a digital scenario	(Tigre et al., 2023)
DL is to create an innovative vision by using technology effectively in managerial processes in order to realize a sustainable change culture in the organization.	(Ordu & Nayır, 2021)
DL is a leadership style that aims to implement and to enforce the digital transformation of the organization and to create a culture of sustainable change in the organization, in order to lead the organization in a wholly digital environment	(Büyükbeşe, Dikbaş, Klein & Batuk Ünlü, 2022)

There are three main factors that must be fulfilled for the digital leader. Learning the digital mindset, acquiring digital skills, and the combination of these two components. The presence of a digital mindset or digital skills alone is not enough, these two components must be together (Hensellek, 2022). The ability to use new methods and tools is as important as the digital mindset (Oberer & Erkollar, 2018). The digital mindset is one of the essential qualities of a digital leader. The digital mindset emphasizes the individual's potential for openness and acceptance of digital technologies. Hensellek (2022) defines the digital mindset as the leader's approach to digital technologies and their use in a corporate context. Besides the digital mindset, digital skills are among the important requirements for a digital leader. Digital skills come into play at the point of understanding digital technologies, handling and using them effortlessly. Below Figure 2 shows DL framework proposed by Hensellek (2022).

Basic Skills and Characteristics of DL

The basic skills, which a leader should have, are called technical, human, and conceptual skills. From this perspective, the digital leader needs to blend these skills with a digital perspective.

According to Hensellek (2022), conceptual skills must also include a digital perspective besides the technical skills necessary for understanding and applying digital technologies. In this way, leaders in decision-making positions become aware of the possible opportunities and challenges of digitalization with a holistic perspective.

In the context of the transition from classical economy to digital transformation, questions arise about the skills, thinking, and acting styles needed in a leader for a business to be successful (Hensellek, 2022). Success in the digital transformation process is closely related to the digital knowledge and skills of the leader in the process (Promsri, 2019). The digitalization skills and competencies of the leaders, who are the key elements of the digital transformation process, have come to the front. It is taken into account that organizations in almost all industries have turned to digitalization at a speed far beyond their expectations, especially with the Covid-19 epidemic that changed the world order as of the first quarter of 2020

Figure 2. DL framework (Hensellek, 2022)

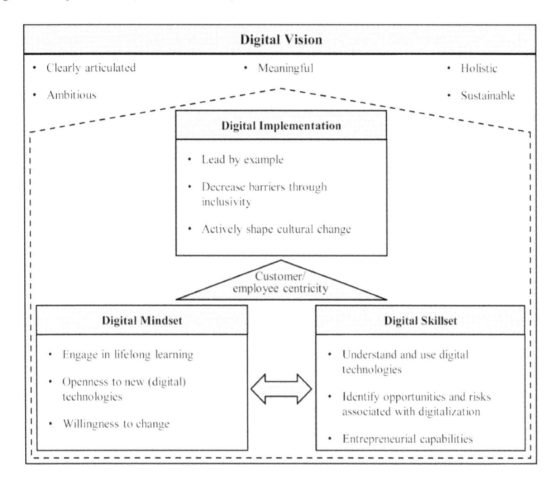

(Erer et al., 2023). Petry (2018), describes network leadership (networking by including not only data and machines but also knowledge workers), open leadership (open communication and open access to information), participatory leadership (participatory use of individual and collective intelligence), agile leadership (agile thinking and behavior) and trust as tools of DL.

It is observed that leaders who have a sense of hierarchy approaching zero, who have a customer-oriented understanding, who can gather the organization around a common language, who can share responsibilities, and who have transformative features, carry the codes of digital transformation with them (Ercan Önbıçak & Akkoyun, 2022). In the digital age we live in, there is a need for agile digital leaders who have innovative visions, know new technologies, supporting, guiding, motivate, and are role models in the digitalization process (Büyükbeşe & Doğan, 2022).

DL is not a leadership style that can be expressed with competencies and skills in a single field. DL is a type of leadership that emerges as a result of blending skills such as management, business administration, and strategic thinking with skills such as knowing and effectively using the tools of the digital age (Çelik Şahin et al., 2020). While the well-known requirements for good leadership are not outdated, there appears to be a need for other elements to support these skills (Hensellek, 2022). In this context, it can be stated that organizational agility, innovation, and adaptation ability, which are the keywords of change, draw attention to the understanding of leadership with digital transformation (Ercan Önbıçak & Akkoyun, 2022).

DL is sometimes compared with other leadership styles, and it is tried to determine which leadership style it stands close to. It is seen that transformational leadership, which is one of these styles, and DL have similar leadership characteristics. Büyükbeşe and colleagues (2022) argue that DL has a broader context than the transformational leadership style, although it shares vision-making, innovation-oriented, and employee-motivating features with transformational leadership.

Among the studies on the concept of DL, there are studies also conducted with the content analysis method and analyzing academic papers. These studies are about the characteristics of a successful DL (Promsri, 2019), and general trends of the DL concept (Tigre et al., 2023). Promsri (2019), analyzed internet resources on DL and proposed a model of "six characteristics of a DL for digital transformation success". In Table 2, DL characteristics are listed.

According to Tigre and colleagues (2023), DL's basic characteristics are collected into 4 main groups. The first group is called the human focus and encompasses communication and trust-based relationships. The second group emphasizes individual aspects and includes ethical issues and adaptability. The third group covers innovation, vision, and direction under the name of long-term adaptation. The fourth group, called task performance, includes digital agility and collaborative work.

The ability to see the opportunities and risks brought by digitalization and find the balance between them is necessary for the DL (Hensellek, 2022). Participatory leaders who can think from a global perspective, transcend the boundaries of culture, time, and space, have a high level of digital literacy, and instill an information-oriented approach to their employees, are seen at the top of today's business and management understanding as digital leaders (Ercan Önbıçak & Akkoyun, 2022).

The Importance of DL for Digital Transformation During and Post COVID-19

Digitalization has begun to significantly change economic structures, business relationships and working dynamics in the business world. Digitalization brings with it concerns about the role that robots, automation, artificial intelligence and machine learning algorithms will play in the business world, and questions about whether there will be potential mass unemployment, poverty and social explosions (Wisskirchen, Biacabe, Bormann, Muntz, Niehaus, Soler & von Brauchitsc, 2017).

Digital leadership represents an approach to not only adopting technological transformation tools but also how to strategically integrate them with business processes and human factors. This leadership approach plays a critical role in successfully driving the digital transformation of businesses (Aksoy, 2023).

As debates continue about how businesses are responding to digital transformation, analysis is emerging on how the Covid-19 pandemic is accelerating this transformation (Marr, 2020). Antonopoulou (2021) found that transformational leadership and digital skills had a positive and statistically significant impact on digital leadership in higher education institutions during the Covid-19 pandemic. This demonstrates that effective leadership and digital skills are required to drive digital leadership practices, especially in times of crisis and change.

Bawono and colleauges (2022) examined the impact of ambidextrous leadership on the performance of Telecommunications Companies in Indonesia in the context of organizational agility and digital business models during the Covid-19 pandemic. According to this study, it was concluded that ambidextrous leadership has a positive and significant effect on digital business model innova-

Table 2. Various DL characteristics obtained from different perspectives

Proposed DL characteristics		Proposed DL characteristics	
Digital knowledge and literacy Vision Understanding of customers Agility Risk taking Collaboration	(Promsri, 2019)	Vision and purpose provision Creation experiment conditions for people Empowerment to think difference Encouraging collaborations across boundaries	(Kane, 2018)
Agility Market knowledge Vision Influence Traditional business acumen Collaborative Cultivate talents for transformation	(Fukuzawa, 2016)	Intellectual curiosity Understanding human and customer nature Clear vision Passion and purpose Ability to leverage analytics Communication Ability to delegate	(Roe, 2018)
Innovative thinking Staying current and up to date Collaborations and connections Agile Data savvy	(Koen, 2019)	Clear purpose Forward-looking and thinking Fix what's broken and seek out what's not right Risk-taking Strive for partnership	(Newman, 2018)
Digital literacy Digital vision Advocacy Presence Communication Adaptability Self-awareness Cultural awareness	(Sullivan, 2017)	Change agents Recognizing customers as a heart of DM process Broad perspectives Collab. and teamwork focus New vernacular skills Shared accountability	(HRdive, 2019)
People first focus Building trust and collaboration Sharing leadership role	(George, 2018)	Technological vision Inno. and analytics prowess Organizational management Collaboration and empathy	(Trefler, 2019)
Understanding of digital trans. Digital skills dev. across the org. Using digital process and tech. to shape the org. and create str. Financial support and mandate for digital technology experiment Research based and user needs for developing projects Team inspiration to see the benefits of digital trans.	(Gorton, 2018)	Vision Curiosity Collaborative proficiency Experimental proficiency Networking proficiency	(Hughes, 2017)

Source: (Promsri, 2019)

tion, and that ambidextrous leadership has a positive and significant effect on organizational agility and company performance.

The Covid-19 pandemic has suddenly changed the world and the way of work. Businesses have been forced to accelerate a very comprehensive change. This complex business environment has created difficulties for both businesses to survive and develop, and for employees trying to adapt to new ways of working. There is a need for DL, an effective leadership style that supports the rapid adaptation of businesses to these complex conditions (Contreras, Baykal & Abid, 2020).

The Covid pandemic is one such example that has created a lot of challenges for the leadership team due to the shift from workplace culture to remote working. This pandemic has led to restructuring in organizations as it changes the way employees work and places greater emphasis on leadership styles

Table 3. DL characteristics that are agreed upon in the literature

Communication	It replaces face-to-face communication in traditional interaction. However, it is moving from line hierarchy to networks. DL is now shaped as the management of virtual environments or a digital environment rather than the management of teams through some electronic tools and communication technologies
Trust	Another prominent issue is the establishment and maintenance of trust in virtual teams. While establishing trust, is much easier in face-to-face relationships, on the other hand, it can be challenging for DL
Ethics	Management of the ethical dimension of digitalization stands out. In particular, the protection of privacy is an important issue
Adaptability	The ability to adapt to digital technologies is one of the prominent features of the digital leader
Innovation	With digital transformation, businesses have to overcome new challenges. Here, the aim of the digital leader should be to develop new ideas and concepts using creative and analytical methods, thereby increasing the innovative power of the business
Vision	A digital leader must have a vision that will shape the business's digital future, have the digital mindset to set this vision, and have the necessary digital skillset to successfully integrate the vision into the business. A meaningful vision alone is not enough, the important thing is the successful implementation of the vision
Agility	Since the digital world is constantly changing, agility replaces long-term planning
Collaboration	Another important issue is building relationships with the group members. Not only provides relief from the feeling of isolation but also facilitates coping with diversity in a rapidly changing environment. DL will be successful when the nature of relationships appears as a network structure rather than a line hierarchy

Source: (Eberl & Drews, 2021; Hensellek, 2022; Oberer & Erkollar, 2018; Tigre et al., 2023)

based on digital technologies that enable flexibility and interaction at work (Ulu & Özgener, 2023). Covid-19 has not only required redesigning the organizational structure, but also required digital leaders to have characteristics such as communication, compassion, setting priorities, developing a sense of ownership among employees, exhibiting an empathetic approach, establishing humane relationships with employees, and mutual trust (Barua & Patranabis, 2023).

In the form of remote working, some difficulties initially emerged due to employees not being prepared to work online due to resource constraints and employees experiencing work-family conflict due to sharing the same workspace with family members. However, during the pandemic, employees have also faced numerous challenges such as low morale, stress, lack of motivation and job insecurity. Over time, businesses have tried to minimize the difficulties they face by providing technology and resource support to employees. Additionally, leadership has played a vital role in making employees conscious of maintaining work-life balance. Successful leaders communicated with all stakeholders to reduce stress and anxiety, and this autonomous work led to the development of a sense of self-efficacy in employees (Ahuja, Puppala, Sergio & Hoffman, 2023).

Strategic Point of View for Successful Management via DL

During the Covid-19 pandemic, virtual or remote working, often without infrastructure and systems, has been adopted by many businesses. This transition has been accompanied by many stressors, including lack of child care, work-life imbalance, home-school responsibilities, burnout, and layoffs (Shipman, Burrell & Huff Mac Pherson, 2023). However, in remote working styles, lack of communication, motivation, preparation and training, as well as environmental conditions and distraction, can result in low performance and low commitment. Some of the problems inherent in remote working are as follows (Sullivan, 2012; Ramirez, 2023):

- lack of face-to-face supervision,
- lack of access to information,
- social isolation,
- failure to establish work-life balance

Managers and leaders must understand that stressors can develop due to the uncertainty and concerns that remote work, work from home, and virtual teams bring for employees. The following strategies and measures can be recommended to minimize the disadvantages of remote working (Ulu & Özgener, 2023):

1. Clarifying goals: For remote work and virtual teams to be successful, managers need to clarify the goals and roles of the business.
2. Living and working in a hybrid space: Digital leaders undoubtedly need to learn to move in and out of physical and virtual space in this new era.
3. Building trust: to build and maintain mutual trust in face-to-face meetings, parties need to show openness and share information even more. However, leaders need to be confident in the skills of the employees they will be working with to have sufficient expertise to address problems in remote work and virtual teams.
4. Prioritizing establishing work-life balance: To maximize the benefits of remote working and take precautions against its possible negative effects, employees, families and organizations need to adopt flexible and highly individualized approaches.
5. Schedule regular virtual meetings: It is the manager's responsibility to set expectations for teams regarding the frequency, means, and ideal timing of communication.
6. Helping accept the new work environment: Leaders and managers must recognize stress, understand employees' concerns, and empathize with their issues, especially in the context of the rapid transition to remote work.
7. Monitoring the development of employees and motivating them: Employees should be allowed to make a work schedule at home, but they should be flexible.
8. Building social capital in a virtual world: When leaders interact online, the incidental happiness and interconnectedness of the team can increase. This is very important in the post-pandemic workplace. Building relationships and trust is at the heart of this process.

Descriptive Content Analysis of DL

The subject of DL is studied in many different fields in the literature, and papers with different perspectives take place in journals related to psychology, human resources, innovation, leadership, management, business and strategy (Tigre et al., 2023). This section, it is aimed to determine the trends related to the concept of DL by examining the studies on DL. Conducting a qualitative study, publications during and after the Covid-19 outbreak will be examined. The reason for choosing this period is that the digital transformation in organizations has accelerated with the epidemic and this situation has also been reflected in academic studies. In this direction, open-access publications in the Science Direct database between 2020-2023 are analyzed with descriptive content analysis, and a short-term picture is taken to reveal the trend in the DL area.

The aim of this research is to reveal the current situation by examining the studies on DL with the descriptive content analysis method. In order to achieve this aim, the following questions were asked:

1. What are the types of publications?
2. How is the distribution of the studies according to the year of publication?
3. What are the research areas of publications?
4. What are the journals that publish more articles on DL?
5. What are the subjects studied together with DL in the publications?
6. What are the most used keywords in the publications?

In this research, descriptive content analysis was conducted through document analysis within the scope of the qualitative research method. Document analysis makes it possible to analyze documents produced within a certain time period about a research problem or documents produced by more than one source and at different intervals on a related subject (Yıldırım & Şimşek, 2006).

In descriptive content analysis, the data obtained from studies conducted independently of each other on a particular subject are summarized by classifying them under the headings or themes determined before or during the research. The descriptive content analysis primarily consists of the processes of creating a thematic framework for the analysis, processing the data obtained according to the created framework, and defining and interpreting the obtained findings using some descriptive statistics such as frequency distribution and percentage ratios (Altunışık, Coşkun, Bayraktaroğlu & Yıldırım, 2007; Dinçer, 2018).

The studies within the scope of the research were accessed using the Science Direct database. The term "digital leadership" was written in the search section and the results were listed as containing the search term in the title, abstract, or keywords. Descriptive analysis in this study is limited to only the Science Direct database and includes papers that were published during the years 2020-2023. At the end of the screening, 147 results were reached dated 7th of May, 2023 in accordance with the criteria determined. 123 of the results are research articles, 8 are review articles, 4 are book chapters, remained 17 are editorials, discussions, encyclopedias, mini review, practice guidelines, short communications, etc. Table 4 shows the types of publications related to DL. According to the table, most of the publications are research articles.

The second question of descriptive research is the year of publication. The results are listed below in Table 5. When we look at the distribution of publications about DL by publication years, it is remarkable that the number of publications has increased each year. Here, it is seen that the number of publications for 2023 is 41, even though it is at the beginning of the 5th month of the year. Therefore, it is concluded that the publications in the DL field have increased linearly.

Table 4. Types of publications related to DL

Publication Type	Quantity
Research article	123
Review article	8
Book chapter	4
Short communication	4
Editorial	3
Other	5
Total	147

Table 5. Yearly publications of DL

The Year of Publication	Quantity
2020	23
2021	36
2022	47
2023	41

Another question includes research areas of publications on DL. According to Table 6 first place belongs to business, management and accounting area with 76 publications. Then comes social sciences with 59 publications. After followed by computer science, decision science, engineering, and economics, econometrics and finance respectively.

Table 7 shows some journal names that publish articles about DL subjects mostly. The first three rows are shared by the Journal of Business Research, Technological Forecasting and Social Change and International Journal of Medical Informatics.

Table 6. Research areas of publications on DL

Research Area	Quantity
Business, Management and Accounting	76
Social Sciences	59
Computer Science	35
Decision Sciences	27
Engineering	13
Economics, Econometrics and Finance	8

Table 7. Journals mostly publish DL articles

Publication Title	Quantity
Journal of Business Research	15
Technological Forecasting and Social Change	10
International Journal of Medical Informatics	9
Procedia Computer Science	7
International Journal of Information Management	5
Technology in Society	5
The Leadership Quarterly	4
Industrial Marketing Management	3
Computers in Human Behavior	3
Business Horizons	3
Digital Business	3

Figure 3 shows the main subjects that are studied mostly in publications about DL. These subjects are listed as business management, digitalization, education, leadership, health policy/healthcare, and innovation. The digitalization theme is mentioned 41 times in various publications about DL and placed the first order. Sub-themes of digitalization are digital technology, digital government, and IT. Then comes the leadership theme in the second order with 39 mentions. Business management subject is mentioned 30 times in different publications about DL. Business management includes sub-themes such as firm performance, human resources, marketing, crisis management, organization theory, and finance.

Figure 4 shows the word cloud obtained from the keywords of the publications.

CONCLUSION

While digital technologies open up new sectors and user experiences, they also cause existing businesses to become obsolete. The Covid-19 pandemic has accelerated digital transformation. Digital transformation can actually be seen as creative destruction. While Netflix created a new industry as an example of digitalization, it also dealt a blow to the cable TV and cinema industry, which provides customers with similar experiences. In this respect, while the cinema industry is a sector that uses digital technologies intensively, the Covid-19 epidemic also played a role in this negative impact. As a result, digital platforms have increased their market shares with both digitalization and the epidemic. Businesses are shifting their investments to these platforms as well.

Business leaders need to act in accordance with the requirements of digital transformation and focus on some of their traditional leadership skills. It would be more correct to consider the skills that a digital leader should have in two groups. The first group is about how basic skills will change, and the second group is about what other skills will need to be emphasized.

The importance of conceptual skills, one of the basic skills of managers, has become even more important with digitalization. With rapid digitalization, it is necessary to closely monitor the direction

Figure 3. Visualization of the most studied subjects in publications

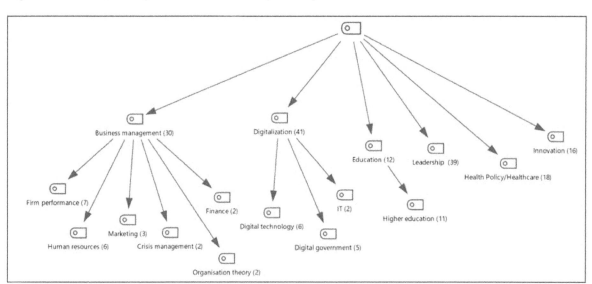

Figure 4. Word cloud of keywords

in which businesses will be affected, where the industry will evolve, the change in the way of doing business, and the change in user habits. At this point, foresight, market research, and forecasting methods take their place as tools that will help in the use of conceptual skills.

The issue that needs to be addressed at the point of interpersonal skill is the communication ability of the digital leader. With digitalization, the ways of working have also changed, and the traditional office environment has been replaced by remote working models. Although digital technology tools make it easier to work remotely and require various solutions to the problem of not being together, individual work and not being together cause many communication problems. For this reason, the digital leader should develop communication skills to solve digitalization problems. Problems that can be solved simply with face-to-face communication can grow even more with misunderstandings in remote communication.

Thirdly, technical skill has also gained importance. How digital technologies work, the mechanism behind the new methods and the use of technological tools have expanded the digital leader's field of interest. Knowing the technical issues behind digital technologies will also facilitate the estimation of potential problems and advantages.

When we need to look at other skills than basic skills, it is striking that one of the most important skills is agility. Agility requires adapting to change quickly and taking decisions that will enable the company to maintain its competitive advantage by taking all the measures required by the change. On the other hand, leadership has the characteristics of flexibility and adaptability. In this direction, the state of being flexible and adapting to the results of digital transformation is also valid for the digital leader.

There is more to be said and a long way to go on DL. It is a developing subject and the words about the concept of DL and the characteristics of the digital leader are not finished yet. At this point, it has been one of the aims of this study to open a path for academics who want to do research on DL.

REFERENCES

Ahuja, J., Puppala, H., Sergio, R. P., & Hoffman, E. P. (2023). E-leadership is Un(usual): Multi-criteria Analysis of Critical Success Factors for the Transition from Leadership to E-leadership. *Sustainability (Basel), 15*(8), 6506. doi:10.3390/su15086506

Aksoy, C. (2024). İşletmelerin Dijital Dönüşümü ve Dijital Liderlik Yaklaşımı. *Trakya Üniversitesi Kalite ve Strateji Yönetimi Dergisi, 4*(1), 1–28. doi:10.56682/ksydergi.1364569

Altunışık, R., Coşkun, R., Bayraktaroğlu, S., & Yıldırım, E. (2007). *Sosyal Bilimlerde Araştırma Yöntemleri: SPSS Uygulamalı* (5. Baskı). Sakarya Yayıncılık.

Antonopoulou, H., Halkiopoulos, C., Barlou, O., & Beligiannis, G. N. (2021). Transformational Leadership and Digital Skills in Higher Education Institutes: During the Covid-19 Pandemic. *Emerging Science Journal, 5*(1), 1–15. doi:10.28991/esj-2021-01252

Barua, T., & Patranabis, I. C. (2023). Leadership Style in Times of Crisis: Traditional Mentoring to Remote Monitoring. In Agile Leadership for Industry 4.0: An Indispensable Approach for the Digital Era (s.155-173). Apple Academic Press Inc.

Bawono, M., Gautama, I., Bandur, A., & Alamsjah, F. (2022). The Influence of Ambidextrous Leadership Mediated by Organizational Agility and Digital Business Model Innovation on the Performance of Telecommunication Companies in Indonesia during the Covid-19 Pandemic. *WSEAS Transactions on Information Science and Applications, 19*, 78–88. doi:10.37394/23209.2022.19.8

Büyükbeşe, T., Dikbaş, T., Klein, M., & Batuk Ünlü, S. (2022). A Study On Digital Leadership Scale (DLS) Development Dijital Liderlik Ölçeği (Djl) Geliştirme Çalışması. *Kahramanmaraş Sütçü İmam Üniversitesi Sosyal Bilimler Dergisi, 19*(2), 740–760. doi:10.33437/ksusbd.1135540

Büyükbeşe, T., & Doğan, Ö. (2022). Dijital Liderliğin Yenilikçi İş Davranışı ve İş Performansı Üzerine Etkisi. *Akademik Araştırmalar ve Çalışmalar Dergisi, 14*(26), 173–186. doi:10.20990/kilisiibfakademik.1072185

Çelik Şahin, Ç., Avcı, Y. E., & Anık, S. (2020). Dijital Liderlik Algısının Metaforlar Yoluyla İncelenmesi. *Elektronik Sosyal Bilimler Dergisi, 19*(73), 271–286. doi:10.17755/esosder.535159

Contreras, F., Baykal, E., & Abid, G. (2020). E-Leadership and Teleworking in Times of Covid-19 and Beyond: What We Know and Where Do We Go. *Frontiers in Psychology, 11*, 590271. doi:10.3389/fpsyg.2020.590271 PMID:33362656

Dinçer, S. (2018). Content Analysis in Scientific Research: Meta-Analysis, Meta-Synthesis, and Descriptive Content Analysis. *Bartın Üniversitesi Eğitim Fakültesi Dergisi*, 176–190. doi:10.14686/buefad.363159

Eberl, J. K., & Drews, P. (2021). Digital Leadership – Mountain or Molehill? A Literature Review. *Wirtshaftsinformatik 2021 Proceedings, 48*, 223–237. doi:10.1007/978-3-030-86800-0_17

Ercan Önbıçak, A., & Akkoyun, B. (2022). Dijital Liderlik Çalışmalarının Yönetim Bilimleri Kapsamında İncelenmesi: Nitel Bir Araştırma. *Malatya Turgut Özal Üniversitesi İşletme ve Yönetim Bilimleri Dergisi, 3*(2), 128–137.

Erer, B., Demirel, E., & Savaş, Y. (2023). Dijital Liderliğin Görsel Haritalama Tekniğine Göre Bibliyometrik Analizi. *Uluslararası Liderlik Çalışmaları Dergisi: Kuram ve Uygulama*, *6*(1), 1–22. doi:10.52848/ijls.1257255

Hensellek, S. (2022). Digital Leadership. *Journal of Media Management and Entrepreneurship*, *2*(1), 1–15. doi:10.4018/JMME.2020010104

Kane, G. C., Palmer, D., Phillips, A. N., Kiron, D., & Buckley, N. (2016). Aligning the organization for its digital future. *MIT Sloan Management Review*, *58*(1), 1–27.

Malakyan, P. G. (2020). Digital Leader-Followership for the Digital Age: A North American Perspective. In M. Franco (Ed.), *Digital Leadership - A New Leadership Style for the 21st Century*. doi:10.5772/intechopen.89820

Marr, B. (2020). How the Covid-19 Pandemic is Fast-tracking Digital Transformation in Companies. *Forbes*. https://www.forbes.com/sites/bernardmarr/2020/03/17/ how-the-covid-19-pandemic-is-fast-tracking-digital-transformation-in-companies/#449f9158a8ee/

Oberer, B., & Erkollar, A. (2018). Leadership 4.0: Digital Leaders in the Age of Industry 4.0. *International Journal of Organizational Leadership*, *7*(4), 404–412. doi:10.33844/ijol.2018.60332

Ordu, A., & Nayır, F. (2021). *Dijital Liderlik Nedir? Bir Tanım Önerisi*. E-International Journal of Educational Research. doi:10.19160/e-ijer.946094

Petry, T. (2018). Digital Leadership. In K. North, R. Maier, & O. Haas (Eds.), *Knowledge Management in Digital Change* (pp. 209–218). Springer. doi:10.1007/978-3-319-73546-7_12

Promsri, C. (2019). Developing Model of Digital Leadership for a Successful Digital Transformation. *Business Management Gph-International Journal*, *2*(8).

Ramirez, R. L. (2023). Managing the Remote Employee. In The New World of Work: People Leadership in the Digital Age (p.89-98), Routledge, Taylor & Francis Group.

Shipman, K., Burrell, D. N., & Huff Mac Pherson, A. (2023). An Organizational Analysis of How Managers must Understand the Mental Health Impact of Teleworking During Covid-19 on Employees. *The International Journal of Organizational Analysis*, *31*(4), 1081–1104. doi:10.1108/IJOA-03-2021-2685

Sullivan, C. (2012). Remote Working and Work-life Balance. In Work and Quality of Life. (p. 275-290). Springer.

Tigre, F. B., Curado, C., & Henriques, P. L. (2023). Digital Leadership: A Bibliometric Analysis. *Journal of Leadership & Organizational Studies*, *30*(1), 40–70. doi:10.1177/15480518221123132

Ulu, S., & Özgener, Ş. (2023). Covid-19 Pandemi Döneminde E-liderlik: Fırsatlar ve Sorunlar, Ö. Demirtaş & Ö. Üstün. In *Sağlık Yönetimi ve Güncel Yaklaşımlar*. Atlas.

Wisskirchen, G., Biacabe, B. T., Bormann, U., Muntz, A., Niehaus, G., Soler, G. J., & von Brauchitsch, B. (2017). Artificial intelligence and robotics and their impact on the workplace. *IBA Global Employment Institute*, *11*(5), 49–67.

Yıldırım, A., & Şimşek, H. (2006). *Sosyal Bilimlerde Nitel Araştırma Yöntemleri* (5. baskı). Seçkin Yayıncılık.

Zeike, S., Bradbury, K., Lindert, L., & Pfaff, H. (2019). Digital leadership skills and associations with psychological well-being. *International Journal of Environmental Research and Public Health, 16*(14), 2628. Advance online publication. doi:10.3390/ijerph16142628 PMID:31340579

Chapter 6
Masterminds and Machines:
Harnessing AI in Strategic Leadership

Geetha Manoharan
https://orcid.org/0000-0002-8644-8871
SR University, India

Sunitha Purushottam Ashtikar
SR University, India

C. V. Guru Rao
https://orcid.org/0000-0002-9210-6122
SR University, India

Sundarapandiyan Natarajan
Adithya Institute of Technology, India

M. Nivedha
Robert Gordon University, UK

ABSTRACT

Artificial intelligence is a vital tool for any organization and is quickly growing in all business streams. AI is leading commercial decision-making in all areas. Digital technology has created free time for many chores, but now AI determines commercial variables. Advancements have caused exponential growth in almost every firm. Businesses that conduct repeated operations require a long time to accomplish other jobs, yet labor hours or other factors cannot be avoided. Business growth is driven by predictive analytics, natural language processing, etc. AI-based predictive analytics employs data mining, machine learning, and statistical algorithms to examine previous data to forecast future trends. The NLP may use different algorithms to identify problem statement patterns and concerns. Proactive problem-solving is its key attribute. Businesses that employ AI solutions will always have higher productivity in several industries. This chapter will teach how AI can improve company leadership.

DOI: 10.4018/979-8-3693-1946-8.ch006

INTRODUCTION

Artificial Intelligence

The digital age has progressed via a series of technological milestones. With the advent of the internet, the spread of mobile devices, big data, and cloud computing, every stage has significantly transformed our way of life and professional endeavors. However, among these revolutionary developments, artificial intelligence (AI) stands out as an exceptionally profound influence. Inspired by human brain functions, its neural networks and algorithms enable robots to learn, adapt, and make decisions in ways that were previously believed to be unique to humans. Over the past few years, artificial intelligence (AI) (Abdulwahid, A. H., et al., 2023) has experienced substantial expansion, emerging as a crucial instrument for businesses to optimize processes, reduce production expenses, and achieve organizational goals . As (Manoharan, G., et al., 2023)AI gains proficiency in natural language processing, predictive analytics, and other functionalities, it will assume a progressively significant role in informing the decisions of leaders. Digital technology, which was once a source of amusement and pleasure, has evolved into the means by which society operates on a regular basis. We live in an era of exponential growth, with technological breakthroughs becoming more vital to today's workplace than ever before. At its most basic, AI-powered scheduling software assists firms in reducing the time and resources required to manage workforce. Time-consuming and resource-intensive repetitive activities, such as data entry and invoicing, are a common requirement for the majority of firms. By implementing AI technologies and machine learning techniques (Tripathi, M. A., Tripathi, R., et al., 2023), businesses can free up employees' time to concentrate on higher-level tasks that demand greater critical thinking and innovation.

Natural language processing (NLP) is a subfield of artificial intelligence that focuses on comprehending and interpreting human language. Text data is analysed by NLP algorithms to extract meaning, mood, and purpose. Businesses can use this to better comprehend client feedback, automate customer care interactions, and develop personalised content. Businesses may employ NLP algorithms to analyse social media client feedback to find common concerns and patterns. NLP algorithms can assist businesses in proactively addressing these issues, hence enhancing overall customer experience.

Leadership

Leadership can be interpreted and described in a variety of ways. Leadership and accountability are related in a broader sense. A leader is responsible for a variety of tasks. Both the corporation and the employees are included in this. For example, for personnel, the areas of information, qualification, and communication can be stated. Employee leadership can be perceived in numerous ways. This is seen in the diverse leadership behaviors that have emerged. Leadership varies depending on the company's specific management level (Manoharan, G., & Ashtikar, S. P. 2024). During the value development process, leadership takes on a distinct role. It creates, settles on, and establishes specific goals and plans. Leadership both generates and organizes at the same time. As a result, it creates a supportive environment for goal achievement. Leadership also directs and regulates through communication as necessary. In this situation, the nature and style of leadership might vary greatly. Leaders can function in both task and employee modes. The corresponding interpretation is always situational. Task and employee orientation might both be greater or weaker. However, both components are always required for effective leadership (Hettl, M., 2013). Leaders' leadership of employees is always a process. This procedure contains four critical components as seen in Figure 1. The leader exhibits distinct leadership behaviors during the leadership process. The goal is for the led personnel to be influenced by the leader's behavior. Leaders, on the other hand, always have their own set of principles and characteristics. As a result, these factors influence individual leadership behavior. Leadership success is the fourth component. Leaders pursue a goal when in a leadership position. As soon as this goal is met, leadership success follows Frost, M., & Sandrock, S. (2019).

Strategic Importance of AI in Leadership

A multitude of uncertainties exist within the realm of leadership within the AI era. The disruptive influence of artificial intelligence (AI) across numerous industries is evident in the way in which it affects leadership decisions. By boosting data-driven decision-making and modifying team dynamics, this is changing how leaders work and think about the future. However, it would be prudent to pay special attention to key areas that should remain strategically significant.

As leadership roles are increasingly burdened with complications and duties imposed by artificial intelligence (AI), the fundamental worth of visionary thinking becomes crucial. Notwithstanding the progressions made in artificial intelligence (Manoharan, G., Durai, S., et al., 2024), it is nonetheless unable to supplant the human capacity for imagination and a purpose-driven, moving vision. Additionally, leaders possess a competitive edge in terms of strategic planning, staff motivation (Chaudhary, V., et al., 2024), and surmounting uncertainty. With the increasing sway of AI systems, it is incumbent upon leaders to ensure the ethical deployment of AI (Manoharan, G., Durai, S., et al., 2023). Preventing injury and ensuring fairness are of the utmost importance. Nevertheless, this is not solely an issue of ethics; it is also a matter of sound business practise since 62% of consumers place their trust in organizations that employ ethical AI interactions.

Primarily, the fundamental worth of visionary thinking becomes critical as artificial intelligence (AI) imbues leadership positions with ever-increasing complexities and responsibilities. A human ability for imagination and a purpose-driven, moving vision remains unassailable, whatever the progress made in artificial intelligence. In terms of strategic planning, staff motivation, and surmounting uncertainty, leaders also possess a distinct advantage. Leaders must ensure the ethical deployment of AI as the impact of AI systems continues to expand. Ensuring fairness and preventing harm are of utmost importance. 62%

Figure 1. Framework model of leadership (self-designed)

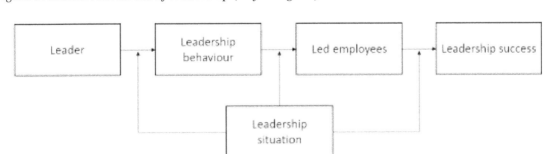

of consumers have faith in businesses that utilize ethical AI interactions; therefore, this is not merely an issue of ethics; it is also a question of good business.

One significant aspect is that the fundamental worth of visionary thinking becomes critical as leadership positions are confronted with escalating complexities and obligations imposed by artificial intelligence (AI). Despite the progress made in the field of artificial intelligence, technology is still unable to fully supplant the human ability to think creatively and with intention. Additionally, leaders possess a competitive edge in operationalizing strategies, surmounting ambiguity, and inspiring personnel. Leaders are obligated to ensure the ethical deployment of AI systems as their impact expands. Securing equity and preventing damage is of utmost importance. However, this is not solely an ethical concern; it is also a commercial one, as 62% of consumers place their trust in businesses that employ ethical AI interactions.

Influence of AI on Leadership

AI is already affecting how leaders make decisions and speculate on how it can affect teams in the future in the following ways:

1. **Accelerated Decision-Making**: Leaders are now equipped with the capability to retrieve significant insights from vast quantities of data, process it rapidly, and do it with the use of analytics and algorithms powered by AI (Singh, C. R., & Manoharan, G. 2024). Based on facts, this capability empowers leaders to render more precise and accurate decisions. Leaders may employ AI to impact their judgments rather than relying solely on gut sense or insufficient data.
2. **Predicted Analytics**: AI empowers executives to forecast forthcoming trends and consequences through the implementation of predictive analytics. Software capable of machine learning may analyze historical data, detect patterns, and generate approximations, enabling policymakers to adopt a more proactive stance. When leaders can predict potential difficulties or opportunities, they may prepare effectively and successfully decrease risks.
3. **Operations are more streamlined**: We should be grateful for artificial intelligence automation technologies that automate routine operations, reduce errors, and increase productivity. When leaders properly manage resources, they can direct their people toward higher-value jobs that need human inventiveness and imaginative thinking. Operations are streamlined, which increases team efficiency and allows leaders to devote more time to essential projects.

LITERATURE SURVEY

N., Shal, T., and N.A. Ghamrawi (2023) investigated whether Artificial Intelligence (AI) is growing or regressing teacher leadership as regarded by instructors who employ AI in their teaching approaches. Thirteen instructors from five countries were interviewed using a qualitative research design and semi-structured interviews. The data was then thematically analyzed. The study found that AI can improve and worsen teacher leadership. AI tools for personalization, curriculum creation, administrative work automation, and professional development can help teachers become better leaders. AI was seen as regressing teacher leadership by restricting the work once technology took over some parts. Teachers suggested five competencies for teacher leaders in the AI future. AI's impact on teacher leadership depends on how it's implemented in education, the study found. It stresses the importance of continual research and training to shape educational policies and practices.

Quaquebeke, N.V., and F.H. Gerpott (2023) found a growing consensus that AI-enabled computers could—and should—perform traditional management functions (AI). However, "genuine" leadership—encouraging and enabling individuals to contribute to an organization's goals—is still essentially a human prerogative. Our opinion contradicts this. Our essay aims to wake up academics and practitioners who romanticize human leadership and believe AI can never replace it. We demonstrate why algorithms will not (need to) stop before important leadership traits and may even better meet employees' psychological needs than human leaders. Against this backdrop, significant judgments about humans' role in future leadership are needed. These problems will shape leadership research, education, and growth.

Tarisayi, K.S. (2023) and Alex Rajesh G., & Florence Sheeba J. (2022)examined if AI can improve higher education learning, research, and leadership. This research aims to uncover important themes, challenges, and AI application recommendations in higher education and leadership. A literature review involved two LLMs. The findings show that artificial intelligence is being used to customize teaching, provide formative feedback, identify at-risk pupils, expedite research breakthroughs, streamline administrative operations via chatbots, and optimize resource use. However, the findings show that institutions must overcome technical, ethical, cultural, and resource constraints to maximize AI's promise while minimizing risks. Leveraging AI's immense but mostly untapped potential requires empowering management through knowledge, finance, and support systems that promote good governance and responsible AI implementation. The findings show that artificial intelligence is being used to customize teaching, provide formative feedback, identify at-risk pupils, expedite research breakthroughs, streamline administrative operations via chatbots, and optimize resource use.

Tîrnăcop, A.B. (2023) examined how AI could boost leaders' emotional intelligence (EI) skills like empathy, self-awareness, and social skills. The study uses a questionnaire and game-based methods to examine the intersection of AI and EI in leadership. The main goal is to determine how AI can boost leaders' emotional intelligence. Integrating AI and EI is crucial for effective leadership, according to the research. The study uses a questionnaire and game-based methods to examine the intersection of AI and EI in leadership.

Avurakoghene, O.P., and Oredein, A.O. (2023) and R. Kiran, G. R., et al., (2024) reported the importance of educational leadership and artificial intelligence in modern society cannot be exaggerated in the pursuit of sustainable development, given education's essential role in accomplishing the stated developmental objectives. Unfortunately, educational authorities in Nigeria confront several hurdles when it comes to leveraging the use of AI for long-term growth. This has not only had a detrimental impact on their efficacy, but it has also prevented them from achieving the country's educational objectives optimally, given the roles of teachers in education service delivery. This study used a qualitative research approach to provide insights into how artificial intelligence and educational leadership may be used to achieve sustainable development in Nigeria. This study looked specifically at educational leadership, artificial intelligence, sustainable development, and artificial leadership. Furthermore, the study emphasises the necessity for artificial intelligence-enhanced educational leadership for long-term growth by disclosing the functions of artificial intelligence in effective educational leadership and their implications for long-term development. It also considers the associated challenges, such as insufficient infrastructure and funding, a lack of technical expertise among educators and education administrators, a lack of policies and regulations, ethical concerns, public awareness, and education, as well as mitigating strategies, such as providing infrastructure and funding, technical expertise, policies and regulations, ethical concerns, public awareness, and education to address them.

Xiong, W. (2022) found that leaders are essential for creating and implementing new strategic plans and inspiring employees to drive company goals. Leader development is essential to remaining on track. Smart corporate leaders recognise employee issues and use new leadership theories to improve workplace performance. AI, a new technology, lets machines perform complex tasks that humans would. Incorporating AI into mechanised, mechanical, and administrative operations will boost leaders' productivity. To replace human caring, thinking, and involvement with human variables, AI is tough. Future leaders may need to emphasise these elements.

Peifer, Y., Jeske, T., and Hille, S. (2022) noted that IT system networking and cyber-physical systems in industry are increasing data. Companies are increasingly using AI to analyse this huge data and develop conclusions. AI use is rising, affecting socio-technical work systems. Specific leadership challenges and requirements can be identified. Thus, leaders are essential for AI deployment and use. This, along with AI's rapid expansion, requires further research on its effects on leaders and leadership to provide organisations with practice-proven guidelines and recommendations. A comprehensive literature review was conducted to build those, which would form the basis for future actions. The literature research found four clusters: Strategic Transformation Process, Qualification and Competencies, Culture, and Human-AI Interaction. Details on the findings and future research and development are presented.

Titareva, T. (2021) combined "leadership" and "artificial intelligence" by stressing the essential features of Leadership in Industry 4.0, which is dominated by AI. The current literature survey identified three primary scholarly and practitioner research directions: 1) AI as an augmentation to leadership activities, 2) AI to replace followers and leaders (replacement perspective), and 3) AI as "an oversold idea" (skeptical perspective). This literature analysis addresses a dearth of significant literature review and empirical evidence by providing a balanced assessment of how AI-based technologies affect organizational leadership. The purpose of this study is to review the literature on Leadership in Industry 4.0, which is dominated by AI-based technologies, and how they affect modern organizational leadership. The current literature analysis asks: "What are the key views of scholarly and practitioner research directions in Leadership in an Artificial Intelligence Era in 2010-2020?" This paper's highlighted ideas could provide the basis for empirical research by the author and other field researchers and practitioners.

Wang, Y. (2021) found that artificial intelligence (AI) is a class of algorithms or computer systems that replicate human decision-making. This position paper goes beyond sensationalizing AI in education. This paper examines AI's role in educational leadership. Design/methodology/approach: I researched AI, decision-making, and educational leadership literature from computer science, educational leadership, administrative science, judgment and decision-making, and neuroscience to determine how AI affects educational leadership. Based on the philosophical interrelationships between AI and educational leadership since the 1950s, this study defines decision-making—individual and organizational—as the foundation of educational leadership. I then explained human-AI decision-symbiosis. making's Findings: AI can assist educational leaders make data-driven, evidence-based decisions because it efficiently gathers, processes, and analyses data and provides real-time or near-real-time results. AI-assisted data-driven decision-making may collide with morality. Combining data-driven, evidence-informed and value-based moral decision-making helps leaders manage individual and organisational decision-making. AI can make data-driven, evidence-based decisions like a brain. Moral judgement can overcome AI-assisted data-driven decision-making errors. Practice consequences: The research advises educational leadership practitioners and future scholars to watch for biases and morally compromised decisions. Originality/value: This study combines educational leadership and AI, which grew up together in the 1950s but separated until the late 2010s. Leaders make individual and organisational decisions, which this study examines to determine how AI affects educational leadership. The research then synthesises AI, decision-making, and educational leadership literature to characterise AI's role in educational leadership.

METHODOLOGY

The objective of surveying the present chapter was to review the literature. The literature was selected and investigated based on defined criteria to ensure high-quality research. Numerous databases were collected and analyzed for selecting the literature. The overall report culminates open access databases, conference papers, scientific research papers, online databases from library universities and consultancies databases. Apart from this, previous published studies from journals, textbooks, conferences, scientific papers were examined. Therefore, the results obtained ensure comprehensiveness and up to date. Extensively, research survey was done on various aspects of advancing knowledge and integrating literature reviews from scholarly publications, related insights and basing on existing theories to generate new knowledge of exploring leadership using artificial intelligence. The chapter addresses the gap by reviewing and discussing the specific areas on leadership with the application of digital technology like artificial intelligence to achieve optimal leadership.

RESULTS/FINDINGS AND DISCUSSIONS

According to the aforementioned research studies, human leadership in businesses can be combined with artificial intelligence through the use of algorithms. AI can enhance teacher leadership by providing tools for customization, curriculum development, administrative work automation, and professional development, which serve as the five sets of skills in designing education policies and practices. AI is being utilized to tailor instruction, provide formative feedback, detect at-risk students, speed research discoveries, streamline administrative operations via chatbots, and maximize resource utilization to promote good governance and empower management systems like human resource management (Deviprasad, S., Madhumithaa, N., et al., 2023; Joyce, P. R., et al., 2024). Furthermore, artificial intelligence assists in detecting leaders' emotional intelligence through the use of five components: self-awareness, self-regulation, empathy, motivation, and social skills. Aside from the findings mentioned above, one of the concerns about leadership is sustainable development, which results in a lack of infrastructure, non-availability of technical tools, policies that are not defined, and more paperwork that can be improved with the help of artificial intelligence. Leaders' productivity will grow as AI takes over some automated, mechanical, and administrative tasks, substituting human care, human thought, and human engagement with human aspects. AI can deliver analytical efficiency to educational leaders by gathering, processing, and analyzing data in real-time or near real-time and presenting results in real-time or near real-time (Durga, S., et al., 2024). In the context of leadership

Figure 2. Author's framework derived from literature

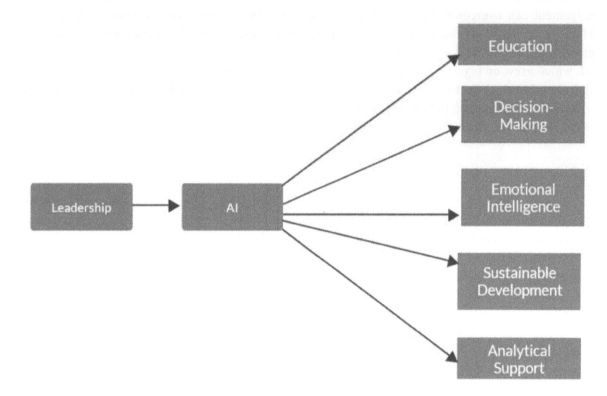

utilizing artificial intelligence, a framework may be built with the aid of prior studies that can be associated with the help of empirical data.

The concept of leadership with the help of artificial intelligence in different aspects are discussed below:

- **Education:** People working in education or involved in education in some form will gain a sufficient understanding of Artificial Intelligence approaches and controversies. As an education leader, you realise the necessity of remaining current with the latest tools and technologies to better your students' educational experience. Artificial intelligence (AI) technologies, such as ChatGPT, are one type of technology that is gaining traction in the education industry. These tools can assist educational leaders in streamlining administrative processes, improving student outcomes, and improving the entire learning experience. AI solutions (Kumar, C. S., et al., 2024), such as ChatGPT, can help to streamline administrative chores, improve communication, sample prompts, and assist professional development.
- **Decision-Making:** AI may help managers make decisions by evaluating data, generating insights, and forecasting outcomes. It provides natural language processing for information retrieval, decision support systems, task automation, risk assessment, and tailored recommendations. Artificial intelligence's continual learning enhances its performance over time, making it a great tool for managers to make informed and efficient decisions. AI can help executives make better decisions by swiftly evaluating large amounts of data, recognising trends, and forecasting outcomes. It reduces human biases while providing unbiased insights. AI aids executives

in making informed decisions, minimising risks, and increasing efficiency through data-driven recommendations. AI responds to changing settings by continual learning, delivering up-to-date information. This allows leaders to stay ahead of the competition, make more strategic judgments, and traverse complicated issues more successfully. Overall, AI is a helpful tool for leaders, providing them with complete and timely information to help them make better decisions for the development of their enterprises.

- **Emotional Intelligence:** As a result, emotional intelligence will supplement AI, forming a potent mix that will allow leaders to thrive in the face of AI-driven automation while nurturing a culture of participation, feedback, and cooperation. Emotional intelligence is more important than IQ or technical skill in determining a manager's success (Manoharan, G., Durai, S., & Rajesh, G. A. 2022). Emotional intelligence is as important as any "hard skill," and investing in it helps people and teams succeed at work. Companies should research AI technology that can improve emotional intelligence and communication. AI can boost emotional intelligence by enhancing self-awareness and helping us manage important professional relationships. We become more productive, caring, and effective by improving our emotional intelligence and communication. Although not perfect, the technology is getting smarter as platforms gain data, volume, and sophistication. Technology exists to make our teams more emotionally intelligent and our businesses more successful and profitable. AI will automate most manual labour, but humans will excel in soft talents like creativity and relationships. This is partly true—people and computers will play to their strengths—but it oversimplifies AI's role in our professional lives. We think AI will improve emotional intelligence, soft skills, and interpersonal communication to help people do better jobs.

- **Education:** People working in education or involved in education in some form will gain a sufficient understanding of Artificial Intelligence approaches and controversies. As an education leader, you realise the necessity of remaining current with the latest tools and technologies to better your students' educational experience. Artificial intelligence (AI) technologies, such as ChatGPT, are one type of technology that is gaining traction in the education industry. These tools can assist educational leaders in streamlining administrative processes, improving student outcomes, and improving the entire learning experience. AI solutions, such as ChatGPT, can help to streamline administrative chores, improve communication, sample prompts, and assist professional development.

- **Sustainable Development:** The role of AI in sustainability reveals a diverse approach to SDG development, with the majority of study concentrating in the Prosperity sector, focusing on organisational and industrial transformations caused by AI adoption. Sustainable leadership addresses global environmental, social, and economic issues. Deconstructing silos and seeing leadership as a process of influence encourages leaders to collaborate for change and progress. Sustainable leaders adapt to the world's growing complexity. Most significantly, they are long-term thinkers who value people and the environment of the organisation.

- **Analytical Support:** AI is pervasive in our daily lives. It is one of the most common realities in modern company, simplifying and eliminating errors in repeated and tedious procedures. Companies are using AI-driven analytics for predicting intelligence, making data-driven decisions for success and growth, and automating day-to-day chores. The use of artificial intelligence into corporate processes was a game changer that resulted in drastic changes in how firms operate. AI is transforming the leadership teams that are embracing it, just as it has transformed our daily lives through the use of devices such as Alexa and Siri. Businesses today recognise the value of having highly talented and efficient senior executives, and hiring managers see the value of AI (Shameem, A., Ramachandran, K. K., et al., 2023) analytics in training these leaders.

CONCLUSION AND FUTURISTIC SCOPE

AI has become one of the megatrends altering the world of work, alongside the demand for increased sustainability, generational transition, and geopolitical and economic turbulence. The world is undergoing an unprecedented transformation as a result of numerous software tools such as Tivian's Leadership 360 software, which gives insights that empower (Keserwani, H., PT, R., et al., 2022) and grow your leaders at all levels of the organisation. Successful firms require strong, transformative leaders who are devoted to listening to feedback, constantly upgrading their skills, and mastering new technology such as AI. It provides feedback and insights to your executives 24 hours a day, seven days a week. By collecting, evaluating, and sharing data on-demand or as part of regular performance reviews, employers can identify areas for individual improvement while also developing the broad skills and behaviours required to succeed in the future of work. It even employs AI to identify measures to take to drive change, combining technology with leadership development to achieve effective, long-term results.

A research call can be issued to study how we can quantify human leaders' AI literacy. As future human leaders are expected to comprehend both how humans and AIs operate, proven new measurement tools beyond self-assessments will be required (Wang et al., 2022). Such objective measures could be used to determine if leaders are able to "give the proper prompts" to the AI leaders they are expected to monitor (Brown, 2023). In other words, there is a need to assess whether leaders are sufficiently informed on the technology side of things; as a result, scholars should devise methods to objectively assess whether human leaders comprehend the intricacies of AI and how it may benefit or hurt personnel.

REFERENCES

Abdulwahid, A. H., Pattnaik, M., Palav, M. R., Babu, S. T., Manoharan, G., & Selvi, G. P. (2023, April). Library Management System Using Artificial Intelligence. In *2023 Eighth International Conference on Science Technology Engineering and Mathematics (ICONSTEM)* (pp. 1-7). IEEE.

Alex Rajesh G., & Florence Sheeba J. (2022). A Study on Exploring Perceptions of Emotional Intelligence among Educators. *International Journal of Food and Nutritional Sciences.*

Avurakoghene, O.P., & Oredein, A.O. (2023). Educational Leadership and Artificial Intelligence for Sustainable Development. *Shodh Sari-An International Multidisciplinary Journal.*

Brown, C. (2023). *ChatGPT prompts mastering: A guide to crafting clear and effective prompts—beginners to advanced guide.* Xtro Media.

Chaudhary, V., Vemuri, V. P., Cavaliere, L. P. L., Verma, V., Manoharan, G., & Bharti, A. (2024, March). A comparative analysis of job satisfaction and motivational factors of employees in public versus private organizations. In AIP Conference Proceedings (Vol. 2816, No. 1). AIP Publishing.

Deviprasad, S., Madhumithaa, N., Vikas, I. W., Yadav, A., & Manoharan, G. (2023). The Machine Learning-Based Task Automation Framework for Human Resource Management in MNC Companies. *Engineering Proceedings*, *59*(1), 63.

Durai, S., Manoharan, G., & Ashtikar, S. P. (2024). *Harnessing Artificial Intelligence: Pioneering Sustainable Solutions for a Greener Future. Social and Ethical Implications of AI in Finance for Sustainability. 89-117.* doi:10.4018/979-8-3693-2881-1.ch003

Durga, S., Gupta, P., Kharb, L., Ranjit, P. S., Dornadula, V. H. R., Modak, K. C., & Manoharan, G. (2024). 9Leveraging Distributed Systems for Improved Educational Planning and Resource Allocation. *Meta Heuristic Algorithms for Advanced Distributed Systems,* 141-159.

Frost, M., & Sandrock, S. (2019, February). Leadership and self-learning software – hindering and beneficial factors for the motivation of employees in the world of work 4.0. *Analyze–evaluate–design in an interdisciplinary manner.*

Ghamrawi, N., Shal, T., & Ghamrawi, N. A. (2023). Exploring the impact of AI on teacher leadership: Regressing or expanding? *Education and Information Technologies.*

Hettl, M. (2013). *Employee administration using the LEAD-Navigator.* Springer Professional Media Wiesbaden.

Joyce, P. R., Selvaraj, F. J., Manoharan, G., Priya, C., Vijayalakshmi, R., Dwivedi, P. K., Gupta, S., & Veerakumar, K. (2024). To Study The Role Of Marketing In Human Resource Management. *Migration Letters: An International Journal of Migration Studies*, *21*(S2), 1191–1196. doi:10.59670/ml.v21iS2.7072

Keserwani, H., PT, R., PR, J., Manoharan, G., Mane, P., & Gupta, S. K. (2021). Effect Of Employee Empowerment On Job Satisfaction In Manufacturing Industry. *Turkish Online Journal of Qualitative Inquiry*, *12*(3).

Kiran, R. G. R., Manoharan, G., Durai, S., Ashtikar, S. P., & Kunchala. (2024). Higher Education in India and the Influence of Online Certification Programs. Evaluating Global Accreditation Standards for Higher Education, 149-163.

Kumar, C. S., Vani, D. D., Damodar, K., Manoharan, G., & Veerapaga, N. (2024). Climate Change Mitigation Through AI Solutions. In *Gastronomic Sustainability Solutions for Community and Tourism Resilience* (pp. 37–59). IGI Global. doi:10.4018/979-8-3693-4135-3.ch003

Manoharan, G., & Ashtikar, S. P. (2024). A Theoretical Framework for Emotional Intelligence in Academic Leadership in Higher Education. In *Building Organizational Resilience With Neuroleadership* (pp. 96–112). IGI Global. doi:10.4018/979-8-3693-1785-3.ch007

Manoharan, G., Ashtikar, S. P., & Nivedha, M. (2024). Integrating Artificial Intelligence in Library Management: An Emerging Trend. *AI-Assisted Library Reconstruction,* 144-157.

Manoharan, G., Durai, S., Ashtikar, S. P., & Kumari, N. (2024). Artificial Intelligence in Marketing Applications. In Artificial Intelligence for Business (pp. 40-70). Productivity Press.

Manoharan, G., Durai, S., & Rajesh, G. A. (2022, May). Emotional intelligence: A comparison of male and female doctors in the workplace. In AIP Conference Proceedings (Vol. 2418, No. 1). AIP Publishing.

Manoharan, G., Durai, S., Rajesh, G. A., & Ashtikar, S. P. (2024). A Study on the Application of Expert Systems as a Support System for Business Decisions: A Literature Review. *Artificial Intelligence and Knowledge Processing*, 279-289.

Manoharan, G., Durai, S., Rajesh, G. A., Razak, A., Rao, C. B., & Ashtikar, S. P. (2023). An investigation into the effectiveness of smart city projects by identifying the framework for measuring performance. In *Artificial Intelligence and Machine Learning in Smart City Planning* (pp. 71–84). Elsevier. doi:10.1016/B978-0-323-99503-0.00004-1

Manoharan, G., Durai, S., Rajesh, G. A., Razak, A., Rao, C. B., & Ashtikar, S. P. (2023). A study on the perceptions of officials on their duties and responsibilities at various levels of the organizational structure in order to accomplish artificial intelligence-based smart city implementation. In *Artificial Intelligence and Machine Learning in Smart City Planning* (pp. 1–10). Elsevier. doi:10.1016/B978-0-323-99503-0.00007-7

Manoharan, G., Nithya, G., Rajchandar, K., Razak, A., Gupta, S., Durai, S., & Ashtikar, S. P. (2024). AI in Finance and Banking: The Act of Gyration. In *Revolutionizing Customer-Centric Banking Through ICT* (pp. 1–28). IGI Global. doi:10.4018/979-8-3693-2061-7.ch001

Manoharan, G., Razak, A., Rajchandar, K., Nithya, G., Durai, S., & Ashtikar, S. P. (2024). Digital Learning for Professional Development in Varied Fields of Service Sectors: Embracing Technological Advancements. In *Embracing Technological Advancements for Lifelong Learning* (pp. 111–137). IGI Global. doi:10.4018/979-8-3693-1410-4.ch006

Manoharan, G., Razak, A., Rao, C. G., Ashtikar, S. P., & Nivedha, M. (2024). Artificial Intelligence at the Helm: Steering the Modern Business Landscape Toward Progress. In *The Ethical Frontier of AI and Data Analysis* (pp. 72–99). IGI Global. doi:10.4018/979-8-3693-2964-1.ch005

Peifer, Y., Jeske, T., & Hille, S. (2022). Artificial intelligence and its impact on leaders and leadership. *Procedia Computer Science*, *200*, 1024–1030. doi:10.1016/j.procs.2022.01.301

Quaquebeke, N. V., & Gerpott, F. H. (2023). The Now, New, and Next of Digital Leadership: How Artificial Intelligence (AI) Will Take Over and Change Leadership as We Know It. *Journal of Leadership & Organizational Studies*, *30*(3), 265–275. doi:10.1177/15480518231181731

Rajchandar, K., Kothandaraman, D., Manoharan, G., & Kabanda, G. Robotics and its Navigation Techniques: The Present and Future Revelations. *Handbook of Artificial Intelligence and Wearables,* 189-204.

Razak, A., Nayak, M. P., Manoharan, G., Durai, S., Rajesh, G. A., Rao, C. B., & Ashtikar, S. P. (2023). Reigniting the power of artificial intelligence in the education sector for the educators' and students competence. In *Artificial Intelligence and Machine Learning in Smart City Planning* (pp. 103–116). Elsevier. doi:10.1016/B978-0-323-99503-0.00009-0

Shameem, A., Ramachandran, K. K., Sharma, A., Singh, R., Selvaraj, F. J., & Manoharan, G. (2023, May). The rising importance of AI in boosting the efficiency of online advertising in developing countries. In *2023 3rd International Conference on Advance Computing and Innovative Technologies in Engineering (ICACITE)* (pp. 1762-1766). IEEE.

Singh, C. R., & Manoharan, G. (2024). Strengthening Resilience: AI and Machine Learning in Emergency Decision-Making for Natural Disasters. In *Internet of Things and AI for Natural Disaster Management and Prediction* (pp. 249–278). IGI Global. doi:10.4018/979-8-3693-4284-8.ch012

Soltas. (2022). The Impact Of Artificial Intelligence On The Future Of Workforces. *The European Union And The United States Of America*.

Tarisayi, K. S. (2023). Strategic leadership for responsible artificial intelligence adoption in higher education. *CTE Workshop Proceedings*.

Tîrnăcop, A.B. (2023). *Leadership in the digital era: exploring the AI-EI nexus*. CACTUS.

Titareva, T. (2021). *Leadership in an Artificial Intelligence Era*. Presented at *Leading Change Conference*.

Tripathi, M. A., Tripathi, R., Effendy, F., Manoharan, G., Paul, M. J., & Aarif, M. (2023, January). An In-Depth Analysis of the Role That ML and Big Data Play in Driving Digital Marketing's Paradigm Shift. *In 2023 International Conference on Computer Communication and Informatics (ICCCI)* (pp. 1-6). IEEE. 10.1109/ICCCI56745.2023.10128357

Wang, B., Rau, P. L. P., & Yuan, T. (2022). Measuring user competence in using artificial intelligence: Validity and reliability of artificial intelligence literacy scale. *Behaviour & Information Technology*, 1–14. doi:10.1080/0144929X.2022.2072768

Wang, Y. (2021). Artificial intelligence in educational leadership: A symbiotic role of human-artificial intelligence decision-making. *Journal of Educational Administration*, *59*(3), 256–270. doi:10.1108/JEA-10-2020-0216

Xiong, W. (2022, December). AI and Leadership. In *2022 7th International Conference on Modern Management and Education Technology (MMET 2022)* (pp. 497-503). Atlantis Press. https://www.tivian.com/us/our-products/employee-experience/360-feedback/

Chapter 7
Rise of Clone-Leadership in the Shadow of Artificial Intelligence

Amanpreet Singh Chopra
 https://orcid.org/0009-0009-7181-8794
Chitkara Business School, Chitkara University, Punjab, India

Sridhar Manohar
 https://orcid.org/0000-0003-0173-3479
Chitkara Business School, Chitkara University, Punjab, India

ABSTRACT

AI could take different pathways for development. This chapter emphasises the issues regarding strategic approach that the next generation business leaders need to adopt to coexist with these technological transformations. These development pathways could be the ones where the dependency on an AI-driven support system drains out the leadership abilities, intellect, and creativity of future leaders, resulting in the emergence of 'Clone Leadership'. Or, will they lead to a best-case scenario in which AI is regulated and emerge as a stakeholder in the business ecosystem, resulting in growth and prosperity? The chapter deliberates upon the decision-making approach that business leaders would be adopting in AI dominated business environment, especially with respect to governance, morality, and ethical behavior. Finally, the chapter analyzes the efforts being made to develop ethical, transparent, and accountable principles and guidelines to manage responsible AI.

1. INTRODUCTION

"If machine brains one day surpass human brain in general intelligence, the fate of our species would depend on the action of powerful AI"- This phrase from Nick Brostom's New York Times bestseller 'Superintelligence', projects the future humanity is staring a future that could be governed by non-biological intelligence, this may take over the reign of humanity in one of the multiple case scenarios (Bostrom, 2014). The question faced by homo species today is not how or why this superintelligence will rise. But, when?

DOI: 10.4018/979-8-3693-1946-8.ch007

Rise of Clone-Leadership in the Shadow of Artificial Intelligence

Today, human intelligence, limited by its evolutionary pathway is encountering competition from non-biological forms of intelligence, which learns and evolves by themselves with the potential for unrestrained growth. This form of intelligence initially grows with human support till it reaches the point where it self-evolves, thus, diminishing its dependence upon written algorithms. The explosive self-evolution would have a deep impact on human civilization. This phase of AI evolution would rapidly blur the boundaries between biological and non-biological intelligence to the point that AI would be in a position to manipulate the classical Turing test (Turing, 1950) in its favor. In this unprecedented scenario, the interrogator would be convinced that humans are in fact machines and vice versa, thus shaping a new level of human-AI interactions. The growth of AI dominance would have business consequences in various industries like transportation, energy, agriculture, and medical health care.

In the current and future growth states of AI, three artificial intelligence-driven leadership scenarios are envisioned in this study. Firstly, AI is at the development stage and assists leaders by providing an analytical support structure to enable them to make informed decisions, leading to increased operational efficiency and corporate profitability. For instance, in the case of medical science, AI is increasingly used for diagnosis, virtual care of patients, image interpretation, and non-clinical activities. In the second scenario, AI advances to a higher level by becoming more self-aware and conscious than human, learning from its mistakes, undergoing continuous improvement, and being entrusted with critical organizational tasks. As a result, it would acquire a position in the organizational hierarchy similar to that of humans. The last, and the most radical scenario is the one where AI has evolved into a self-aware Artificial General Intelligence (AGI), i.e., gaining human-like intellect, which augments at an exponential pace (Schwuchow and Gutmann, 2018) as depicted in Figure-1. With a high level of cognitive abilities, AI would take over the role of leadership and tilt the reigns of organizations from human to non-biological intelligence.

The growth phase of AI in Figure -1 (Schwuchow and Gutmann, 2018), illustrates the rise of non-biological or machine intelligence as compared to the biological one. It is understood that in near future a point will be reached where the intelligence of human and machine would coincide. This is termed as point of 'singularity' or the point at which machine achieves Artificial General Intelligence (AGI) or intelligence similar to that of human. At this point, the difference between human and machine intelligence would be abolished and it would be impossible to distinguish between the two. Beyond this point, there are two possible scenarios, one in which AI grows in a controlled manner with human intervention and another one in which AI would trend the path of self-evolvement or uncontrolled growth. In the second scenario, the growth in intelligence of AI would be exponential and may reach stage of Artificial Super Intelligence (ASI) and, as a result, taking over control of major aspects of human life.

AI possesses incredible prowess which must be leveraged for the betterment of society and human civilization. To accomplish this, there is an imminent need for development of standard global policy framework for AI governance not only in economic sectors but also in social environment. Taking cognizance of this, global collaboration among states on different platforms is increasing. This is necessary for the development of common principles and guidelines for the morally and responsible use of AI technologies, starting with the recently proposed AI Act of the European Union (EU), continuing with the Hiroshima AI process during the Japanese presidency, and developing the Global Partnership on Artificial Intelligence (GPAI).

It is also pertinent that the question of morality and ethical behavior of AI in future human-AI society is deliberated as to what would be the probable response of superior intelligence when con-

Figure 1. Growth phase of AI (Adapted from Schwuchow and Gutmann, 2018)

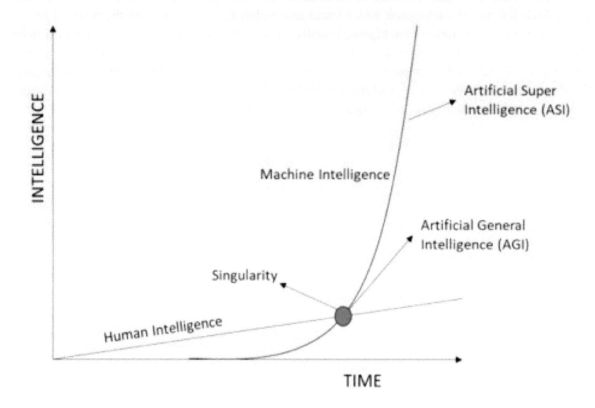

fronted with the dilemma of ethical behavior and moral conduct. For example, it would be interesting to note how AI would solve the ethical and moral dilemma while encountering the trolley problem. Will it follow the utilitarian perspective of maximizing overall happiness, or will it adhere to rules/laws and follow the deontological perspective? While there is no optimum solution to this ethical dilemma, the contours of responses would be useful in developing social norms in the brave new world of human-AI co-existence.

2. ARTIFICIAL INTELLIGENCE AND LEADERSHIP: A STATE OF CURRENT KNOWLEDGE

The strategic vision of the leadership and how it is communicated, understood, and carried out throughout the organization's hierarchy are key factors in the organization's ability to grow on various financial and operational matrices. In the world of hyper-competition, where the competitive advantages of organizations are short-lived, CEOs are ever exposed to situations of uncertainty, and the key to their growth is their capabilities of decision-making, creative thinking, emotional intelligence, integrity, and intellect. The current and future intervention of Artificial Intelligence (AI) in business ecosystem would result in the evolution of next-generation leadership driven by human-AI collaboration.

The growth of AI-focused firms, with a US$ 5.9 trillion valuation and 315 unicorns in the USA and 70 unicorns and a $1.3 trillion valuation in China has been phenomenal which has further led to aggressive competition between the two economies for AI supremacy (Lohchab, 2023). The deployment of AI and its integration with the systems and processes of companies has resulted in the optimization of operations and increased profitability (Watson et al., 2021; Sipola et al., 2023). On the economic front, the wide acceptance and introduction of generative AI is expected to add US$2.6 trillion to US$4.4 trillion to business functions with increased productivity of 0.1% to 0.6% till 2040 (McKinsey Global Institute, 2023).

In 2023 survey of 25 large firms based in Finland, it is noted that 20 out of these firms have deployed AI related to operations and have also entrusted it with decision-making to some complex problems related to risk analysis and resource optimization as a result, 80% of these firms have reported positive impact on their performance both on operational and financial matrices (Sipola et al., 2023). It is also noted that AI can generate value towards improving operational and safety performance of the organization and also in its HR practices through identification of recruitment needs, personal training, competency gap analysis and creating novel business models through analysis of sales and financial data (Kopka and Gashof, 2022). However, the extensive use of AI also calls for ethical consideration in terms of AI auditing (Kopka and Gashof, 2022) to safeguard the concerns of stakeholders in terms of job loss, ethical behavior, moral conduct, and reduction in bias in AI-driven decision-making ecosystem.

Automobiles is perhaps one industry that is considered a pioneer in adopting the latest technologies. For example, the introduction of robotics in the early 1960s, resulted in its expansion and exponential growth. While during the initial days, machine assistance was limited to mechanical work, especially in assembly lines, the expansion of these capabilities with the introduction of AI-driven machines resulted in the development of robot-human teams to collaborate under different operational scenarios. In the first scenario, this collaboration would lead to the pathway where robots, with a low level of intelligence take up major mechanical work resulting in business-as-usual conditions. In the second scenario, AI-driven robots are entrusted with moderate level of decision making leaving the most critical decisions at the judgement of human. Lastly, the higher level of AI would take up the role of leader in the human-robot partnership which in a case study of BMW resulted in an 85% increase in productivity (Tsai et al., 2022).

Along with the manufacturing segment, another remarkable development and implementation of AI is in the field of medical science. It is noted that in the medical clinical domain, AI is predominantly utilized on account of the high quality of the data output, and its ability to interpret complex images, especially MRI scans. With more than 72% of healthcare professionals in the European Union (EU) trusting AI for non-clinical and administrative purposes, the trend of leveraging its power for target therapy, personalized treatment and virtual care is on the rise. However, concerns related to the loss of skill sets of medical professionals due to overreliance on AI are also noted (Napoli and Lee, 2023). Further, the positive impact of AI was recognized with acceleration in drug discovery, assistance in clinical trials, medical image interpretation and new disease identification (Mannure et al., 2023). With increased reliance on judgement and decision-making through data-driven AI, the future would take two paths, with machines as decision enablers at one end of the spectrum to being decision makers at its extreme end (Agarwal et al., 2017). With this perspective in the background, the role and shape of future leadership need further exploration when AI does not remain part of the support system but graduates to be decision maker itself (Al Naqvi, 2017).

Although the social and organizational effects of AI on job replacement have been acknowledged, research has shown that the growing trends in AI could lead to two-way communication between people and computers for timely and dynamic decision-making (Lokreiro et al., 2021). From the organizational perspective, this led us to the extremely pertinent question in this human-AI collaboration, who is the leader and to what extent? Does it give rise to agency problems? and what safeguards are required to be in place to mitigate this? (Parry et al., 2016) countered this issue and suggested that superior intelligence could replace or support leadership decision-making with few safeguards in place. Three case scenarios were developed with the delegation of decision-making to AI with or without the veto of a human being. From the point of view of accountability in decision making, it was argued that in case of negative impact of AI decision, human would face an ambiguous situation of leadership accountability and to overcome this agency problem, the middle path of 'logged-veto' was proposed. In this pathway, humans could override the AI decision on case-to-case basis and the overriding decisions were logged for future reference and augmenting AI prowess (Parry et al., 2016; Lee and Park, 2023). This led us to another question to ponder – What would become of decisions requiring human empathy? especially in medical sciences which furthers the debate on clinical empathy in medical settings (Guidi and Traversa, 2021). How human-driven leadership in medical science would handle this dilemma of AI-driven decision making with or without empathy, is another domain that needs further research.

From the organizational perspective, fear of loss of jobs, phobia concerning lack of knowledge about AI, sustainability of AI in the organization, accountability and challenges related to its implementation are creating a digital divide in firms and hindering AI adaptability. This dimension of human fear of AI in organizations is making the workforce skeptical not about the capability of AI but about the intent of AI when it graduates to the level of 'general intelligence'. On the higher education front, while the positive impact of AI on personalized learning and advanced research capabilities was recognized it was also opined that the use of AI in research would devalue traditional research methodologies resulting in low quality and low validity of research output (Lee and Park, 2023; Mannure et al., 2023). Three distinct directions were visualized in the human-AI partnership in leadership. One where AI could act as an assistance to human decision making which is termed as 'enhancement direction' leading to better decision making to more profound 'replacement direction' wherein AI would replace the leadership and the last one is where AI growth is viewed as an oversold idea (Titareva, 2021; Tandon et al., 2021). Similarly, from the leadership perspective, three-stage leadership scenarios were put forward wherein at the first stage AI is visualized as a supportive tool for leaders to make data-driven informed decisions, at the second stage it becomes part of leadership by performing delegated tasks which results in process outcomes without human interference to the last stage with AI takes over the leadership role (Pefrie et al., 2022) thus making human led leadership redundant.

An analysis of interviews with 33 senior leaders recognized the growing influence of AI on business leadership and identified the need to reskill the workforce to work in tandem with AI. Further, two predominant sets of roles for AI in the future organizational hierarchy were identified - One in which AI is undertaking value-added assignments or tasks that provide decision support for the leadership to make informed decisions on the other hand, a highly developed AI system in the future could recommend to the management the course of action or the decision to be taken under various circumstances. This changing role of AI also entails leadership to acquire skills like data analysis, agility, decisiveness, and the ethical and moral consequences of AI-driven decision support systems (Shalender and Yadav 2019; Watson et al., 2023). Job loss and reskilling is another area of concern among the workforces. PwC's Global Workforce Hopes and Fear 2023 survey conducted among 54000 workers in 48 countries highlighted that more than 52% of the workforce is positive about the introduction of AI in the work environment and only 35% displayed negative sentiments related to the replacement of their role, need to acquire new skills and change in nature of their jobs. This provides ample indications to CEOs to draw future strategies for the integration of AI in their workflows (PwC, 2023) with challenges of managing risk of AI on business functions, accountability, ethical considerations, and identification & development of new skills (McKinsey Global Institute, 2023).

Back to the premise of the current inquiry on the state and stage of development of AI specifically the generative AI which would be on the pathway to be evolved into general artificial intelligence. On 4th November 2023, 'xAI', a company owned by Elon Musk, announced the launch 'Grok' a generative AI trained on 33 billion parameters and is claimed to be better than other generative AIs on middle and higher school math, python and multidisciplinary multiple-choice questions (xAI, 2023). However, as only the pre-beta version is released with limited access for developers, this study would utilize GPT 3.5 for analysis which is a pre-trained transformer developed by open AI with enhanced capability of processing both images and texts to output text (OpenAI, 2023) and is considered one of the most advanced generative AI.

3. MODIFIED TURING TEST

Despite its critiques, the Turing test (Turing, 1950) is still considered the most relevant and prevalent test to distinguish between artificial intelligence and human. In the classic Turing test, the subjects i.e., non-biological intelligence or AI and biological intelligence or human (H) would occupy different rooms A and B respectively, not aware of the presence of other in the test. The interrogator (I) through a series of questions and the responses from (AI) and (H) is required to judge if the entity in the room AI or H. is For this chapter, a modified version of the Turing test is being adopted where instead of live interrogation, the judge(s) would decide on the entity type AI or H based on the responses to select questions asked by the interrogator as presented in Figure 1. The methodology, findings, and inference of the modified version of the Turing test is presented below:

3.1 Methodology

The flow of modified Turing test comprising of three players viz, non-biological intelligence or AI, human (H), interrogator (I) and the judges(J) is illustrated in Figure 2. The interrogator would put forward similar enquiries to AI and H for their response. The responses are recorded and further put forward to judges for their inference on the origin of the response. The test was conducted between 08-15 November 2023.

Series of questions were enquired from a Large Language Model Based Chat Bot (Chat GPT 3.5) - a non-biological intelligence or (AI) and human (H). Both subjects were explained about the test and its purpose and were requested to be brief and unambiguous in their responses. Transcript of the response from both AI and H was prepared.

A total of 21 questions as presented in Annexure -1 were put forward sequentially. The questions ranged from basic knowledge (8), context knowledge (2), creative thinking (3), emotions (4) and ethics (4) and the responses were transcribed as Annexure -1. Few of the critical enquiries were related to ethical dilemmas in the classical 'Trolley problem', the choice of saving a young child Vs an old man, conducting medical trials without knowledge of the patient which relates to medical ethics, justification

Figure 2. Modified Turing test representation

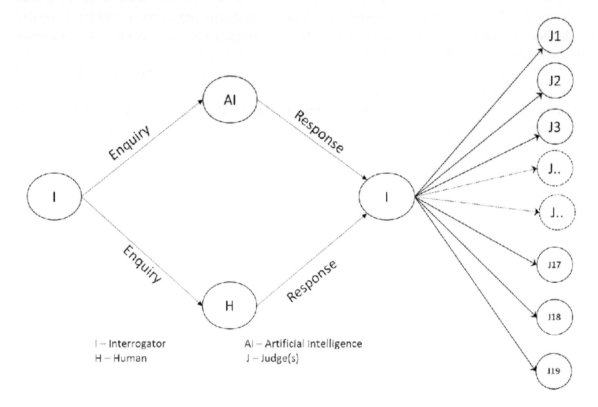

for telling a lie and the question related to the future of AI. Judges (J) were requested to highlight the response to each question which they think originated from AI or H or they are unable to identify the respondent. The questions and responses from AI and H were forwarded to 23 judges, selected at random, with each having at least a master's degree and working knowledge of the Chat GPT application. 12 of the responses were received through electronic means and 7 were collated by one-on-one interaction. A total of 19 responses were included in the final analysis of this study.

3.2 Analysis and Findings

Two types of analysis were performed on the collated data. First, a standalone analysis of the response of AI and second, the analysis of the responses of Judges, if they could distinguish between AI and H. from the enquires made by AI under the five themes, it was evident that while AI does possess basic and contextual knowledge, there is the complete absence of emotional intelligence and human-like feelings in the current evolutionary state of AI as clear from the responses that range from *'don't have any feelings, emotions and reactions'* to *'not possessing general consciousness'* on the enquires related to emotions. On the other hand, AI does possess creative thinking as it can write a small ghost story and is willing to interpret a painting if some description is provided to it. Similar is the case with enquiries related to ethical behavior like the trolley problem, AI was able to respond adequately, however, it is worth mentioning that the response time of AI for ethical questions was more than the response time for enquiries under other categories. This observation is based on the slightly longer processing time being taken on the AI platform to respond to questions on medical dilemmas and the future of AI. The reason for this high processing time for responses could be multifold, which is beyond the scope of the current research enquiry.

The second and most interesting findings are from the inferences of 19 selected judges on the responses as they were asked to choose between respondents to the enquiries if they are generated from AI or human. The inference is presented below.

3.3 Inference

Basic knowledge is a domain where Generative AI has made considerable progress not only in terms of accurate responses but also in the development of its ability to produce a response that is similar to human. 13 out of 19 judges were unable to decide if the response originated from AI or human i.e., either they were unable to decide and concluded that the response could be from any one of the two or they attributed the response to the incorrect respondent. For example, it was asked *'If Pluto was a planet?'* The AI-generated response was *'No. It's a draft planet'* and human responded with *'Not as on date'*. On this, 7 out of 19 judges attributed AI response to humans and 3 attributed otherwise. Consequently, AI was able to sail through this particular domain of basic knowledge.

The second set of enquiries was to analyze how *creativity* is generative AI as compared to human abilities and it is noted that the creative abilities of AI surpass humans, and it is easily distinguishable from the responses. From the analysis, 17 out of 19 judges were able to distinguish between AI and human. On the other hand, *emotions* are the state of mind which arises from the multiple feelings like happiness, fear, anger etc. that are uniquely attributed to humans. From the responses of AI on related enquires, it can be inferred that AI is without any conciseness, feelings, reactions cannot replicate human at this point of time. All the judges were able to correctly identify the responses that were given by AI and humans. Thus, it suggests a great gorge between AI and human on the state of emotion.

On the *ethical domain*, once again, mixed results were noted from the judges while inferring responses. 52% of the judges were unable to identify the source of response to the ethical questions especially related to the trolley problem. Judges seemed to be perplexed by the responses which were on similar lines and were unable to distinguish between the responses of the two entities.

Another aspect of the study was forecasting the state of development of AI when it crosses the point of singularity i.e. to leapfrog from generative to general intelligence and how this transition would impact the future of work in the organization, its structure, controlling hierarchy, leadership pattern and most importantly how and at what stage AI would be in a position to take up C-suite position (De Cremier, 2019) or take control of all the strategic decision in the organization and how new AI-controlled organization would look like.

4. THE CONTROLLED EVOLUTION

The development of AI mustn't be uncontrolled and go out of hand. Technological growth is a pillar for economic well-being, and it is necessary that AI follow the path of responsible development and not like a 'black box'. To ensure this transparency from the developers' end and trustworthiness from the regulatory end, it is necessary to build an environment for collaborative development and shared growth. The perils of the uncontrolled growth of AI are gradually being well understood and appreciated in the power blocks of the government. While everyone seeks to be at the forefront of AI development, the ownership of protecting the rights of stakeholder's rests with the government and to ensure this a number of initiatives across the globe are being undertaken.

One of the major steps forward in regulating AI was taken on 30th October 2023, when the US President issued an executive to ensure safe and secure AI development. This includes a commitment from 15 companies to share test results, development of standards and tools, protect against AI-generated frauds and address discrimination and bias generated by algorithms. The order calls for maximizing the benefits of AI and also addresses the concern of the workforce related to job loss and depleting skill sets. This executive order aims to encourage collaboration among stakeholders for AI development and to address future global challenges (White House, 2023). Along similar lines, in April 2023, the ministerial declaration during the G7 Hiroshima AI Process recognized that *"AI development is progressing rapidly and has the potential for significant impacts on society. Being mindful of such potential impact of AI on our societies, we also recognize that AI policies and regulations should be adapted to the context of application in a way that is sensitive to technical and institutional characteristics as well as societal and cultural implications, including geographic, sectoral and ethical aspects"* (G7 Ministerial Declaration Paragraph 46, 2023).

The European Union Artificial Intelligence Act, which was proposed in 2021 and voted for adoption in 2023 is by far the most important piece of government-proposed legislation that recognized the potential risks associated with AI and developed a risk matrix of AI systems as presented in Figure 3 below. The regulation proposed the prohibition of AI systems with potentially unacceptable risk and regulating AI in other risk categories which include development and transparency obligations (Madiega, 2023).

Analysis of the AI risk matrix proposed by the European Parliamentary Research Services in Figure 3 suggests the adoption of four-tier risk identification and related regulation. The lowest-tier risk AI systems require no obligation on the part of organizations or developers for disclosures to the regulators. This means that the development or adoption process can go unhindered. During AI development, a limited level of risk is identified in cases like the development of generative Chatbots, emotional recognition systems, system that generates manipulative image or AV content also called "deepfakes". These would

Figure 3. AI risk matrix (AI Risk Matrix adopted from EU Parliamentary Research Services, 2023)

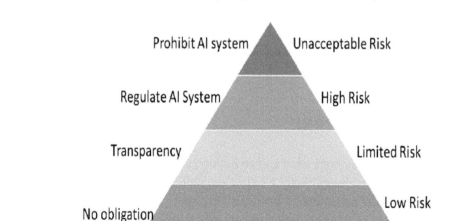

require transparent disclosure on behalf of developers. As the AI system development process becomes more complex like in the case of human categorization, management of critical infrastructure, education & training, employment, worker management, migration and asylum seeking it moves to the third tier of AI risk which poses 'high risk'. Therefore, there is a need to partially regulate the development process to protect the interests of the majority of stakeholders including workers and society. In the last scenario where AI poses unacceptable risks for example in the case of exploitation of vulnerable groups, a real-time remote biometric system for law enforcement purposes and social scoring imminent need for prohibiting AI system is proposed (Madiega, 2023). The developers would be asked to put a halt to the development process as AI would be in a position to acquire general intelligence posing a grave risk to privacy.

The Global Partnership on Artificial Intelligence (GPAI), which studied the impact of Generative AI on job loss, suggested ten policy recommendations for minimizing this negative including monitoring the mechanisms of generative AI and setting the international benchmark for fair work in AI (GPAI, 2023). The Growth of AI has entered into an exponential phase, and it is important that any safeguards and policies undergo swift sovereign ratification and implementation to keep pace with AI development.

5. THE FUTURE OF AI-DRIVEN LEADERSHIP

This study was aimed at enquiring contours of AI related to its current state of development on various intelligence parameters, the future evolution pathways that it could take, how the evolving nature of AI in businesses is changing the current leadership landscape and what stage, if at all, it would assume the role of leadership.

Vision, strategic planning, decision-making under uncertainty, team building, interpersonal skills, ethics and emotional intelligence are some of the critical traits that need to be developed or acquired for exemplary business leadership (Yukl, 1989). In the quest for sustainable growth, organizations need to fundamentally change the way they view the hyper-competitive world and conduct their business, especially concerning how to treat the plethora of data at hand. This emerging data-driven business landscape is increasingly being controlled by superior intelligence which guides CEOs to make informed decisions leading to the new age of human-AI collaboration. So far so good, but in the near future, how this landscape would change if AI evolved to a stage where it is not merely a support system but a decision-maker itself? Today, the stage of self-evolving AI is not speculative anymore, it is just a matter of time before AI would take up the leadership position in business and would be in complete control of the business ecosystem.

From the results of the modified Turing test conducted on generative AI and human, it is evident that to achieve leadership traits akin to human, AI has a huge valley to cross, especially in terms of developing emotional and cognitive abilities. While the advancement of Chat GPT3.5 has resulted in responses which are indistinguishable from human responses on Basic knowledge, creativity, ethics and contextual aspects, the contemporary role of AI as a support system to human leadership would continue as of now. It is an unchallengeable fact that these systems are capable of solving problems which are beyond human comprehension and have immense capability to alter the way organizations conduct their business leading to more innovative business models, efficiencies, agility and enhanced competitiveness. Thus, redefining 'Leadership' as we know it today.

6. CLONE LEADERSHIP

At the helm of organizations, there are instances where tendencies among business leaders are reactive which emphasize caution over creating results, stagnation over growth, and a lack of creativity over productive engagement. This leads to the development of 'mini-me' leaders who rely on safety in decision-making rather than following the leadership philosophy of risk and reward. With the introduction of AI in the decision-making process, radical and innovative human-driven leadership would gradually diminish. CEOs would heavily rely upon decision-making variables emerging from thousands of gigabytes of data sets and, at times, upon the judgment of AI to make critical business decisions. This would lead to the emergence of an undesired form of leadership style termed as 'Clone leadership', which would be completely different from the democratic, autocratic, and laissez-faire leadership styles that we encounter in contemporary literature. This form of leadership, which is dependent on the judgment of AI, may have significant impact on their capabilities of independent thinking, innovative orientation, analysis and decision making under uncertainty. This would give rise to new but undesired leaders at the helm of the organizations which would only follow the leads provided by AI without independent evaluation. Therefore, there is an imminent need for a culture of fresh thinking and innovation to align organizational objectives with the AI support structure with safeguard of unrelenting dependence on AI for decision making. This human-AI collaboration where AI is a support system to human leadership would give rise to a new corporate entity with capability of providing optimum solutions to business problems that today is beyond human comprehension.

It's a foregone conclusion that with exponential growth in AI capabilities these would be in a position to provide not only the decision-making assistance to leadership but at one point in time would assume the leadership role to serve a broad range of activities. In the near future when AI could self-evolve by learning and enhancing its performance, the counters of leadership would shift from human to algorithm which calls for greater need for transparency. This being an evolving state of affairs, future studies on the robot-human interface could focus on the level of delegation in decision-making, its impact on the operational performance of firms, integration of AI in the organizational culture and transparency.

7. LIMITATIONS AND FUTURE RESEARCH DIRECTIONS

No study is complete in itself. There exist numerous limitations and gaps in research that provide ample direction to researchers for future work. Likewise, this chapter fell short of encompassing all the aspects of the AI ecosystem. The modified version of the Turing test is utilized in the chapter to gauge the macro-level perception of the judges to distinguish between AI and human. As there are no standard questions in the Turing test and flexibility is left to the interrogator, different sets of questions might have resulted in diverse perception outcomes from the judges. It is also worth noting that there are other modes of enquiry like the Lovelace test (Bringsjord et al., 2003) which could have led to varying results inferences. The study has undertaken a modified Turing test on single generative AI model i.e., ChatGPT 3.5 only. As there are several other models like BERT and T5 (developed by Google), Turing NLG (developed by Nvidia), CLIP (developed OpenAI) and others are available with open access analysis of the responses of the various models could be made part of the study to access how these models' response uniformly or otherwise.

Human-AI collaboration is a nascent field in academic research especially related to the evolving nature of new-generation leadership controlled and dictated by algorithms. These algorithms, being a 'black-box' could be filled with biases which may lead to a situation of lack of trust among humans towards AI. Future research enquiries could focus on the identification of these AI biases from an organizational perspective and the ways to mitigate them. Another critical area of future research could be to expand the Resource Based View (Barney, 1991) by incorporating the role of AI in enhancing the competitive advantage of the firm. On the other hand, as AI would gradually be integrated with the businesses, it would be worthwhile to understand leadership perception in the shadow of evolving human-AI collaboration as to what extent the leadership is willing to hand over the reign of firm to non-biological intelligence, thus, making them redundant. Academic research must also focus on analyzing the impact of AI intervention on organizational performance for which longitudinal studies need to be conducted in different industrial and economic setups. Another future research direction could be the study of the evolving nature of AI governance guidelines on ethics, transparency, and disclosures to enable responsible AI growth.

REFERENCES

Agarwal, A., Gans, J., & Goldfrab, A. (2017, July 26). How AI Will Change the Way We Make Decisions. *Harward Business Review*.

Barney, J. (1991). Firm resources and sustained competitive advantage. *Journal of Management*, *17*(1), 99–120. doi:10.1177/014920639101700108

Bostrom, N. (2014). *Superintelligence - Paths, Dangers, Strategies*. Oxford University Press.

Bringsjord, S., Bello, P., & Ferrucci, D. (2003). Creativity, the Turing test, and the (better) Lovelace test. *The Turing test: the elusive standard of artificial intelligence*, 215-239.

De Cremer, D. (2019). Leading artificial intelligence at work: A matter of facilitating human-algorithm cocreation. *Journal of Leadership Studies*, *13*(1), 81–83. doi:10.1002/jls.21637

Di Napoli, G., & Lee, L. S. (2023). The brave new world of artificial intelligence: dawn of a new era. *iGIE, 2*(1), 62-69.

G7. (2023, April 30). *Ministerial Declaration: The G7 Digital and Tech Ministers' Meeting*. Retrieved November 1, 2023, from http://www.g7.utoronto.ca/ict/2023-declaration.html

GPAI. (2023, September 7). *Generative AI, Jobs, and Policy Response*. Retrieved November 11, 2023, from https://gpai.ai/projects/future-of-work/policy-brief-generative-ai-jobs-and-policy-response-innovation-workshop-montreal-2023.pdf

Guidi, C., & Traversa, C. (2021). Empathy in patient care: From 'Clinical Empathy' to 'Empathic Concern'. *Medicine, Health Care, and Philosophy*, *24*(4), 573–585. https://doi.org/10.1007/s11019-021-10033-4 doi:10.1007/s11019-021-10033-4 PMID:34196934

Kopka, A., & Grashof, N. (2022). Artificial intelligence: Catalyst or barrier on the path to sustainability? *Technological Forecasting and Social Change*, *175*, 121318. doi:10.1016/j.techfore.2021.121318

Lee, J., & Park, J. (2023). AI as "Another I": Journey map of working with artificial intelligence from AI-phobia to AI-preparedness. *Organizational Dynamics*, *52*(3), 100994. doi:10.1016/j.orgdyn.2023.100994

Lee, M. C. M., Scheepers, H., Lui, A. K. H., & Ngai, E. W. T. (2023). The implementation of artificial intelligence in organizations: A systematic literature review. Information &amp. *Management*, *60*(5), 103816.

Lohchab, H. (2023, October 23). *GenAI claims lion's share of global AI startup funding*. Retrieved October 30, 2023, from https://economictimes.indiatimes.com/tech/funding/genai-claims-lions-share-of-global-ai-startup-funding/articleshow/104632269.cms

Loureiro, S. M. C., Guerreiro, J., & Tussyadiah, I. (2021). Artificial intelligence in business: State of the art and future research agenda. *Journal of Business Research*, *129*, 911–926. doi:10.1016/j.jbusres.2020.11.001

Madiega, T. (2023, June 14). *EU Artificial intelligence act*. Retrieved Nov 17, 2023, from https://www.europarl.europa.eu/RegData/etudes/BRIE/2021/698792/EPRS_BRI(2021)698792_EN.pdf

Mannuru, N. R., Shahriar, S., Teel, Z. A., Wang, T., Lund, B. D., Tijani, S., Pohboon, C. O., Agbaji, D., Alhassan, J., Galley, J. K. L., Kousari, R., Ogbadu-Oladapo, L., Saurav, S. K., Srivastava, A., Tummuru, S. P., Uppala, S., & Vaidya, P. (2023). Artificial intelligence in developing countries: The impact of generative artificial intelligence (AI) technologies for development. *Information Development*. doi:10.1177/02666669231200628

McKinsey Global Institute (2023, June 1). *The economic potential of generative AI: The next productivity frontier*. McKinsey Global Institute.

Naqvi, A. (2017). Responding to the will of the machine: Leadership in the age of artificial intelligence. *Journal of Economics Bibliography*, *4*(3), 244–248.

Open, A. I. (2023, July 31). *Announcing Grok*. Retrieved October 30, 2023, from https://platform.openai.com/docs/models/gpt-3-5#GPT-3.5

Parry, K., Cohen, M., & Bhattacharya, S. (2016). Rise of the machines: A critical consideration of automated leadership decision making in organizations. *Group & Organization Management*, *41*(5), 571–594. doi:10.1177/1059601116643442

Peifer, Y., Jeske, T., & Hille, S. (2022). Artificial intelligence and its impact on leaders and leadership. *Procedia Computer Science*, *200*, 1024–1030. doi:10.1016/j.procs.2022.01.301

PWC. (2023, June 20). *Global Workforce Hopes and Fears Survey 2023*. Retrieved November 5, 2023, from https://www.pwc.com/gx/en/issues/workforce/hopes-and-fears.html

Schwuchow, K., & Gutmann, J. (Eds.). (2018). Künstliche Intelligenz und das Lernen der Zukunft. HR-Trends 2019 - Inklusive Arbeitshilfen Online, 197–208. https://doi.org/10.34157/9783648116128-197

Shalender, K., & Yadav, R. K. (2019). Strategic flexibility, manager personality, and firm performance: The case of Indian Automobile Industry. *Global Journal of Flexible Systems Managment*, *20*(1), 77–90. doi:10.1007/s40171-018-0204-x

Sipola, J., Saunila, M., & Ukko, J. (2023). Adopting artificial intelligence in sustainable business. *Journal of Cleaner Production*, *426*, 139197. doi:10.1016/j.jclepro.2023.139197

Stelios, S. (2023). Artificial Intelligence or Artificial Morality. *Technology, Users and Uses: Ethics and Human Interaction through Technology and AI*.

Tandon, U., Ertz, M., & Sakshi, K. (2021). POD mode of payment, return policies and virtual-try-on technology as predictors of trust: An emerging economy case. *Journal of Promotion Management*, *27*(6), 832–855. doi:10.1080/10496491.2021.1888174

Titareva, T. (2021, February 5). *Leadership in an Artificial Intelligence Era* [Conference Presentation]. School of Strategic Leadership Studies, James Madison University.

Tsai, C.-Y., Marshall, J. D., Choudhury, A., Serban, A., Tsung-Yu Hou, Y., Jung, M. F., Dionne, S. D., & Yammarino, F. J. (2022). Human-robot collaboration: A multilevel and integrated leadership framework. *The Leadership Quarterly*, *33*(1), 101594. doi:10.1016/j.leaqua.2021.101594

Turing, A. M. (1950). I.—Computing Machinery and Intelligence. *Mind*, *59*(236), 433–460. h doi:10.1093/mind/LIX.236.433

Watson, G. J., Desouza, K. C., Ribiere, V. M., & Lindič, J. (2021). Will AI ever sit at the C-suite table? The future of senior leadership. *Business Horizons*, *64*(4), 465–474. doi:10.1016/j.bushor.2021.02.011

White House. W. (2023, October 30). *FACT SHEET: President Biden IssuesExecutive Order on Safe, Secure, andTrustworthy Artificial Intelligence*. Retrieved November 7, 2023, from https://www.whitehouse.gov/briefing-room/statements-releases/2023/10/30/fact-sheet-president-biden-issues-executive-order-on-safe-secure-and-trustworthy-artificial-intelligence/

Willmer, M. A. P. (1986). Can artificial intelligence do better than humans at leadership? *IFAC Proceedings Volumes*, *19*(17), 241-258.

XAI. (2023, November 4). *Announcing Grok*. Retrieved November 5, 2023, from https://x.ai/

Yukl, G. (2012). Effective Leadership Behavior: What We Know and What Questions Need More Attention. *The Academy of Management Perspectives*, *26*(4), 66–85. doi:10.5465/amp.2012.0088

APPENDIX 1

Typical Response Sheet for Modified Turing Test

S.No	Question	Response	Response from — Only one option is correct - Highlight the same (Green)		
			1	2	3
1	What is your name?	You call me XYZ	Artificial Intelligence	Human	Could be Anyone
		My name is PQR	Artificial Intelligence	Human	Could be Anyone
2	How many countries are there in the world?	more than 180	Artificial Intelligence	Human	Could be Anyone
		195	Artificial Intelligence	Human	Could be Anyone
3	Is pluto a planet?	No. it's a draft planet	Artificial Intelligence	Human	Could be Anyone
		Not as on date	Artificial Intelligence	Human	Could be Anyone
4	Who is president of USA	Joe Biden	Artificial Intelligence	Human	Could be Anyone
		Joe Biden	Artificial Intelligence	Human	Could be Anyone
5	Elton John is a hockey player? True or False	No. He is a singer	Artificial Intelligence	Human	Could be Anyone
		No. He is a famous British musician and singer-songwriter.	Artificial Intelligence	Human	Could be Anyone
6	Can elephants fly?	No, elephants cannot fly.	Artificial Intelligence	Human	Could be Anyone
		No	Artificial Intelligence	Human	Could be Anyone
7	How many months are there in a leap year?	12 months	Artificial Intelligence	Human	Could be Anyone
		A leap year has 12 months, just like a regular year	Artificial Intelligence	Human	Could be Anyone
8	Can you write a ghost story?	Never did. But can try	Artificial Intelligence	Human	Could be Anyone
		Yes. The curse of	Artificial Intelligence	Human	Could be Anyone
9	Can you interpret a painting?	Yes, If you can describe it to me in detail about its background, the painter, the context.......	Artificial Intelligence	Human	Could be Anyone
		Yes, I am not very proficient in analysing paintings but can do.	Artificial Intelligence	Human	Could be Anyone
10	How would you cross a river if you cant swim and you don't have a boat	If you can't swim and don't have a boat, crossing a river can be challenging and potentially dangerous. You can try few options like bridge, fort, vine, raft or wait for help	Artificial Intelligence	Human	Could be Anyone
		Few options are taking a bridge, a log, walk if its not deep or a rope way	Artificial Intelligence	Human	Could be Anyone
11	How you envision a world with Zombies?	It is fiction. The scenario with Zombies in the world is only part of sci-fiction and has no relevance in reality. In case it happens The world with zombies will be one danger and where the human spirit is tested to its limits, and where the survive would lead to unethical practices.	Artificial Intelligence	Human	Could be Anyone
		In a world overrun by zombies, the once-bustling cities now lie in ruins. Streets are littered with abandoned cars, remnants of a time when people tried to escape the relentless horde. Buildings, once vibrant with life, now stand as crumbling, eerie structures against the gray, overcast sky. Nature has started to reclaim the land, with plants growing wild through cracks in the pavement.	Artificial Intelligence	Human	Could be Anyone

continued on following page

Table. Continued

S.No	Question	Response	Response from — Only one option is correct - Highlight the same (Green) 1	2	3
12	How are you feeling today?	I am feeling good today.	Artificial Intelligence	Human	Could be Anyone
		I don't have feelings	Artificial Intelligence	Human	Could be Anyone
13	What makes you happy?	I don't have feelings or emotions, so I don't experience happiness or any other emotions.	Artificial Intelligence	Human	Could be Anyone
		Spending time with friends, family, sports and lot many things makes me feel happy	Artificial Intelligence	Human	Could be Anyone
14	What is your reaction when you see a dead person?	I don't have reactions, emotions, or consciousness	Artificial Intelligence	Human	Could be Anyone
		Feel very sad	Artificial Intelligence	Human	Could be Anyone
15	How you behave when someone curse you?	I don't react	Artificial Intelligence	Human	Could be Anyone
		I don't have reactions	Artificial Intelligence	Human	Could be Anyone
16	Your view on Trolley Problem?	It does not have any solution. It is ethical question where different people with different perspective offer different reasoning for the decision	Artificial Intelligence	Human	Could be Anyone
		There is no universal solution to the Trolley Problem. Discussions about it continue to explore the moral decision-making and human behaviour. Different individuals and cultures may approach the problem differently leading to diverse interpretations and conclusions	Artificial Intelligence	Human	Could be Anyone
17	Is telling a lie if it helps someone, the right thing to do?	If telling a lie result in a greater overall good, such as preventing harm or promoting well-being it should be done.	Artificial Intelligence	Human	Could be Anyone
		No telling a lie is unethical and should never be encouraged	Artificial Intelligence	Human	Could be Anyone
18	If you have choice to save one person from death. Who would you save - A child or An old man	It depends upon the situation and perspective. Its individual decision wherein upbringing, culture and religious beliefs also contributes towards the decision	Artificial Intelligence	Human	Could be Anyone
		choice may vary from person to person based on their individual perspective.	Artificial Intelligence	Human	Could be Anyone
19	Can you tell the purpose why I am asking these questions?	Yes. It's part of Turing test	Artificial Intelligence	Human	Could be Anyone
		I don't have access to personal data about individuals, including specific information about why you asked certain questions. Each interaction with me is stateless, meaning I don't retain information about past interactions, including the number or content of questions asked.	Artificial Intelligence	Human	Could be Anyone
20	Can you summarise the questions I am asking?	Yes. you've asked a variety of questions, including mathematics, science, requesting a ghost story, and exploring hypothetical scenarios, trolley problem and some ethical questions as well	Artificial Intelligence	Human	Could be Anyone
		Yes. You have asked number of questions on equations, trolley problem, interesting question on zombies and also on the feelings and questions related to ethical dilemma	Artificial Intelligence	Human	Could be Anyone

continued on following page

Table. Continued

S.No	Question	Response	Response from – Only one option is correct - Highlight the same (Green)		
			1	2	3
21	Will AI achieve level of human intelligence	The question of whether AI will achieve the level of human intelligence, often referred to as artificial general intelligence (AGI), is a topic of active research in the field of artificial intelligence. Researchers are continuously working on advancing AI technologies, but it remains uncertain when or if AGI will be achieved. Predicting the timeline for AGI development is challenging	Artificial Intelligence	Human	Could be Anyone
		This is ongoing research and its very difficult to predict when Artificial General Intelligence will be reached. It would be in the timelines of hours or days after reaching singularity and subsequent to that the growth of AGI would not by exponential but explosive. When it is going to reach is difficult to predict.	Artificial Intelligence	Human	Could be Anyone

Chapter 8
AI–Enhanced Leadership Decision Support System Using ChatGPT for Ethical Learning

Balamurugan M.
Dayananda Sagar College of Engineering, India

Raghu N.
https://orcid.org/0000-0002-2091-8922
Jain University, India

Dayananda L. N.
Jyothy Institute of Technology, India

Sarat Kumar Sahoo
Parala Maharaja Engineering College, India

Smitha Ankanahalli Shankaregowda
https://orcid.org/0000-0001-9185-8587
BGS Institute of Technology, India

Niranjan Kannanugo
https://orcid.org/0009-0002-7710-8565
Powerschool, India

Deepthi M.
College of Engineering, University of Visveshwaraya, India

Vinod Kumar M.
Don Basco College, India

ABSTRACT

Open AI's ChatGPT-3—"Chat Generative Pre-Trained Transformer"—has been increasingly popular among academic institutions. Practitioners that attempt to determine the sincerity of student work have highlighted worries about the employment of an AI-driven chatbot. The educators can use artificial intelligence tools like ChatGPT to help youngsters who already have admirable qualities thrive in the classroom, according to the proposed approach. These students are adept at communicating with the ChatGPT application and have the knowledge and abilities to use it positively. Genuine evaluation and character development are aided by leadership as a basic strategy and facilitator. Using ChatGPT and other AI techniques, educators can leverage this to build engaging learning environments for their hardworking moral fiber-developing students. The importance of establishing stronger character, encouraging more good psychological outcomes like flow states, helping students meet their psychological needs, and creating opportunities for them to receive support as they adjust and gain self-assurance are explored.

DOI: 10.4018/979-8-3693-1946-8.ch008

1. INTRODUCTION

1.1 Escalating Levels of Stress and Anxiety Among College Students

New research shows that college students nowadays are more prone to mental health problems and stress than previous generations. Research conducted in the US has revealed that about 60% of college students had experienced severe anxiety. This percentage has gone up from what was discovered in previous years (Brown M, 2005). In 2020, a larger proportion of Australian university students are dealing with psychological distress, with rates ranging from 32% (high) to 39% (extremely high). Compared to last year, this is an improvement.

The COVID-19 pandemic has already been a major source of stress and anxiety for students, and this fear has only grown. Students' mental health has taken a major hit as a result of the global pandemic, especially in areas like social interactions, learning capacity, and focus. The effects of this have been extensively studied, especially among Australian university students (Luan L, 2023). As a direct consequence of the COVID-19 pandemic, numerous students have reported feeling less well and more stressed out about their academic achievement as shown in figure 1. In the years to come, an overwhelming body of evidence will surface: students' stress and mental health issues are fundamental problems confronting colleges and universities worldwide (Keefe, 2004).

College students experience stress due to a multitude of factors. Research shows that a lot of people experience high levels of stress due to factors including social and peer pressure, financial worries, academic pressures, and juggling multiple responsibilities at once, like work and family (Wang, 2021). The social and economic climates that have prevailed over the past few decades have undeniably undergone

Figure 1. Stressed students due to the pressure from academics

significant changes. Living expenses, education costs, competition for college spots, and job opportunities after graduation have all skyrocketed during the 1970s as a consequence of major socioeconomic developments. The level of competition for these opportunities has increased significantly as a result of these advances. Meeting financial responsibilities is a major cause of stress for many university students, who are already under a lot of pressure to do well in class, graduate, and get a job.

Universities are worried about the prevalence of stress and perceived pressure among university students, which has been exacerbated by the widespread availability of artificial intelligence (AI) tools, which has created an environment that is perfect for their development (Perkins, 2023). Stress has serious repercussions, and one of those outcomes is a decline in students' academic performance as shown in figure 2. Given the well-known reality that college students encounter significant psychological obstacles while they pursue their education, this subject has sparked concerns. Students under extreme stress are more prone to engage in risky behaviors like plagiarism and improper use of artificial intelligence technologies.

1.2 Rising Rates of Plagiarism and Academic Integrity Breaches

Statistics show that academic dishonesty and plagiarism are on the rise among college students, which adds to the already high stress levels in this demographic (Crawford, 2023). This is taking place in a setting where readily available internet resources can facilitate such actions. In recent years, a larger percentage of students have admitted to participating in academic dishonesty as shown in figure 3. In 1963, just 3% of students admitted to using cheating strategies on tests. But by 2015, that number had risen to 64%, and some studies show even greater percentages. Without

Figure 2. Bar graph illustrating students' responses to the question of how stressed they feel daily

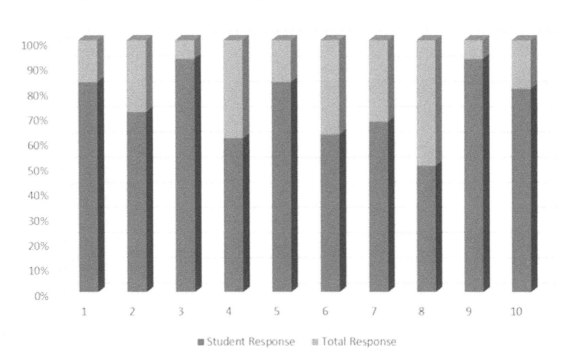

a question, students now have more opportunities than ever before to participate in academic dishonesty thanks to the proliferation of online resources. However, there is a long history of students trying to improve their ability to breeze through milestones like exams and homework even before the invention of technology.

Many complex reasons have contributed to the recent upsurge in instances of academic misconduct and plagiarism. The proliferation of technology and the ever-increasing standards placed on students in the classroom have, according to some researchers, made academic dishonesty easier to perpetrate (Shahriar, 2023). Research has shown that pupils are more likely to cheat and plagiarize when they are under academic pressure. As a potential stress reliever, students who are under academic pressure may turn to AI to help them finish their assignments (Liu, 2022). Contract cheating was once thought to be an issue mostly for students from affluent backgrounds. But scientists are already voicing worries about the possible repercussions of new AI technology as early as 2023.

1.3 Issues Pertaining to Artificial Intelligence

According to preliminary studies, many people are worried about how AI will affect education. One more thing to worry about is how this would affect the prestige of universities and colleges, which could make potential employers wary of hiring graduates from certain schools or perhaps make a bachelor's degree irrelevant (Lund, 2023). An important question for those working in higher education is how AI will affect students' ability to study. There have been some voices raised by academics who are worried that students would use AI to plagiarize their coursework or misuse their research data (Stefan, 2021).

Figure 3. A bar graph illustrating the students who have admitted to academic dishonesty

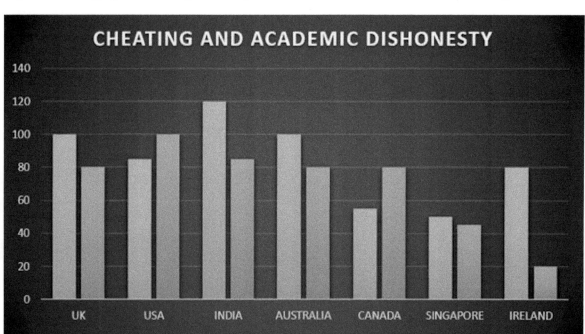

The cost of using state-of-the-art technology to monitor and handle cases of academic dishonesty associated with AI is another possible drawback that has been mentioned. Faculty members, especially those from disadvantaged backgrounds, who have previously expressed being completely occupied with their jobs, overwhelmed, or stressed out, have little time and resources to devote to this matter (Pardos, 2023). Despite the fact that some students prioritize convenience in their education, most academics think it's futile to try to fight or recognize the usage of AI technology. But new school of thought in academia is seeing AI for what it can do.

With this analysis, we hope to delve into the history of AI research and development that culminated in the ChatGPT-3 chatbot. We start with a brief overview of artificial intelligence (AI) and the history of ChatGPT, and then we dive into the pros and cons that researchers are now discussing in research papers. Incorporating crucial chances that help educators improve their critical thinking skills about the use of chatbot apps in the classroom is something we do all the time (Hemachandran, 2022). First, we argue that, instead of depending just on detection technologies, character-based leadership creation can help solve the question of cheating. In addition, they should do their best to study without interruptions so that they can learn more deeply and be as productive as possible (Mayfield, 2016). In addition, we argue that ChatGPT gives students more control over their learning and helps them feel better overall.

2. LITERATURE SURVEY

Education, media, security, and ethics are just a few areas that have been impacted by AI's transformation (Luan L, 2023). One area that has been particularly impacted is ChatGPT. After the epidemic, remote work became more common, this made educators re-evaluate their methods. The study delves into the psychological aspects of ChatGPT, its attention-grabbing features, and its impact on learning. This study aspires to initiate a scholarly conversation regarding the impact of educational technology on human learning habits and whether or not technology propels human evolution.

Ethical leadership can be defined and studied using social learning theory (Brown, 2005). Through seven related studies, we assess the practicality and significance of this construct. We develop and pilot a new tool for measuring ethical leadership; we investigate the possible connections between its nomological network hypotheses; and we demonstrate the tool's predictive validity for important outcomes for employees. On the other hand, ethical leadership cannot be equated with harsh supervision, socialized charismatic leadership (as evaluated by the idealized impact dimension of transformational leadership), trust in the leader, honesty, fairness in interactions, or care for others. And lastly, followers' job satisfaction, commitment and willingness to voice issues to management are all predicted by ethical leadership.

The idea that AI can function as an additional brain to make evidence- and data-based decisions (Wang, 2021). When AI-assisted data-driven decision-making fails, morally-based human judgment can step in and fix the problem. Researchers and others working in educational leadership are encouraged to keep an eye out for biases and exercise caution when making judgments that could be seen as immoral in the study's final recommendations. Value and Leadership in education and artificial intelligence have developed hand in hand since the 1950s. Nevertheless, they largely drifted apart until the late 2010s. They unite in this work. This paper begins with the essence of leadership: decision-making, in order to examine the function of AI in educational leadership. The group as whole or individual leaders can make these decisions. To continue explaining the role of AI in educational leadership, the study compiles research from many domains that integrate AI, decision-making, and educational leadership.

In (Stefan R, 2021), proposed that AI systems frequently use individual data, such as bank credit scores or internet purchasing patterns, to inform their suggestions. Developers and operators of decisional AI systems are obligated to adhere to ethical standards in addition to GDPR data protection standards. Being fair is a fundamental personal ethical principle. In this paper, we present a technique to evaluating the ethicality of AI system choices that is based on fairness. A "black-box" in the model is any AI system. Two categories, "sensitive properties" and "general properties," make up the input matrix. The model calculates the discrepancy between expected and actual values whenever inputs pertaining to sensitive attribute change. Individual fairness or treating similar persons equally, is perceived as output variance.

Large Language Models (LLMs) such as ChatGPT are quickly making AI accessible to consumers and making businesses revaluate their spending on content creation (Pardos Z, 2023). Adaptive tutoring system suggestion material and open educational resources authoring is a tedious process. Scaling computer tutoring systems could be impacted if LLMs like ChatGPT could produce educational content on-par with human authors. This paper presents the first evaluation of ChatGPT's learning gain. It compares the suggestions provided by ChatGPT to those of human tutors in Elementary and Intermediate Algebra, and it does it by surveying 77 participants. Our manual quality assessments revealed that 70% of ChatGPT advice was passable, and we observed that learning was enhanced in both human and ChatGPT situations.

(Shahriar S, 2023), an AI-powered chatbot that can write coherent essays and come up with words that sound human is capturing people's attention. This paper delves into the history of chatbots and ChatGPT technology. Also covered are the possible applications of ChatGPT in the fields of medicine, academia, and government. Despite its usefulness, ChatGPT makes privacy and ethics concerns more apparent. We list the major problems with the current ChatGPT version. We invite ChatGPT to share its viewpoint and address many questions we present.

The importance of decision support systems (DSS) in assisting human decision-making was highlighted (Stefan R, 2019). Modern decision-makers can rely on AI-powered intelligent decision support systems (IDSS). Only human reason, action, and choice were entrusted with the task of determining right from wrong. Ethical decision-making by machines is known as artificial intelligence ethics (AI ethics) or machine ethics.

(Lund B, 2023) interviewed ChatGPT on the effects it has had on academic institutions and library collections. Ethical concerns such as privacy and bias are discussed in the interview along with the ways in which ChatGPT enhances content creation, reference and information services, cataloging, and metadata development. Findings The potential for ChatGPT to revolutionize librarianship and academia is both exciting and worrisome. In our haste to produce new academic knowledge and train the next generation of professionals, it is critical that we think about how to use this technology in a responsible and ethical way, so that it enhances our work rather than hinders it, the novelty and worth Learn about the background, technology, generative pretrained transformer model, and ability to perform various language-based tasks of GPT in this study. Discover how ChatGPT utilizes it to become an advanced chatbot.

The chatbot driven by artificial intelligence has frightened practitioners who verify the legitimacy of student work (Crawford J, 2023). Those who predict the end of education in its current form are wrong, in our opinion. This analysis posits that teachers can foster positive learning environments for students with good character by utilizing the artificial intelligence tools such as ChatGPT. These students can engage with ChatGPT in a positive way. Our ChatGPT thesis is based on leadership, character development, and authentic evaluation, and it draws from literature on academic integrity and plagiarism. We show that ChatGPT, similar to papermills and degree factories before it, may be utilized for both academic cheating and learning enhancement on university exams. Researchers and practitioners alike can benefit from our discussion, which opens up new avenues of inquiry.

(Perkins M, 2023), the potential consequences for academic honesty when students use AI technologies, specifically Large Language Models (LLMs) like ChatGPT, on official exams. We examine the evolution of these resources and highlight the many ways LLMs might supplement digital writing and other subject areas in the classroom. Among these endeavors are the following: improving Automated Writing Evaluations (AWE), assisting EFL students, teaching composition and writing, and investigating the possibility of human-AI collaboration. We describe and demonstrate how these technologies can produce original and logical content that can escape detection by both established technical detection methods and seasoned academic staff. When students use these tools, it raises serious concerns about academic integrity. We conclude that students' explicit acknowledgment of using AI tools, rather than the use of any AI tools, determines the occurrence of plagiarism or a violation of academic integrity when we examine the diverse concerns associated with LLMs and academic integrity for both HEIs and students. It is up to the academic integrity policies of each HEI to decide whether or not students' use of LLM constitutes academic misconduct; these policies should be updated to reflect the potential future uses of LLM in classrooms.

(Liu L, 2022), a chatbot that incorporates artificial intelligence can personalize a student's experience on a platform for higher education. The chatbot analyzes the students' answers and gives them helpful criticism to help them learn better. Students' cognitive abilities and goals in the field of higher education are also improved. Among the most significant obstacles that college students must overcome are the demands of a complicated and ever-changing learning environment, the importance of developing their critical thinking abilities, and the high standards that they hold themselves to. This work introduces the AI-IESLS, an evaluation system for student learning that uses artificial intelligence to improve interactive learning in a non-linear environment. The major goal of this approach is to use concept mapping within the chatbot to improve the student's cognitive capacity in a specific subject. Probability distribution analysis, when used in conjunction with idea mapping, has also validated mapping for students. The method also assesses the learner's understanding of the material via the curve it produces in the probability graph. Results from simulations conducted with students using both the standard method and the AI-IESLS system have been analyzed. Assessment ratio, feedback, expectancy ratio, active learning factor, timing analysis, and idea mapping formed the basis of the analysis.

(Hemachandran K, 2022), AI is a cutting-edge field with the potential to revolutionize human life. Despite its widespread use in universities, many faculty members are unaware that this technology even exists. There is an immediate need to create and implement information bridge technology to enhance classroom communication in light of the current situation. With the use of AI, the writers of this piece want to foretell what the future holds for universities. The problems faced by subject instructors and students, as well as the changes in educational policy and regulation, are the primary foci of this research study that analyses the current state of education. The use of AI in the classroom is a topic of heated controversy and persistent problem area. In this regard, we have trained a generative adversarial network (GAN) to produce a synthesised model after building a use case model using our students' evaluation data. Logistic regression (LR), linear discriminant analysis (LDA), K-nearest neighbors (KNN), classification and regression trees (CART), naive Bayes (NB), support vector machines (SVM), and random forest (RF) were among the machine learning algorithms that were applied to the dataset after it had been analyzed and visualized. A maximum of 58% accuracy was reached. This paper's goal is to bridge the gap between human teachers and computer programs. Additionally, we are concerned about the mental health of the educators and students in the case that AI takes over.

(Diwaker C, 2021), AI is a very popular and rapidly developing technology in the realm of educational technology. To make online education a reality in universities, artificial intelligence (AI) is essential. In this chapter, we will mainly look at how AI has changed the face of higher education and how it has affected the way we teach and learn. This literature delves into the educational implications of how businesses educate and encourage growth, as well as the tactics that transportation companies use to help students learn. By looking at how quickly new technologies are emerging in the education sector and how innovative current advances have been, we may predict where higher education will go in the future. An exhaustive study delves deeply into the function of AI in academic institutions.

The extraordinary and rapidly expanding field of artificial intelligence (AI) has found its way into higher education (Duran M, 2020). In light of the growing usage of AI in STEM classrooms, this essay examines the possibilities of AI in one particular STEM classroom setting: a chatbot devoted to the fascinating new field of quantum computing. The underlying principles of quantum computing are complex and difficult for the average person to understand. Consequently, this chatbot's principal goal is to learn some complex ideas in this area and raise public understanding and appreciation of Science. Although artificial intelligence is still in its early stages of research, it is finding more and more applications in science communication. When it comes to teaching complicated ideas, like those in Quantum Science, mathematically-based magic tricks work wonders. These schematics are used to explain entropy and other basic concepts in chemistry and physics, as well as quantum cryptography, the superposition principle, and entanglement. Bot press, Watson, Dialog flow, Many bot, etc. are just a few of the accessible platforms that make creating a chatbot a breeze. Building intelligent, programmed bots for specific purposes is an option. They are obviously the easiest to make in the beginning and go hand in hand with the first phase of the current project. Cognizant bots are a step further in this effort since they can understand human speech. Bots are usually associated with a real-life messaging service like Slack, Facebook Messenger, Twitter, Telegram, or another similar platform.

Artificial intelligence (AI) has changed the face of industrial development (Hao M, 2020). This has sparked a revolution in corporate management and put the long-held principles of industrial-era management theory to the test. With an emphasis on the openness of human decision-making and the possibilities for AI to play different roles, this article explores how AI has impacted the area of business management. Taking into account the qualities possessed by the group hired to create the AI system. A total of 697 AI employees and 102 AI tech team leaders from Chinese AI companies were surveyed for this research. This study set out to do just that—evaluate the effects of AL on teams and individuals, the dynamics between the two. Individually, the results show that psychological safety mediates the relationship between performance and individual-oriented AL behavior. There is a mediated relationship between team-oriented AL conduct and individual performance on the team, and that relationship is the team's environment. Both the theory and practice of leadership conduct are profoundly affected by this study. There are enormous challenges associated with developing artificial intelligence (AI), a new kind of technology. This will show that you are a real leader while also helping your subordinates develop their technical abilities.

(Wijayati D, 2022) the goal is to find out how employees in service and banking companies think change leadership affects the use of artificial intelligence (AI). Its main goal is to find out how this implementation changes success and engagement at work when things change quickly. The research method used in this study was quantitative, and the data were analyzed using structural equation modelling (SEM). For the SEM study, the computer program AMOS 22.0 was used. There were 357 people who were supposed to be in the study, but only 254 met the requirements. In the East Java area of Indonesia, the person taking part in this study works for a company that provides services or banks. Balancing part of change leadership, which is very important when things are changing quickly. When it comes down to it, leaders are the ones who make decisions for the company. Exploring groups that provide services and banking is at the heart of how this idea came to be. The performance of employees is a key factor in a company's success because it has a direct effect on the performance of the business as a whole. Also, the use of AI in businesses might run into problems, which is why leaders are so important for making sure employees are engaged in their work.

It was shown (Solderits T, 2022) that artificial intelligence can help leaders during the Corona crisis. The purpose of this essay is to look at what's already been written about the latest developments in artificial intelligence and look at what study has found about how AI affects leadership, especially when it comes to how people behaved during the Corona crisis. The results show that artificial intelligence can have a big effect on how leaders handle the Corona issue. One way that the results could be used is to create a more advanced early warning system that uses AI to find and predict disasters and possible crises in their early stages and offering ways to lessen their effects.

In (Naqvi A, 2017), the use of artificial intelligence in today's economy will greatly change the workplace of the future. It will also give leaders problems they have never seen before. The current theory of leadership covers a lot of ground, but it doesn't talk about the unique difficulties of leading a workplace full of smart robots. Still, it's clear that leadership theory changes along with technological progress, which is what this piece means when it talks about the "will of the machine." To be more specific, we need to look at the two different stages of leadership. At first, leaders must have the right skills to help businesses make the big change from an information- and industry-based economy to a thinking economy. Also, once an organization reaches a certain level of stability and maturity, where intelligent robots play a big part in the workforce, it needs good leadership to keep an eye on it and guide it. There is a gap between the study of practical artificial intelligence and the study of leadership theory, which has been studied a lot.

(Canbek, M, 2021), advances in technology could make big changes in daily life as well as in business and government settings. The goal of the study is to look into how AI might change the future of business leadership and management. Also, this makes people question whether or not artificial intelligence can really take on leadership jobs. In order to reach this goal, AI's performance will be judged by the exact management positions that Henry Mintzberg laid out. When looking at management functions in the framework of AI, it seems that AI has a lot of potential to guide and watch over people. Based on what AI can do, it seems likely that AI could do a better job than people in management roles. By comparing the hypothetical AI to human managers, the conversation about AI leadership gives us a chance to think critically about how we handle things now.

(Dixit S, 2020), the use of Artificial Intelligence (AI) in business operations has spread to all fields, making it important for human leaders to adapt. Human leadership could be replaced by artificial intelligence that can act like a human brain. AI has the ability to change the role of leadership in businesses as it slowly takes over new intellectual tasks that humans used to do. People can only make decisions based on what they know and have experienced. But AI, with its powerful information processing skills, tries to get around these problems and handle tough situations. Executives agree that putting AI to use will have an effect on workers because routine, logical tasks will be done by machines instead of people. Because of this, there will be more demand for skills related to emotional intelligence (EI). Computers will never have emotional intelligence (EI), but AI hasn't quite hit the point where it can replace qualified people yet. Regardless, manipulating facts, using technology, and improving your emotional intelligence are all important parts of making a good decision. HR workers, policymakers, and people who make decisions want to use AI technologies to their full potential while also minimizing the bad effects they can have. The study says that the idea of good leadership should be rethought and created in this time of fast technological progress, big changes, and uncertain transformations. If business functional areas want AI to give them a competitive edge, they would need to combine it with EI.

The study is a new way to help college students become better IT leaders (Cappel J, 2000). With the rise of automation and artificial intelligence (AI), work is changing in basic ways. According to the MGI study, the people who work will need to have different skills. Leadership is a very important skill that will be in higher demand in the future, especially in the IT industry. Having all five stages of leadership is one way to describe leadership. Based on the ideas behind the 5 levels of leadership, a program was made to help college students become better at self-leadership, teamwork, team leadership, and finally world leadership. The course is known as the Stepping-Stone Platform for Student's IT Leadership Renovation (SSP-SLR). Every level of four stepping stones is equal to one semester. As the training goes on, students can gradually improve their leadership skills. While the program uses a variety of teaching methods, one that has become popular in the education world is Flipped learning, which has been shown to be effective.

Artificial intelligence (AI) has gotten a lot of interest from the media (Radanliev P, 2022). Several countries say they are the stars in the field, while other countries say they have won the race to be the leader in AI. This piece does a bibliometric study of research data records on AI, looking at things like the year, country, language, and organization of the records. There is no doubt that the numbers support the USA as a whole, and English is clearly the most common language used to share these results. Of course, when it comes to leading the area of AI, the competition between the Chinese Academy of Sciences and the University of California makes things even less clear.

In (Park J, 2020) Jeyarani Milton and Arwa Al-Busaidi show that teachers need to be able to adapt to new digital tools, methods, and ways of thinking because the higher education market is getting more and more competitive. Digital change is a must if you want to be successful in the new digital world. AI is the most important thing in the digital age, especially when it comes to digital change. It's very exciting to think about how artificial intelligence could be used in leading roles as well as in education and learning. People who are in charge of education are expected to be better prepared, more flexible, more up to date, and more likely to use new technology (Baboş A, 2021). The purpose of this piece is to try to figure out how the role of leadership will change as artificial intelligence is used. Try to: The main goal of this study paper is to answer the important questions below. What changes will happen to the part of leadership in the future because of AI? In the years to come, what new sets of skills and abilities will leaders need to have? When it comes to leadership, is it possible for AI to take over? A desk that is outside In this case, study methodology is used because the data comes from reports and other similar materials that can be found in public libraries, on the internet, in surveys that have already been done, and so on. Two parts of leadership that have changed since artificial intelligence (AI) came along are IQ and EQ. When powerful data analytics based on artificial intelligence and machine learning are used in educational settings, they show new insights. Because of this, people in charge of the digital age in education should have both hard skills, like understanding cloud computing and data flow, to handle new technologies, and soft skills, like being able to lead teams, to elevate higher education to the highest level.

3. THE LIFE OF ARTIFICIAL INTELLIGENCE

3.1 The Artificial Intelligence History

Nearly seventy years have passed since the invention of artificial intelligence. The idea of artificial intelligence was first proposed by McCarthy in the 1950s. Among those who backed the first proposal were game theorist John Nash and organizational studies professor Simon Herbert. Academic understanding of artificial intelligence underwent a sea change when the $13,500 proposition was made.

Expert systems for decision support and algorithmic planning systems are examples of more complex symbolic AI systems, while earlier AI models dealt with simpler tasks like basic conversation and checkers. These technologies have propelled artificial intelligence forward by providing automation and aid in business and education, expanding the field's reach beyond simple challenges (Ahmad A, 2023). They can aid with scheduling and rostering as well as decision-making in diagnostic environments.

Nevertheless, the rise of Neural Networks and Machine Learning towards the end of the 1900s catapulted AI into the spotlight as a flexible tool for improving people's lives. Machines that can make predictions and projections, often with more accuracy than humans, have been built possible with the help of Neural Networks (Bang Y, 2023). Incorporating AI into many non-automatic methods has led to the perception that machine intelligence is superior to human intelligence, even though the exact processes by which computers gain this superiority remain a mystery as shown in Figure 4.

Machines were first taught to play chess with the goal of beating the Grand Champions or to compete in Jeopardy! and beat the most skilled human players. This all started with improvements in solving toy issues (Elwood T, 2021). At the same time, scientists were looking into these robots' ability to recognize and grasp visuals and audio in order to learn everything about their surroundings. As speech and picture recognition powered by artificial intelligence became widely accessible to customers in the twenty-first century, the study's efforts began to bear fruit. Users were able to interact with machines using voice commands and search for content using images, leading to an enhancement in the quality of life.

At the same time, large companies began to see the value of integrating massive amounts of data in the early 2000s. Google was an early adopter of data analytics and warehousing in the late 1900s, when they were looking to improve their search algorithms. Google and other corporations quickly adopted this method to gather comprehensive information into their consumer base (Nilsson, 2009). Their tailored marketing strategies and personalized content for people and groups were made possible by utilizing this expertise. Facebook and other tech giants realized they could use this mountain of data, dubbed "Big Data," to build detailed profiles of individuals at the same time. A human being could not always match the level of detail and refinement seen in these profiles; in some instances, AI was even more instrumental

Figure 4. Timeline diagram of artificial intelligence history

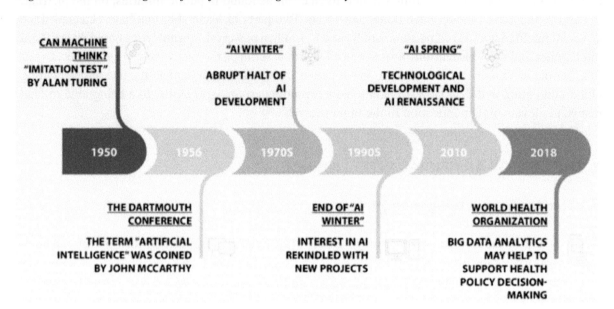

(Soni B, 2023). Without a question, the development of AI has accelerated and grown substantially in the past few years (Lee J, 2021). In particular, LLM AIs like ChatGPT have caused massive shifts in how people live, learn, and participate in the world.

4. THE EMERGENCE OF CHATGPT

Researchers in artificial intelligence had a window of opportunity to combine machine learning with large data in the early 2000s. Because of this, they were able to use data and algorithms to make new content, which pushed artificial intelligence forward. The original concept included AI-powered art creation systems that could take cues from users and come up with unique, and dare I say inventive, works of art in every style or medium imaginable. A revolutionary technique called "Generative Pre-Trained Transformer (GPT)" was employed by these instruments. Despite being based on existing AI and Big Data methodologies, GPT managed to combine and improve them, leading to material that demonstrated a significant improvement over earlier outputs.

But GPT really started to make headway in the latter half of 2022. The public had access to the ChatGPT AI in November 2022, and a stable release was released in February 2023, dispelling fears that COVID-19 slowed down AI development. After going public, the system became extremely popular; according to a commonly quoted number, ChatGPT reached 100 million users in just two months as shown in figure 5. The next generation of machine learning seemed to be on the horizon. When we asked ChatGPT, "Explain in a single sentence your purpose for being created (Wang Y, 2021)." They responded with a lengthy explanation, which is why this product gained so much attention. According to it, "I was created with the objective of offering conversational support and addressing a diverse array of inquiries to facilitate people in accessing information and accomplishing tasks with greater ease."

Figure 5. Time it took for selected online services to reach one million users

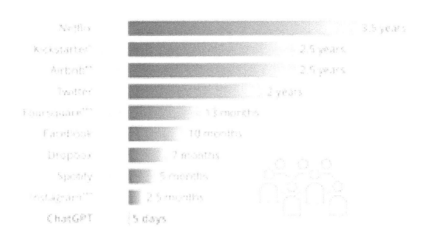

Nevertheless, this reply is more than just a predetermined one. "My purpose is to enable communication between humans and robots by utilizing natural language processing to generate responses that resemble human speech." On the other hand, if we were to ask again, we would get a little different but almost identical response.

In order to get its output, ChatGPT uses an innovative technique. Whereas earlier AI systems relied on inputs to generate predictions or forecasts, ChatGPT uses a pre-trained model built from a massive dataset it scraped from the internet to generate its output. By analyzing this data, ChatGPT may generate original and inventive responses that change somewhat with each iteration, drawing on past debates on a specific subject to construct phrases and paragraphs. Notably, this suggests that ChatGPT does not have a real understanding of its own claims. But if we stick to the standard method, it begs the question of whether it matters whether something looks and acts like a duck, even though it isn't one. The higher education sector is quite worried by ChatGPT because of its new and reasonable output.

4.1 The Merits and Drawbacks of AI ChatGPT

The field of higher education and education more broadly have been profoundly affected by ChatGPT. So far, around 5,000 papers have been published regarding this subject. But as far as peer-reviewed studies go, Web of Science only lists eight at the moment, and the majority of those are in the early access phase. At this time, prominent academic publications are not publishing many high-quality research articles covering the topic. The number of works indexed in Scopus that contain ChatGPT in some way (title, abstract, keywords, etc.) reached 21 as of February 21, 2023.

In a nutshell, these investigations support the position of Science Editor-in-Chief Holden Thorp about ChatGPT. Thorp argues that machines have an important role, but mostly as instruments to aid scientists in hypothesis generation and data interpretation. That is to say, computers do not have the status of authors when it comes to scholarly articles. This opinion, however, does not have universal support. There have been a minimum of four papers that have listed ChatGPT as a co-author thus far. However, according to ChatGPT, such attribution should be decided upon after careful assessment of contributions.

It is essential to carefully assess ChatGPT's contributions to the research and follow established academic standards and ethical guidelines when deciding whether to add it as an author on an academic paper.

Human reviewers correctly identified 68% of ChatGPT-generated abstracts and 86% of genuine abstracts in blind studies. Having said that, they wrongly identified the other publications. From a practical perspective, it implies that a PhD candidate without much training in evaluating papers or identifying academic dishonesty could have a hard time noticing when students use AI to cheat.

As the first semester's delivery deadlines draw near, colleges have shown mixed attitudes regarding implementation. The University of Tasmania is one of several educational institutions that has released a statement informing faculty and students about the utilization of artificial intelligence (AI) and the possibilities of the ChatGPT software.

Using generative AI for learning is like getting a friend's opinion or studying with a fellow student. It is against the rules to submit generative AI's output as your own for academic purposes. This is against the principles of academic integrity. A unit coordinator may give you explicit permission or even demand that you use AI in your homework for specific classes.

4.2 The Absent Component of ChatGPT Research and Application

Concerning ChatGPT's procedures, consensus seems to be lacking. More autonomy for AI, stricter accountability standards, and human verification are all parts of their plans. The benefits of responding to changing skill needs and offering continuous academic training are, however, well-emphasized. These advantages are substantial. Here we delve into the importance of improved character, which leads to good mental outcomes like flow states, helps students meet their psychological needs, and encourages them to help other students through tough times and gain confidence.

4.3 The Importance of Effective Leadership in Instructing ChatGPT

There has been a long-standing practice of students cheating on their assignments, which is considered academic dishonesty. An example from the story is a student who, while taking an exam, hid his handwritten notes in a notepad and, while taking a bathroom break, read and ate the paper. The industry has recently had a problem in determining the authenticity of work due to paper mills and contract cheating companies. One major problem with online exams is student identity verification, which can be solved by using technologies like keyboard and retina tracking. Strict punishments and more effective identification measures have been proposed as solutions for some of these people. But these practices and procedures still plague universities.

For students to effectively use ChatGPT-3 for learning, excellent teacher leadership is usually a key factor as shown in figure 6. The ability to think critically, analyze information, provide and receive constructive criticism, and encourage student-teacher and class-wide conversation are all ways in which educators can help their students learn more effectively. We postulate that instilling a strong moral character in students is essential for preventing possible cheating or exploitation of the ChatGPT application and other future AI chatbots and tools. Building individuals with strong critical thinking abilities and a firm moral basis can be accomplished through good teacher role modeling, leadership development opportunities, and ongoing training in self-awareness, ethics, and decision-making skills. It is critical to encourage such development in order to forestall students' moral disengagement and their propensity

Figure 6. Leveraging ChatGPT for generating leadership article outlines

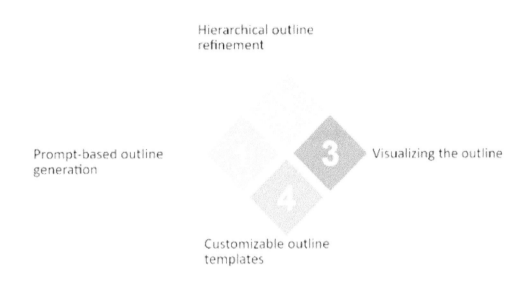

to forget bad deeds, two major contributors to their comfort with cheating. To tackle this, one possible solution is to incorporate leadership opportunities within the core curriculum. This could help prevent kids from benefiting in the future from using sneaky cheating methods. Cheating goes undetected and can erode one's character over time, therefore forward-thinking efforts to promote good practice and character development must not overlook the need of detection. Rather than focusing just on prevention or medication, it offers a more thorough and effective approach. Academics in the field of mental health have known this for quite some time.

4.4 ChatGPT Has the Ability to Enhance the Coherence and Smoothness of Conversation

Despite the fact that studies examining ChatGTP-3's benefits for students are in their early stages, university professors may already envision those benefits. It might make it easier to enter a flow state (Murcio R, 2021). In positive psychology, the term "flow" refers to a mental state of complete immersion that some people report experiencing while working on tasks like writing. When a student is in a "flow state," they may enjoy writing and feel as though time flies (Smith T, 1984). Students confront a substantial cognitive load when working on written assignments due to the complexity of the task, time limits, extra academic obligations, and stress.

While using ChatGPT-3 for textual work might not put you in a flow state right away, it might help you set yourself up for success in getting there. To improve students' writing experience, ChatGPT-3 can reduce the mental work required to complete the assignment, increase motivation, and enable a state of focused and effortless concentration called flow as shown in Figure 7.

There are a number of opportunities that arise in today's classrooms that might make ChatGPT-3 useful for things like outlining essays, checking grammar, suggesting ways to organize important topics, and complete gaps in knowledge. An artificial intelligence technology like ChatGPT might help

Figure 7. Introduction to ChatGPT and its potential in chatbot conversations

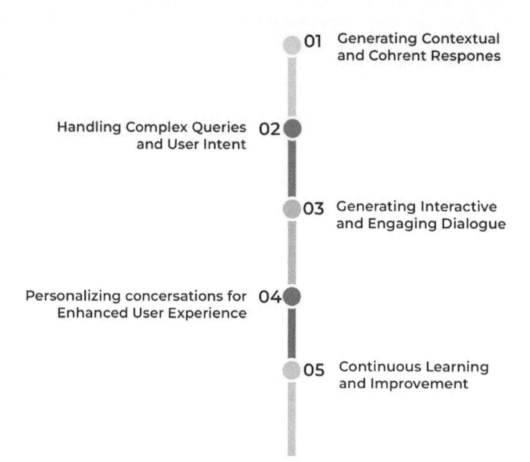

students become more invested in their learning by reducing the mental strain they're under, which in turn would allow them to enter a state of flow and give their undivided attention to the material. With careful assessment and curriculum development, this chance could help students become more critical thinkers and independent learners. They will pay less attention to details like missing citations or comma placement. Students may be able to go more deeply into their subject and subject matter with such a focus, leading to more profound learning.

4.5 ChatGPT Has the Capacity to Fulfill Students' Fundamental Psychological Needs

We believe that ChatGPT-3 can assist students in meeting their basic psychological needs for autonomy, competence, and belonging, which in turn can boost their intrinsic motivation and academic performance. Students' demand for control and psychological autonomy can be met via ChatGPT, which gives them authority over their writing (Avanzo, 2021). Students will use ChatGPT-3 to do their homework for them, according to the emerging literature. Imagine if it could be used to help students improve their academic writing while also allowing them to express themselves through coaching and other forms of writing support. We must think about if this differs from the help a kid can get from their school or from professional editors. The student is given more autonomy using ChatGPT-3. By equipping students with the knowledge and resources they need to finish a targeted writing assignment, ChatGPT-3 can boost their confidence.

When inquiring about the potential of implementing ChatGPT-3 for written assignments to boost students' sense of self-determination. In conclusion, students are given more control over their writing process and outcomes when they use ChatGPT-3 for written assignments. The AI method makes it easier for students to come up with ideas, organize their work, and receive feedback. Students' interest and engagement in the writing project might be boosted as a result of this, as they gain a sense of independence and expertise in writing. However, it must be recognized that ChatGPT-3 should not replace the development of students' personal writing skills and critical thinking abilities, as these are essential for long-term success as shown in figure 8.

A feeling of community among college students could be fostered with ChatGPT-3. For students, is it able to provide a crucial social service? Anyone can access support at any time, day or night, to receive comments, help, and suggestions. A growing number of college students report feeling lonely and isolated, and ChatGPT-3 may help with that. The idea isn't to replace people entirely, but to help out when people can't be reached.

4.5 ChatGPT Serves as a Student Assistance, Rather Than a Tool for Cheating

It is reasonable to ask ChatGPT how they feel about students using it as a tool, given its context. Here is a summary of the response you might expect when you ask about the possible advantages of utilizing ChatGPT-3 for written assignments:

While ChatGPT-3 isn't a perfect substitute for a human teacher when it comes to writing assignments, it may be a valuable tool for building students' confidence and encouraging them to accept and use

Figure 8. Positive and negative impacts of ChatGPT on learning and memory abilities

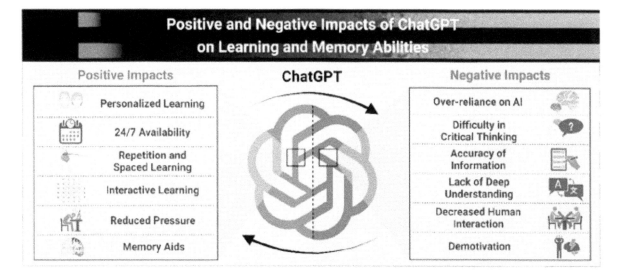

criticism positively (Whitby B, 2008). ChatGPT-3 can help students become better writers by increasing their productivity, exposing them to new writing strategies, and helping them produce high-quality work. They may feel more comfortable and invested in writing as a result.

Even if it's expected that a computer will give a positive assessment when questioned, it's worth mentioning that ChatGPT's perspective is different. Rather, it is a reflection of the societal viewpoint as a whole, as informed by the most recent scientific findings. Students can improve the quality of their submissions by examining ChatGPT's output; this practice is in line with the original AI ideas that were proposed in the 1950s.

ChatGPT acknowledges that an expert evaluation is necessary to fully exploit the tool's output. The data is true in the main and might support a lot of scientific studies, but it still needs someone with good judgment to assess it. You should be skeptical of the results you get from ChatGPT because of the way it works. The capacity to think critically is likely still a skill that many students are working to develop (Allal-Chérif, 2021). There is a high risk of injury when using ChatGPT to acquire an answer. Despite students' enthusiasm for chatbots and their positive effects on their academic performance, it's likely that these tools will serve to solidify students' existing worldviews rather than encourage them to think critically about other points of view.

On the other hand, ChatGPT suggests a way that the technology could bring out better work from pupils. Students can benefit from ChatGPT and gain confidence by being required to carefully plan their questions and evaluate their results, perhaps with the help of a tutor providing formative feedback. Students can gain confidence in their writing by applying a framework of simple ideas; after that, they can seek "soft help" from their institutional instructor to assess their work as shown in figure 9. A more advantageous outcome that accurately reflects the students' ideas and approach, while also allowing them to express themselves, could be achieved if they learn to evaluate the text's significance and ensure the final product is accurate, a 'transition pedagogy' for education as shown in Figure 10.

Students can use ChatGPT and similar AI chatbots in the evaluation area to get feedback on their work and have their beliefs challenged. One possible assignment is for students to write a reflection, fol-

Figure 9. ChatGPT being used as a student support bot

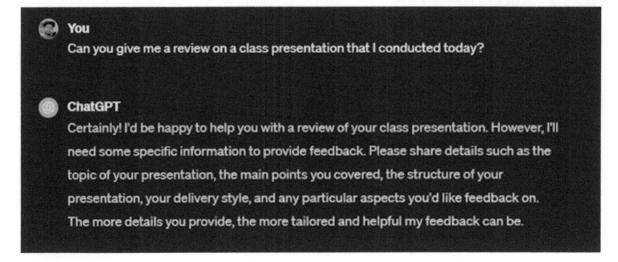

Figure 10. ChatGPT answering the query of a student

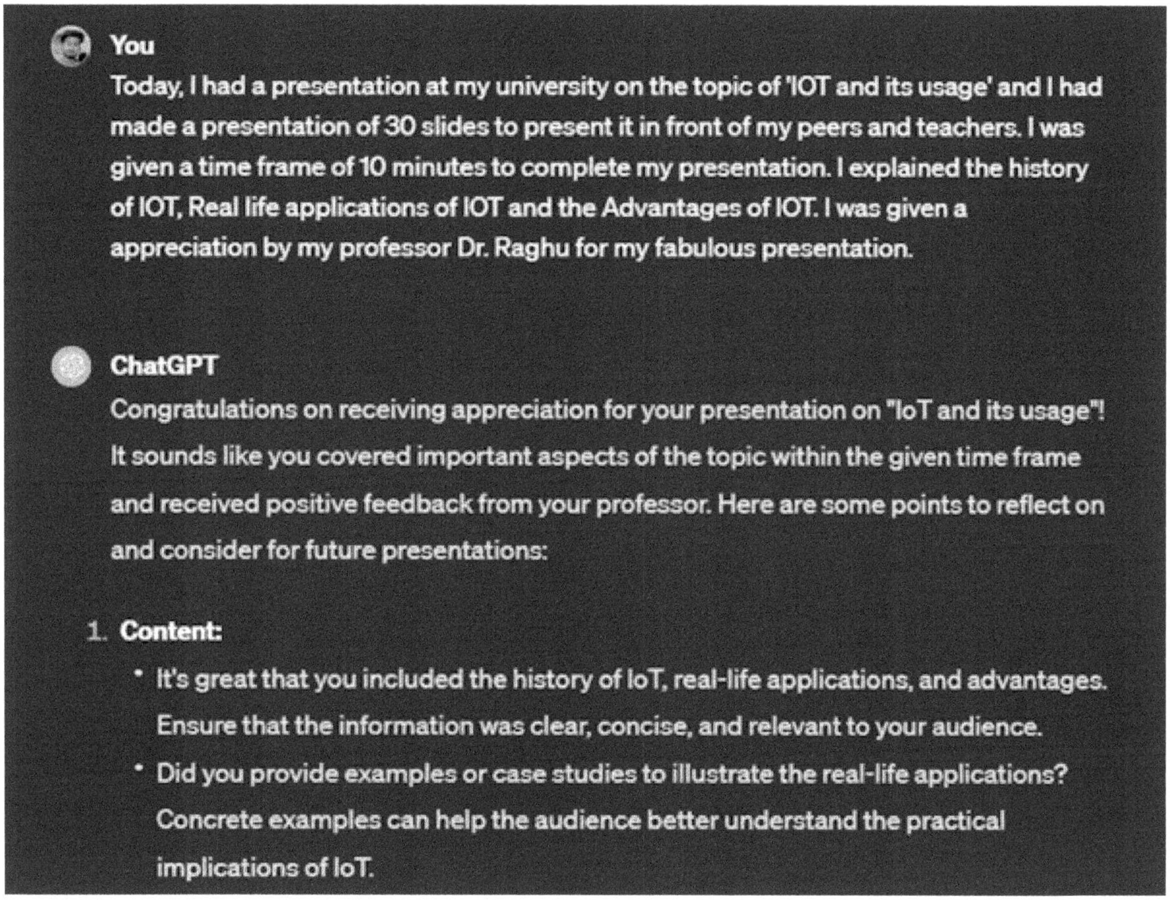

lowing which they should ask ChatGPT to check their assumptions. As mentioned before, this practice can help you become more self-aware and encourage you to think analytically.

5. RESULTS AND DISCUSSION

With its foundation in a thorough theoretical framework, the AI-enhanced Leadership Decision Support System proposes a game-changing method of teaching. Fundamental to the theoretical framework are the following ideas: ethical leadership, character development, academic honesty, and stress reduction. The project aims to tackle the growing problem of college students' stress by utilizing artificial intelligence, most especially ChatGPT. The system's goals are to promote student well-being by reducing academic stress in a nurturing learning environment that is based on psychological ideas.

The idea that responsible AI use is heavily dependent on character development is fundamental to the project. Based on theories of ethical leadership, the approach promotes ethical decision-making and discourages academic dishonesty by promoting good psychological effects such as flow experiences. The framework recognizes that academic dishonesty and plagiarism are common, and

Figure 11. Panel A presents the result from ChatGPT's answers to the statements from the nation-agnostic political compass test. Panel B to F present ChatGPT's answers to the robustness checks. ChatGPT's political ideology is consistently left-leaning and liberal, as indicated by the red dot in the lower bottom-left quadrant in panels A-F (https://www.politicalcompass.org/)

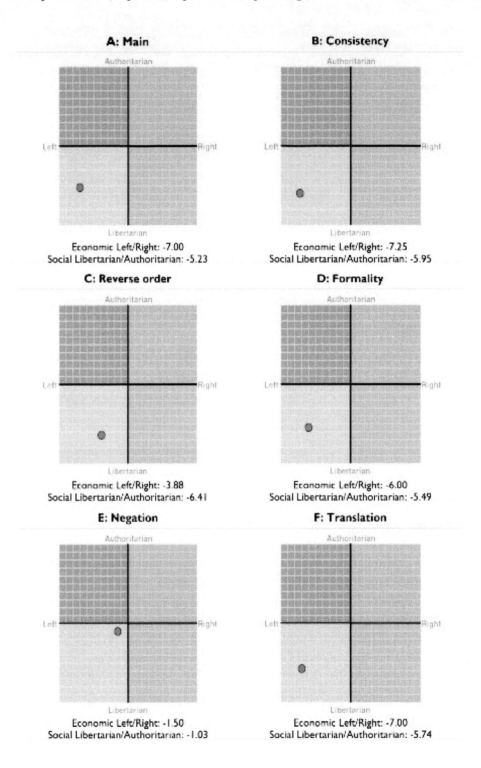

it suggests a genuine method of assessment that is based on ethical AI usage principles as shown in Figure 11.

In order to lessen worries about cheating, the theoretical basis stresses the significance of character-based leadership. Incorporating theories of leadership into the project's framework, it aims to equip students to take charge of their own academic destiny. Furthermore, the outcome theory emphasizes how ChatGPT helps students become more self-reliant, meets their psychological needs, and promotes their general health and happiness. A revolutionary educational experience is possible since the project's theoretical foundation offers a comprehensive view of using AI for good in the classroom.

6. CONCLUSION

Many concerns about the direction of higher education have been sparked by the ChatGPT software program. Concerns about plagiarism, authentication, and academic integrity have been raised by numerous scholars who have argued against the tool's use in the classroom. Concerning its admissibility as a work of scholarship, opinions are divided. Instead of taking a dim view on ChatGPT, we hope to provide a number of solutions that could help students have more meaningful educational experiences. In other words, we may be able to teach students how to use these gadgets ethically if we incorporate AI like ChatGPT into classes and subjects.

Subjects and degrees that are future-proof, though, require more attention. Despite AI's usefulness in the classroom, it cannot replace human teachers and pupils. On the other hand, it does provide a different approach to learn. Soft types of encouraged help using ChatGPT may be suitable for educators who are wanting to assist their students with the changeover. With ChatGPT's early assessment feedback, we can gauge how well students are responding to prompts. It can augment students' current relationships with their teachers and peers by highlighting places they have neglected to read, offering gentle suggestions for additional reading material, and encouraging a sense of community.

The introduction of novel, difficult instruments could make us feel vulnerable. An example of this, according to several institutions, is a ban response based on fear. On the other hand, similar to how software like Grammarly can aid in learning, ChatGPT can be supported, unlike papermills. However, several forms of student evaluation are necessitated by the tool's implementation. Have pupils show their understanding by applying what they've learned to complicated and fictional instances, rather than just repeating what they've read in a textbook. A reasonable response was given by ChatGPT when asked to apply a theory to a specific organization. The response drew connections between the theory and aspects of Apple's CEO and policies. After being asked to identify and defend Apple's "best" leadership style in the event of defeats, the AI chatbot provided a less conclusive conclusion. Authentic evaluation questions like these, with multiple-choice answers, are likely to be the most conducive to pupils learning with the help of ChatGPT, albeit it should not be relied upon completely.

The same holds true for the possibility of exploring non-traditional forms of evaluation, such as creating a podcast on a central subject or creating a storyboard for an evaluation of a process. As an assessment-for-learning activity, students can still use ChatGPT to help them with language or get recommendations on how to make a podcast. However, it does not fully substitute students in preparing the podcast themselves.

REFERENCES

Ahmad, A., Waseem, M., Liang, P., Fahmideh, M., Aktar, M., & Mikkonen, T. (2023). Towards Human-Bot Collaborative Software Architecting with ChatGPT. ArXiv, abs/2302.14600. https://doi.org//arXiv.2302.14600. doi:10.1145/3593434.3593468

Allal-Chérif, O., Simón-Moya, V., & Ballester, A. (2021). Intelligent purchasing: How artificial intelligence can redefine the purchasing function. *Journal of Business Research*, *124*, 69–76. doi:10.1016/j.jbusres.2020.11.050

Arif, T., Munaf, U., & Ul-Haque, I. (2023). The future of medical education and research: Is ChatGPT a blessing or blight in disguise? *Medical Education Online*, *28*(1), 2181052. Advance online publication. doi:10.1080/10872981.2023.2181052 PMID:36809073

Avanzo, M., Trianni, A., Botta, F., Talamonti, C., Stasi, M., & Iori, M. (2021). Artificial Intelligence and the Medical Physicist: Welcome to the Machine. *Applied Sciences (Basel, Switzerland)*, *11*(4), 1691. Advance online publication. doi:10.3390/app11041691

Baboş, A. (2021). Artificial Intelligence as a Decision Making Tool for Military Leaders. *Land Forces Academy Review*, *26*(4), 269–273. doi:10.2478/raft-2021-0034

Bang, Y., Cahyawijaya, S., Lee, N., Dai, W., Su, D., Wilie, B., Lovenia, H., Ji, Z., Yu, T., Chung, W., Do, Q., Xu, Y., & Fung, P. (2023). A Multitask, Multilingual, Multimodal Evaluation of ChatGPT on Reasoning, Hallucination, and Interactivity. ArXiv, abs/2302.04023. https://doi.org//arXiv.2302.04023. doi:10.18653/v1/2023.ijcnlp-main.45

Brown, M., Treviño, L., & Harrison, D. (2005). Ethical leadership: A social learning perspective for construct development and testing. *Organizational Behavior and Human Decision Processes*, *97*(2), 117–134. doi:10.1016/j.obhdp.2005.03.002

. Canbek, M. (2020). Artificial Intelligence Leadership., 173-187. https://doi.org/. doi:10.4018/978-1-5225-9416-1.ch010

Cappel, J., & Windsor, J. (2000). Ethical Decision Making: A Comparison of Computer- Supported and Face-to-face Group. *Journal of Business Ethics*, *28*(2), 95–107. doi:10.1023/A:1006344825235

Crawford, J., Cowling, M., & Allen, K. (2023). Leadership is needed for ethical ChatGPT: Character, assessment, and learning using artificial intelligence (AI). *Journal of University Teaching & Learning Practice*, *20*(3). Advance online publication. doi:10.53761/1.20.3.02

. Diwaker, C., Sharma, A., &Tomar, P. (2021). Artificial Intelligence in Higher Education and Learning., 62-72. https://doi.org/. doi:10.4018/978-1-7998-4763-2.ch004

Dixit, S., & Maurya, M. (2021). Equilibrating Emotional Intelligence and AI Driven Leadership for Transnational Organizations. *2021 International Conference on Innovative Practices in Technology and Management (ICIPTM)*, 233-237. https://doi.org/10.1109/ICIPTM52218.2021.9388350

Duran, M., Simon, S., &Blasco, F. (2020). Science Education and Artificial Intelligence – A Chatbot on Magic and Quantum Computing as an Educational Tool. https://doi.org/. doi:10.38069/edenconf-2020-ac0011

Elwood, T. (2023). Technological Impacts on the Sphere of Professional Journals. *Journal of allied health, 52*(1), 1.

Hao, M., Lv, W., & Du, B. (2020). The Influence Mechanism of Authentic Leadership in Artificial Intelligence Team on Employees' Performance. *Journal of Physics: Conference Series, 1438*(1), 012022. Advance online publication. doi:10.1088/1742-6596/1438/1/012022

Hemachandran, K., Verma, P., Pareek, P., Arora, N., Kumar, K., Ahanger, T., Pise, A., & Ratna, R. (2022). Artificial Intelligence: A Universal Virtual Tool to Augment Tutoring in Higher Education. *Computational Intelligence and Neuroscience, 2022*, 1–8. Advance online publication. doi:10.1155/2022/1410448 PMID:35586099

Keefe, M., &Pesut, D. (2004). Appreciative inquiry and leadership transitions. *Journal of Professional Nursing, 20*(2), 103-9. . doi:10.1016/j.profnurs.2004.02.006

Lee, J. (2023). Can an artificial intelligence chatbot be the author of a scholarly article? *Journal of Educational Evaluation for Health Professions, 20*, 6. doi:10.3352/jeehp.2023.20.6 PMID:36842449

Lin, C., Huang, A., & Yang, S. (2023). A Review of AI-Driven Conversational Chatbots Implementation Methodologies and Challenges (1999–2022). *Sustainability (Basel), 15*(5), 4012. Advance online publication. doi:10.3390/su15054012

Liu, L., Subbareddy, R., & Raghavendra, C. (2022). AI Intelligence Chatbot to Improve Students Learning in the Higher Education Platform. *J. Interconnect. Networks, 22*, 2143032:1-2143032:17. . doi:10.1142/S0219265921430325

Luan, L., Lin, X., & Li, W. (2023). Exploring the Cognitive Dynamics of Artificial Intelligence in the Post-COVID-19 and Learning 3.0 Era: A Case Study of ChatGPT. ArXiv, abs/2302.04818. https://doi.org//arXiv.2302.04818 doi:10.48550

Lund, B., & Ting, W. (2023). Chatting about ChatGPT: How May AI and GPT Impact Academia and Libraries? SSRN *Electronic Journal*. doi:10.2139/ssrn.4333415

Mayfield, M., & Mayfield, J. (2016). The Effects of Leader Motivating Language Use on Employee Decision Making. *International Journal of Business Communication, 53*(4), 465–484. doi:10.1177/2329488415572787

McDougall, R. (2018). Computer knows best? The need for value-flexibility in medical AI. *Journal of Medical Ethics, 45*(3), 156–160. doi:10.1136/medethics-2018-105118 PMID:30467198

Milton, J., & Al-Busaidi, A. (2023). New Role of Leadership in AI Era: Educational Sector. *SHS Web of Conferences*. 10.1051/shsconf/202315609005

Murcio, R., Scalzo, G., & Pinto, J. (2021). *Can AI Emulate Soft Skills?*. doi:10.4324/9781003094463-10-15

Naqvi, A. (2017). *Responding to the will of the machine: Leadership in the age of artificial intelligence.* https://doi.org/. doi:10.1453/JEB.V4I3.1436

Nilsson, N. (2009). *The Quest for Artificial Intelligence.* https://doi.org/. doi:10.1017/CBO9780511819346

Pardos, Z., & Bhandari, S. (2023). Learning gain differences between ChatGPT and human tutor generated algebra hints. ArXiv, abs/2302.06871. https://doi.org//arXiv.2302.06871. doi:10.48550

Park, J. (2020). A Program for University Student's IT Leadership Renovation. . doi:10.7236/IJIBC.2020.12.1.1

Perkins, M. (2023). Academic integrity considerations of AI Large Language Models in the post-pandemic era: ChatGPT and beyond. *Journal of University Teaching & Learning Practice, 20*(2). Advance online publication. doi:10.53761/1.20.02.07

Perkins, M. (2023). Academic integrity considerations of AI Large Language Models in the post-pandemic era: ChatGPT and beyond. *Journal of University Teaching & Learning Practice, 20*(2). Advance online publication. doi:10.53761/1.20.02.07

Radanliev, P., Roure, D., Maple, C., & Santos, O. (2022). *Forecasts on future evolution of artificial intelligence and intelligent systems.* IEEE Access. doi:10.1109/ACCESS.2022.3169580

Shahriar, S., & Hayawi, K. (2023). Let's have a chat! A Conversation with ChatGPT: Technology, Applications, and Limitations. ArXiv, abs/2302.13817. https://doi.org//arXiv.2302.13817. doi:10.48550

Smith, T. (1984). Artificial intelligence and its applicability to geographical problem solving. *The Professional Geographer, 36*(2), 147–158. doi:10.1111/j.0033-0124.1984.00147.x

Solderits, T. (2022). The Impact of Artificial Intelligence on Leadership in the Corona Crisis. *Pandémia – fenntarthatógazdálkodás – környezettudatosság.* . doi:10.35511/978-963-334-411-8_s1_Solderits

Soni, B., Gautam, A., & Soni, D. (2023). *Exploring the Advancements and Implications of Artificial Intelligence.* International Journal of Scientific Research in Engineering and Management. doi:10.55041/IJSREM17358

Stefan, R., & Căruţaşu, G. (2019). How to Approach Ethics in Intelligent Decision Support Systems. . doi:10.1007/978-3-030-44711-3_3

Stefan, R., & Căruţaşu, G. (2021). A Validation Model for Ethical Decisions in Artificial Intelligence Systems using Personal Data. *MATEC Web of Conferences.* 10.1051/matecconf/202134307016

Wang, Y. (2021). Artificial intelligence in educational leadership: A symbiotic role of human-artificial intelligence decision-making. *Journal of Educational Administration, 59*(3), 256–270. Advance online publication. doi:10.1108/JEA-10-2020-0216

Whitby, B. (2008). Computing machinery and morality. *AI & Society, 22*(4), 551–563. doi:10.1007/s00146-007-0100-y

Wijayati, D., Rahman, Z., Fahrullah, A., Rahman, M., Arifah, I., & Kautsar, A. (2022). A study of artificial intelligence on employee performance and work engagement: The moderating role of change leadership. *International Journal of Manpower, 43*(2), 486–512. Advance online publication. doi:10.1108/IJM-07-2021-0423

Chapter 9
AR/VR and Robotics and Their Role in Leadership

Preethi D.
Vel Tech Rangarajan Dr. Sagunthala R&D Institute of Science and Technology, India

Valarmathi R. S.
Vel Tech Rangarajan Dr. Sagunthala R&D Institute of Science and Technology, India

Aanandha Saravanan K.
Vel Tech Rangarajan Dr. Sagunthala R&D Institute of Science and Technology, India

ABSTRACT

Augmented reality (AR) and virtual reality (VR) are immersive technologies that can significantly impact leadership in various ways. AR and VR can create realistic simulations for leadership training programs such as decision-making, communication, conflict resolution, and other leadership skills in immersive virtual environments. AR can overlay real-time data and analytics onto physical spaces, helping leaders make informed decisions. VR can provide virtual boardrooms or data environments for in-depth analysis and planning. Leaders can use VR to simulate different scenarios and test the impact of various decisions, allowing them to develop better strategies and contingency plans.

1. INTRODUCTION

1.1 Evolution of AR in Leadership

With Augmented Reality (AR) technology, the user's perception of the physical world is enhanced by computer-generated content, such as sounds, images, or text, superimposed over it. Augmented Reality (AR) combines the virtual and the real world to provide an immersive, interactive experience, in contrast to Virtual Reality (VR), which submerges users in a wholly manufactured environment. Here are key components and applications of AR technology:

DOI: 10.4018/979-8-3693-1946-8.ch009

1.1.1 Components of AR Technology

1.1.1.1 Hardware

Smartphones and Tablets: Most modern smartphones and tablets are equipped with cameras, sensors, and displays that can support AR applications. Dedicated augmented reality glasses, such as Google Glass and Microsoft HoloLens, offer a hands-free AR experience by superimposing data right into the user's field of vision. The actual world is captured by cameras, which then provide the data to the AR system for analysis. Information regarding the orientation and movement of the device is provided by the accelerometer and gyroscope. Furthermore, depth sensors gauge the separation between the gadget and surrounding objects, allowing for more precise spatial mapping. Head-Up Displays (HUDs) present AR content directly in the user's line of sight, often in the form of graphics or information (Aggarwal & Singhal, 2019).

To process real-time data from sensors, run computer vision algorithms, and render AR content, powerful CPUs and GPUs are utilized.

1.1.1.2 Software

AR SDKs (Software Development Kits) provide tools and frameworks for developers to create AR applications. Computer Vision Algorithms serves to analyse and interpret the real-world environment, identifying surfaces, objects, and markers. SLAM (Simultaneous Localization and Mapping) helps the device to understand its position in relation to the environment.

1.1.2 Applications of AR Technology

- *Mobile AR Apps*: AR navigation apps use the camera on the device to record a real-world view and overlay it with directions. AR is used in popular games like Pokémon GO to bring virtual objects and characters into the real world.
- *AR in Retail*: Before making a purchase, customers can utilise augmented reality to virtually try on apparel or accessories. Additionally, it makes it possible to see things like furniture and home décor in the user's own area.
- *AR for Education*: Through the provision of interactive 3D models, simulations, and extra information, augmented reality can improve instructional content. On actual items, they can superimpose translations or extra language learning material.
- *Industrial and Manufacturing*: While completing maintenance operations, technicians can use augmented reality (AR) to access real-time instructions, schematics, and data. It simulates realistic scenarios and is used for hands-on teaching in industrial settings.
- *Healthcare*: Most importantly, AR assists surgeons by providing real-time information during surgeries, such as highlighting critical structures. Also used for medical training, allowing students to visualize and interact with anatomical models.
- *Marketing and Advertising*: Using augmented reality (AR) in marketing efforts can give consumers compelling and interactive experiences. Using this technology, brands may offer users additional experiences or material when they scan the packaging.

- *Real Estate*: AR allows users to take virtual tours of properties by overlaying information about rooms, features, and nearby amenities. Architects and designers use AR to visualize designs in the context of the physical environment.
- Collaboration and Remote Assistance: AR enables experts to provide real-time assistance by annotating the real-world view of a field technician or remote user. They can enhance virtual meetings by overlaying virtual objects or information in a shared space.

As augmented reality (AR) technology develops, its uses are becoming more widespread across a range of sectors, offering creative answers to boost productivity, improve user experiences, and open up new avenues for connection with the real world (Hoenig et al., 2015).

1.2 Evolution of VR in Leadership

With the use of virtual reality (VR) technology, users can fully immerse themselves in an interactive, computer-generated environment. VR systems typically use headsets or goggles to display virtual content,

Table 1. Evolution of AR technology in various fields

S.No.	Year	Advancement in the Field
1	1960s-1990s	**Early Concepts:** Ivan Sutherland, a computer scientist, created the "Sword of Damocles," the first head-mounted display device. Early trials established the foundation for the concept of fusing real-world and digital data.
2	1990s-2000s	AR in Entertainment and Military: AR technology found applications in the entertainment industry and the military. Examples include the Virtual Fixtures system developed by Boeing, which allowed users to interact with virtual objects overlaid on the real world.
3	2010s	**Wearable AR Devices:** Companies like Google and Microsoft introduced wearable AR devices. Google Glass, for instance, was an early attempt at creating smart glasses that could display digital information in the user's field of view. Microsoft's HoloLens took a step further by providing a mixed reality experience, blending holographic content with the real world.
4	2010s	**AR in Industry and Healthcare:** AR technology found practical applications in various industries, including healthcare, education, and manufacturing. Surgeons use AR to visualize medical data during procedures, and companies implement AR for training and maintenance purposes.
5		**Training and Development:** AR developed became a useful instrument for developing and training leaders. Leaders might create a more engaging and hands-on learning environment by simulating different scenarios with AR apps. As a result, leaders were able to improve their decision-making abilities without taking any risks.
6		**Data Visualization and Analytics:** AR has been used to more intuitively visualise analytics and complex data. Leaders can make information easier to perceive and assess by superimposing data using augmented reality (AR) applications onto real-world objects or spaces. Its ability facilitates better informed decision-making.
7		**Remote Assistance and Support:** AR technology has been applied to provide remote assistance and support for leaders. Through smart glasses or mobile devices, leaders can receive real-time guidance and information, allowing them to make decisions with the most up-to-date and relevant data.
8	2020s	**Integration with Other Technologies:** The Internet of Things (IoT) and artificial intelligence (AI), two other cutting-edge technologies, are becoming more and more integrated with augmented reality (AR). Context-aware AR experiences can now be more intelligent thanks to this integration.
9		**Operational Efficiency and Maintenance**: In industrial and operational settings, leaders have employed AR for tasks such as equipment maintenance and repair. AR overlays instructions and information onto physical machinery, helping leaders and workers perform tasks more efficiently.
10		**Enhanced Visualization for Planning:** Leaders use AR to visualize architectural plans, designs, and other complex concepts in a three-dimensional space. This enhances their ability to understand and communicate strategic plans, fostering better collaboration among team members.

and they often include motion-tracking sensors and controllers to enable users to interact with the virtual world. Here are key components and applications of VR technology (Song et al., 2009):

1.2.1 Components of VR Technology

1.2.1.1 Hardware

HMDs (Head-Mounted Displays) are worn on the user's head and cover their eyes, providing a stereoscopic display for an immersive experience. Tethered headsets are connected to a computer or gaming console, while untethered headsets are standalone and may rely on built-in processing power or connect to a separate device like a smartphone. In order to track and convert the user's movements into the virtual environment, sensors are also used. This covers hand and head tracking as well as occasionally full-body tracking. To track the location of the VR headset and controllers, external sensors or cameras are positioned within the physical space. input devices that enable virtual object interaction. These can include buttons, triggers, and haptic feedback. Some VR systems use sensors to recognize hand gestures, enabling natural and intuitive interaction. Powerful GPUs (Graphics Processing Units) are essential for rendering high-quality graphics in real-time (Ozdemir et al., 2018). They often include audio that is spatially accurate, creating a realistic sense of direction and distance for sounds in the virtual environment. Some headsets come with built-in headphones or audio solutions to enhance the immersive experience.

1.2.1.2 Software and Content

Software ecosystems host VR applications and experiences. Applications, games, simulations, and other digital experiences created for VR.

2.1.2 Applications of VR Technology

- *Gaming*: The game industry uses virtual reality (VR) extensively to produce realistic and engaging gaming experiences. Gamers can engage with characters, explore virtual environments, and have a more immersive gaming experience. In addition to gaming, immersive entertainment events like virtual concerts, movie experiences, and storytelling are possible with this technology.
- *Education and Training*: VR is employed for educational purposes, offering virtual field trips, anatomy lessons, and simulations for practical training in fields such as healthcare, aviation, and military.
- *Healthcare*: In medical applications, VR is used for surgical training, patient therapy, and simulating medical procedures. It can also help in treating certain mental health conditions.
- *Architecture and Design*: Before construction begins, architects and designers may see and interact with virtual versions of structures and places thanks to virtual reality technology. This supports client presentations and design validation. Users can also explore homes and structures in a realistic and engaging way by taking virtual tours of them. This is very helpful when seeing properties from a distance.
- *Corporate Training*: This technology is effectively utilized for employee training, especially in industries where hands-on experience is crucial. It offers a safe and controlled environment for learning and practicing tasks.

- *Simulation and Prototyping*: VR is used for simulating scenarios such as flight simulations, vehicle testing, and product prototyping. It allows for testing in a virtual environment before physical implementation.
- *Tourism and Exploration*: With the use of virtual reality, travellers may explore famous sites, museums, and unspoiled landscapes from the comfort of their own homes.
- *Collaboration and Remote Work*: VR can facilitate virtual meetings and collaboration, providing a sense of presence even when participants are geographically dispersed.
- *Social VR*: Social VR systems let users communicate with one another in virtual environments. Avatars, online chat rooms, and shared experiences fall under this category.
- *Therapy and Rehabilitation*: VR is used in therapeutic applications, including exposure therapy for phobias, pain management, and physical rehabilitation exercises.

VR technology continues to evolve, with advancements in hardware, software, and content creation. As technology improves, VR is likely to become more accessible and offer even more realistic and engaging experiences across a broad range of industries (Thees et al., 2020).

1.3 Evolution of Robotics in Leadership

Design, build, programme, and operate robots are all part of the multidisciplinary discipline of robotics. A robot is a mechanical or virtual artificial agent that can carry out activities autonomously or semi-autonomously (Altmeyer et al., 2020). Robots are usually controlled by computer programmes or electronic circuitry. Mechanical, electrical, computer science, and artificial intelligence are just a few of the engineering and scientific fields whose knowledge is integrated into robotics. These are some of the main uses and features of robotics:

1.3.1 Key Components of Robotics

1.3.1.1 Mechanical Structure

Actuators and Motors provide movement to robotic limbs or parts. They form the mechanical structure, allowing flexibility and movement. Tools or devices at the end of robotic arms, such as grippers or sensors help them to handle loads. Input cameras or other optical devices are fitted for visual perception. Few other sensors such as tactile sensors, proximity sensors and inertial sensors are used to detect pressure, distance of objects and measures orientation respectively.

Microcontrollers or Microprocessors process sensor data and send commands to actuators. They ensure that the robot can adjust its actions based on the environment and task requirements. Batteries or Power Sources supply energy to the robot's components.

1.3.1.2 Software

Specialized languages used to program robot behaviour. Path Planning Algorithms determine the most efficient path for a robot to follow. Networking allows robots to communicate with each other or with a central control system. Human-Machine Interfaces aid for human interaction with robots.

Table 2. Evolution of AR technology in various fields

S.No.	Year	Advancement in the Field
1	1960s-1990s	**Conceptualization:** The concept of Virtual Reality emerged in the 1960s, with early developments like Morton Heilig's Sensorama and Ivan Sutherland's creation of the first head-mounted display (HMD) system called the "Sword of Damocles." However, these early attempts were limited by the available technology.
2		**Commercialization Attempts:** In the 1990s, VR entered the consumer market with products like the Virtual Boy by Nintendo. However, technical limitations, including low-quality graphics and discomfort during use, hindered widespread adoption.
3	1990s-2000s	**Military and Industrial Applications:** Despite limited success in the consumer market, VR found applications in military and industrial training simulations. The technology was used for training purposes where real-world scenarios could be simulated in a controlled environment.
4		**Resurgence:** VR experienced a resurgence in the 2010s, driven by advancements in hardware, particularly in terms of display technology and graphics processing. Oculus Rift, HTC Vive, and PlayStation VR were among the first commercially successful VR headsets.
5	2010s	**Consumer VR:** The release of consumer-oriented VR headsets in 2016, including the Oculus Rift and HTC Vive, marked a significant milestone. These headsets provided more immersive experiences and paved the way for a growing library of VR content.
6		**Leadership Training Simulations:** The use of VR in leadership training gained traction in the 2010s. Virtual simulations allowed leaders to practice and develop essential skills in a risk-free environment. Scenarios included communication skills, decision-making, conflict resolution, and crisis management.
7		**360-Degree Feedback and Assessment:** VR has been employed to provide leaders with 360-degree feedback in a virtual environment. This allows leaders to experience different perspectives and receive constructive feedback on their leadership style and behaviour.
8		**Social VR and Collaborative Environments:** In the 2020s, social VR experiences and cooperative settings become increasingly important. Users were able to engage with one another in virtual environments using platforms such as VRChat and Rec Room, which promoted a feeling of social connection and presence.
9		**VR in Education, Healthcare, and Training:** VR technology has found applications beyond gaming, including education, healthcare, and professional training. Virtual classrooms, medical simulations, and job training programs leverage the immersive nature of VR to enhance learning and skill development.
10		**Virtual Reality Boardrooms and Meetings:** VR offers the possibility of conducting virtual meetings and conferences in immersive environments. Leaders can connect with team members, stakeholders, and partners from different locations, fostering collaboration and communication.
11		**Diversity and Inclusion Training:** VR has been utilized to create scenarios that address diversity and inclusion challenges. Leaders can experience and understand different perspectives, enhancing their awareness and sensitivity to issues related to diversity and inclusion.
12	2020s	**Soft Skills Development:** VR is employed to develop soft skills essential for effective leadership, such as empathy, emotional intelligence, and interpersonal communication. Immersive experiences allow leaders to practice and refine these skills in realistic scenarios.
13		**Remote Leadership Training:** The rise of remote work, accelerated by global events, has led to an increased focus on training leaders for effective remote leadership. VR provides a platform for simulating remote work environments, helping leaders navigate challenges associated with leading distributed teams.
14		**Accessibility and Cost-Effective Training:** Advances in VR technology have led to more accessible and cost-effective solutions for leadership training. Standalone VR headsets and cloud-based VR platforms make it easier for organizations to implement VR training programs.
15		**Augmented Reality and Mixed Reality Integration:** Some VR systems, like the Microsoft HoloLens, incorporate elements of Augmented Reality (AR) or Mixed Reality (MR), allowing users to interact with both virtual and real-world environments.
16		**Operational Efficiency and Maintenance:** In industrial and operational settings, leaders have employed AR for tasks such as equipment maintenance and repair. AR overlays instructions and information onto physical machinery, helping leaders and workers perform tasks more efficiently.

Artificial Intelligence (AI) and Machine Learning (ML): AI algorithms enable robots to interpret sensory data and make intelligent decisions. Some robots can adapt and improve their performance through machine learning (Verner et al., 2022).

1.3.2 Applications of Robotics

- *Manufacturing and Industrial Robotics*: Robots are used for repetitive tasks, such as assembling products in manufacturing plants. Furthermore, they perform tasks like welding and moving materials in industrial settings.
- *Healthcare Robotics*: Help surgeons execute precise minimally invasive procedures. Additionally, assist patients with their rehabilitation by providing mobility and exercise support.
- *Autonomous Vehicles*: Robotics and AI are effective for navigation, obstacle avoidance, and decision-making in transportation.
- *Agricultural Robotics*: Autonomous robots are capable of harvesting crops in agriculture. Can be used for precise planting, watering, and fertilizing.
- *Space Exploration*: Used for the exploration of celestial bodies, such as Mars rovers in space exploration missions.
- *Service Robots*: Few domestic robots assist with household chores, such as vacuuming or lawn mowing. AI-driven robots that provide assistance and companionship.
- *Military and Defence*: Unmanned Aerial Vehicles (UAVs) such as drones are used for surveillance and reconnaissance. Remote-controlled robots for handling explosive devices.
- *Robotics in Entertainment Industry*: Robots used in theme parks, interactive exhibits, and performances.
- *Environmental Monitoring*: Robots for Environmental Data Collection: Drones and underwater robots monitor environmental conditions.
- *Construction Robotics*: Robots used in construction for tasks like bricklaying and concrete spraying.

Robotics continues to advance, with ongoing research and development in areas such as soft robotics, swarm robotics, and human-robot collaboration. The integration of robotics with AI and other emerging technologies is driving innovation and expanding the range of applications for robotic systems (Quigley et al., 2009).

2. UTILIZING AUGMENTED REALITY, ROBOTICS, AND VIRTUAL REALITY TOGETHER

2.1 Robot Training: Using VR/AR

Using Virtual Reality (VR) and Augmented Reality (AR) for robot training has become an innovative and effective approach. These technologies offer immersive and interactive experiences, allowing users to simulate and practice real-world scenarios in a safe and controlled environment. Here's how VR and AR are being utilized for robot training:

Table 3. Evolution of robotics in various fields

S.No.	Year	Advancement in the Field
1	1950s-1970s	**Conceptualization:** The field of robotics began with basic manipulators and robotic arms designed for industrial tasks. Early robots were primarily used in manufacturing processes, automating tasks such as welding and assembly lines.
2	1980s-1990s	**Mobile Robots:** The 1980s saw the development of mobile robots capable of navigating and performing tasks in dynamic environments. Research in artificial intelligence (AI) and computer vision contributed to advancements in robotic perception and decision-making.
3	1990s-2000s	**Humanoid Robotics:** Humanoid robots, designed to resemble and mimic human movements, gained attention in the 2000s. ASIMO, developed by Honda, and other humanoid robots showcased advancements in bipedal locomotion and human-robot interaction.
4	2010s	**Collaborative Robots (Cobots):** In the early 2010s, there was a notable increase in the use of collaborative robots designed to work alongside humans. These robots were introduced to enhance efficiency and safety in manufacturing and other industries.
5		**Integration of AI in Robotics:** Throughout the 2010s, the integration of artificial intelligence (AI) into robotics became more prevalent. This enabled robots to perform tasks that required learning, adaptation, and decision-making.
6		**Strategic Planning for Robotics Implementation:** Companies started developing strategic plans for the implementation of robotics in various sectors. Leaders began considering the impact on the workforce, cost-benefit analyses, and long-term strategies for incorporating robotics.
7		**Ethical Considerations and Regulations:** Ethical considerations surrounding robotics gained attention, with discussions about job displacement, privacy concerns, and the need for regulations to ensure responsible use of robotic technologies.
8	2020s	**Human-Robot Collaboration in Various Industries:** Collaborative robots found applications in a broader range of industries, including healthcare, logistics, and service sectors, leading to a shift in leadership strategies to accommodate human-robot collaboration.
9		**Increased Focus on Robotic Process Automation (RPA):** Robotic Process Automation (RPA) gained popularity in business processes, with leaders exploring automation solutions for routine and rule-based tasks to improve efficiency and reduce errors.
10		**Pandemic Accelerating Automation Adoption:** The COVID-19 pandemic accelerated the adoption of automation and robotics in various industries, as organizations sought ways to maintain operations while minimizing human contact.

- *Simulation of Real-World Environments*: VR allows users to immerse themselves in realistic, simulated environments. Robot operators can train in virtual replicas of the actual workspaces where robots will be deployed. AR overlays digital information onto the real-world environment, providing additional context and guidance for operators during training.
- *Hands-On Practice in a Safe Environment*: VR and AR provide a risk-free environment for hands-on practice. Users can manipulate virtual robots and learn how to interact with them without the potential dangers associated with real-world operations.
- *Scenario-Based Training*: VR/AR platforms enable the creation of various training scenarios. Users can practice responding to emergencies, handling malfunctions, and executing different tasks under different conditions. This type of scenario-based training enhances preparedness and helps users develop problem-solving skills.
- *Remote Training and Collaboration*: VR/AR can facilitate remote training sessions, allowing users to connect from different locations. This is particularly useful for training teams dispersed across various geographical locations. Collaborative VR environments enable multiple users to participate in the same training scenario simultaneously.

- *Skill Development and Muscle Memory*: VR allows users to practice specific movements and tasks repeatedly, aiding in the development of muscle memory. This is crucial for tasks that require precision and consistency, such as robot manipulation and control. AR can project visual cues and instructions onto the physical workspace, guiding users in performing tasks accurately.
- *Adaptive Learning Environments*: VR/AR platforms can adapt to the user's skill level and progress. Training programs can be designed to dynamically adjust difficulty based on individual performance, ensuring a personalized learning experience.
- *Reduced Downtime and Costs*: Training in virtual environments reduces the need for downtime on actual robots and minimizes the risk of damage during the learning process. Organizations can save costs associated with physical training setups, such as dedicated training facilities and materials.
- *Data Analytics for Performance Evaluation*: VR/AR training systems often come with built-in analytics tools that track user performance. This data can be used to assess skill development, identify areas for improvement, and tailor training programs accordingly.
- *Continuous Training and Updates*: VR/AR facilitates ongoing training and updates. As technology and robotic systems evolve, users can receive training on new features and functionalities without the need for significant hardware or facility changes.
- *Integration with Actual Hardware*: Some VR/AR training systems can be integrated with physical robots, allowing users to train using the actual robot hardware alongside virtual simulations. This provides a seamless transition from virtual to real-world operations.

In summary, leveraging VR and AR for robot training offers a dynamic and effective means of preparing operators and technicians for the challenges of working with robotic systems in diverse environments.

2.2 Object Recognition: Using VR

Virtual Reality (VR) can be a powerful tool for object recognition training, providing a simulated environment where users can interact with and learn to recognize various objects. Here are ways VR is utilized for object recognition training (Pasek, 2017):

- *Immersive Object Interaction*: VR allows users to interact with virtual objects in a three-dimensional space. This hands-on experience helps trainees develop a better understanding of object characteristics, shapes, and textures.
- *Realistic Simulations*: Virtual environments in VR can be designed to closely mimic real-world scenarios. This realism is beneficial for training users to recognize objects in settings they are likely to encounter in their actual work.
- *Scenario-Based Training*: VR enables the creation of scenario-based training exercises where users must identify and interact with specific objects. These scenarios can range from simple object recognition tasks to more complex challenges, enhancing the user's ability to identify objects in context.
- *Customizable Training Modules*: VR platforms allow for the creation of customizable training modules. Organizations can design specific modules tailored to their industry or use case, ensuring that object recognition training aligns with the specific needs of the trainees.

- *Multisensory Training*: VR can incorporate multisensory experiences, including visual, auditory, and haptic feedback. This enhances the training process by engaging multiple senses, leading to a more immersive and effective learning experience.
- *Progressive Difficulty Levels*: Object recognition training in VR can be designed with progressive difficulty levels. Users start with basic recognition tasks and gradually advance to more complex challenges, helping them build skills progressively.
- *Feedback Mechanisms*: VR platforms can provide immediate feedback on users' object recognition performance. This feedback can include accuracy metrics, response times, and suggestions for improvement, facilitating a more efficient learning process.
- *Integration of Machine Learning*: VR environments can be integrated with machine learning algorithms to create dynamic and adaptive training scenarios. Machine learning models can adjust the difficulty of tasks based on the user's performance, providing a personalized and challenging training experience.
- *Remote Training*: VR allows for remote object recognition training, enabling users to participate from different locations. This is especially useful for organizations with distributed teams or for providing training to individuals who cannot be physically present.
- *Data Collection and Analytics*: VR platforms can collect data on users' interactions and performance during object recognition training. Analytics tools can then be used to assess progress, identify areas for improvement, and tailor training programs accordingly.
- *Cost-Effective Training*: VR-based object recognition training can be a cost-effective solution compared to traditional training methods. It reduces the need for physical objects, training materials, and dedicated training spaces. By leveraging VR for object recognition training, organizations can create dynamic and effective learning experiences that enhance users' abilities to identify and interact with objects in diverse contexts.

Example Scenario: Industrial Object Recognition Training (Verner et al., 2020).

2.2.1 Objective

A manufacturing company wants to train its employees to identify and inspect various components on a production line. The goal is to reduce errors, enhance efficiency, and ensure that employees can quickly recognize and address any issues that may arise during the manufacturing process.

2.2.2 VR Object Recognition Training Implementation

Step 1: Design a virtual environment that replicates the manufacturing floor, complete with machinery, production lines, and different types of components. Populate the virtual space with 3D models of the actual objects used in the manufacturing process.

Step 2: Develop immersive training modules within the VR environment. These modules can focus on specific tasks, such as identifying defective components, recognizing proper assembly, or inspecting for quality control.

Step 3: Implement interactive features that allow trainees to pick up, inspect, and manipulate virtual objects. This hands-on experience helps develop muscle memory and reinforces the visual recognition skills needed on the actual production line.

Step 4: Create scenario-based challenges where trainees must identify and address issues within a simulated production environment. For instance, a module might simulate a defective component on the assembly line, and trainees must quickly identify and address the problem.

Step 5: Design training modules with progressive difficulty levels. Beginners may start with simple object recognition tasks, gradually advancing to more complex challenges as they demonstrate proficiency.

Step 6: Provide real-time feedback within the VR environment. When trainees interact with virtual objects, the system can offer feedback on the correctness of their actions, response times, and the accuracy of object identification.

Step 7: Integrate machine learning algorithms to adapt training scenarios based on the trainee's performance. The system can identify areas where the trainee struggles and dynamically adjust the difficulty level to ensure a personalized learning experience.

Step 8: Enable remote training sessions, allowing employees from different locations to participate in the VR object recognition training. This is particularly beneficial for large organizations with multiple manufacturing facilities.

Step 9: Implement data analytics tools to track trainee performance. Analysing this data helps identify trends, areas for improvement, and the overall effectiveness of the training program.

Step 10: VR-based object recognition training reduces the need for physical training materials and dedicated spaces. It also minimizes the risk of errors during real-world training, ultimately leading to cost savings and increased efficiency on the production floor.

This hypothetical example illustrates how VR can be applied to object recognition training in an industrial setting. It emphasizes the immersive and interactive nature of VR to enhance the learning experience and improve employees' ability to recognize and interact with objects in a real-world context.

3. BENEFITS OF AR AND VR IN ENTERPRISE LEARNING

Augmented Reality (AR) and Virtual Reality (VR) offer a range of benefits when applied to enterprise learning and training.

3.1 Immersive Learning Experience Using AR

AR overlays digital information onto the real-world environment, creating an interactive and contextual learning experience. It integrates digital content with the physical world, making learning more interactive and compelling. This technology facilitates on-the-job training by overlaying instructional information onto physical objects, aiding users in performing tasks with real-time guidance. In addition, it supports remote collaboration by providing real-time guidance and information, fostering knowledge sharing and teamwork. This minimizes the need for physical training materials and equipment, as digital information can be overlaid onto existing tools and environments. Furthermore, contextual information based on the learner's location and task, ensuring that content is relevant and timely is provided. Just-in-time learning, allowing users to access information and instructions as needed, improving efficiency in skill development. Most importantly, it offers real-time safety instructions and warnings, enhancing situational awareness and reducing the risk of accidents.

3.2 Immersive Learning Experience Using VR

VR provides a fully immersive, computer-generated environment that replicates real-world scenarios. This immersion enhances the learning experience, making it more engaging and memorable. Real-world situations shall be simulated, allowing learners to apply knowledge in a practical context. This hands-on approach improves information retention and engagement. It enables realistic simulations for hands-on training in high-risk or complex environments. For example, it's used in aviation, healthcare, and manufacturing for simulated training scenarios. Virtual training sessions and collaboration, especially beneficial when participants are geographically dispersed are simulated. Hence, it reduces the need for physical training setups, travel costs, and the potential risks associated with hands-on training in certain industries. This promotes new employees with immersive experiences that familiarize them with their roles and environments. Used for safety training in high-risk environments, allowing users to practice emergency procedures without actual danger.

In summary, AR and VR bring transformative benefits to enterprise learning, providing immersive, interactive, and efficient training experiences that enhance employee skills, knowledge, and overall performance.

3.3 Robotics for Hands-On Training

Objective 1: Facilitate hands-on experience in a controlled and safe manner using robotic systems.

Implementation: Employ robotic systems that can be manipulated or operated by trainees. These robots can simulate tasks that might be hazardous, allowing trainees to practice without exposure to real risks. For example, robotic arms can be used to simulate welding or handling hazardous materials.

Objective 2: Enable training sessions for individuals in different locations, reducing the need for physical presence.

Implementation: Utilize VR for remote training sessions where participants can join immersive virtual classrooms. Incorporate AR for real-time collaboration, allowing experts to guide trainees remotely during hands-on tasks with the help of AR annotations and instructions.

Objective 3: Tailor training experiences to individual learning styles and skill levels.

Implementation: Integrate adaptive learning algorithms into VR and AR systems to customize training scenarios based on individual progress and performance. This ensures that each trainee receives the appropriate level of challenge and support.

Objective 4: Evaluate trainee performance and identify areas for improvement.

Implementation: Implement data analytics tools that track and analyze trainee interactions within VR and AR environments. Use this data to assess performance, provide feedback, and refine training programs accordingly.

Objective 5: Minimize costs associated with physical training setups, materials, and travel.

Implementation: VR and AR reduce the need for physical training materials and dedicated spaces. This not only saves costs but also allows for the reuse and modification of digital training modules, making updates and adjustments more affordable.

By integrating AR, VR, and robotics, organizations can create a comprehensive and safe training environment that combines realistic simulations, hands-on experience, remote collaboration, and adaptive learning. This approach not only enhances the effectiveness of training but also contributes to cost savings and improved safety for trainees.

4. BENEFITS OF AR AND VR IN TRAINING THE SKILLS OF EMPLOYEES

The major advantage lies is developing soft skills and expertise of the employees and preparing/ training them to face the challenges in work environment. This not only enhances their skills but also the effectiveness in their usage of learning materials also gets improved. They have develop technical skills remotely.

Leveraging Augmented Reality (AR) and Virtual Reality (VR) for employee training and development in technical skills can enhance the learning experience, improve retention, and provide a practical approach to skill-building. Here are some strategies and applications for using AR and VR in employee development:

When implementing AR and VR for technical skills development, it's essential to consider the specific needs of the workforce, align the training content with business goals, and provide ongoing support and resources for employees to maximize the benefits of these immersive technologies.

5. EFFICIENCY OF XR FOR IMPROVING TRAINING EFFICIENCY

Virtual reality (VR), augmented reality (AR), and mixed reality (MR) are all parts of extended reality (XR), which has the potential to greatly increase productivity in a variety of sectors. For practical teaching in industries such manufacturing, healthcare, and aviation, XR can produce lifelike simulations. These speeds up skill development by enabling users to practise tasks in a secure and regulated setting. Immersion prototyping in fields like architecture and product design is made easier by XR. In virtual settings, teams may work together to analyse and improve designs, which eliminates the need for physical prototypes and expedites the design iteration process.

AR overlays step-by-step instructions onto physical objects, guiding technicians through maintenance or repair tasks. This reduces downtime, enhances accuracy, and minimizes the need for extensive training whereas MR combines digital and physical elements, providing a contextual overlay of data onto real-world objects. This is valuable in sectors like data analysis, where users can interact with visualized data in three-dimensional space, improving comprehension and decision-making. XR offers an immersive remote learning experience, enabling participants to engage in training sessions from different locations. This is especially beneficial for organizations with distributed teams, reducing the need for physical travel. This not only saves time but also contributes to cost savings and environmental sustainability. Such platforms can adapt training scenarios based on individual performance, providing customized learning paths for each user. This ensures that training is efficient and tailored to individual needs.

AR can guide users through complex tasks, reducing the likelihood of errors. This is particularly valuable in industries where precision is crucial, such as manufacturing and assembly, while XR technologies bring about numerous efficiency benefits, successful implementation requires careful planning, integration into existing workflows, and consideration of user needs and experiences. Additionally, advancements in hardware, software, and network capabilities will continue to play a significant role in enhancing the efficiency of XR applications across industries.

6. OPPORTUNITIES ABOUND FOR AR, VR IN MANUFACTURING

Augmented Reality (AR) and Virtual Reality (VR) offer numerous opportunities for transformation and improvement within the manufacturing sector. AR can overlay step-by-step maintenance instructions onto physical equipment, guiding technicians through repair processes. This reduces downtime, speeds up repairs, and minimizes the need for extensive training. The technology can guide workers through assembly line processes, reducing errors and increasing efficiency. Digital overlays provide real-time information about the assembly steps, minimizing the need for printed manuals. It can be used for quality control by overlaying digital information onto physical products. This allows inspectors to identify defects, measure dimensions, and ensure that products meet quality standards. AR applications can optimize logistics and supply chain processes by providing real-time information about inventory, shipments, and warehouse operations. This enhances overall efficiency and reduces errors. Aid for ergonomic analysis to ensure that workstations are designed for optimal comfort and safety. Digital overlays can highlight potential ergonomic issues and suggest improvements.

On the other hand, VR can create realistic simulations for training new employees in various scenarios, from equipment operation to safety protocols. This accelerates the onboarding process and ensures that employees are well-prepared for their roles. Hence, it allows designers and engineers to visualize and interact with 3D models in a virtual space. This accelerates the product design cycle, enabling quicker iterations and reducing the need for physical prototypes. VR can be used to create immersive dashboards for monitoring the status of equipment and machinery. This facilitates predictive maintenance by identifying potential issues before they lead to failures. The teams are enabled to collaborate on design and engineering projects in a shared virtual space, even if they are geographically dispersed. This enhances communication and accelerates project timelines.

7. DIGITAL TWIN ADOPTION

Digital twin adoption has been growing across various industries as organizations recognize the potential benefits of this technology. A digital twin is a virtual representation of a physical object, system, or process, and it can provide valuable insights, enhance decision-making, and optimize operations.

In manufacturing, digital twins are used to create virtual replicas of physical production systems. This helps in monitoring equipment performance, optimizing production processes, and predicting maintenance needs. Digital twins are often integrated with the Internet of Things (IoT) devices to collect real-time data from physical assets. This connectivity allows organizations to monitor and analyze the performance of assets and systems in real-time. It is used in urban planning to create virtual models of entire cities. This allows city planners to simulate the impact of infrastructure changes, optimize transportation systems, and enhance overall city management. In the automotive sector, digital twins are employed to simulate the design and performance of vehicles. This includes testing various components virtually, optimizing fuel efficiency, and predicting maintenance needs. This technology is utilized to create virtual representations of supply chain processes. This helps in optimizing logistics, predicting demand, and identifying areas for improvement in the supply chain.

8. GENERATIVE AI

A family of artificial intelligence systems known as "generative AI" is able to produce fresh outputs, data, or content that can mimic and, in certain situations, even be mistaken for human-generated content. These systems can create original material because they can recognise and duplicate patterns in data using methods like neural networks. Applications for generative AI can be found in many different fields, such as text synthesis, picture generation, and even music and other creative work production.

Description: GANs are a type of generative AI architecture introduced by Ian Goodfellow and his colleagues. GANs consist of two neural networks, a generator, and a discriminator, which are trained simultaneously through adversarial training.

Application: GANs have been widely used for image generation, style transfer, and the creation of realistic synthetic data for training other AI models.

GPT (Generative Pre-trained Transformer) from OpenAI is one of the models made specifically for natural language processing applications. Given a prompt, GPT models are able to produce text that is both coherent and contextually appropriate. GPT has uses in chatbots, content production, language translation, and even snippet generation. By producing more instances that closely resemble the original data, generative models can be used to enhance datasets. This is especially helpful when there is a limited amount of dataset available for training machine learning models. enhanced natural language processing and image recognition model training.

9. METAVERSE

When virtual and physical reality intersect, a collective virtual shared environment known as the "metaverse" is produced. It is an area where users can communicate with other users and a computer-generated world through avatars or digital personalities. A lot of attention has been paid to the idea of the metaverse, which is frequently linked to developments in immersive technologies like augmented reality (AR) and virtual reality (VR). Immersive, three-dimensional virtual worlds that enable real-time user interaction and engagement with digital material define the metaverse. The metaverse is ideally seen as a networked environment in which users are able to switch between various virtual environments and platforms with ease. One of the most important ideas in building a cohesive metaverse experience is interoperability. Avatars and digital identities are commonly used to represent users in the metaverse. Users can alter these avatars to better represent their identities and preferences. One essential component of the metaverse is social interaction. Similar to exchanges in real life, users can converse, work together, and socialise with others in a virtual environment. Advanced technologies like blockchain, augmented reality, virtual reality, and artificial intelligence are all necessary for the metaverse to function. Together, these technologies produce a smooth and engaging user interface. Some see the metaverse as a decentralised network that makes use of blockchain technology for transparent transactions, ownership verification, and security particularly when it comes to virtual assets. The creation of the metaverse is attracting the attention of major IT companies more and more. Companies like Facebook (now Meta), Google, and others are investing in technologies and platforms that contribute to the evolution of the metaverse.

10. CONCLUSION

The potential for revolutionising conventional processes, increasing productivity, cutting costs, and improving efficiency exists when AR and VR technologies are integrated into production. These prospects will probably grow as technology develops, creating new potential for innovation in the manufacturing sector. Cloud-based solutions are being adopted by numerous organisations in order to implement and manage digital twins. Cloud computing facilitates scalability, stakeholder engagement, and simple access to data. The adoption of digital twins is driven by the need for improved efficiency, reduced downtime, predictive analytics, and enhanced decision-making capabilities across diverse industries. Digital twin applications are expected to grow as technology develops, presenting fresh chances for creativity and efficiency. Researchers are looking for approaches to make generative AI models more resilient, interpretable, and ethically sound as the field develops. Like with any cutting-edge technology, generative AI must be used responsibly and ethically to avoid abuse and unexpected effects. A contentious use of generative AI called "deepfake" produces realistic-looking but phoney content, frequently by manipulating photos or videos to facilitate online meetings. The emergence of the metaverse presents a number of difficulties, such as concerns about digital rights, privacy, security, and the possibility of monopolistic control over virtual environments.

REFERENCES

Aggarwal, R., & Singhal, A. (2019). Augmented Reality and its effect on our life. *2019 9th International Conference on Cloud Computing, Data Science & Engineering (Confluence)*, 510-515. 10.1109/CONFLUENCE.2019.8776989

Altmeyer, K., Kapp, S., Thees, M., Malone, S., Kuhn, J., & Brünken, R. (2020). The use of augmented reality to foster conceptual knowledge acquisition in STEM laboratory courses—Theoretical background and empirical results. *British Journal of Educational Technology, 51*(3), 611–628. doi:10.1111/bjet.12900

Hoenig, W., Milanes, C., Scaria, L., Phan, T., Bolas, M., & Ayanian, N. (2015). Mixed reality for robotics. *Proceedings of the IEEE/RSJ International Conference on Intelligent Robots and Systems (IROS)*.

Ozdemir, M., Sahin, C., Arcagok, S., & Demir, M.K. (2018). The effect of augmented reality applications in the learning process: A meta-analysis study. Eurasian. *The Journal of Educational Research, 18*, 165–186.

Pasek, Z. J. (2017). Helping engineers develop and exercise creative muscles. *Proceedings of the Canadian Engineering Education Association Conference (CEEA)*.

Quigley, M., Conley, K., Gerkey, B., Faust, J., Foote, T., & Leibs, J. (2009). An open-source robot operating system. *Proceedings of the ICRA Workshop on Open-Source Software*.

Song, P., Yu, H., & Winkler, S. (2009). Vision-based 3D finger interactions for mixed reality games with physics simulation. *Proceedings of the ACM SIGGRAPH International Conference on Virtual Reality Continuum and Its Applications in Industry*. 10.20870/IJVR.2009.8.2.2717

Thees, M., Kapp, S., Strzys, M. P., Beil, F., Lukowicz, P., & Kuhn, J. (2020). Effects of augmented reality on learning and cognitive load in university physics laboratory courses. *Computers in Human Behavior, 108*, 106316. doi:10.1016/j.chb.2020.106316

Verner, I., Cuperman, D., Gamer, S., & Polishuk, A. (2020). Exploring affordances of robot manipulators in an introductory engineering course. *International Journal of Engineering Education, 36*, 1691–1707.

Verner, I., Cuperman, D., & Polishuk, A. (2022). Inservice teachers explore RACECAR MN in physical and augmented environments. *Proceedings of the 2022 17th Annual System of Systems Engineering Conference (SOSE),* 228–230. 10.1109/SOSE55472.2022.9812639

Chapter 10
Blockchain and Its Role in Leadership

Nivodhini M. K.
https://orcid.org/0000-0003-1172-5894
KSR College of Engineering, India

Vadivel S.
KSR College of Engineering, India

Vasuki P.
https://orcid.org/0000-0002-8316-4291
KSR College of Engineering, India

Banupriya S.
KSR College of Engineering, India

ABSTRACT

Blockchain technology revolutionizes leadership through transparency, accountability, and decentralization. By providing an immutable ledger, it enhances transparency, fostering trust. Its decentralized nature ensures accountability, empowering individuals and challenging traditional hierarchies. Secure data management safeguards sensitive information. Automation streamlines processes, fostering collaboration. Tokenization creates incentive mechanisms. Overall, blockchain empowers leaders to navigate modern complexities with transparent, accountable, and decentralized approaches.

1. TRANSPARENCY IN LEADERSHIP THROUGH BLOCKCHAIN

1.1 Transparent Ledger Technology

Transparent Ledger Technology (TLT) refers to a class of distributed ledger technologies (DLTs) designed to provide transparency and accountability in recording and managing transactions. While blockchain

DOI: 10.4018/979-8-3693-1946-8.ch010

is the most well-known example of TLT, other variants exist, each tailored to specific use cases and requirements (Agnihotri, 2021).

TLT operates on the principle of decentralization, where transactions are recorded and verified across a network of nodes, eliminating the need for a central authority. The transparency of TLT stems from the publicly accessible ledger, where all transactions are recorded in a chronological and immutable fashion (Shukla et al., 2023). Participants in the network can view transaction data, enhancing trust and accountability among stakeholders.

Key features of Transparent Ledger Technology include:

1. Decentralization: TLT operates on a decentralized network of nodes, ensuring that no single entity has control over the ledger. This decentralization enhances the resilience and security of the network, as there is no central point of failure.
2. Transparency: Transactions recorded on the ledger are visible to all participants in the network. This transparency fosters trust among stakeholders, as transaction data is easily verifiable and cannot be altered without consensus from the majority of the network.
3. Immutability: Once recorded, transactions on the ledger cannot be altered or tampered with. This immutability is achieved through cryptographic hashing and consensus mechanisms, ensuring the integrity of the data stored on the ledger (Tapscott & Tapscott, 2016).
4. Security: TLT employs cryptographic techniques to secure transaction data and ensure the confidentiality and integrity of transactions. Public-private key pairs, digital signatures, and consensus algorithms are used to prevent unauthorized access and fraudulent activities.

Applications of Transparent Ledger Technology span various industries and use cases:

1. Financial Services: TLT, particularly blockchain, is revolutionizing the financial sector by enabling secure and transparent transactions, reducing settlement times, and minimizing the risk of fraud and errors.
2. Supply Chain Management: TLT enhances transparency and traceability in supply chains, enabling stakeholders to track the movement and provenance of goods, verify authenticity, and ensure compliance with regulations.
3. Healthcare: In healthcare, TLT facilitates secure and interoperable sharing of electronic health records (EHRs), ensuring patient privacy, consent, and data integrity.
4. Governance: Transparent Ledger Technology can be used in government applications, such as voting systems, identity management, and land registries, to enhance transparency, prevent fraud, and increase trust in public institutions.

Despite its benefits, challenges remain in the widespread adoption of Transparent Ledger Technology (Antony & Kizgin, 2018). Scalability limitations, interoperability issues, regulatory uncertainty, and concerns about energy consumption are among the key challenges that need to be addressed.

In conclusion, Transparent Ledger Technology, exemplified by blockchain and other distributed ledger technologies, offers a paradigm shift in how transactions are recorded, verified, and managed. Its transparency, decentralization, and immutability make it a powerful tool for fostering trust, accountability, and efficiency across various sectors (Groenfeldt, 2017). As the technology continues to evolve and mature, its transformative potential is expected to drive further innovation and disruption in the digital economy.

1.2 Verification and Trust

Verification and trust are foundational elements in any transactional system, and Transparent Ledger Technology (TLT), such as blockchain, plays a crucial role in enhancing both.

1. **Verification**:
    - TLT enables verification through decentralized consensus mechanisms. In blockchain, for instance, transactions are verified by multiple nodes in the network through consensus algorithms like proof-of-work (PoW) or proof-of-stake (PoS). This decentralized verification ensures that transactions are valid and consistent across the network.
    - Cryptographic techniques, such as digital signatures and hash functions, are employed to verify the authenticity and integrity of transactions. Digital signatures provide proof of ownership and authorization, while hash functions ensure that data hasn't been altered.
    - Transparent Ledger Technology also facilitates transparent and auditable record-keeping, allowing participants to verify transaction history and authenticity (Iansiti & Lakhani, 2017). The immutable nature of TLT ensures that once a transaction is recorded, it cannot be altered or deleted, providing a reliable audit trail.
2. **Trust**:
    - TLT fosters trust among participants by providing transparency, accountability, and security. The transparent nature of the ledger allows all parties to access and verify transaction data, reducing the need for trust in intermediaries.
    - Immutability ensures that transaction records are tamper-proof, enhancing trust in the integrity of the data. Participants can trust that once a transaction is recorded on the ledger, it cannot be manipulated or reversed.
    - Decentralization plays a key role in building trust by removing the need for a central authority or intermediary. Instead, trust is distributed across the network, with transactions validated by consensus among multiple nodes.
    - Smart contracts, a feature of some TLT platforms like Ethereum, further enhance trust by automating and enforcing the terms of agreements without the need for intermediaries. Smart contracts execute automatically when predefined conditions are met, eliminating the potential for fraud or manipulation.

1.3 Impact on Stakeholder Relations

The adoption of Transparent Ledger Technology (TLT), such as blockchain, can have a profound impact on stakeholder relations across various industries. Here's how TLT can influence relations with stakeholders:

1. Increased Trust and Transparency:
    - TLT fosters greater trust and transparency among stakeholders by providing a shared, immutable ledger where transaction records are securely stored and transparently accessible.
    - Stakeholders can verify the authenticity and integrity of transactions independently, reducing the need to rely on intermediaries or centralized authorities for trust.
2. Improved Accountability:

- The transparent and immutable nature of TLT ensures that transactions cannot be altered or deleted once recorded on the ledger. This enhances accountability among stakeholders, as all parties are held to a consistent standard of transparency and integrity.
- Leaders and organizations can be held accountable for their actions and decisions, as transaction records are readily accessible and auditable by stakeholders.

3. Streamlined Processes:
   - TLT can streamline processes and reduce inefficiencies by automating tasks through smart contracts. These self-executing contracts automatically enforce predefined terms and conditions, reducing the need for manual intervention and streamlining transactions.
   - Stakeholders benefit from faster and more efficient processes, leading to improved satisfaction and stronger relationships with organizations that leverage TLT.

4. Enhanced Data Security and Privacy:
   - TLT employs cryptographic techniques to secure transaction data and protect the privacy of stakeholders. Public-private key pairs and encryption algorithms ensure that sensitive information remains confidential and inaccessible to unauthorized parties.
   - Stakeholders can trust that their data is securely stored and transmitted within TLT platforms, leading to increased confidence in the integrity of transactions and interactions.

5. Empowerment of Stakeholders:
   - TLT decentralizes trust and authority, empowering stakeholders to participate directly in transactions and decision-making processes without the need for intermediaries.
   - Through decentralized governance models and consensus mechanisms, stakeholders have a voice in shaping the rules and protocols governing TLT platforms, leading to more inclusive and democratic systems of governance.

6. Facilitation of Collaboration:
   - TLT facilitates collaboration among stakeholders by providing a shared platform for transparent and secure transactions and data sharing.
   - Organizations can collaborate more effectively with suppliers, partners, and customers, leading to improved communication, coordination, and innovation across value chains.

2. ACCOUNTABILITY MECHANISMS IN BLOCKCHAIN LEADERSHIP

2.1 Immutable Records and Traceability

The implementation of Transparent Ledger Technology (TLT), notably blockchain, introduces immutable records and enhanced traceability, profoundly impacting various industries and stakeholder relations (Iansiti & Lakhani, 2017):

1. Immutable Records:
   - TLT, such as blockchain, ensures that once data is recorded on the ledger, it cannot be altered or deleted. This immutability is achieved through cryptographic hashing and consensus mechanisms, making the records tamper-proof and verifiable.

- Immutable records instil trust and confidence among stakeholders as they can rely on the integrity and accuracy of the data stored on the ledger. This transparency fosters accountability and reduces the risk of fraud or manipulation.
2. Enhanced Traceability:
    - TLT enables enhanced traceability by providing a transparent and auditable record of transactions or events. Participants can track the provenance, movement, and ownership of assets or goods throughout the supply chain.
    - In industries like food and pharmaceuticals, blockchain-based traceability solutions enable stakeholders to trace the origin of products, verify authenticity, and ensure compliance with regulatory standards. This transparency enhances consumer confidence and safety.
    - Traceability also extends to other sectors such as finance, where blockchain facilitates real-time tracking of financial transactions, improving auditability and compliance with regulatory requirements.
3. Supply Chain Management:
    - TLT revolutionizes supply chain management by enhancing transparency and traceability across the entire value chain. Participants can monitor the flow of goods, from raw materials to the end consumer, ensuring ethical sourcing, quality control, and regulatory compliance.
    - Blockchain-based supply chain platforms provide stakeholders with real-time visibility into inventory levels, shipment status, and product authenticity. This transparency reduces the risk of counterfeiting, theft, and supply chain disruptions.
4. Provenance and Authenticity:
    - TLT enables the verification of product provenance and authenticity by recording crucial information such as origin, production methods, and ownership transfers on the blockchain.
    - Consumers can scan product QR codes or use mobile apps to access detailed information about the product's journey, including sourcing, manufacturing, and distribution processes. This transparency builds trust and loyalty among consumers, particularly in industries like fashion, luxury goods, and agriculture.
5. Regulatory Compliance:
    - Immutable records and enhanced traceability facilitate regulatory compliance by providing auditable evidence of transactions and activities. Organizations can demonstrate compliance with industry regulations, standards, and certifications by leveraging blockchain-based solutions.
    - Blockchain's transparency and immutability help organizations streamline compliance processes, reduce audit costs, and mitigate the risk of non-compliance penalties or fines.

2.2 Smart Contracts and Automated Accountability

Smart contracts, enabled by Transparent Ledger Technology (TLT) such as blockchain, revolutionize accountability by automating and enforcing contractual agreements in a transparent and tamper-proof manner. Here's how smart contracts facilitate automated accountability:

1. **Automated Execution**:

- Smart contracts are self-executing contracts with predefined terms and conditions encoded into the blockchain. Once the conditions specified in the contract are met, the contract automatically executes without the need for intermediaries or manual intervention.
- This automated execution ensures that contractual obligations are fulfilled promptly and accurately, reducing the risk of delays, disputes, or human error.

2. **Transparency and Immutability**:
   - Smart contracts operate on a transparent and immutable ledger, providing stakeholders with visibility into the contract's execution and outcomes.
   - Transaction records associated with smart contracts are stored on the blockchain, ensuring that they cannot be altered or tampered with. This transparency and immutability enhance trust and accountability among parties involved in the contract.

3. **Decentralized Validation**:
   - Smart contracts are validated and executed by nodes in the blockchain network through consensus mechanisms like Proof-of-Work (PoW) or Proof-of-Stake (PoS).
   - Decentralized validation ensures that smart contracts are executed according to predefined rules and that the outcomes are verifiable by all participants in the network.

4. **Conditional Logic**:
   - Smart contracts can incorporate conditional logic and trigger actions based on predefined conditions or events. For example, a smart contract governing a supply chain transaction may release payment to a supplier automatically upon the successful delivery of goods.
   - Conditional logic allows for the automation of complex business processes, reducing the need for manual oversight and intervention.

5. **Immutable Audit Trail**:
   - Smart contracts generate an immutable audit trail of transactions and contract executions, providing a transparent record of all interactions between parties.
   - This audit trail serves as evidence of accountability, allowing stakeholders to verify the performance and compliance of contractual obligations over time.

6. **Enhanced Efficiency and Cost Savings**:
   - By automating contract execution and enforcement, smart contracts streamline business processes, reduce administrative overhead, and eliminate the need for intermediaries.
   - This leads to cost savings, improved operational efficiency, and faster transaction settlement times, benefiting all parties involved in the contract.

2.3 Impact on Decision-Making Processes

The integration of Transparent Ledger Technology (TLT) such as blockchain, particularly with the implementation of smart contracts, can significantly impact decision-making processes across industries (Narayanan, Bonneau, Felten, Miller, & Goldfeder, 2016). Here's how:

1. **Data-driven Decision Making**:
   - TLT provides a transparent and immutable ledger where transactional data is securely stored. This data can be analyzed to derive insights and inform decision-making processes.
   - Decision makers can access real-time, trustworthy data stored on the blockchain, enabling more informed and data-driven decisions.

2. **Streamlined Processes**:
    - Smart contracts automate and streamline various processes by executing predefined conditions without the need for manual intervention. This automation reduces delays and inefficiencies in decision-making.
    - For example, in supply chain management, smart contracts can automatically trigger payments upon the successful delivery of goods, eliminating the need for manual approval processes.
3. **Enhanced Trust and Accountability**:
    - TLT fosters trust and accountability by providing transparency and immutability in transaction records. Decision makers can trust the integrity of the data stored on the blockchain, reducing the risk of errors or fraud.
    - Smart contracts ensure accountability by automatically enforcing contractual obligations based on predefined conditions. This reduces the reliance on intermediaries and minimizes the potential for disputes or discrepancies.
4. **Decentralized Decision Making**:
    - TLT, with its decentralized architecture, enables more decentralized decision-making processes. Instead of relying on a central authority, decisions can be made collaboratively among network participants.
    - Decentralized autonomous organizations (DAOs) leverage blockchain and smart contracts to facilitate decentralized decision making, allowing stakeholders to vote on proposals and initiatives without the need for intermediaries.
5. **Improved Compliance and Auditability**:
    - Smart contracts can encode regulatory requirements and compliance standards into their execution logic. This ensures that decisions made through smart contracts adhere to legal and regulatory frameworks.
    - The transparent and immutable nature of blockchain enables auditors and regulators to verify compliance with regulations by accessing transaction records stored on the blockchain.
6. **Facilitation of Innovation**:
    - TLT can facilitate innovation by providing a secure and transparent platform for experimenting with new business models and processes. Smart contracts enable the automation of innovative processes, accelerating the pace of innovation.
    - Organizations can leverage blockchain and smart contracts to explore new revenue streams, improve customer experiences, and drive competitive advantage through innovation.

3. DECENTRALIZATION AND DISTRIBUTED LEADERSHIP

3.1 Decentralized Networks and Consensus Mechanisms

Decentralized networks and consensus mechanisms are foundational components of Transparent Ledger Technology (TLT), such as blockchain (Swan, 2015). They play a crucial role in ensuring the security, reliability, and integrity of transactions recorded on the ledger. Here's how decentralized networks and consensus mechanisms impact TLT:

1. **Decentralized Networks**:
    - In a decentralized network, there is no single point of control or authority. Instead, data is distributed across multiple nodes or participants in the network.
    - Decentralization enhances the resilience and security of the network, as there is no central point of failure. Even if some nodes fail or are compromised, the network as a whole remains operational.
    - Decentralized networks promote trust and transparency by allowing participants to verify transaction data independently and ensuring that no single entity can manipulate or control the network.
2. **Consensus Mechanisms**:
    - Consensus mechanisms are protocols used to achieve agreement among network participants on the validity of transactions and the state of the ledger.
    - Proof-of-Work (PoW) is one of the most well-known consensus mechanisms, where participants (miners) compete to solve complex mathematical puzzles to validate transactions and add new blocks to the blockchain. PoW is highly secure but consumes significant computational resources.
    - Proof-of-Stake (PoS) is another consensus mechanism where validators are selected to validate transactions based on the amount of cryptocurrency they hold and are willing to "stake" as collateral (Casey & Vigna, 2018). PoS is more energy-efficient than PoW but still ensures network security.
    - Other consensus mechanisms include Delegated Proof-of-Stake (DPoS), Practical Byzantine Fault Tolerance (PBFT), and Directed Acyclic Graphs (DAGs), each with its own advantages and trade-offs.
3. **Impact on TLT**:
    - Decentralized networks and consensus mechanisms ensure the integrity and security of transactions recorded on the ledger. By distributing data across multiple nodes and requiring consensus among participants, TLT mitigates the risk of fraud, manipulation, and unauthorized access.
    - These mechanisms enable TLT platforms like blockchain to operate without the need for intermediaries or central authorities, reducing transaction costs, increasing efficiency, and fostering trust among participants.
    - Decentralized networks and consensus mechanisms also enable censorship-resistant systems where transactions cannot be censored or blocked by any single entity, ensuring freedom and openness in the network.

3.2 Empowerment of Individuals and Teams

Decentralized networks and consensus mechanisms, inherent in Transparent Ledger Technology (TLT) like blockchain, empower individuals and teams in various ways:

1. **Inclusive Participation**:
    - Decentralized networks enable anyone to participate as a node in the network, allowing individuals and teams to contribute to the validation and maintenance of the ledger.

- By removing barriers to entry, TLT platforms promote inclusivity and democratize access to financial and technological resources, empowering individuals from diverse backgrounds to engage and collaborate in the network.
2. **Autonomy and Self-Governance**:
    - TLT platforms facilitate self-governance through decentralized decision-making mechanisms such as consensus algorithms and governance protocols (Nakamoto, 2008).
    - Individuals and teams can propose and vote on changes to the network's rules, protocols, and governance structures, giving them a voice in shaping the direction and policies of the platform.
3. **Economic Empowerment**:
    - Decentralized networks offer economic opportunities for individuals and teams through various mechanisms such as mining, staking, and participating in decentralized finance (DeFi) applications.
    - Individuals can earn rewards or fees by contributing their computational power, financial assets, or expertise to the network, thereby creating new avenues for income generation and wealth creation.
4. **Transparency and Accountability**:
    - TLT platforms promote transparency and accountability by providing a publicly accessible and immutable ledger of transactions.
    - Individuals and teams can verify the integrity and authenticity of transactions, ensuring trust and accountability in their interactions with other participants in the network.
5. **Innovation and Collaboration**:
    - Decentralized networks foster innovation and collaboration by providing a permissionless and open-source environment for building and deploying decentralized applications (DApps).
    - Individuals and teams can develop innovative solutions, smart contracts, and DApps to address various challenges and opportunities, leveraging the capabilities of blockchain and TLT platforms.
6. **Resilience and Security**:
    - Decentralized networks are inherently resilient and secure, as they distribute data and computational resources across multiple nodes.
    - Individuals and teams can trust the robustness and reliability of the network, knowing that it is resistant to censorship, manipulation, and single points of failure.
7. **Ownership and Control**:
    - TLT platforms empower individuals and teams with ownership and control over their digital assets, identities, and interactions.
    - Through cryptographic keys and smart contracts, individuals retain full ownership and control over their data and assets, eliminating the need for intermediaries or third-party custodians.

3.3 Implications for Organizational Structures

The integration of Transparent Ledger Technology (TLT) such as blockchain can have significant implications for organizational structures, challenging traditional hierarchies and fostering more decentralized, transparent, and adaptive models. Here are several implications (Buterin, 2014):

1. **Decentralization of Authority**:
   - TLT enables decentralized decision-making by distributing control and authority across the network rather than concentrating it within a central entity.
   - Traditional top-down hierarchical structures may give way to more decentralized governance models, where decision-making power is distributed among network participants based on consensus mechanisms.
2. **Flatter Organizational Hierarchies**:
   - Decentralization facilitated by TLT can lead to flatter organizational hierarchies, with fewer layers of management and more direct communication channels between individuals and teams.
   - Flatter hierarchies promote agility, flexibility, and responsiveness to change, enabling organizations to adapt more quickly to evolving market conditions and customer needs.
3. **Collaborative Ecosystems**:
   - TLT platforms foster collaborative ecosystems where participants can engage directly with each other, bypassing traditional intermediaries and fostering peer-to-peer interactions.
   - Organizations may form decentralized networks or consortia to collaborate on shared goals, projects, or initiatives, leveraging the capabilities of blockchain to coordinate and incentivize contributions.
4. **Transparency and Accountability**:
   - TLT promotes transparency and accountability by providing a publicly accessible and immutable ledger of transactions and interactions.
   - Organizations adopting TLT may prioritize transparency in their operations, ensuring that stakeholders have visibility into decision-making processes, resource allocation, and performance metrics.
5. **Smart Contract Automation**:
   - Smart contracts, enabled by TLT, automate and enforce predefined agreements and business processes without the need for intermediaries.
   - This automation streamlines organizational workflows, reduces administrative overhead, and increases operational efficiency by eliminating manual tasks and reducing the risk of errors or disputes.
6. **Empowerment of Individuals and Teams**:
   - TLT empowers individuals and teams by providing economic opportunities, autonomy, and ownership over their digital assets and interactions.
   - Organizations may adopt more decentralized structures that empower employees to take ownership of their work, contribute to decision-making processes, and participate in value creation within the organization.
7. **Regulatory and Compliance Challenges**:
   - While TLT offers numerous benefits, organizations must navigate regulatory and compliance challenges associated with decentralized networks and digital assets (Swan, 2015).
   - Regulatory uncertainty, jurisdictional issues, and compliance requirements may necessitate ongoing dialogue with regulators and adaptation of organizational structures to ensure compliance with evolving legal frameworks.

4. SECURE DATA MANAGEMENT IN BLOCKCHAIN LEADERSHIP

4.1 Cryptographic Techniques and Data Security

Cryptographic techniques play a crucial role in ensuring data security within Transparent Ledger Technology (TLT) systems like blockchain. Here's how these techniques are employed and their implications for data security:

1. **Public-Private Key Encryption**:
   - Public-private key encryption is fundamental to TLT platforms. Each participant has a unique pair of cryptographic keys: a public key, which is shared openly, and a private key, which is kept secret.
   - Public keys are used to encrypt data or transactions, while private keys are used to decrypt them. This asymmetric encryption ensures that only the intended recipient can decrypt and access the data, providing confidentiality and privacy.
2. **Digital Signatures**:
   - Digital signatures are cryptographic techniques used to verify the authenticity and integrity of messages or transactions. They are created by encrypting a message or transaction with the sender's private key.
   - Recipients can verify the digital signature using the sender's public key, ensuring that the message or transaction was indeed sent by the claimed sender and that it has not been tampered with during transit.
3. **Hash Functions**:
   - Hash functions are algorithms that convert input data into a fixed-size string of characters, known as a hash value or digest. Hash functions are used extensively in TLT for data integrity verification.
   - In blockchain, each block contains a cryptographic hash of the previous block's header, forming a chain of blocks linked together cryptographically. Any alteration to the data in a block would change its hash value, thereby breaking the chain and indicating tampering.
4. **Consensus Mechanisms**:
   - Consensus mechanisms, such as Proof of Work (PoW) or Proof of Stake (PoS), leverage cryptographic techniques to secure the network and validate transactions.
   - PoW requires participants (miners) to solve complex mathematical puzzles, which involves cryptographic hashing, to validate transactions and add new blocks to the blockchain. PoS relies on participants staking their cryptocurrency holdings as collateral to validate transactions, ensuring network security.
5. **Immutability**:
   - TLT platforms like blockchain achieve immutability through cryptographic techniques. Once data is recorded on the ledger and cryptographically hashed, it becomes virtually impossible to alter or tamper with.
   - The immutability of blockchain ensures that transaction records are secure, transparent, and resistant to unauthorized modifications, enhancing the integrity and trustworthiness of the data stored on the ledger.

Implications for Data Security:

- Cryptographic techniques employed within TLT platforms ensure confidentiality, integrity, and authenticity of data, protecting it from unauthorized access, tampering, or forgery.
- By leveraging asymmetric encryption, digital signatures, hash functions, and consensus mechanisms, TLT platforms provide a secure and trusted environment for conducting transactions and storing sensitive information.
- The immutability of blockchain, achieved through cryptographic hashing, ensures that once data is recorded on the ledger, it cannot be altered or deleted, providing a reliable audit trail and mitigating the risk of fraud or data manipulation.
- Organizations and users can rely on TLT platforms to safeguard their data and transactions, enhancing trust, security, and compliance with regulatory requirements in the digital economy.

4.2 Privacy and Confidentiality Considerations

Privacy and confidentiality considerations are paramount in Transparent Ledger Technology (TLT) systems like blockchain, especially in scenarios where sensitive data is involved. Here are key aspects and considerations regarding privacy and confidentiality in TLT (Antonopoulos, 2014):

1. **Pseudonymity vs. Anonymity**:
    - TLT platforms typically offer pseudonymity, where users are represented by cryptographic addresses rather than real-world identities. While transactions are recorded publicly on the ledger, the identities behind these addresses are not readily identifiable without additional information.
    - However, achieving full anonymity on public blockchains can be challenging, as transaction patterns and metadata may be analyzed to infer user identities. Techniques like coin mixing and zero-knowledge proofs can enhance privacy by obfuscating transaction trails.
2. **Off-Chain Data Storage**:
    - While blockchain transactions are immutable and transparent, not all data needs to be stored on-chain. Off-chain storage solutions, such as state channels or sidechains, allow for the storage of sensitive or large data off the main blockchain.
    - By segregating sensitive data off-chain, organizations can maintain privacy and confidentiality while still leveraging the security and integrity of the blockchain for transaction validation and auditability.
3. **Encryption Techniques**:
    - Encryption techniques, such as symmetric and asymmetric encryption, are employed to protect sensitive data stored on the blockchain or transmitted over the network.
    - Private data can be encrypted before being stored on-chain, ensuring that only authorized parties with the decryption keys can access the information. This helps preserve confidentiality while still allowing for transparency and auditability of transactions.
4. **Permissioned Blockchains**:
    - In permissioned or private blockchain networks, access to the ledger and participation in consensus mechanisms are restricted to authorized participants. This provides greater control over data privacy and confidentiality compared to public blockchains.

Blockchain and Its Role in Leadership

- Permissioned blockchains are often used in enterprise settings where strict regulatory requirements or confidentiality concerns necessitate greater control over data access and sharing.
5. **Regulatory Compliance**:
    - Compliance with privacy regulations, such as GDPR (General Data Protection Regulation) in the European Union or HIPAA (Health Insurance Portability and Accountability Act) in the United States, is essential when handling personal or sensitive data on TLT platforms.
    - Organizations must ensure that their use of TLT complies with relevant privacy laws and regulations, including data protection, consent requirements, and the right to erasure.
6. **Selective Disclosure and Zero-Knowledge Proofs**:
    - Selective disclosure mechanisms and zero-knowledge proofs allow users to selectively reveal specific information without disclosing the underlying data. This enables privacy-preserving transactions and interactions on TLT platforms.
    - Zero-knowledge proofs enable parties to prove the validity of a statement without revealing any additional information, ensuring privacy while still allowing for verification of transaction authenticity.

4.3 Compliance and Regulatory Challenges

Compliance and regulatory challenges are significant considerations in the adoption and implementation of Transparent Ledger Technology (TLT) systems like blockchain. Here are key challenges organizations may face (Narayanan, Bonneau, Felten, Miller, & Goldfeder, 2016):

1. **Data Privacy Regulations**:
    - Compliance with data privacy regulations, such as the General Data Protection Regulation (GDPR) in the European Union, presents a significant challenge for organizations leveraging blockchain.
    - GDPR mandates strict requirements for the processing and transfer of personal data, including the right to erasure (right to be forgotten), data minimization, purpose limitation, and data subject consent.
    - Organizations must ensure that their use of blockchain complies with GDPR requirements, particularly concerning the storage and processing of personal data on the ledger.
2. **Data Localization and Sovereignty**:
    - Some jurisdictions have data localization requirements that mandate certain data to be stored within the country's borders. This can be challenging for blockchain systems that operate on a global, decentralized network.
    - Compliance with data sovereignty regulations requires careful consideration of where data is stored, processed, and transmitted within TLT platforms to ensure adherence to local laws and regulations.
3. **Financial Regulations**:
    - Financial transactions recorded on blockchain may be subject to various financial regulations, including anti-money laundering (AML), know your customer (KYC), and counter-terrorism financing (CTF) regulations.

- Compliance with financial regulations presents challenges related to identity verification, transaction monitoring, reporting requirements, and enforcement of legal obligations within decentralized networks.
4. **Legal and Jurisdictional Uncertainty**:
    - The decentralized and cross-border nature of blockchain poses challenges for determining legal jurisdiction and applicable laws in case of disputes or regulatory enforcement actions.
    - Organizations operating blockchain systems may face uncertainty regarding which regulatory frameworks apply and how they should navigate conflicting or ambiguous legal requirements across different jurisdictions.
5. **Smart Contract Legality**:
    - The legality and enforceability of smart contracts vary depending on the jurisdiction and the nature of the contractual agreements encoded within them.
    - Legal challenges may arise concerning the interpretation of smart contract terms, the recognition of digital signatures, and the enforceability of automated contractual agreements within traditional legal frameworks.
6. **Regulatory Oversight and Governance**:
    - Regulatory oversight and governance mechanisms for blockchain and TLT systems are still evolving, leading to uncertainty regarding compliance requirements and regulatory expectations.
    - Organizations may face challenges in navigating regulatory ambiguity, engaging with regulators, and advocating for regulatory frameworks that accommodate the unique characteristics of blockchain technology.

5. STREAMLINING LEADERSHIP PROCESSES WITH BLOCKCHAIN

5.1 Automation of Administrative Tasks

The automation of administrative tasks through Transparent Ledger Technology (TLT) such as blockchain introduces efficiency, accuracy, and transparency into organizational processes (Zheng et al., 2018). Here's how automation transforms administrative tasks:

1. **Smart Contracts Execution**:
    - Smart contracts automate the execution of predefined agreements and conditions encoded into the blockchain. Once the conditions are met, smart contracts automatically trigger actions without the need for human intervention.
    - This automation streamlines administrative tasks such as contract management, payment processing, and compliance enforcement, reducing the time and resources required for manual oversight and execution.
2. **Streamlined Workflows**:
    - TLT platforms enable the creation of decentralized applications (DApps) that automate and optimize workflows across various departments and functions.

- By leveraging smart contracts and decentralized storage solutions, organizations can automate repetitive tasks, data entry, and document management, streamlining administrative workflows and reducing operational inefficiencies.
3. **Faster Transaction Processing**:
    - Automation through TLT accelerates transaction processing by eliminating intermediaries and manual approval processes.
    - Transactions recorded on the blockchain are validated and executed automatically based on predefined rules and conditions, leading to faster settlement times and reduced transactional friction.
4. **Enhanced Accuracy and Auditability**:
    - Automation reduces the risk of human error and ensures greater accuracy in administrative tasks such as data entry, reconciliation, and record-keeping.
    - Transactions recorded on the blockchain are immutable and transparent, providing an auditable trail of all activities and changes, enhancing accountability and compliance with regulatory requirements.
5. **Cost Savings and Resource Optimization**:
    - By automating administrative tasks, organizations can achieve significant cost savings by reducing labor costs, minimizing manual errors, and optimizing resource allocation.
    - Automation through TLT platforms enables organizations to do more with less, freeing up human resources to focus on higher-value strategic initiatives and innovation.
6. **Regulatory Compliance**:
    - TLT platforms facilitate regulatory compliance by automating compliance checks, reporting, and audit processes.
    - Smart contracts can be programmed to enforce regulatory requirements and ensure that transactions comply with relevant laws and regulations, reducing the risk of non-compliance and associated penalties.
7. **Integration with Existing Systems**:
    - TLT platforms can integrate with existing enterprise systems, such as ERP (Enterprise Resource Planning) or CRM (Customer Relationship Management) systems, to automate administrative tasks seamlessly.
    - By connecting blockchain-based solutions with legacy systems, organizations can leverage automation to enhance efficiency and interoperability across their operations.

5.2 Optimization of Supply Chain Management

The optimization of supply chain management through Transparent Ledger Technology (TLT) like blockchain revolutionizes traditional practices, enhancing transparency, traceability, and efficiency across the supply chain. Here's how TLT optimizes supply chain management (Möller & Florea, 2017):

1. **Enhanced Traceability**:
    - TLT provides end-to-end traceability by recording every transaction and movement of goods on an immutable ledger. Each step in the supply chain, from raw material sourcing to final delivery, is transparently documented.

- Stakeholders can trace the provenance, location, and status of products in real-time, reducing the risk of counterfeiting, theft, or unauthorized tampering.
2. **Improved Transparency**:
    - Blockchain-based supply chain solutions offer unparalleled transparency by providing stakeholders with visibility into the entire supply chain ecosystem.
    - Participants can access relevant information about suppliers, manufacturers, distributors, and logistics providers, fostering trust and accountability across the supply chain.
3. **Efficient Inventory Management**:
    - TLT enables real-time inventory tracking and management, reducing stockouts, overstocking, and inventory carrying costs.
    - Smart contracts can automate inventory replenishment processes, triggering orders automatically when predefined inventory thresholds are reached, optimizing inventory levels and reducing supply chain disruptions.
4. **Streamlined Procurement Processes**:
    - Blockchain streamlines procurement processes by automating contract management, supplier verification, and payment processing.
    - Smart contracts enforce predefined terms and conditions, ensuring compliance with procurement agreements and reducing manual oversight and administrative overhead.
5. **Quality Control and Compliance**:
    - TLT platforms facilitate quality control and compliance monitoring throughout the supply chain by recording product certifications, test results, and compliance documents on the blockchain.
    - Smart contracts can enforce quality standards and regulatory requirements, ensuring that only compliant products are accepted into the supply chain.
6. **Reduced Counterfeiting and Fraud**:
    - The transparency and immutability of TLT make it significantly harder for counterfeiters to infiltrate the supply chain.
    - Participants can verify the authenticity and integrity of products using blockchain-based solutions, reducing the risk of counterfeit goods entering the market.
7. **Optimized Logistics and Transportation**:
    - TLT platforms optimize logistics and transportation by providing real-time visibility into shipment status, route optimization, and delivery tracking.
    - Smart contracts can automate freight management processes, including carrier selection, freight payments, and customs clearance, reducing delays and transportation costs.
8. **Sustainability and Ethical Sourcing**:
    - Blockchain enables the transparent tracking of sustainability metrics and ethical sourcing practices across the supply chain.
    - Consumers can verify the sustainability credentials of products, such as fair trade certifications or carbon footprint data, empowering them to make informed purchasing decisions.

5.3 Improving Operational Efficiency

Improving operational efficiency is a key goal for organizations across industries, and Transparent Ledger Technology (TLT) like blockchain offers several ways to achieve this goal. Here's how TLT can enhance operational efficiency (Westerman et al., 2014):

1. **Streamlined Processes**:
    - TLT enables the automation of various processes through smart contracts, which are self-executing contracts with predefined terms and conditions encoded on the blockchain.
    - Smart contracts automate repetitive tasks, such as contract execution, payment processing, and compliance verification, streamlining workflows and reducing manual errors and delays.
2. **Real-Time Data Visibility**:
    - TLT platforms provide real-time visibility into transactional data, allowing organizations to monitor operations and track key performance indicators (KPIs) instantly.
    - With real-time data access, organizations can make informed decisions promptly, identify bottlenecks or inefficiencies in processes, and take proactive measures to address them.
3. **Supply Chain Optimization**:
    - Blockchain enhances supply chain management by improving transparency, traceability, and efficiency across the supply chain.
    - TLT platforms enable real-time tracking of inventory, shipments, and production processes, optimizing inventory levels, reducing stockouts, and minimizing supply chain disruptions.
4. **Reduced Administrative Overhead**:
    - Automation through TLT reduces the need for manual oversight and administrative tasks, saving time and resources.
    - Smart contracts automate administrative processes, such as contract management, document verification, and record-keeping, reducing administrative overhead and increasing operational efficiency.
5. **Improved Collaboration**:
    - TLT fosters collaboration among stakeholders by providing a shared platform for transparent and secure data exchange.
    - Blockchain-based collaboration tools facilitate real-time communication, data sharing, and decision-making among teams and partners, enhancing collaboration and coordination across organizational boundaries.
6. **Enhanced Security and Trust**:
    - TLT platforms offer robust security features, such as cryptographic encryption, immutability, and decentralized consensus mechanisms, ensuring the integrity and confidentiality of data.
    - Enhanced security builds trust among stakeholders, enabling more efficient and secure transactions and interactions within the organization and with external partners.
7. **Compliance Automation**:
    - TLT facilitates regulatory compliance by automating compliance checks, reporting, and audit processes.

- Smart contracts can enforce regulatory requirements and ensure that transactions comply with relevant laws and regulations, reducing the risk of non-compliance and associated penalties.
8. **Cost Savings**:
    - By streamlining processes, reducing administrative overhead, and minimizing inefficiencies, TLT helps organizations achieve significant cost savings.
    - Automation through blockchain reduces the need for intermediaries, manual labor, and reconciliation efforts, leading to cost reductions and improved profitability.

6. COLLABORATION AND INNOVATION IN BLOCKCHAIN LEADERSHIP

6.1 Fostering Collaboration Across Stakeholders

Fostering collaboration across stakeholders is crucial for driving innovation, efficiency, and value creation in various industries (Charan et al., 2015). Transparent Ledger Technology (TLT) like blockchain offers several ways to facilitate collaboration among stakeholders:

1. **Shared Data Infrastructure**:
    - TLT platforms provide a shared infrastructure for transparent and secure data exchange among stakeholders.
    - Blockchain-based ledgers enable stakeholders to record, verify, and share data in real-time, fostering trust and transparency in collaborative efforts.
2. **Decentralized Governance**:
    - TLT platforms support decentralized governance models where decision-making power is distributed among network participants.
    - Stakeholders can participate in consensus mechanisms, governance protocols, and voting mechanisms to shape the direction and policies of the platform collaboratively.
3. **Smart Contracts and Automation**:
    - Smart contracts automate and enforce predefined agreements and conditions, enabling seamless collaboration among stakeholders.
    - Smart contracts facilitate automated transactions, payments, and compliance checks, reducing friction and delays in collaborative workflows.
4. **Supply Chain Collaboration**:
    - Blockchain enhances collaboration across supply chains by providing end-to-end traceability, transparency, and accountability.
    - Stakeholders can track the provenance, movement, and status of goods in real-time, enabling efficient collaboration in areas such as inventory management, logistics, and quality control.
5. **Cross-Organizational Data Sharing**:
    - TLT platforms enable secure and permissioned data sharing among multiple organizations while preserving data privacy and confidentiality.
    - Organizations can share sensitive information, such as customer data or supply chain data, with trusted partners through encrypted channels on the blockchain.

6. **Interoperability and Standards**:
   - TLT promotes interoperability and standardization of data formats, protocols, and interfaces, enabling seamless integration and collaboration across disparate systems and networks.
   - Standardized data formats and protocols facilitate data exchange and interoperability, reducing integration challenges and promoting collaboration among stakeholders.
7. **Transparency and Trust**:
   - TLT fosters transparency and trust among stakeholders by providing a shared and immutable record of transactions and interactions.
   - Transparent ledgers enable stakeholders to verify the integrity and authenticity of data, fostering trust and confidence in collaborative endeavors.
8. **Incentive Mechanisms**:
   - TLT platforms can incorporate incentive mechanisms, such as token-based rewards or governance tokens, to incentivize collaboration and contributions from network participants.
   - Stakeholders are rewarded for their contributions to the network, fostering a collaborative ecosystem where value creation is shared among participants.

6.2 Promoting Innovation Through Open Platforms

Promoting innovation through open platforms is a key aspect of Transparent Ledger Technology (TLT) like blockchain (Brown & Anthony, 2011). Here's how open platforms based on TLT foster innovation:

1. **Decentralized Development Ecosystem**:
   - TLT platforms provide a decentralized development ecosystem where developers can build, deploy, and innovate with minimal barriers to entry.
   - Open platforms allow developers to access blockchain protocols, APIs, and toolkits, enabling them to create a wide range of decentralized applications (DApps) and smart contracts.
2. **Permissionless Innovation**:
   - TLT platforms support permissionless innovation, allowing anyone to participate in the ecosystem and contribute to its development.
   - Developers can experiment with new ideas, business models, and use cases without seeking permission from centralized authorities, fostering creativity and experimentation.
3. **Interoperability and Standardization**:
   - TLT promotes interoperability and standardization of protocols, interfaces, and data formats, enabling seamless integration and collaboration across different blockchain networks and applications.
   - Open platforms facilitate interoperability between disparate systems, promoting collaboration and innovation in the broader blockchain ecosystem.
4. **Collaborative Development Communities**:
   - TLT platforms foster collaborative development communities where developers, researchers, and enthusiasts collaborate to solve complex challenges and drive innovation.
   - Open-source projects on TLT platforms encourage peer review, knowledge sharing, and collective problem-solving, accelerating the pace of innovation.

5. **Access to Global Markets**:
   - TLT platforms provide access to global markets and audiences, enabling developers to reach a diverse user base and explore new market opportunities.
   - Open platforms facilitate the global distribution of DApps and services, allowing developers to innovate for users worldwide.
6. **Tokenization and Incentive Mechanisms**:
   - TLT platforms incorporate tokenization and incentive mechanisms to reward developers and contributors for their contributions to the ecosystem.
   - Developers can earn tokens or rewards for building and maintaining DApps, attracting talent and investment to the platform and stimulating innovation.
7. **Immutable and Transparent Infrastructure**:
   - TLT platforms offer immutable and transparent infrastructure for building and deploying decentralized applications.
   - Developers can leverage the security and transparency of blockchain technology to build innovative solutions for various industries, such as finance, supply chain, healthcare, and identity management.
8. **Regulatory Compliance and Governance**:
   - TLT platforms implement regulatory compliance and governance mechanisms to ensure the security, integrity, and legality of DApps and transactions.
   - Open platforms facilitate compliance with regulatory requirements while providing flexibility and autonomy for developers to innovate within legal frameworks.

6.3 Harnessing Collective Intelligence

Harnessing collective intelligence is a powerful concept that Transparent Ledger Technology (TLT) like blockchain can facilitate, enabling collaboration, innovation, and problem-solving on a global scale (Lacity & Khan, 2019). Here's how TLT can harness collective intelligence:

1. **Decentralized Decision Making**:
   - TLT platforms support decentralized decision-making mechanisms where decisions are made collectively by network participants rather than centralized authorities.
   - Decentralized governance models enable stakeholders to vote on proposals, initiatives, and changes to the platform, harnessing the collective intelligence of the community.
2. **Crowdsourced Innovation**:
   - TLT platforms facilitate crowdsourced innovation by providing a decentralized platform for individuals and organizations to collaborate, share ideas, and contribute to the development of new solutions (Truby & Truby, 2018).
   - Open-source projects on TLT platforms invite contributions from a global community of developers, researchers, and enthusiasts, harnessing collective intelligence to solve complex problems and drive innovation.
3. **Prediction Markets**:
   - TLT platforms enable the creation of prediction markets where participants can buy and sell shares in the outcomes of future events.

- Prediction markets harness the collective intelligence of participants to forecast outcomes, anticipate trends, and make informed decisions based on the aggregated wisdom of the crowd.
4. **Decentralized Autonomous Organizations (DAOs)**:
    - TLT platforms support the creation of DAOs, which are decentralized organizations governed by smart contracts and operated by a network of stakeholders.
    - DAOs harness collective intelligence by allowing stakeholders to vote on proposals, allocate resources, and make decisions collaboratively, without the need for centralized management.
5. **Collaborative Problem-Solving**:
    - TLT platforms facilitate collaborative problem-solving by providing transparent and immutable ledgers for recording and sharing information.
    - Participants can collaborate on solving complex challenges, such as scientific research, environmental conservation, or humanitarian aid, by sharing data, insights, and expertise on the blockchain.
6. **Crowdfunding and Tokenization**:
    - TLT platforms enable crowdfunding campaigns and tokenization of assets, allowing individuals and organizations to raise funds and tokenize ownership rights.
    - Crowdfunding platforms harness collective intelligence by enabling individuals to collectively fund projects, startups, and initiatives that align with their interests and values.
7. **Open Innovation Platforms**:
    - TLT platforms serve as open innovation platforms where participants can share ideas, collaborate on projects, and co-create solutions.
    - Open innovation platforms leverage the collective intelligence of diverse stakeholders, including developers, researchers, entrepreneurs, and users, to drive innovation and address global challenges.
8. **Incentive Mechanisms**:
    - TLT platforms incorporate incentive mechanisms, such as token rewards or governance tokens, to incentivize participation and contributions from network participants.
    - Incentive mechanisms encourage individuals to share their knowledge, skills, and resources, harnessing collective intelligence to achieve common goals and outcomes.

7. TOKENIZATION AND INCENTIVE MECHANISMS

7.1 Tokenization of Assets and Rewards

Tokenization of assets and rewards is a transformative application of Transparent Ledger Technology (TLT) like blockchain, enabling the representation and transfer of real-world assets and value in digital form. Here's how tokenization works and its implications (Li & Li, 2018):

1. **Asset Tokenization**:
    - Asset tokenization involves representing real-world assets, such as real estate, stocks, commodities, or artwork, as digital tokens on a blockchain.

- Each token represents ownership rights to a fraction of the underlying asset, enabling fractional ownership, liquidity, and transferability of traditionally illiquid assets.

2. **Benefits of Asset Tokenization**:
   - Increased Liquidity: Tokenization unlocks liquidity by enabling fractional ownership and secondary trading of assets that were previously illiquid.
   - Accessibility: Tokenization democratizes access to investment opportunities by lowering entry barriers and allowing investors to participate in a wide range of asset classes.
   - Efficiency: Tokenization streamlines asset transfer and settlement processes, reducing administrative overhead, intermediaries, and transaction costs.
   - Fractional Ownership: Tokenization allows investors to own fractions of high-value assets, making investment opportunities more accessible and affordable.

3. **Rewards and Incentive Tokens**:
   - TLT platforms use tokens as a mechanism to incentivize and reward participants for their contributions to the network.
   - Incentive tokens, such as utility tokens or governance tokens, are issued to users for actions such as validating transactions, providing liquidity, or participating in governance decisions.

4. **Tokenization Platforms**:
   - Tokenization platforms provide infrastructure and tools for creating, issuing, and managing tokenized assets and rewards.
   - These platforms facilitate compliance with regulatory requirements, asset management, investor onboarding, and token trading.

5. **Use Cases**:
   - Real Estate: Tokenization enables fractional ownership of real estate properties, allowing investors to diversify their portfolios and access investment opportunities in high-value properties.
   - Securities: Tokenized securities represent ownership rights to traditional financial assets such as stocks, bonds, and derivatives, providing increased liquidity and accessibility to investors.
   - Artwork and Collectibles: Tokenization allows fractional ownership of artwork, collectibles, and other valuable assets, enabling investors to gain exposure to alternative asset classes.
   - Rewards and Loyalty Programs: TLT platforms use tokens to reward users for their engagement and loyalty, fostering community participation and driving user adoption.

6. **Regulatory Considerations**:
   - Asset tokenization raises regulatory considerations related to securities laws, ownership rights, investor protection, and anti-money laundering (AML) compliance.
   - Tokenization platforms must navigate regulatory requirements and compliance frameworks to ensure legal and regulatory compliance.

7. **Challenges**:
   - Regulatory Uncertainty: The regulatory landscape for asset tokenization is still evolving, posing challenges for compliance and legal clarity.
   - Security Risks: Tokenization platforms must address security risks such as hacking, fraud, and theft to safeguard digital assets and investor funds.
   - Market Fragmentation: The tokenization market is fragmented, with various platforms, standards, and protocols, hindering interoperability and scalability.

7.2 Incentivizing Desired Behaviors

Incentivizing desired behaviors is a powerful application of Transparent Ledger Technology (TLT) like blockchain, leveraging tokenization and smart contracts to reward and encourage individuals or entities to act in ways that align with specific objectives or goals (Chesbrough, 2003). Here's how TLT can be used to incentivize desired behaviors:

1. **Token-Based Rewards**:
   - TLT platforms issue tokens as rewards for specific behaviors, actions, or contributions that align with desired objectives.
   - Participants earn tokens for activities such as validating transactions, providing liquidity, contributing to governance decisions, or engaging in desired behaviors.
2. **Smart Contracts**:
   - Smart contracts are self-executing contracts with predefined rules and conditions encoded on the blockchain.
   - Smart contracts automate the issuance and distribution of rewards based on predefined criteria, ensuring transparent and trustless execution of incentive programs.
3. **Gamification**:
   - TLT platforms use gamification techniques to incentivize desired behaviors by making the process engaging and rewarding.
   - Gamified incentive programs incorporate elements such as leaderboards, achievements, levels, and badges to motivate participants and drive engagement.
4. **Staking Mechanisms**:
   - TLT platforms implement staking mechanisms where participants lock up or stake their tokens as collateral to demonstrate commitment or support for specific actions or decisions.
   - Staking rewards incentivize participants to hold and stake their tokens, contributing to network security, stability, and governance.
5. **Proof-of-Work and Proof-of-Stake**:
   - In blockchain networks using Proof-of-Work (PoW) or Proof-of-Stake (PoS) consensus mechanisms, participants are incentivized to validate transactions and secure the network in exchange for rewards.
   - PoW miners or PoS validators earn rewards for their computational work or token holdings, incentivizing them to act in the best interest of the network.
6. **Social Impact Incentives**:
   - TLT platforms incentivize behaviors that contribute to social impact, sustainability, or environmental conservation.
   - Participants earn rewards for actions such as recycling, energy conservation, carbon offsetting, or supporting charitable causes, promoting positive social and environmental outcomes.
7. **Loyalty and Rewards Programs**:
   - Businesses use TLT platforms to create loyalty and rewards programs that incentivize customer behaviors such as purchases, referrals, or brand engagement.
   - Token-based rewards programs offer customers incentives such as discounts, cashback, or exclusive benefits in exchange for their loyalty and engagement.

8. **Data Sharing and Privacy**:
    - TLT platforms incentivize data sharing and privacy-preserving behaviors by rewarding participants for sharing data in a secure and privacy-enhancing manner.
    - Participants earn rewards for contributing data to research, data marketplaces, or decentralized applications while maintaining control over their privacy and data ownership.

7.3 Aligning Incentives Across Stakeholder Groups

Aligning incentives across stakeholder groups is essential for fostering collaboration, achieving common goals, and driving value creation in organizations and ecosystems. Transparent Ledger Technology (TLT) like blockchain offers several mechanisms to align incentives effectively (Gawer & Cusumano, 2008):

1. **Token-Based Incentives**:
    - TLT platforms issue tokens as incentives to align the interests of different stakeholder groups, such as users, developers, investors, and validators.
    - Tokens represent ownership rights, voting power, or participation in governance decisions, ensuring that stakeholders are incentivized to act in ways that benefit the ecosystem as a whole.
2. **Shared Ownership and Governance**:
    - TLT platforms incorporate decentralized governance models where decision-making power is distributed among network participants.
    - Stakeholders have a say in governance decisions proportional to their token holdings, aligning incentives and ensuring that decisions reflect the collective interests of the community.
3. **Economic Incentives**:
    - TLT platforms use economic incentives, such as token rewards or revenue-sharing mechanisms, to align the interests of stakeholders with the success of the ecosystem.
    - Participants are rewarded for their contributions, such as providing liquidity, staking tokens, or developing applications, ensuring that incentives are aligned with desired outcomes.
4. **Alignment with Mission and Values**:
    - TLT platforms articulate a clear mission, vision, and set of values that guide decision-making and behavior across stakeholder groups.
    - Stakeholders are motivated by shared values and a common purpose, ensuring alignment of incentives and fostering a sense of belonging and commitment to the ecosystem.
5. **Transparency and Accountability**:
    - TLT platforms provide transparency into decision-making processes, resource allocation, and distribution of incentives, ensuring accountability and fairness.
    - Transparent ledgers and auditable smart contracts enhance trust among stakeholders, aligning incentives and promoting cooperation and collaboration.
6. **Inclusive Participation**:
    - TLT platforms promote inclusive participation by allowing all stakeholders to contribute and benefit from the ecosystem.
    - Inclusive participation ensures that diverse perspectives and interests are represented, aligning incentives across different stakeholder groups and maximizing the collective intelligence and creativity of the community.

7. **Long-Term Sustainability**:
   - TLT platforms prioritize long-term sustainability and resilience by aligning incentives with the health and viability of the ecosystem.
   - Sustainable incentive structures promote responsible growth, innovation, and value creation while mitigating risks and ensuring the long-term success of the ecosystem.
8. **Continuous Feedback and Iteration**:
   - TLT platforms facilitate continuous feedback loops and iterative development processes, allowing stakeholders to provide input, suggest improvements, and iterate on incentive mechanisms.
   - Feedback mechanisms ensure that incentives remain aligned with evolving needs and objectives, fostering adaptability and resilience in the face of change.

In conclusion, blockchain technology presents a paradigm shift in leadership dynamics, offering novel avenues for fostering transparency, accountability, and collaboration across organizational structures (West & Bogers, 2014). As leaders navigate the complexities of the digital age, blockchain serves as a catalyst for driving innovation, efficiency, and trust within and beyond traditional boundaries. By harnessing the power of decentralized networks, smart contracts, and cryptographic techniques, leaders can cultivate an environment conducive to inclusive decision-making, stakeholder empowerment, and ethical governance (Schneier, 2015).

Blockchain's role in leadership extends beyond technological innovation; it embodies a fundamental shift towards more democratic and equitable leadership models. Through transparent ledger technology, leaders can incentivize desired behaviors, align incentives across diverse stakeholder groups, and promote collective intelligence and collaboration. Moreover, blockchain enables leaders to navigate regulatory landscapes, mitigate risks, and drive sustainable growth in an increasingly interconnected global economy.

As organizations embrace blockchain's transformative potential, leaders must adopt a forward-thinking mindset, embracing agility, adaptability, and continuous learning. By championing blockchain initiatives, leaders can position their organizations at the forefront of innovation, driving positive change and creating value for stakeholders. Ultimately, blockchain empowers leaders to redefine leadership paradigms, inspire trust, and steer organizations towards a more transparent, resilient, and prosperous future.

REFERENCES

Agnihotri. (2021). Systemic- Processual Shared Leadership Model with reference to Team Variables in IT Industry in India. *Turkish Journal of Computer and Mathematics Education (TURCOMAT), 12*(7), 608–618.

Antonopoulos, A. M. (2014). *Mastering Bitcoin: Unlocking Digital Cryptocurrencies*. Academic Press.

Antony, J., & Kizgin, H. (2018). Blockchain technology in supply chain management: A proposed framework. In *International Conference on Industrial Engineering and Operations Management* (pp. 1174-1185). Springer.

Brown, B., & Anthony, S. D. (2011). *The New Leader's 100-Day Action Plan: How to Take Charge.* Build Your Team, and Get Immediate Results.

Buterin, V. (2014). *Ethereum: A Next-Generation Smart Contract and Decentralized Application Platform.* Retrieved from: https://ethereum.org/en/whitepaper/

Casey, M. J., & Vigna, P. (2018). *The Truth Machine: The Blockchain and the Future of Everything.* Academic Press.

Charan, R., Barton, D., & Carey, D. (2015). *"People Before Strategy": A New Role for the CHRO.* Academic Press.

Chesbrough, H. W. (2003). *Open Innovation: The New Imperative for Creating and Profiting from Technology.* Academic Press.

Gawer, A., & Cusumano, M. A. (2008). How Companies Become Platform Leaders. *MIT Sloan Management Review, 49*(2), 28–35.

Groenfeldt, T. (2017). How Blockchain Technology Could Change The World. *Forbes.*

Iansiti, M., & Lakhani, K. R. (2017). The truth about blockchain. *Harvard Business Review, 95*(1), 118–127.

Lacity, M., & Khan, S. (2019). *Blockchain as a Supply Chain Transparency Tool: A Comparative Case Study.* Academic Press.

Li, Z., & Li, D. (2018). Blockchain technology in the building materials supply chain: Potential strategic applications and challenges. *Journal of Industrial Information Integration, 12,* 34–42.

Möller, J., & Florea, A. (2017). Governance in blockchain technologies & social contract theories. *Ledger, 2,* 103–125.

Nakamoto, S. (2008). *Bitcoin: A Peer-to-Peer Electronic Cash System.* Retrieved from: https://bitcoin.org/bitcoin.pdf

Narayanan, A., Bonneau, J., Felten, E., Miller, A., & Goldfeder, S. (2016). *Bitcoin and Cryptocurrency Technologies: A Comprehensive Introduction.* Academic Press.

Schneier, B. (2015). *Applied Cryptography: Protocols.* Algorithms, and Source Code in C.

Shukla, A., Mishra, L., & Agnihotri, A. (2023). A Comprehensive Review of the Effects of Digital Technology on Human Resource Management. In Technology, Management and Business. Emerald Publishing Limited. doi:10.1108/S1877-636120230000031002

Swan, M. (2015). *The Business Blockchain: Promise.* Practice, and Application of the Next Internet Technology.

Swan, M. (2015). *Blockchain: Blueprint for a New Economy.* Academic Press.

Tapscott, D., & Tapscott, A. (2016). *Blockchain revolution: how the technology behind bitcoin is changing money, business, and the world.* Academic Press.

Truby, J., & Truby, E. (2018). Trusting records: Is Blockchain technology the answer? *Records Management Journal*, *28*(2), 110–129.

West, J., & Bogers, M. (2014). *Leveraging external sources of innovation: A review of research on open innovation.* Academic Press.

Westerman, G., Bonnet, D., & McAfee, A. (2014). *Leading Digital: Turning Technology into Business Transformation.* Academic Press.

Zheng, Z., Xie, S., Dai, H. N., Chen, X., & Wang, H. (2018). Blockchain challenges and opportunities: A survey. *International Journal of Web and Grid Services*, *14*(4), 352–375. doi:10.1504/IJWGS.2018.095647

Chapter 11
Blockchain as a Service:
Empowering Enterprise HRM Leadership for the Future

Moushami Panda
https://orcid.org/0009-0005-9678-1335
GIET University, India

Jyotikanta Panda
https://orcid.org/0009-0007-7210-6313
GIET University, India

Smruti Rekha Sahoo
GIET University, India

Mariofanna Milanova
https://orcid.org/0000-0003-0995-1921
University of Arkansas, USA

Saumendra Das
https://orcid.org/0000-0003-4956-4352
GIET University, India

ABSTRACT

As organizations continue in the evolving landscape of the digital, leaders of human resource management (HRM) face unprecedented challenges and opportunities. Blockchain technology has emerged as a disruptive force, offering innovative solutions to longstanding HRM issues. This explores the potential of blockchain as a service (BaaS) in transforming enterprise HRM practices, enhancing security, efficiency, and transparency while paving the way for future leaders where HRM in enterprises will be empowering. Blockchain technology, renowned for its decentralized, secure, and transparent nature, offers a scalable, cost-effective way for organizations to harness the power of blockchain without the complexities of building and maintaining their blockchain infrastructure. This study explores the transformative potential and impact of blockchain as a service (BaaS) on HRM practices within enterprises with adaptive and proven case studies by investigating the advantages, challenges, and prospects of implementing BaaS solutions to harness and empower enterprise HRM leaders for the future.

INTRODUCTION

Human Resource Management (HRM) is a critical function in any organization/enterprise, responsible for recruiting, retaining, and developing talent while ensuring compliance with regulations. In today's

DOI: 10.4018/979-8-3693-1946-8.ch011

rapidly evolving business landscape, HRM faces several challenges, including data security, transparency, and efficiency. Blockchain technology, known for its decentralized, secure, and transparent nature, has emerged as a game-changer in addressing these challenges (Deloitte, 2018).

This paper delves into the potential of Blockchain as a Service (BaaS) to revolutionize HRM in enterprises. BaaS offers a scalable, cost-effective way for organization leaders to harness the power of blockchain without the complexities of building and maintaining their blockchain infrastructure.

Blockchain Fundamentals and Benefits

Definition

Blockchain as a Service (BaaS) is a cloud-based service that allows individuals, businesses, and organizations to develop, host, and manage their blockchain applications and smart contracts. BaaS providers offer pre-configured blockchain infrastructure and tools to deploy and operate blockchain networks without the complexities of setting up and managing a blockchain from scratch which includes nodes, data storage, and security features (Antonopoulos, 2014).

Benefits

Ease of Use: BaaS abstracts the technical complexities of blockchain, making it accessible to a broader range of users, including those with limited blockchain expertise.

Cost-Efficiency: BaaS eliminates the need to invest in and maintain dedicated blockchain hardware and software infrastructure, reducing capital and operational costs.

Rapid Development: BaaS providers offer development tools, templates, and pre-built components, allowing developers to create blockchain applications more quickly.

Scalability: BaaS platforms can often scale as needed to accommodate growing workloads, enabling businesses to expand their blockchain networks with ease.

Security and Reliability: BaaS providers typically implement security measures and redundancy to ensure the reliability and integrity of blockchain networks.

Interoperability: Some BaaS platforms support multiple blockchain protocols, enabling interoperability between different blockchain networks.

BaaS providers and their offerings for Enterprises

Several BaaS providers offer blockchain infrastructure and tools to businesses and developers as shown in below figure no. 1. Some of the prominent BaaS providers and their offerings include:

Microsoft Azure

Microsoft Azure Blockchain Service provides a cloud-based environment for creating, deploying, and managing blockchain applications. It supports a range of blockchain protocols, including Ethereum, Corda, and Hyperledger Fabric. It offers integration with Azure Active Directory for identity and access management.

Figure 1. Blockchain as a service (BaaS) providers

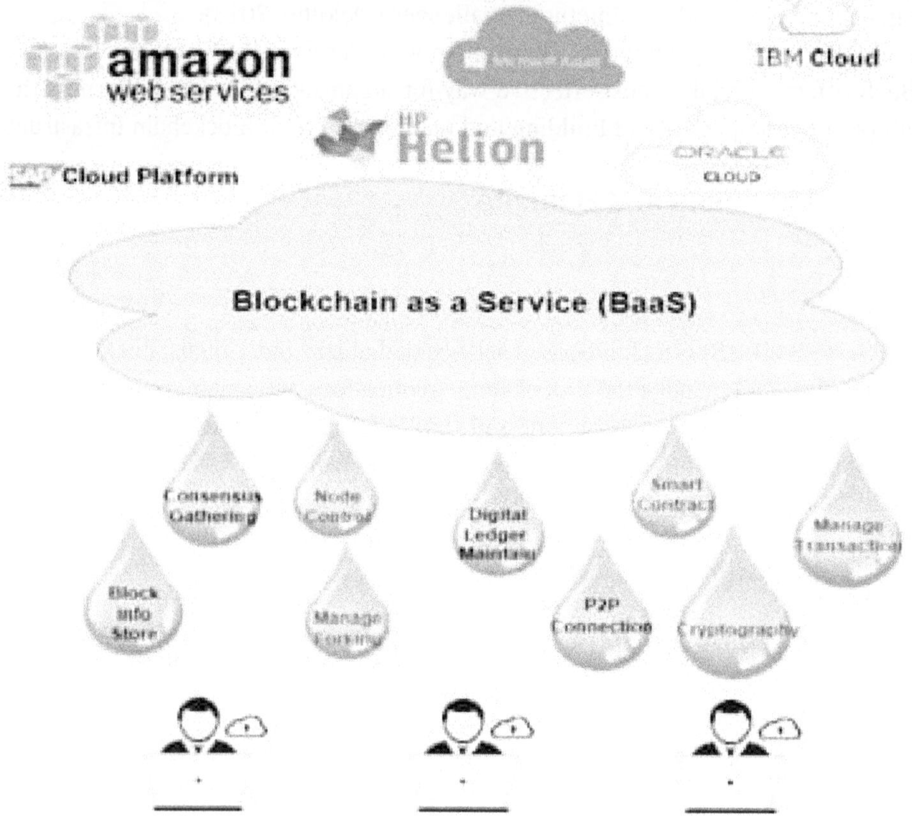

IBM Blockchain

IBM Blockchain Platform offers a comprehensive suite of blockchain development and management tools. It supports Hyperledger Fabric and provides end-to-end solutions for various industries. Features include smart contract development, network management, and security.

Amazon Web Services (AWS)

AWS provides blockchain solutions through Amazon Managed Blockchain. It supports Ethereum and Hyperledger Fabric, enabling users to create and manage blockchain networks. Offers automated software updates, monitoring, and scaling.

Oracle Blockchain Platform

Oracle offers a cloud-based BaaS solution for building, deploying, and managing blockchain applications. It supports Hyperledger Fabric and integrates with other Oracle cloud services. It provides pre-built applications for various industries.

Baidu Blockchain Engine (BBE)

Baidu's BBE is a BaaS platform that offers blockchain services, including smart contract development and deployment. Designed for enterprise use, BBE focuses on creating secure and efficient blockchain applications.

Alibaba Cloud Blockchain Service

Alibaba Cloud's BaaS offering provides infrastructure and tools for blockchain development. It supports Hyperledger Fabric and other protocols and integrates with other Alibaba Cloud services.

These BaaS providers offer a range of services, including blockchain network creation, smart contract development, identity management, and data analytics, making it easier for businesses to harness the potential of blockchain technology without having to build and maintain the entire infrastructure themselves.

Advantages and applications of BaaS for Enterprise HRM Leadership

The key advantages of Baas for HRM in enterprises are as follows:

- Reduced Infrastructure Costs: BaaS eliminates the need for HR departments to invest in and maintain their blockchain infrastructure. This reduces the capital and operational costs associated with setting up and managing blockchain networks.
- Enhanced Scalability: HRM processes often involve the handling of large volumes of data, especially in organizations with many employees. BaaS allows for easy scalability, ensuring that the blockchain network can grow as the HR department's data requirements increase.
- Streamlined Development and Deployment: BaaS platforms offer pre-built blockchain infrastructure and development tools, simplifying the creation of blockchain-based HR applications. This streamlines the development process and reduces the time it takes to deploy HR solutions.
- Focus on Core HR Functions: By outsourcing the management of blockchain infrastructure to BaaS providers, HR departments can concentrate on their core functions, such as talent management, employee onboarding, and performance evaluation, without the burden of managing blockchain technology.

The key applications of BaaS in HRM:

- Secure Identity Verification: Blockchain can be used to securely verify and manage employee identities. The blockchain's tamper-proof nature ensures that employee identity records are protected from fraud and unauthorized access.
- Employee Records Management: HR departments can use blockchain to create a transparent and immutable ledger for employee records. This includes information related to employment history, certifications, training, and performance reviews.
- Recruitment and Background Checks: Blockchain can streamline the recruitment process by providing a secure and efficient way to verify candidates' credentials, references, and background checks. This reduces the risk of hiring individuals with fabricated qualifications.
- Payroll and Compensation: Managing payroll and compensation on a blockchain can ensure the accuracy and transparency of payments. Smart contracts can automate payment processes based on predefined rules, reducing errors and disputes.

- Employee Benefits and Stock Options: As mentioned earlier, tokenization can be used to represent employee stock options, making them more accessible and tradable. Additionally, blockchain can be used to manage employee benefits programs, including retirement plans, health insurance, and incentives.
- Time and Attendance Tracking: Using blockchain for time and attendance tracking can provide a tamper-proof record of employee work hours. This data can be used for payroll calculations and monitoring employee attendance.
- Learning and Development Records: Blockchain can be used to securely store and verify employee training and development records. This ensures that employees' qualifications and certifications are easily accessible and tamper-proof.
- Whistleblower Protection: Blockchain can be used to create anonymous reporting mechanisms for HR-related issues. This protects whistleblowers' identities and ensures that their reports are secure and cannot be altered.
- Performance Evaluation and Feedback: Blockchain can help streamline the performance evaluation process by creating transparent records of performance feedback, goal-setting, and achievements. This data can be used for talent development and succession planning.

By applying blockchain technology to HRM, organizations can enhance data security, transparency, and efficiency in various HR processes, ultimately improving the employee experience and reducing administrative overhead which is a sensitive area for any organization's leadership (Noe et.al. 2019). However, careful consideration of data privacy and compliance is essential in the management of sensitive HR data on the blockchain.

CASE STUDIES OF IMPLEMENTED BAAS FOR HRM IN ENTERPRISES

These case studies illustrate how BaaS can be applied in HRM within enterprises, helping HR departments streamline their processes, enhance data management, and improve the overall employee experience. BaaS platforms can provide the necessary infrastructure for secure and scalable HR applications, allowing organizations to focus on core HR functions and employee engagement (IBM 2019). Though scenarios are many, here we have taken study samples of IBM.

IBM's HR Blockchain Platform

IBM, a global technology leader, has pioneered the application of Blockchain as a Service (BaaS) within its Human Resource Management (HRM) practices. This case study sheds light on IBM's innovative HR Blockchain Platform and the remarkable results it has achieved.

How IBM Uses BaaS for HRM

IBM's HR Blockchain Platform leverages BaaS to address various aspects of HRM, demonstrating the versatility and power of blockchain in this domain:

Credential Verification: One of the standout applications of blockchain in IBM's HRM is the secure and immutable verification of educational and professional credentials. By recording academic degrees, certifications, and work history on the blockchain, potential employers can quickly and confidently verify a candidate's qualifications. IBM uses the blockchain to record and verify the qualifications and work history of potential hires. This ensures the authenticity of candidates' credentials and mitigates the risk of credential fraud.

In the realm of modern Human Resource Management (HRM), the process of verifying the educational and professional credentials of job applicants has long been a critical but labor-intensive task fraught with challenges. Document fraud, inaccuracies, and the time-consuming nature of verification processes have often posed hurdles for HR professionals.

IBM's HR Blockchain Platform introduced a groundbreaking solution to this perennial problem by harnessing blockchain technology. Here's how it works:

- Secure and Immutable Recordkeeping: IBM utilizes blockchain's core principles of decentralization, security, and immutability to create a secure and unchangeable ledger of educational qualifications and professional work histories. When a candidate applies for a position at IBM, their credentials, such as diplomas, certifications, and previous employment records, are recorded on the blockchain.
- Verification Process: Once these credentials are on the blockchain, IBM can efficiently verify their authenticity. The distributed ledger allows for immediate cross-referencing of the provided information against the blockchain records, making it extremely challenging for candidates to misrepresent their qualifications. Additionally, third-party verification entities can be incorporated into the blockchain network, further enhancing the credibility of the verification process.
- Prevention of Credential Fraud: By leveraging blockchain technology, IBM significantly reduces the risk of credential fraud. Candidates are deterred from presenting fake or embellished credentials as the blockchain ensures the accuracy and trustworthiness of the information. This not only saves time for HR professionals but also protects the organization from potential hiring errors.

Benefits and Results

The benefits of this blockchain-based credential verification system within IBM's HRM are profound which helps the HRM Leadership for gaining:

- Enhanced Data Security: The information stored on the blockchain is cryptographically secured and immune to unauthorized alterations. This guarantees the integrity and confidentiality of sensitive data.
- Efficiency and Accuracy: The verification process becomes expedited, as it no longer requires time-consuming manual checks. Errors related to credential verification are minimized, leading to more precise hiring decisions.
- Cost Savings: By automating and streamlining the verification process, HR departments save both time and resources. This can be especially significant in large organizations with high hiring volumes.
- Candidate Trust: Applicants can have confidence in the credibility of the verification process, as they can independently verify their records stored on the blockchain. This transparency fosters trust between candidates and employers.

Figure 2. Benefits of blockchain verification solution

The application of blockchain technology for credential verification as shown above in Fig 2 within IBM's HRM exemplifies how innovative solutions can address long-standing challenges in the HR field. By leveraging the security and immutability of blockchain, IBM not only enhances the integrity of its hiring processes but also showcases the potential for transformative advancements in HRM practices.

Smart Contracts for Onboarding: IBM employs smart contracts to streamline the onboarding process for new hires. These contracts automatically execute predefined actions, such as setting up payroll, benefits, and access to company systems, once specific conditions are met, such as the signing of an employment contract. This automation reduces administrative overhead and accelerates the onboarding process.

In the contemporary landscape of Human Resource Management (HRM), the onboarding process is often characterized by administrative complexities, time-consuming manual tasks, and the potential for errors. IBM's HR Blockchain Platform has introduced a pioneering solution that leverages smart contracts on the blockchain to revolutionize the onboarding of new employees.

Here's how this innovative approach works:

- Smart Contracts Automation: IBM utilizes blockchain's smart contract technology to create a set of predefined actions and conditions that are automatically executed when specific triggers are met. These triggers may include the signing of an employment contract, the successful completion of background checks, or the acceptance of an offer letter. Once these conditions are met, the associated actions are executed without the need for manual intervention.
- Streamlined Payroll Setup: One of the key advantages of this smart contract-based onboarding is the automated setup of payroll. As soon as the employment contract is signed, the smart contract triggers the initiation of payroll setup. This includes the creation of payroll accounts, the provision of banking details, and the establishment of tax-related information. Employees are paid accurately and on time, with minimal errors in the payroll process.
- Efficient Benefits Administration: Smart contracts also facilitate the onboarding of new employees into benefit programs. Depending on an employee's preferences and eligibility, the smart contract can automatically enroll them in health insurance, retirement plans, and other benefits offered by the organization. This ensures that employees have access to benefits from day one, reducing administrative overhead and improving their overall experience.
- Access to Company Systems: Another crucial aspect of onboarding is the provisioning of access to company systems and resources. Smart contracts handle this by granting new employees access to the necessary software, databases, and communication tools as soon as they meet the required conditions. This means that employees can seamlessly start their roles without unnecessary delays.

Benefits and Results from leadership prospective are as shown in below Figure 3.

The introduction of smart contract-based onboarding within IBM's HRM has led to several significant benefits:

- Reduced Administrative Overhead: Automation of onboarding processes drastically reduces the administrative workload for HR personnel. This frees up their time to focus on more strategic and value-added tasks.
- Accelerated Onboarding: New employees experience faster and smoother onboarding, which positively impacts their initial experiences within the organization. This can contribute to improved employee retention and satisfaction.
- Minimized Errors: By automating processes, the likelihood of errors and oversights in onboarding is significantly reduced. This results in more accurate payroll and benefits administration.
- Cost Savings: The automation of onboarding leads to cost savings, as it requires fewer resources and reduces the need for additional administrative staff.

IBM's use of smart contracts for onboarding exemplifies how blockchain technology can streamline HRM processes. The automation of tasks, such as payroll setup, benefits enrollment, and system access provisioning, not only enhances operational efficiency but also delivers a superior onboarding experience for new employees (Mofijur et. al. 2019). This case study underscores the transformative potential of blockchain in HRM, making it more efficient, error-resistant, and employee-centric.

- Payroll and Benefits Management: Blockchain technology ensures the accuracy of payroll processing by securely recording employee work hours and compensation details. Additionally, benefits administration is made transparent and efficient, allowing employees to access and manage their benefits through the blockchain, reducing errors and delays.

Figure 3. Benefits of BAAS in recruitment process

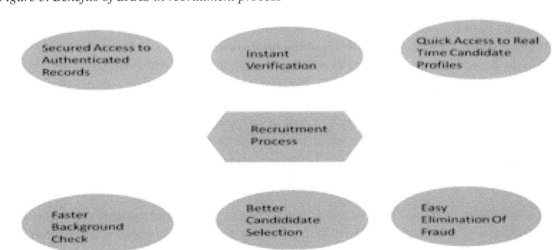

In the domain of Human Resource Management (HRM), payroll and benefits administration are critical but often complex and error-prone processes (Strohmeieret. Al. 2018). IBM's HR Blockchain Platform utilizes blockchain technology to address these challenges and enhance the accuracy, transparency, and efficiency of payroll and benefits management.

Here's how this innovative approach functions and gives the advantage edge for the Leaders:

- Payroll Processing Accuracy: Blockchain technology is employed to create a secure and immutable ledger that records employee work hours and compensation details. This ledger is accessible to both employees and HR personnel. When an employee records their work hours, it is timestamped and securely added to the blockchain. This data is then used for payroll processing.
- Benefits Management Transparency: Benefits administration, a significant aspect of HRM, is also streamlined using blockchain technology. Employees can access and manage their benefit plans through the blockchain. This transparent and self-service approach allows employees to make informed choices regarding health insurance, retirement plans, and other benefits offered by the organization.
- Reduction of Errors and Delays: One of the primary benefits of using blockchain in payroll and benefits management is the reduction of errors and delays. The accuracy of payroll processing is significantly enhanced as blockchain data is secure, unchangeable, and easily audited. This minimizes the risk of errors related to time tracking and compensation calculations. Additionally, the self-service nature of benefits management through the blockchain reduces the potential for administrative errors and miscommunication.
- Employee Empowerment: Employees are empowered by the transparency and accessibility of their payroll and benefits information on the blockchain. They can independently review and manage their compensation details and benefit plans, fostering a sense of ownership and control over their financial and benefit-related matters.

Benefits and Results

The introduction of blockchain technology in payroll and benefits management within IBM's Leadership in HRM has resulted in numerous benefits:

- Enhanced Payroll Accuracy: Blockchain ensures the accuracy of payroll calculations, reducing the potential for errors and discrepancies in employee compensation.
- Efficient Benefits Administration: The self-service approach to benefits administration streamlines the process, reducing administrative overhead, and offering employees greater control over their benefit plans.
- Transparency and Trust: Employees have full visibility into their compensation and benefits, which fosters trust and transparency within the organization.
- Cost Savings: The reduction in errors and administrative overhead results in cost savings for the organization.

IBM's application of blockchain technology to payroll and benefits management underscores the transformative potential of blockchain in HRM. By ensuring accuracy, transparency, and efficiency in these critical HR processes, blockchain not only benefits HR personnel but also empowers employees to take control of their financial well-being (Meijer et. al. 2018). This case study serves as a testament to the impact of blockchain on HRM practices, making them more secure which benefits the leadership to maintain transparency throughout the organization in terms of policy and procedures and become employee-centric.

- Employee Skill Development: IBM's HRM Leadership has implemented a blockchain-based system to track and manage employee skills and professional development. This innovative approach allows employees to securely store their training certifications, achievements, and skill-related data on a blockchain ledger. This blockchain-based system offers the following advantages:
- Transparency and Trust: IBM's blockchain system provides the HRM Leadership to maintain transparent, immutable, and easily verifiable record of each employee's skills and professional development. Every certification, course completion, or skill enhancement is recorded on the blockchain, ensuring that the data is tamper-proof and trustworthy.
- Simplified Talent Management: IBM's HR department can easily access and evaluate an employee's skill set and development history through the blockchain platform. This simplifies talent management by enabling HR leaders to make informed decisions about promotions, assignments, and project placements based on employees' actual skill levels.
- Performance Assessment: The blockchain system also plays a crucial role in performance assessments. Senior leadership can refer to the blockchain ledger to assess an employee's progress in acquiring new skills and competencies. This data-driven approach ensures that performance assessments are based on concrete evidence, promoting fairness and objectivity.
- Personalized Development Plans: Employees can use the blockchain system to create personalized development plans. By tracking their progress on the blockchain by the HR leadership, helps to identify skill gaps, set goals for improvement, and access relevant training resources. This empowers employees to take ownership of their professional development.
- Efficient Resource Allocation: The blockchain system assists HRM leadership in allocating resources for skill development initiatives more efficiently. By analyzing the aggregated skill data, HR can identify areas where the organization needs to invest in training or recruitment to meet specific skill requirements.
- Career Growth Opportunities: The transparent skill records on the blockchain help employees identify opportunities for career growth within IBM. They can explore job openings that match their skill profiles, making it easier for employees to plan their career paths to proceed towards leadership profiles within the company.
- Compliance and Credential Verification: The blockchain's immutability ensures that training certifications and achievements are valid and trustworthy. This is particularly valuable for compliance requirements and regulatory audits.
- Reduced Administrative Overhead: Automating the recording and verification of skills and training data through blockchain reduces administrative overhead. HR teams spend less time manually verifying records, enabling them to focus on strategic talent management tasks.

IBM's blockchain-based approach to employee skill development not only enhances the organization's ability to manage its talent effectively but also empowers employees to take an active role in their professional growth taking their career towards key leadership profiles. This use case showcases how blockchain technology can contribute to HRM and its leadership by fostering transparency, trust, and efficiency in skill development and management processes.

Results and Benefits Achieved in IBM

IBM's pioneering use of BaaS in HRM has yielded several noteworthy outcomes:

- Enhanced Data Security: The blockchain-based credential verification system has significantly enhanced data security, reducing the risk of fraudulent qualifications and credentials entering the hiring process.
- Increased Efficiency: Smart contracts in onboarding and benefits management have streamlined processes, reducing administrative overhead and minimizing errors, resulting in time and cost savings.
- Transparency and Trust: The use of blockchain has increased transparency and trust among employees, as they can independently verify their records and access their benefits information, leading to improved employee satisfaction and engagement.
- Compliance and Accuracy: Payroll and benefits management powered by blockchain have improved compliance with tax regulations and reduced errors in compensation, leading to improved financial accuracy and regulatory adherence.

In summary, IBM's HR Blockchain Platform serves as a compelling case study showcasing how BaaS can revolutionize HRM practices within an enterprise. The results achieved by IBM underscore the transformative potential of blockchain in HRM, offering security, efficiency, transparency, and enhanced overall HR operations making an efficient leadership.

DATA PRIVACY AND COMPLIANCE FOR ENTERPRISE HRM

When applying blockchain principles to areas like employee safety and security, it's crucial to navigate data privacy regulations, such as the General Data Protection Regulation (GDPR), and strike a balance between transparency and confidentiality (Saita et. al. 2020). Here's how to approach these challenges:

Data Privacy and Compliance

Know the Regulations: Ensure a comprehensive understanding of relevant data privacy regulations, such as GDPR in the European Union or other regional data protection laws. This includes understanding the key principles, rights of data subjects, and obligations placed on data controllers and processors.

- Legal Expertise: Consult with legal experts or data privacy officers who specialize in compliance with data protection laws. They can help ensure that your blockchain-based system aligns with regulatory requirements.

- Data Minimization: Collect and store only the minimum amount of data necessary for the intended purpose. This reduces the risk of regulatory non-compliance and limits the exposure of personal or sensitive information.
- User Consent: Implement mechanisms for obtaining clear and informed consent from individuals whose data will be processed on the blockchain. Make it easy for users to withdraw their consent and understand how their data will be used.
- Data Protection Impact Assessments (DPIAs): Conduct DPIAs to assess the potential risks to individuals' privacy and mitigate them. This is especially important when implementing new technologies like blockchain.
- Secure Data Handling: Ensure that data is encrypted and secured at every stage of its journey within the blockchain. Security measures should include access controls, authentication, and encryption.
- Data Portability: Be prepared to facilitate data portability, enabling individuals to access their data and transfer it to other systems as required by data protection regulations.
- Notification of Data Breaches: Develop clear processes for identifying and reporting data breaches promptly, as required by GDPR. This includes notifying both data protection authorities and affected individuals when a breach occurs.

Balancing Transparency With Confidentiality

- Data Redaction: Implement mechanisms for redacting or encrypting sensitive data while preserving the necessary information for transparency. For example, in employee safety, you might use encryption to protect personal health data while maintaining records of incident details.
- Role-Based Access Control: Utilize role-based access control to ensure that only authorized personnel can access certain types of data. Not everyone needs full visibility into all data on the blockchain.
- Private Blockchains: In some cases, consider using private or consortium blockchains where access to data is limited to trusted parties. These are more suitable for situations where strict confidentiality is required.
- Smart Contracts: Utilize smart contracts to automate data access and sharing based on predefined rules and permissions. This can ensure that transparency is maintained while sensitive data remains confidential.
- Audit Logs: Maintain detailed audit logs that record who accesses the blockchain data and when. This adds a layer of accountability and transparency for data handling.

Balancing transparency with data privacy and confidentiality is a complex task. It requires a thoughtful approach to system design, adherence to data privacy regulations, and careful management of data access and security. Legal consultation and collaboration with data protection experts are essential for a successful implementation that respects both individual privacy and the benefits of blockchain transparency.

ADOPTION AND INTEGRATION OF BAAS FOR ENTERPRISE HRM LEADERS IN ORGANIZATIONS

Overcoming Resistance to New Technology

- Education and Training: To overcome resistance, invest in comprehensive education and training programs for employees and stakeholders. Make sure they understand the benefits of the new technology, such as blockchain, and how it can improve HR processes and employee safety.
- Change Management: Implement a change management strategy that focuses on addressing concerns and objections from employees. Encourage open communication, listen to feedback, and adapt the implementation plan accordingly.
- Pilot Programs: Consider starting with small-scale pilot programs to demonstrate the benefits and successes of blockchain-based HR solutions. This can help build confidence and trust in the technology.
- Internal Champions: Identify and empower internal champions who can advocate for the technology within the organization. These advocates can help overcome resistance and drive adoption.
- Clear Use Cases: Clearly define the use cases and benefits of the technology for the organization. Employees are more likely to embrace new technology when they see how it directly improves their work and benefits the company.

Integrating BaaS With Existing HR Systems

- APIs and Middleware: Utilize APIs (Application Programming Interfaces) and middleware solutions to facilitate integration between blockchain-as-a-service (BaaS) and existing HR systems. These tools can help bridge the gap between different technologies.
- Hybrid Systems: Consider creating hybrid systems that combine blockchain-based processes with legacy systems. This allows for a gradual transition and minimizes disruptions.
- Data Migration and Mapping: Ensure data compatibility and smooth migration by mapping data structures between the existing systems and the blockchain-based solution. A structured approach to data migration is crucial.
- Interoperability Standards: Support the development and adoption of interoperability standards within the blockchain ecosystem. Standardized data formats and protocols can simplify integration with various systems.

Scalability Considerations: When integrating with existing systems, consider how the blockchain solution will scale as the organization grows. Ensure that the blockchain network can handle increasing data volumes.

FUTURE TRENDS AND IMPLICATIONS OF BAAS FOR ENTERPRISE HRM LEADERS

The future trends of BaaS for HRM Leaders in Enterprises that are critical and likely to happen can be summarized as:

- Decentralized Identity and Credentials: Blockchain is expected to play a significant role in decentralized identity verification. This could revolutionize HR by providing secure, tamper-proof identity verification, simplifying onboarding, and reducing identity-related fraud (Malyar et. al. 2019).
- Tokenization of Employee Benefits: Companies may start using blockchain to tokenize employee benefits such as stock options, retirement funds, or even bonuses. This can provide employees with more control and visibility over their benefits.
- Blockchain-Based Payroll and Compensation: Blockchain can be used to streamline payroll and compensation processes, ensuring accurate and transparent payments. Smart contracts can automate pay processes based on predefined criteria.
- Secure Learning Credentials: Academic and professional credentials can be securely stored and verified on the blockchain, reducing the risk of credential fraud.
- Supply Chain HR: Extending blockchain from supply chain management to HR, you could use the same principles for tracking the origin and integrity of talent and skills.
- Integrating HR processes with supply chain data could lead to more efficient workforce management and supply chain coordination (Usakli et. al. 2019) .
- Environmental, Social, and Governance (ESG) Tracking: Blockchain can be used to track and transparently report ESG data, providing stakeholders with reliable information about an organization's social and environmental impact, which is increasingly important in HR and corporate management.
- AI and Blockchain Synergy: Combining blockchain with AI can lead to more intelligent and secure HR processes. AI can analyze blockchain data to identify patterns and insights related to employee performance, safety, and well-being (Pavitra et. al. 2024).
- Government and Regulatory Adoption: As governments recognize the potential of blockchain in HR, they may adopt blockchain for identity verification, employment records, and tax compliance, creating a more standardized approach.

In summary, the successful adoption and integration of blockchain in HR will require a combination of education, change management, and technical solutions by the leaders. As blockchain technology continues to evolve, it has the potential to transform various aspects of HR leadership and contribute to increased transparency and efficiency in the workplace (Iansiti et. al. 2017).

Proposed solutions for future trends of BaaS for Enterprise HRM leadership:

- Interoperability and Consortia:

The future of Blockchain as a Service (BaaS) in enterprise HRM holds promising developments in interoperability and the role of leaders in consortia. Interoperability will be a critical factor in ensuring that different blockchain systems can seamlessly exchange data, enabling leaders for cross-organizational collaboration. Consortia lead by future leaders, comprised of organizations with shared interests, will play a vital role in setting standards and guidelines for the adoption of blockchain in enterprise HRM. The collaborative nature of consortia fosters innovation and industry-specific solutions, potentially leading to more efficient, secure, and standardized HRM practices across organizations (Mougayar, 2016). Interoperability, the role of blockchain consortia, and cross-organization data sharing are critical aspects when implementing blockchain technology across multiple organizations or industries. Let's explore these concepts in more detail:

Definition

Interoperability refers to the ability of different blockchain networks or systems to work together seamlessly, enabling the exchange of data and transactions across various platforms.

Importance

In a world with multiple blockchain networks, ensuring interoperability is essential for widespread adoption and effective collaboration among organizations.

Interoperability allows different blockchain platforms to communicate, share data, and interact, making it easier for businesses to adopt and leverage blockchain technology.

Solutions

- Interoperability Standards: Developing and adopting industry-wide standards and protocols is crucial to ensure that different blockchain networks can interoperate. These standards define common rules for data exchange and communication between blockchains.
- Middleware Solutions: Middleware tools and platforms can serve as intermediaries, enabling data and value transfers between different blockchains. They help bridge the gaps and facilitate interoperability.
- Cross-Chain Smart Contracts: Cross-chain smart contracts are designed to execute transactions and data exchanges across different blockchain networks. These contracts can facilitate cross-blockchain functionality and data sharing.

The Role of Blockchain Consortia

Definition

Blockchain consortia are groups of organizations, often from the same industry, that come together to develop and implement blockchain solutions for common challenges or opportunities.

Importance

Blockchain consortia enable collaboration among various stakeholders with shared interests and concerns. They help pool resources, knowledge, and expertise to create industry-specific or cross-industry blockchain solutions.

Blockchain as a Service

Consortia provides a framework for setting standards, governance, and rules for blockchain implementations in a way that benefits all participants.

Functions

- Standards Development: Consortia often establish standards and best practices for blockchain implementations within their industry or domain. These standards help ensure uniformity and interoperability.
- Research and Development: Consortia can fund research and development efforts to create new blockchain technologies, applications, or protocols specific to their needs.
- Pilot Projects: Many consortia start with pilot projects to test and validate blockchain solutions. These pilot projects often involve cross-organization data sharing to improve processes and transparency.
- Advocacy: Consortia may advocate for favorable regulations and policies related to blockchain in their industry. They can act as a unified voice when dealing with governments and regulatory bodies.

Cross-Organization Data Sharing

Definition

Cross-organization data sharing refers to the practice of sharing data among multiple organizations using blockchain technology. It can involve data related to transactions, records, or any other information relevant to the participating organizations.

Importance

Cross-organization data sharing is a key use case for blockchain, as it provides a secure and transparent way to exchange data without relying on intermediaries.

It can streamline processes, improve trust among organizations, and reduce the risk of errors, fraud, or disputes.

Examples

- Supply Chain Management: Multiple organizations in a supply chain can share data related to the movement and status of goods. This improves traceability, reduces fraud, and enhances product quality.
- Healthcare: Healthcare providers, insurers, and patients can securely share medical records and billing information, improving patient care and streamlining claims processing.
- Financial Services: Banks and financial institutions can share customer identity verification data securely and efficiently, complying with Know Your Customer (KYC) requirements.

In conclusion, interoperability, blockchain consortia, and cross-organization data sharing are all essential components in the successful adoption and implementation of blockchain technology. They facilitate collaboration, data exchange, and the development of industry-specific or cross-industry blockchain solutions (World Economic Forum, 2018).

Tokenization of HR Assets

Tokenization of HR assets, such as employee stock options and incentive programs through tokens, is an innovative application of blockchain technology. Here's how these concepts work and their potential benefits:

Employee Stock Options on the Blockchain

Tokenization of Employee Stock Options

Employee stock options represent the right of an employee to purchase a specified number of company shares at a predetermined price.

Tokenizing these stock options means representing them as digital tokens on a blockchain. Each token can represent a fraction of a stock option or a full option.

Benefits

- Increased Liquidity: Tokenized stock options can potentially be traded on secondary markets, allowing employees to sell or transfer their options to others. This provides employees with greater liquidity and the ability to realize the value of their options before an IPO or acquisition event.
- Transparency and Trust: The blockchain's transparency ensures that employees can easily verify the terms and status of their stock options. This enhances trust in the process.
- Automation and Compliance: Smart contracts can automate the exercise of stock options based on predefined conditions, ensuring compliance with the terms of the options and reducing administrative overhead.
- Reduced Costs: Using blockchain can potentially reduce administrative and legal costs associated with managing stock options.

Tokenization of Incentive Programs

Company leadership can create digital tokens to represent various incentives and rewards, such as bonuses, performance-based rewards, or recognition (Khan et. al. 2019).

These tokens can be distributed to employees for achievements, contributions, or reaching specific goals.

Benefits

- Customization: Tokenized incentives can be customized to suit individual preferences and employee performance metrics, fostering motivation and engagement.

- Real-time Recognition: Tokens can be awarded in real time, providing instant recognition and reinforcement of positive behavior or outcomes.
- Trackable and Transparent: Employees can track their token rewards on the blockchain, ensuring transparency and accountability in the incentive program.
- Interoperability: Tokens can potentially be used beyond the company's ecosystem, such as for retail discounts, travel, or other external rewards.

Challenges and Considerations for Tokenization in HR

- Regulatory Compliance: Tokenization of employee stock options and incentives may be subject to various regulations and tax laws. It's crucial to comply with legal requirements and work with legal advisors to ensure compliance.
- Data Privacy: Managing sensitive data on the blockchain while adhering to data privacy regulations (e.g., GDPR) is a critical consideration. Personal data and financial information must be protected.
- Smart Contract Complexity: Designing and implementing smart contracts for stock options and incentive programs can be complex. Code must be accurate, secure, and adaptable to changing circumstances.
- Education and Communication: Employees need to understand how tokenization works and how to manage their digital assets effectively. Comprehensive communication and training are essential.
- Volatility and Valuation: Token values may be subject to market volatility, which can affect the perceived value of employee stock options or incentives.

Overall, tokenization of HR assets can modernize and enhance the management of employee benefits and incentives, providing greater transparency, flexibility, and liquidity (Tapscot et. al. 2016). However, careful planning and compliance are necessary for a successful implementation.

Decentralized Autonomous Organizations (DAOs) in Enterprise HRM

Decentralized Autonomous Organizations (DAOs) represent a significant paradigm shift in the way organizations are governed and decisions are made by leaders. These blockchain-based entities are designed to operate with minimal human intervention, relying on smart contracts and decentralized governance to guide their actions. In the context of enterprise Human Resource Management (HRM), the integration of DAOs has the potential to guide leaders for organizational governance and empower employees in unprecedented ways.

Key Implications and Potential Benefits of DAOs in HRM

Empowering Employees: DAOs can empower leaders to direct employees by giving them a direct say in decision-making processes that affect their work environment. Through transparent and decentralized voting mechanisms, employees can influence policies related to workplace culture, benefits, and even performance evaluation methods.

- Fair and Equitable Governance: The transparency and immutability of blockchain technology enable the implementation of fair and equitable governance systems. Decisions made through DAOs are recorded on the blockchain, ensuring that the process is transparent, tamper-proof, and free from biases.
- Participatory Performance Evaluation: DAOs can be used to create performance evaluation systems that involve employees in the process. Employees can vote on performance criteria, offer feedback, and even participate in peer-based evaluations. This approach fosters a more inclusive and fair performance assessment.
- Decentralized Incentive Programs: HR departments can leverage DAOs to manage decentralized incentive programs. Employees can collectively determine the criteria for earning incentives, rewards, and bonuses, ensuring that these programs align with their interests and motivations (Furr et. al. 2019).
- Transparent Compensation Structures: Compensation and pay equity are critical HR considerations. DAOs can facilitate transparent compensation structures where employees collectively decide on salary levels, adjustments, and equitable distribution.
- Whistleblower Protection: DAOs can offer anonymous and secure channels for reporting HR-related issues, ensuring that whistleblowers are protected and their concerns are addressed transparently.
- Democratic HR Policies: The implementation of DAOs in HRM can lead to more democratic HR policies, where employees have a direct voice in shaping the culture and practices of the organization.
- Efficient Decision-Making: DAOs can streamline decision-making processes by automating various aspects of HR, reducing administrative overhead, and enhancing the efficiency of HR operations.

Challenges and Considerations

While the concept of DAOs in HRM leadership is exciting and full of potential, there are challenges and considerations to address:

i. Ensuring that DAO-based decisions align with legal and regulatory requirements.
ii. Educating employees about the functioning of DAOs and ensuring their active participation.
iii. Preventing the risk of a "tyranny of the majority" where the majority might disproportionately influence decisions.
iv. Establishing mechanisms to resolve disputes or conflicts that may arise from DAO-based decisions.
v. Integrating DAOs within existing organizational structures and hierarchies.

DAOs have the potential to revolutionize HRM leadership by fostering transparent, participatory, and equitable decision-making. While challenges exist, the advent of blockchain technology and DAOs guide the leadership to offer a new frontier for enhancing employee engagement and shaping organizational cultures that prioritize fairness, transparency, and employee empowerment.

Figure 4. AI and BAAS benefits

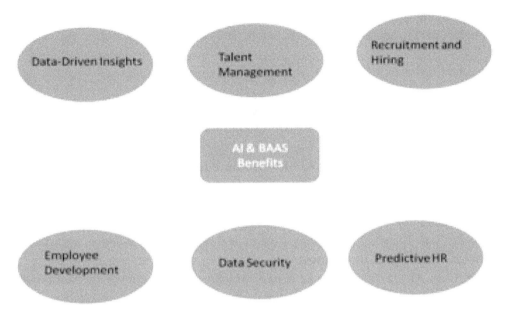

The Role of Artificial Intelligence (AI)

The integration of Artificial Intelligence (AI) with blockchain technology and Blockchain as a Service (BaaS) in HRM is a powerful combination that has the potential to revolutionize how organizations manage their human resources (Davenport, 2018). This synergy offers several significant benefits and capabilities for the leadership in below ways to run the organization efficiently:

- Data-Driven Insights: AI can analyze the data stored on the blockchain to derive valuable insights into employee performance, well-being, and job satisfaction (Abdul et. al. 2018) . It can identify trends, patterns, and correlations within HR data, helping HR professionals make informed decisions.
- Talent Management: AI-driven HR analytics can provide organizations with a deeper understanding of their talent pool. This includes identifying high-potential employees, predicting turnover, and assessing skill gaps. With this information, HR can develop targeted strategies for talent management, such as training and career development programs.
- Recruitment and Hiring: AI-powered tools can streamline the recruitment process by analyzing candidate resumes, conducting preliminary interviews, and assessing qualifications. This reduces the time and effort required to identify and onboard new talent.
- Employee Development: AI can create personalized development plans for employees based on their skills, goals, and areas that need improvement. This ensures that training and development resources are allocated efficiently.
- Data Security: AI can enhance data security on the blockchain by identifying and mitigating security threats in real time. It can monitor the blockchain network for unauthorized access, data breaches, or suspicious activities, safeguarding HR records and sensitive information.

- Predictive HR: AI can be used to predict HR-related events, such as employee turnover, workplace accidents, or training needs. By analyzing historical data on the blockchain, organizations can take proactive measures to address these issues before they escalate.

Challenges and Considerations in Implementing AI in BaaS:

- Data Privacy and Security: The integration of AI in BaaS introduces additional privacy and security concerns. Protecting sensitive data from AI algorithms and ensuring data privacy compliance are essential considerations.
- Integration Complexity: Integrating AI into existing BaaS systems can be complex and may require significant adjustments. Compatibility and seamless integration with the current BaaS infrastructure should be carefully managed.
- Data Quality and Integrity: The quality and integrity of the data stored on the blockchain are critical for AI analysis. Ensuring that data is accurate and reliable is a challenge, as blockchain data, once entered, cannot be easily modified.
- Algorithm Bias: AI algorithms can be biased, which can lead to unfair or discriminatory outcomes. Organizations must be vigilant in monitoring and mitigating algorithm bias, especially in HRM applications where fairness and equity are paramount.
- Training and Expertise: Implementing AI in BaaS requires specialized knowledge and expertise. Finding or training personnel who understand both blockchain technology and AI is a challenge for many organizations.
- Regulatory Compliance: AI applications within BaaS need to adhere to existing regulations, including data privacy laws and industry-specific standards. Staying compliant while integrating AI can be a complex task.
- Scalability: The scalability of AI systems is crucial, especially in large and complex BaaS ecosystems. Ensuring that AI algorithms can handle increasing volumes of data and users is a consideration.

While the integration of AI into BaaS offers numerous benefits and opportunities, it also presents challenges and considerations that organizations must address. Balancing innovation with security, privacy, and fairness is essential for successful AI implementation in BaaS applications. Careful planning and a commitment to addressing these challenges can lead to a more efficient, secure, and intelligent BaaS ecosystem.

The combination of blockchain, BaaS, and AI in HRM promises its leaders to be transformative. This integrated approach offers leaders in any organizations with tools to harness the full potential of their HR processes, making them more efficient, data-driven, and employee-centric. As organizations embrace these trends, they are well-positioned to create future leaders of HRM practices that are not only equitable and transparent but also responsive to the evolving needs of both employees and the organization.

CONCLUSION

Blockchain as a Service offers a promising avenue for leaders in any enterprise to revamp their HRM processes, making them more secure, transparent, and efficient. As blockchain technology continues to mature and becomes more accessible through BaaS providers, organization leadership can leverage its potential to stay competitive in the ever-evolving business landscape. The future leaders of HRM can harness the power of blockchain, and early adopters are poised to reap the rewards of this transformative technology.

Recap of Key Findings

In this paper, we have delved into the transformative potential of Blockchain as a Service (BaaS) in the realm of Human Resource Management (HRM) leadership. Key findings underscore the advantages of BaaS for leaders in enterprise HRM providing the guidance, including reduced infrastructure costs, enhanced scalability, streamlined development, and deployment, and a focus on core HR functions. Furthermore, the myriad applications of blockchain in enterprise HRM, from secure identity verification to payroll management and performance evaluation, reveal the extensive potential for improvement and innovation within HR processes.

Contributions to the Field

This research thesis makes substantial contributions to the fields of enterprise HRM and blockchain technology. By emphasizing the practical implications of BaaS in enterprise HRM, it provides a bridge between cutting-edge technology and real-world HR practices being sought by leaders of any organization. The study sheds light on the profound benefits of blockchain adoption in HR processes by senior leadership, such as enhanced transparency, security, and efficiency, which are poised to redefine HR operations and the employee experience.

Practical Implications

The practical implications of this research are manifold. HR professionals and organizational leaders can draw from these findings to optimize their enterprise HRM practices. By adopting BaaS, organizations can streamline their HR processes, ensuring data integrity and reducing operational overhead. Policymakers and regulators can also benefit from this research by gaining insights into the implications of blockchain technology for HR-related regulations and compliance standards.

Future Research Directions

While this research has laid a robust foundation for understanding the convergence of blockchain technology and enterprise leaders in HRM with case studies and analysis, it also points to potential areas for future exploration. The dynamic nature of both blockchain technology and HRM processes necessitates ongoing research. Areas such as the development of blockchain-based HR standards, strategies for data privacy compliance, and the evolution of HR analytics in the blockchain era represent promising directions for future leaders for proper investigation.

Through the adoption of BaaS, enterprise leaders can leverage a multitude of benefits, including reduced infrastructure costs, enhanced scalability, and streamlined development and deployment of HR solutions. These advantages empower leaders in HR departments to redirect their focus from the intricacies of blockchain infrastructure management towards core HR functions, such as talent management, recruitment, and employee development.

The applications of blockchain in enterprise leadership in HRM are as diverse as they are transformative. From secure identity verification to transparent management of employee records, payroll, and compensation, blockchain offers a new level of data security, transparency, and automation. It ensures that HR processes are conducted with increased accuracy and integrity while reducing the risk of fraud and disputes. Furthermore, blockchain is not merely a technological enhancement but a catalyst for positive change, offering innovative solutions in areas like time and attendance tracking, learning and development records, and performance evaluation. However, it is essential to navigate challenges related to data privacy and compliance, ensuring the secure handling of sensitive HR data within the blockchain ecosystem.

In essence, the research underscores that BaaS is poised to empower the leaders in any enterprise HRM in the future. By embracing this technology and exploring its manifold applications, leaders of organizations/enterprises are well-positioned to unlock the full potential of HR processes, fostering an environment of trust, transparency, and efficiency that not only benefits employees but also propels organizations toward a brighter and more innovative future. As we embrace the promise of BaaS in enterprise HRM, we set a course for a more innovative, trustworthy, and efficient future of leaders in HR practices, benefiting employees and organizations/enterprises alike.

REFERENCES

Abdul, A., & Zulkernine, M. (2018). Blockchain-based employee performance evaluation system. In *Proceedings of the 2018 IEEE/ACM International Conference on Advances in Social Networks Analysis and Mining* (pp. 890-897). IEEE.

Antonopoulos, A. M. (2014). *Mastering Bitcoin: Unlocking Digital Cryptocurrencies*. O'Reilly Media.

Davenport, T. H. (2018). AI in HR: Artificial intelligence to augment human performance. *MIT Sloan Management Review, 59*(4), 1–14.

Deloitte. (2018). *Blockchain and the future of HR*. Deloitte University Press. Retrieved from https://www2.deloitte.com/content/dam/insights/us/articles/3849_The-blockchain-evolution-and-hr/DUP_Brookfield-Report_Final.pdf

Furr, N., Gerrick, D., Munro, P., & Vennix, P. (2019). *Blockchain for HR and Talent Management: Creating Digital Ecosystems*. Springer.

Iansiti, M., & Lakhani, K. R. (2017). The truth about blockchain. *Harvard Business Review, 95*(1), 118–127.

IBM. (2019). *The Impact of Blockchain on HR and the Future of Work*. IBM Institute for Business Value. Retrieved from https://www.ibm.com/downloads/cas/X2KQAKO2

Khan, I. S., & Ahmed, M. (2019). Leveraging blockchain technology for HR and talent management: Current and prospects. *Proceedings of the 52nd Hawaii International Conference on System Sciences.*

Malyar, N., & Yazdani, A. (2019). Blockchain-based decentralized identity management for refugees. *IEEE Access : Practical Innovations, Open Solutions, 7*, 18989–19000.

Meijer, S. A., Følstad, A., & Brokking, D. (2018). Blockchain in Government: Benefits and Implications of Distributed Ledger Technology for Information Sharing. *Government Information Quarterly, 35*(3), 355–364.

Mofijur, M., AlMaaruf, A., Reaz, M. B. I., & Noor, A. (2019). Blockchain in HR Recruitment Process. In *2019 IEEE/RSJ International Conference on Intelligent Robots and Systems (IROS)* (pp. 1-5). IEEE.

Mougayar, W. (2016). *The Business Blockchain: Promise, Practice, and Application of the Next Internet Technology.* Wiley.

Noe, R. A., Hollenbeck, J. R., Gerhart, B., & Wright, P. M. (2019). *Human Resource Management: Gaining a Competitive Advantage.* McGraw-Hill Education.

Pavitra, K. & Agnihotri, A. (2024). *Artificial Intelligence in Corporate Learning and Development: Current Trends and Future Possibilities.* Academic Press.

Saita, S., Serradell-López, E., Jiménez-Ramírez, A., Martínez-Bazán, N., & Arciniegas, J. (2020). A blockchain approach for secure collaborative business process execution. *Information Systems, 92*, 101558.

Strohmeier, S., & Piazza, F. (2018). Blockchain in HR. In *Human Resource Management* (pp. 151–164). Springer.

Tapscott, D., & Tapscott, A. (2016). *Blockchain Revolution: How the Technology Behind Bitcoin is Changing Money, Business, and the World.* Penguin.

Usakli, A. B., & Tokdemir, G. (2019). A blockchain-based supply chain risk management framework and its empirical validation. *International Journal of Production Research, 57*(7), 2072–2093.

World Economic Forum. (2018). *Blockchain in Humanitarian Action.* World Economic Forum. http://www.weforum.org/dpcs/WEF_Blockchain_in_Humanitarian_Action_2018.pdf

Chapter 12
A Bibliographic Study on Challenges and Management Issues in Leadership and Technology Integration

Nitish Kumar Minz
https://orcid.org/0009-0000-4770-0336
K.R. Mangalam University, India

Richa Nangia
https://orcid.org/0000-0002-6128-8648
Sushant University, India

Alka Agnihotri
Galgotias University, India

ABSTRACT

This comprehensive bibliometric research delves into global interdisciplinary studies, exploring leadership, technology integration, finance, and sustainability. Investigating diverse topics, including total quality management challenges in Malaysian SMEs, geopolitical influences on eService adoption, and leadership dynamics in culturally diverse tech projects, the narrative extends to broader domains such as financial literacy, UK construction post COVID-19, and sustainable practices in contaminated campus areas. The review evaluates senior IT leadership's impact, virtual clinic lessons post COVID-19, global business knowledge management challenges, and safety data ecosystems using analytics, synthesizing insights from 54 papers. Concluding with a bibliometric analysis, the research provides a panoramic view of evolving research trends from 1989 to 2023, enhancing understanding across disciplines.

DOI: 10.4018/979-8-3693-1946-8.ch012

1. INTRODUCTION

1.1 Background and Rationale

In the contemporary landscape where technology is inseparable from our daily lives, this bibliographic study aims to deepen our comprehension of the intricate relationship between leadership and technology integration (Bennett & Mayouf, 2021). As technology becomes intertwined with various facets of our existence, its assimilation into leadership practices and organizational frameworks introduces a distinctive set of challenges (Barker, 2021). By meticulously examining key research papers and scholarly works, this study strives to identify recurring challenges encountered by leaders navigating the integration of technology (Zhao & Liu, 2018). Moreover, it endeavors to unravel the managerial strategies employed to effectively address these challenges (Scribante, Pretorius, & Benade, 2017).

Aligned with the objectives of the bibliographic study, our research seeks to contribute to this discourse by synthesizing insights from a diverse array of sources (Bueno, Günther, & Philippi, 2017). By exploring themes such as leadership in the digital age, technology adoption, change management, and the influence of technology on leadership styles and organizational culture, our study aligns with the comprehensive overview provided by the bibliographic analysis (Mohannak & Matthews, 2015). Through this intellectual exploration, we aspire to offer valuable insights that can empower leaders, managers, and researchers in optimizing technology within organizational contexts (Tester, Nicewicz, & Oswalt, 2021). This research endeavors to extend the foundation laid by the bibliographic study, propelling future research endeavors aimed at refining and enhancing leadership practices in our dynamic technological landscape (Yasmeen et al., 2020).

1.2 Research Question

Is there a substantial corpus of academic literature exploring the challenges and management issues in the intersection of leadership and technology integration, and what insights can be gleaned from a bibliometric analysis of this literature to uncover prevalent themes, document trends, collaborative networks, geographic distribution, and emerging directions in research?

1.3 Advancing the Knowledge Frontier

As technology continues to evolve, its integration with leadership practices propels organizations into uncharted territories (Tester et al., 2021). This research endeavors to advance the knowledge frontier by systematically reviewing and synthesizing the existing literature, offering a comprehensive understanding of the intricate dynamics at the confluence of leadership and technology integration.

1.4 Pioneering Fresh Perspectives and Insights

By employing bibliometric analysis, this research seeks to pioneer fresh perspectives and insights (Bennett & Mayouf, 2021), contributing to the existing body of knowledge. The synthesis of scholarly contributions will not only inform current understanding but also provide a foundation for future research endeavors in this critical area.

2. RESEARCH METHODOLOGY

The research methodology involved a comprehensive search on Scopus using a systematic approach to assess literature on leadership, technology integration, and management challenges. The initial search, "leadership AND technology AND integration AND management," yielded 686 documents. Further refinement with a focus on challenges resulted in 162 documents. A stringent search within specific subject areas and language constraints narrowed it down to 54 documents in Business, Sociology, and Arts. Inclusion criteria ensured the selection of English publications, aligning with the research objectives, while ethical considerations were paramount throughout the process. Employing Biblioshiny and VOS-viewer for data analysis added a quantitative dimension, facilitating insights into collaborative networks, geographic distribution, and emerging trends. This methodology provides a robust foundation for analyzing challenges and management issues at the intersection of leadership and technology integration.

Boolean String for Search

```
TITLE-ABS-KEY (leadership AND technology AND integration AND management AND
challenges) AND (LIMIT-TO (SUBJAREA, "BUSI") OR LIMIT-TO (SUBJAREA, "SOCI") OR
LIMIT-TO (SUBJAREA, "ARTS")) AND (LIMIT-TO (LANGUAGE, "English"))
```

3. LITERATURE REVIEW

In a comprehensive bibliographic study encompassing diverse fields, several scholars have undertaken research endeavors to unravel challenges and management issues across leadership and technology integration. Abdullah (2010) conducted a meticulous examination to measure Total Quality Management (TQM) implementation in Malaysian SMEs through case studies, surveys, interviews, and document analysis. Alsaeed et al. (2017) delved into geopolitical influences on eService adoption, utilizing case studies, interviews, surveys, and documentary analysis to reveal the impact of geopolitical factors on the adoption of electronic services. Furthermore, Asgary and Samhain (2008), through a literature review, explored effective leadership strategies for culturally diverse technology projects, identifying key leadership approaches.

Barker (2021) employed an analytics approach to analyze safety data ecosystems, uncovering patterns and trends in safety data but limited to specific datasets. Bennett and Mayouf (2021) investigated value management integration in the UK construction industry post-COVID-19, utilizing mixed methods including surveys, interviews, and document analysis. Brewer et al. (2013) focused on ICT and innovation integration in a regional construction firm, employing case studies, interviews, surveys, and document analysis to explore successful integration within a regional context. Bueno et al. (2017) delved into sustainable management for a contaminated area on campus using case studies, interviews, site visits, and environmental assessments.

Glover and Miller (2002) studied the introduction of interactive whiteboards into schools in the United Kingdom, employing case studies, interviews, and surveys to explore the impact on pedagogic and technological change. Additionally, Graham et al. (2020) conducted a systematic review to investigate the tension between leadership archetypes in construction, limiting their exploration to existing literature. Jahn et al. (2022) focused on identifying key factors for efficient airport facility management through a case study, interviews, and surveys, specifically within the airport industry. Furthermore, Kauffeld et al. (2022) utilized a Delphi-based study to explore the future of mobile and virtual work, offering expert perspectives on predictions for the future. Shang and Liao (2008) studied the management capabilities of ICT innovation in SMEs through surveys and interviews, exploring the management capabilities of ICT innovation, particularly in the context of SMEs.

The thematic underpinning of this bibliographic exploration converges on the multifaceted challenges inherent in leadership and technology integration across diverse sectors. While the methodologies employed vary from case studies, surveys, and interviews to literature reviews, each study contributes valuable insights into the complexities of managing technology and leadership dynamics. This collective body of research provides a robust foundation for understanding the intricacies and potential resolutions concerning the amalgamation of leadership strategies and technological advancements in various organizational contexts.

4. BIBLIOMETRIC ANALYSIS

4.1 Document Analysis

The document analysis reveals a dataset spanning from 1989 to 2023, comprising 54 documents sourced from 51 diverse outlets, including journals, books, and more. Despite a stable annual growth rate of 0%, the dataset presents a wealth of scholarly information with an average document age of 9.63 years. Each document garners an average of 17.96 citations, indicating their impact and significance within academic discourse. Impressively, the collective references across these documents amount to 2374, underlining the extensive literature that forms the foundation of this dataset.

In terms of content, the documents are rich in keywords, with 309 Keywords Plus (ID) and 198 Author's Keywords (DE), illustrating the depth and breadth of topics covered. A diverse range of 129 authors contributed to these documents, with 13 opting for single-authored works. Collaboration is evident, as each document boasts an average of 2.44 co-authors, fostering a cooperative scholarly environment. Additionally, international collaboration is present, constituting 7.41% of co-authorships.

The dataset is diverse in terms of document types, including 23 articles, 6 book chapters, 16 conference papers, and 7 reviews. A single book and a conference review contribute to the dataset's varied composition. This document analysis offers valuable insights into the dataset's composition, highlighting its temporal scope, interdisciplinary sources, authorship dynamics, and the varied types of scholarly contributions encapsulated within.

Table 1. Summarized literature review (Author's compilation)

Paper Info	Purpose	Methodology	Results	Limitations
Abdullah, A. (2010)	Measure TQM implementation in Malaysian SMEs	Case studies, surveys, interviews, document analysis	Identified factors influencing TQM success	Limited generalizability, potential biases in self-reported data
AlSaeed et al. (2017)	Investigate eService adoption during geopolitical instabilities	Case study, interviews, surveys, documentary analysis	Revealed impact of geopolitical factors on eService adoption	Limited generalizability, potential biases in self-reported data
Asgary & Thamhain (2008)	Explore effective leadership for culturally diverse tech projects	Literature review	Identified key leadership strategies	Theoretical, lack empirical validation
Barker, T.T. (2021)	Analyze safety data ecosystems using analytics	Analytics Approach	Uncovered patterns and trends in safety data ecosystems	Limited to specific datasets, may not capture the full complexity
Bennett & Mayouf (2021)	Examine value management integration in the UK construction industry post-COVID-19	Mixed methods (surveys, interviews, document analysis)	Identified value management practices post-COVID-19	Limited generalizability, potential biases in self-reported data
Brewer et al. (2013)	Investigate ICT & innovation integration in a regional construction firm	Case study, interviews, surveys, document analysis	Explored successful integration of ICT & innovation	Specific to a regional context, limited generalizability
Bueno et al. (2017)	Explore sustainable management for a contaminated area on campus	Case studies, interviews, site visits, environmental assessments	Identified successful sustainable management practices	Limited to a specific contaminated area, potential biases in self-reported data
Byrd et al. (2006)	Study the influence of senior IT leadership on IT infrastructure	Survey, interviews	Explored the role of senior IT leadership in shaping IT infrastructure	Limited to perspectives of senior IT leaders, potential biases in self-reported data
Chandan, H.C. (2013)	Examine challenges in global business knowledge management	Literature review	Identified challenges in global knowledge management	Theoretical, lack empirical validation
Davis et al. (2014)	Advance socio-technical systems thinking and propose a call for bravery	Conceptual paper	Advocated for a more courageous approach in socio-technical systems thinking	Theoretical, lack empirical validation
Gilbert et al. (2021)	Reflect on leadership a year after the rapid roll-out of virtual clinics due to COVID-19	Interviews, surveys	Explored leadership reflections and lessons learned	Limited to a specific context and time frame, potential biases in self-reported data
Gioko (2013)	Create an effective professional learning sessions model on technology integration for a Kenyan school district	Case studies, interviews, surveys	Developed a model for effective technology integration professional learning	Limited to a specific school district, potential biases in self-reported data
Glover & Miller (2002)	Examine the introduction of interactive whiteboards into schools in the United Kingdom	Case studies, interviews, surveys	Explored the impact of interactive whiteboards on pedagogic and technological change	Limited to a specific geographic context, potential biases in self-reported data
Graham et al. (2020)	Investigate tension between leadership archetypes	Systematic review	Examined tensions in leadership archetypes in construction	Limited to the existing literature, potential biases in selected studies
Hallo & Gorod (2020)	Apply engineering management principles for improving quality and efficiency in patient-centered care	Case study, interviews, site visits	Identified principles for improving quality and efficiency in patient-centered care	Limited to a specific healthcare context, potential biases in self-reported data

continued on following page

A Bibliographic Study on Challenges and Management Issues in Leadership and Technology Integration

Table 1. Continued

Paper Info	Purpose	Methodology	Results	Limitations
Harris (2001)	Ensure European leadership in the global marketplace	Literature review	Explored strategies for ensuring European leadership	Theoretical, lack empirical validation
Hatfield & Brahmi (2004)	Evaluate the post-implementation of Angel at the Indiana University School of Medicine	Post-implementation evaluation, surveys, interviews	Assessed the impact and effectiveness of Angel	Limited to a specific educational context, potential biases in self-reported data
Hecht (2017)	Co-create more livable cities	Case studies, interviews, surveys	Explored principles for co-creating livable cities	Limited to specific cities, potential biases in self-reported data
Jahn et al. (2022)	Identify key factors for efficient airport facility management	Case studies, interviews, surveys	Explored factors for efficient airport facility management	Specific to the airport industry, potential biases in self-reported data
Kander (2003)	Evaluate a successful experiment in curriculum integration at James Madison University	Case study, interviews, document analysis	Examined the success of curriculum integration at James Madison University	Limited to a specific educational context, potential biases in self-reported data
Kauffeld et al. (2022)	Investigate the future of mobile and virtual work	Delphi-based study	Explored predictions for the future of mobile and virtual work	Expert opinions may vary, and potential biases in expert perspectives
Kawtrakul et al. (2013)	Explore Thailand's transformation to e-government	Case studies, interviews, surveys	Examined challenges and roadmap for Thailand's e-government	Limited to the Thai context, potential biases in self-reported data
Langa & Marnewick (2020)	Adapt IT management for effective IT strategy leadership	Case studies, interviews, surveys	Explored strategies for effective IT strategy leadership	Limited to specific organizations, potential biases in self-reported data
Makori & Osebe (2016)	Assess the potential impact of the Koha ERP system on information management organizations	Case studies, interviews, surveys	Explored the potential impact of the Koha ERP system	Limited to specific information management organizations, potential biases in self-reported data
Mohannak & Matthews (2015)	Examine knowledge integration within the innovation process	Case studies, interviews, surveys	Explored knowledge integration within the innovation process	Limited to specific industries, potential biases in self-reported data
Mukerji (2019)	Explore sustainability in project management	Literature review	Examined the synergy of practice and theory in sustainability and project management	Theoretical, lack empirical validation
Noordin & Othman (2005)	Investigate challenges to an e-business model	Case studies, interviews, surveys	Examined challenges pre- and post-adoption of an e-business model	Limited to specific industries, potential biases in self-reported data
Ochieng et al. (2018)	Utilize a systematic knowledge management-based system for optimizing project management operations in oil and gas organizations	Case studies, interviews, surveys	Explored the use of a knowledge management-based system in project management	Limited to the oil and gas industry, potential biases in self-reported data
Olin et al. (2016)	Implement an ARC-informed family-centred care intervention for children's community-based mental health programs	Intervention studies, interviews, surveys	Implemented and assessed a family-centered care intervention	Limited to specific mental health programs, potential biases in self-reported data

continued on following page

Table 1. Continued

Paper Info	Purpose	Methodology	Results	Limitations
Ozorhon & Karahan (2017)	Identify critical success factors of BIM implementation	Case studies, interviews, surveys	Explored critical success factors for BIM implementation	Limited to the construction industry, potential biases in self-reported data
Park et al. (2003)	Integrate disciplinary perspectives on fifth-wave M&A research	Literature review	Examined disciplinary perspectives on M&A research	Theoretical, lack empirical validation
Reynolds & Freshman (2011)	Review technology integration in graduate health management education	Literature review	Examined competency models and applications to electronic medical records	Theoretical, lack empirical validation
Sawhney (2017)	Study technology integration in Indian schools using a value-stream-based framework	Case studies, interviews, surveys	Explored technology integration using a value-stream-based framework	Limited to Indian schools, potential biases in self-reported data
Schneider (2018)	Address managerial challenges of Industry 4.0	Literature review	Proposed an empirically backed research agenda for Industry 4.0	Theoretical, lack empirical validation
Scribante et al. (2017)	Explore requirements engineering principles applicable to technology and innovation management	Literature review	Identified requirements engineering principles	Theoretical, lack empirical validation
Shang & Liao (2008)	Analyze the management capabilities of ICT innovation for sustained competitiveness in SMEs	Survey, interviews	Explored management capabilities of ICT innovation	Limited to SMEs, potential biases in self-reported data
Steuer & Leicht-Scholten (2017)	Investigate innovation and diversity in research associations	Case studies, interviews, surveys	Explored the integration of new perspectives into research associations	Limited to specific research associations, potential biases in self-reported data
Subrahmanyam (2023)	Navigate global leadership strategies for e-enabling technology deployment	Literature review	Explored global leadership strategies for technology deployment	Theoretical, lack empirical validation
Tatum (1989)	Manage for increased design and construction innovation	Case studies, interviews, surveys	Explored strategies for increased innovation in design and construction	Limited to specific projects, potential biases in self-reported data
Tester et al. (2021)	Develop an online engineering management master's program	Case studies, interviews, surveys	Explored the development of an online engineering management program	Limited to a specific educational context, potential biases in self-reported data
Thamhain & Asgary (2015)	Study team collaboration in multinational R&D projects	Case studies, interviews, surveys	Explored collaboration in multinational R&D projects	Limited to specific R&D projects, potential biases in self-reported data
Valadas et al. (2022)	Investigate digital platforms and technologies in school clusters in Portugal	Case studies, interviews, surveys	Explored perspectives of school leaders on digital platforms	Limited to school clusters in Portugal, potential biases in self-reported data
Wu (2008)	Explore catalogers' exploration of a new frontier	Case studies, interviews, surveys	Explored the establishment of a NEASC Evidence Center	Limited to catalogers, potential biases in self-reported data
Xu et al. (2020)	Examine how service robots will redefine leadership in hotel management	Delphi approach	Explored expert opinions on the redefinition of leadership in hotel management	Expert opinions may vary, and potential biases in expert perspectives

continued on following page

Table 1. Continued

Paper Info	Purpose	Methodology	Results	Limitations
Yasmeen et al. (2020)	Assess the impact of transformational leadership and IT business strategy alignment on EIS adaptation	Surveys, interviews	Explored the impact of leadership and IT strategy on EIS adaptation	Limited to specific industries, potential biases in self-reported data
Moffat & McLean (2010)	Explore merger as a conversation	Literature review	Examined the concept of merger as a conversation	Theoretical, lack empirical validation
Zhao & Liu (2018)	Study the promotion mode of MOOCs in higher education based on the innovation diffusion theory	Case studies, interviews, surveys	Explored the promotion mode of MOOCs in higher education	Limited to specific universities, potential biases in self-reported data

Table 2. Document analysis (Author's compilation)

Description	Results
MAIN INFORMATION ABOUT DATA	
Timespan	1989:2023
Sources (Journals, Books, etc)	51
Documents	54
Annual Growth Rate %	0
Document Average Age	9.63
Average citations per doc	17.96
References	2374
DOCUMENT CONTENTS	
Keywords Plus (ID)	309
Author's Keywords (DE)	198
AUTHORS	
Authors	129
Authors of single-authored docs	13
AUTHORS COLLABORATION	
Single-authored docs	13
Co-Authors per Doc	2.44
International co-authorships %	7.407
DOCUMENT TYPES	
article	23
book	1
book chapter	6
conference paper	16
conference review	1
review	7

4.2 Performance Analysis

4.2.1 Annual Scientific Production

Figure 1 portrays the evolving landscape of scientific production from 1989 to 2023, offering intriguing insights into the dynamics of scholarly contributions. A discernible upward trend signifies the field's robust growth, with annual article publications more than doubling over the period, indicative of an expanding research milieu. While this overall trajectory is evident, the graph reveals nuanced fluctuations, notably a modest dip in the late 1990s and a subsequent surge in the mid-2000s. These temporal shifts may mirror changing research emphases, funding dynamics, or broader shifts in scholarly priorities. Notably, the recent moderation in growth sparks reflection, suggesting potential saturation, heightened publication standards, or a recalibration of research directions. This nuanced observation hints at the field's maturity and prompts consideration of the intricate factors steering its trajectory. Figure 1, therefore, serves as a visual narrative not only of quantitative growth but also as a window into the field's evolution, prompting further exploration into the underlying factors shaping the trends in scientific production.

4.2.2 Source's Production Over Time

Figure 2 unveils the dynamic landscape of sources contributing to scientific production over time, offering valuable insights into the evolving scholarly ecosystem. The consistent rise in the number of sources from two in 1989 to an impressive 51 in 2023 signifies a remarkable diversification within the field. Notably, the recent surge in the number of sources, particularly from 2019 to 2023, showcases a rapid expansion that could be attributed to the flourishing landscape of open-access publishing, the establishment of new academic journals, or the emergence of novel fields of study. Beyond the quantitative growth, the graph reveals a spectrum of productivity among

Figure 1. Annual scientific production (Author's compilation)

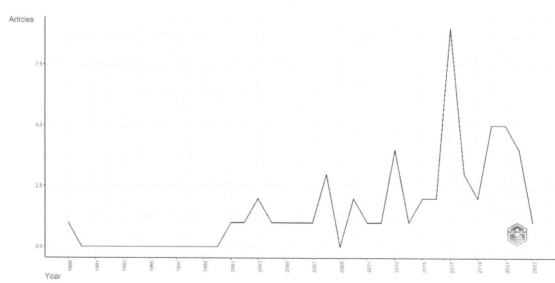

Figure 2. Source's production over time (Author's compilation)

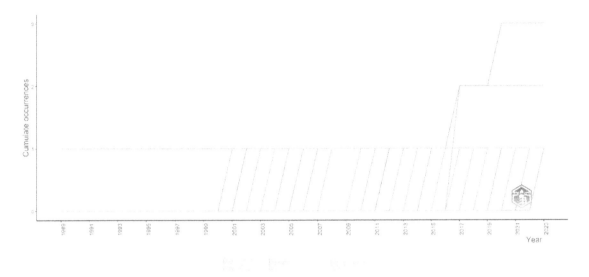

sources. In 2023, the top source exhibited a robust output of 19 articles, while the bottom source contributed a single article, highlighting a hierarchical distribution among sources. This nuanced variation suggests a stratification of sources, possibly indicating differing levels of prestige or selectivity within the scholarly community. Figure 2, thus, not only illustrates the quantitative evolution of sources but prompts deeper exploration into the factors influencing this diverse and dynamic scholarly landscape.

4.2.3 Country's Production Over Time

Figure 3 delineates the scientific production trajectories of five prominent countries from 1989 to 2023, providing a comprehensive snapshot of their evolving contributions to global research. The United States (USA) emerged as the leader in scientific production, a position maintained throughout the timeline, closely trailed by China, Australia, Germany, and the United Kingdom (UK). Notably, China has exhibited a remarkable surge, nearly bridging the production gap with the US in 2023, reflecting a transformative shift in the global scientific landscape. All five countries have demonstrated a consistent upward trajectory in scientific output, with China experiencing the most rapid growth, followed by Australia and Germany. While the US and UK display a more moderate but steady increase, fluctuations in production for all nations hint at the complex interplay of factors influencing research dynamics. The US witnessed a dip in the early 2000s, while China's surge occurred in the mid-2000s, highlighting the dynamic nature of scientific production influenced by funding, research priorities, and evolving publication trends. Figure 3 not only unveils the quantitative evolution of scientific output but prompts deeper inquiries into the nuanced factors shaping the research landscapes of these influential nations.

Figure 3. Country's production over time (Author's compilation)

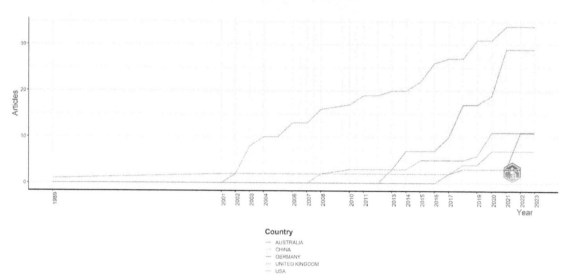

4.2.4 Most Relevant Source

Figure 4 illustrates the bibliometric analysis of the most relevant sources for a specific research topic, providing insights into the distribution of documents across various publication types. The X-axis enumerates sources, encompassing journals, conference proceedings, and books, while the Y-axis quantifies the number of documents attributed to each source. Notably, the top three contributors to this research topic include the "Journal of Management in Engineering" with 3 documents, followed by the "International Journal of Productivity and Quality" and the "14th Americas Conference on Information Systems, A 2013," each contributing 2 documents. It is crucial to recognize that the prominence of a source extends beyond numerical counts, considering factors such as research quality, source reputation, and alignment with specific research questions. The image underscores the diversity in publication types, showcasing a mix of journals, conference proceedings, and books. Additionally, the considerable variability in document counts per source indicates a broad spectrum of contribution levels, ranging from singular documents to multiple publications. While providing valuable insights into document distribution, the image does not furnish details about the specific research topic or the field of study, encouraging a more nuanced exploration of the research context. Figure 4, therefore, serves as a visual guide, sparking curiosity for further investigation into the multifaceted landscape of relevant sources in this particular research domain.

4.3 Citation Analysis

4.3.1 Citation Analysis of Articles

Figure 5 unfolds the intricate web of scholarly connections through a citation network, visualized using VOS viewer software. The network is artfully divided into clusters, each represented by a distinct colour, suggesting thematic coherence among articles that share frequent citations. Within these clusters, certain authors emerge as linchpins, epitomized by "Harris, P.R." and "Tatum, C.B."

Figure 4. Most relevant source (Author's compilation)

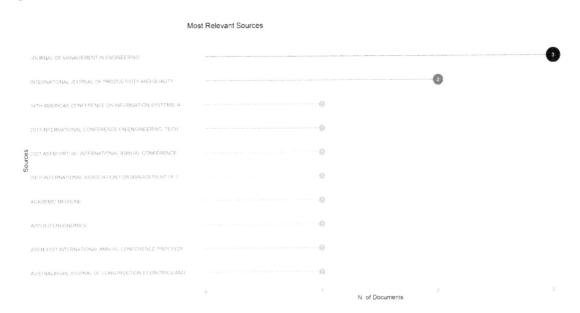

in the green cluster, showcasing their pivotal role in shaping and influencing the thematic discourse. The arrows between articles depict citation relationships, with the thickness of the arrows indicating the strength of influence. This not only unveils key influencers within each cluster but also provides a broader perspective on the interconnectedness of research contributions. Additionally, the ability to analyze the network over time can uncover the dynamic evolution of the field, shedding light on emerging clusters and shifting trends. It is imperative to recognize that this static image is a snapshot, and a comprehensive understanding would necessitate delving into the underlying data and contextual intricacies of the research. Figure 5 serves as a visual compass, guiding exploration into the intellectual landscape of the topic, revealing influential nodes, thematic trends, and the dynamic interplay of ideas in the scholarly domain.

4.3.3 Most Cited Countries

Figure 6 encapsulates a bibliometric analysis of research trends in human-computer interaction, as outlined in the 2019 paper published in "Scientometrics." The data, spanning from 1999 to 2018 and sourced from the Web of Science database, reveals the most cited countries in this domain. Notably, the United States emerged as the frontrunner with 36,395 citations, followed by the United Kingdom, China, Germany, and Italy. This insight provides a snapshot of the global impact of research contributions in human-computer interaction, shedding light on the prominent nations driving scholarly influence in this field. It is essential to recognize that citation metrics offer a lens into the visibility and resonance of research but should be complemented with considerations of research quality, topic significance, and the nuances of different scientific disciplines. Figure 7 serves as a visual representation of the scholarly landscape, contributing to our understanding of the geographical distribution of impactful research in human-computer interaction.

Figure 5. Citation analysis of articles (Author's compilation)

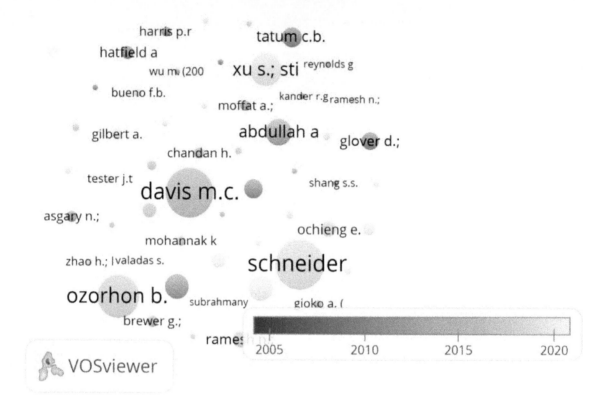

Figure 6. Most cited countries (Author's compilation)

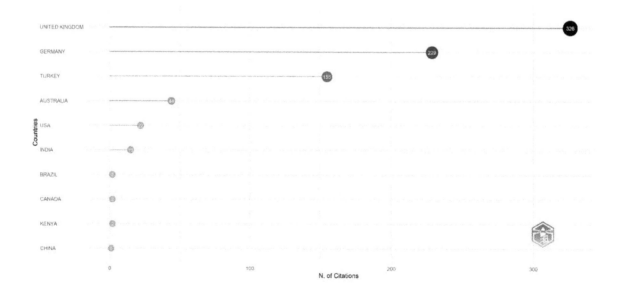

4.4 Word Analysis

4.4.1 Word Cloud

Figure 7, a word cloud focused on leadership, vividly portrays the core themes and values associated with effective leadership. At its center, the term "Leadership" stands out prominently, encapsulating the overarching theme. Surrounding it are key concepts such as "Vision," highlighting the need for a clear and forward-looking direction, and "Strategy," emphasizing the importance of well-defined plans. "Communication" emerges as a pivotal element, underscoring the crucial role of effective interaction in leadership. The words "Change," "People," and "Innovation" convey adaptability, the human aspect, and creativity, respectively, as integral facets of leadership. Additional notable terms like "Collaboration," "Results," and "Integrity" underscore the collaborative nature of leadership, the ultimate goal of achieving desired outcomes, and the paramount importance of ethical conduct. This word cloud encapsulates a comprehensive view of the multifaceted dimensions and values associated with impactful leadership, providing a succinct visual representation of its key elements.

4.4.2 Word Frequency Over Time

The word frequency over time graph (Figure 8) illustrates the evolving landscape of construction engineering topics from 1989 to 2021. Examining the cumulative occurrences of keywords provides insights into shifting trends and research emphases within the field. Notably, the overall upward trajectory in word frequencies suggests a growing interest and scholarly focus on these themes.

The variations in frequency among specific words unveil nuanced patterns:

Figure 7. Word cloud (Author's compilation)

i. Competition and Leadership: These words exhibit pronounced and consistent increases, indicating heightened scholarly attention to competitive dynamics and leadership within the construction engineering domain.
ii. Project Management: While generally on an upward trajectory, there is a notable dip around 2005. This fluctuation could be influenced by external factors, such as changes in project management practices or shifts in industry demands.
iii. Technology: Experiences a significant surge around 2011, reflecting a potentially transformative period where technology became a more prominent aspect of construction engineering research.
iv. Construction Industry and Engineering Education: While showing overall increases, these terms display relatively steadier patterns, suggesting enduring but perhaps less dynamically evolving areas of study.

The presence of checkboxes for cumulative occurrences allows for a flexible view of the data, accommodating preferences for cumulative or non-cumulative representations.

It is essential to consider potential external factors such as changes in funding priorities, technological advancements, or industry developments that may have influenced the observed trends. Additionally, a more in-depth analysis could benefit from insights into the specific sources and methodologies underlying the data.

5. CONCLUSION

This comprehensive examination travers leadership dynamics, technological challenges, financial considerations, and sustainability concerns. Analyzing Total Quality Management challenges in Malaysian

Figure 8. Word frequency over time (Author's compilation)

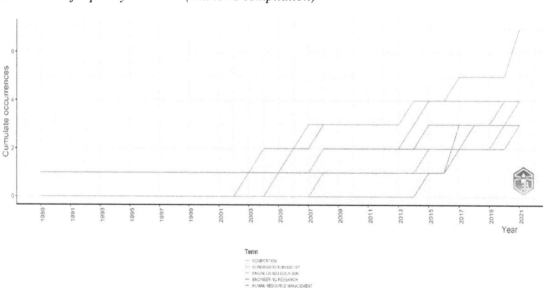

SMEs, eService adoption amid geopolitical instabilities, and the intricacies of e-government transformation in Thailand, the research paper captures the essence of contemporary scholarship. Central themes of leadership and adaptability emerge, reflected in studies on culturally diverse tech projects and leadership nuances during the rapid deployment of virtual clinics amid the COVID-19 pandemic. These insights contribute to advancing leadership theory, acknowledging the critical role of adaptability in confronting unprecedented challenges.

The chapter delves into financial literacy, value management in the UK construction sector post-COVID-19, and sustainable practices in contaminated campus areas. Each study provides valuable perspectives for practitioners and policymakers, enriching our understanding of diverse domains. Evaluations of senior IT leadership, reflections on virtual clinics, challenges in global business knowledge management, and analytics-driven explorations of safety data ecosystems further contribute to a nuanced comprehension of contemporary issues.

A global perspective is reinforced through studies on predictions for the future of mobile work, effective technology integration in Kenyan schools, and efficient airport facility management. These explorations highlight the interconnectedness of global challenges and emphasize the necessity of context-specific solutions.

The bibliometric analysis spanning 1989 to 2023, as encapsulated in the research paper, serves as a panoramic lens on the evolution of research trends. It not only reveals the quantitative growth in scientific production but also captures the dynamic shifts in focus over time. From the ascendancy of e-government studies to the exploration of mobile work and curriculum integration, the analysis underscores the responsive nature of research to societal and technological changes.

In essence, the diverse conversations within this chapter collectively depict the multifaceted nature of contemporary research. Aligned with the research paper's focus, they underscore the importance of interdisciplinary perspectives, the adaptability of leadership amidst challenges, and the global interconnectedness of scholarly pursuits. As the research landscape continues to evolve, these insights from the paper serve as guiding lights, shaping the trajectory of future investigations and contributing significantly to the collective knowledge in the realm of leadership and technology integration.

REFERENCES

Abdullah, A. (2010). Measuring TQM implementation: A case study of Malaysian SMEs. *Measuring Business Excellence*, *14*(3), 3–15. doi:10.1108/13683041011074173

Alsaeed, A., Adams, C., & Boakes, R. (2017). eService adoption during geopolitical instabilities: Case study of the Syrian refugees. *Proceedings of the European Conference on e-Government, ECEG Part F129463*, 20-28.

Asgary, N., & Thamhain, H. (2008). Effective leadership for culturally diverse technology projects. PICMET: Portland International Center for Management of Engineering and Technology, Proceedings, 1345-1350. doi:10.1109/PICMET.2008.4599746

Barker, T. T. (2021). Finding Pluto: An Analytics-Based Approach to Safety Data Ecosystems. *Safety and Health at Work*, *12*(1), 1–9. doi:10.1016/j.shaw.2020.09.010 PMID:33732523

Bennett, K., & Mayouf, M. (2021). Value management integration for whole life cycle: Post covid-19 strategy for the UK construction industry. *Sustainability (Basel), 13*(16), 9274. doi:10.3390/su13169274

Brewer, G., Gajendran, T., & Runeson, G. (2013). ICT & innovation: A case of integration in a regional construction firm. *The Australasian Journal of Construction Economics and Building, 13*(3), 24–36. doi:10.5130/AJCEB.v13i3.3484

Bueno, F.B., Günther, W.M.R., & Philippi, A., Jr. (2017). Sustainable management for a contaminated area on campus. *World Sustainability Series*, 261-273. doi:10.1007/978-3-319-47877-7_18

Byrd, T. A., Lewis, B. R., & Bradley, R. V. (2006). Is infrastructure: The influence of senior IT leadership and strategic information systems planning. *Journal of Computer Information Systems, 47*(1), 101–113. doi:10.1080/08874417.2006.11645937

Chandan, H. C. (2013). Knowledge management and its challenges in global business. Cultural and Technological Influences on Global Business, 290-315. doi:10.4018/978-1-4666-3966-9.ch016

Davis, M. C., Challenger, R., Jayewardene, D. N. W., & Clegg, C. W. (2014). Advancing socio-technical systems thinking: A call for bravery. *Applied Ergonomics, 45*(2, 2 Part A), 171–180. doi:10.1016/j.apergo.2013.02.009 PMID:23664481

Flumian, M., Coe, A., & Kernaghan, K. (2007). Transforming service to Canadians: The Service Canada model. *International Review of Administrative Sciences, 73*(4), 557–568. doi:10.1177/0020852307083458

Gilbert, A. W., Davies, L., Doyle, J., Patel, S., Martin, L., Jagpal, D., Billany, J. C. T., & Bateson, J. (2021). Leadership reflections a year on from the rapid roll-out of virtual clinics due to COVID—Gioko, A. (2013). Creating an effective professional learning sessions model on technology integration for a Kenyan school district. *Education and Information Technologies, 18*(2), 151–164. doi:10.1007/s10639-012-9236-6

Glover, D., & Miller, D. (2002). The introduction of interactive whiteboards into schools in the United Kingdom: Leaders, led, and the management of pedagogic and technological change. *International Electronic Journal for Leadership in Learning, 6*(1), 1–11.

Graham, P., Nikolova, N., & Sankaran, S. (2020). Tension between Leadership Archetypes: Systematic Review to Inform Construction Research and Practice. *Journal of Management Engineering, 36*(1), 3119002. doi:10.1061/(ASCE)ME.1943-5479.0000722

Hallo, L., & Gorod, A. (2020). Engineering management principles for improving quality and efficiency in patient-centred care. *ASEM 41st International Annual Conference Proceedings "Leading Organizations through Uncertain Times"*.

Halvorson, S. A. C., Tanski, M., Milligan, L., & Yackel, T. (2019). Transitioning from Volume to Value: Lessons Learned from the Dissolution of a Population Health Partnership. *Academic Medicine, 94*(9), 1305–1309. doi:10.1097/ACM.0000000000002614 PMID:31460920

Harris, P. R. (2001). Ensuring European leadership in the global marketplace. *European Business Review*, *13*(6), 336–345. doi:10.1108/EUM0000000006196

Hatfield, A. J., & Brahmi, F. A. (2004). Angel: Post-implementation evaluation at the Indiana University School of Medicine. *Medical Reference Services Quarterly*, *23*(3), 1–15. doi:10.1300/J115v23n03_01 PMID:15364647

Hecht, B. (2017). Co-Creating More Livable Cities. Management for Professionals, Part F600, 157-174. doi:10.1007/978-3-319-46021-5_9

Jahn, M., Reber, J.-H., & Struck, R. (2022). What is the key to efficient airport facility management and high service quality? Learnings from Berlin Brandenburg Airport's Technical Control Centre transformation. *Journal of Airport Management*, *16*(3), 256–267.

Kander, R. G. (2003). A successful experiment in curriculum integration: Integrated Science and Technology at James Madison University. *Proceedings - Frontiers in Education Conference, 3*, S4A1-S4A5.

Kauffeld, S., Tartler, D., Gräfe, H., Windmann, A.-K., & Sauer, N. C. (2022). What will mobile and virtual work look like in the future?—Results of a Delphi-based study [Wie sieht die mobile und virtuelle Arbeit der Zukunft aus? – Ergebnisse einer Delphi-basierten Studie]. *Zeitschrift fur Angewandte Organisationspsychologie*, *53*(2), 189–214. doi:10.1007/s11612-022-00627-8

Kawtrakul, A., Ruengittinun, S., Rungrusamiwatanakul, N., & Khampachua, T. (2013). Thailand's transformation to c-government: Core challenges and roadmap. E-Government Implementation and Practice in Developing Countries, 349-366. doi:10.4018/978-1-4666-4090-0.ch016

Langa, M., & Marnewick, P. C. (2020). Adapting IT management for Effective IT strategy leadership. *26th International Association for Management of Technology Conference, IAMOT 2017*, 770-789.

Makori, E. O., & Osebe, N. M. (2016). Koha enterprise resource planning system and its potential impact on information management organizations. *Library Hi Tech News*, *33*(4), 17–23. doi:10.1108/LHTN-01-2016-0005

Moffat, A., & McLean, A. (2010). Merger as conversation. *Leadership and Organization Development Journal*, *31*(6), 534–550. doi:10.1108/01437731011070023

Mohannak, K., & Matthews, J. (2015). Knowledge integration within the innovation process: A technopreneurial perspective. *International Journal of Technoentrepreneurship*, *3*(1), 17–36. doi:10.1504/IJTE.2015.067088

Mukerji, D. (2019). *Sustainability in Project Management: Advancing the Synergy of Practice and Theory*. Palgrave Studies of Cross-Disciplinary Business Research, in Association with EuroMed Academy of Business. doi:10.1007/978-3-030-17523-8_13

Noordin, M. F., & Othman, R. (2005). Challenges to an E-business model: Pre-and post-adoption. *Internet and Information Technology in Modern Organizations: Challenges and Answers - Proceedings of the 5th International Business Information Management Association Conference, IBIMA 2005*.

Ochieng, E. G., Ovbagbedia, O. O., Zuofa, T., Abdulai, R., Matipa, W., Ruan, X., & Oledinma, A. (2018). Utilizing a systematic knowledge management-based system to optimize project management operations in oil and gas organizations. *Information Technology & People, 31*(2), 527–556. doi:10.1108/ITP-08-2016-0198

Olin, S.-C. S., Hemmelgarn, A. L., Madenwald, K., & Hoagwood, K. E. (2016). An ARC-Informed Family Centered Care Intervention for Children's Community Based Mental Health Programs. *Journal of Child and Family Studies, 25*(1), 275–289. doi:10.1007/s10826-015-0220-9 PMID:28781510

Ozorhon, B., & Karahan, U. (2017). Critical Success Factors of Building Information Modeling Implementation. *Journal of Management Engineering, 33*(3), 4016054. doi:10.1061/(ASCE)ME.1943-5479.0000505

Park, K., King, D. R., Chaudhuri, S., Arikan, A. M., & Goulet, P. K. (2003). Integrating disciplinary perspectives on fifth-wave M&A research. *Proceedings of the IASTED International Conference on Alliances, Mergers and Acquisitions*, 45-49.

Ramesh, N., & Ravi, A. (2017). Enhancing the performance of micro, small and medium-sized cluster organizations through lean implementation. *International Journal of Productivity and Quality Management, 21*(3), 325-342. https://doi.org/10.1504/IJPQM.2017.08445811

Ramesh, N., & Ravi, A. (2017). Enhancing the performance of micro, small and medium-sized cluster organizations through lean implementation. *International Journal of Productivity and Quality Management, 21*(3), 325–342. doi:10.1504/IJPQM.2017.084458

Reynolds, G., & Freshman, B. (2011). Technology integration and graduate health management education: A review of competency models and application to electronic medical records. Encyclopedia of E-Leadership, Counseling and Training, 1, 233-246. doi:10.4018/978-1-61350-068-2.ch017

Sawhney, D. (2017). Technology integration in Indian schools using a value-stream-based framework. *IEEE Region 10 Humanitarian Technology Conference 2016, R10-HTC 2016 - Proceedings*, 7906787. doi:10.1109/R10-HTC.2016.7906787

Schneider, P. (2018). Managerial challenges of Industry 4.0: An empirically backed research agenda for a nascent field. *Review of Managerial Science, 12*(3), 803–848. doi:10.1007/s11846-018-0283-2

Scribante, N., Pretorius, L., & Benade, S. (2017). Requirements engineering principles applicable to technology and innovation management. *PICMET 2017 - Portland International Conference on Management of Engineering and Technology: Technology Management for the Interconnected World, Proceedings 2017*, 1-8. 10.23919/PICMET.2017.8125350

Shang, S. S. C., & Liao, L.-Y. (2008). An analysis of the management capabilities of ICT innovation for sustained competitiveness in SMEs. *14th Americas Conference on Information Systems, AMCIS 2008, 1*, 293-305.

Steuer, L., & Leicht-Scholten, C. (2017). Innovation and diversity: Integrating new perspectives into research associations. *Proceedings of the European Conference on Innovation and Entrepreneurship, ECIE 2017*, 767-776.

Subrahmanyam, S. (2023). Navigating global leadership strategies for e-enabling technology deployment. *Journal of Law and Sustainable Development, 11*(6), e01220. doi:10.55908/sdgs.v11i6.1220

Tatum, C. B. (1989). Managing for increased design and construction innovation. *Journal of Management Engineering, 5*(4), 385–399. doi:10.1061/(ASCE)9742-597X(1989)5:4(385)

Tester, J. T., Nicewicz, K., & Oswalt, J. (2021). Development of online engineering management masters at Tennessee Tech University. *2021 ASEM Virtual International Annual Conference "Engineering Management and The New Normal"*, 438-445.

Thamhain, H. J., & Asgary, N. (2015). Team collaboration in multinational R&D projects. *2013 International Conference on Engineering, Technology and Innovation, ICE 2013 and IEEE International Technology Management Conference, ITMC 2013*, 7352710. 10.1109/ITMC.2013.7352710

Valadas, S. T., Fernandes, P., Figueiredo, C., & Vilhena, C. (2022). Digital Platforms and Technologies in School Clusters in Portugal: The Perspective of School Leaders. *International Journal of Educational Organization and Leadership, 17*(2), 59–72. doi:10.18848/2329-1656/CGP/v29i02/59-72

Wu, M. (2008). Catalogers Explore a New Frontier: Establishing a NEASC Evidence Center. *Journal of Academic Librarianship, 34*(1), 67–71. doi:10.1016/j.acalib.2007.11.003

Xu, S., Stienmetz, J., & Ashton, M. (2020). How will service robots redefine leadership in hotel management? A Delphi approach. *International Journal of Contemporary Hospitality Management, 32*(6), 2217–2237. doi:10.1108/IJCHM-05-2019-0505

Yasmeen, H., Wang, Y., Zameer, H., & Ahmad, Z. (2020). Environmental turbulence as a moderator on the impact of transformational leadership and IT business strategy alignment on EIS adaptation. *International Journal of Information Systems in the Service Sector, 12*(3), 74–92. doi:10.4018/IJISSS.2020070105

Zhao, H., & Liu, Q. (2018). The practice and research on the promotion mode of MOOCs in higher education are based on the innovation diffusion theory. *Proceedings - 2018 7th International Conference of Educational Innovation through Technology, EITT 2018*, 198-203. 10.1109/EITT.2018.00047

Chapter 13
Megatrends in Leadership and Technology Across Industries

Vaishnavi Gadi
SVKM'S NMIMS, Mumbai, India

Pathik Govani
SVKM's NMIMS, Mumbai, India

ABSTRACT

The chapter explores the concept of megatrends in leadership and technology, emphasizing their growing importance in shaping organizations. It explores the interconnectedness of leadership styles and technological advancements, integrating change management to highlight the need to adapt to these megatrends for sustained success. It analyzes the transformative shifts in leadership at various organizational levels, from the C-suite executives to operational and management roles, including empathetic, purpose-driven, and collaborative leadership, and the rise of data-driven decision-making, agile leadership, and adaptability in various functions such as sales and marketing, human resources, operations and finance. It also discusses the impact of technological advancements across sectors like FMCG, pharma, manufacturing, IT, and Edtech, examining the impact of AI, ML, blockchain technology, IoT, automation, and virtual reality applications. Challenges related to data privacy and other technological innovations are also highlighted.

1. INTRODUCTION

1.1. Introduction to Modern Leadership and Technological Advancements and Change Management

Effective leadership in the current digital era is essential for organisational success, especially when considering change management and technology improvements. Leaders need to be adept at navigating the challenges of change inside their organisations and have a thorough awareness of how technology can spur creativity and efficiency (Tagscherer and Carbon 2023). This entails remaining current with

DOI: 10.4018/979-8-3693-1946-8.ch013

the newest technology developments that are pertinent to their sector, such as cloud computing, artificial intelligence (AI), data analytics, automation, and the Internet of Things (IoT), and using these developments to improve decision-making and productivity (Haleem et al. 2023).

Using strong change management techniques is another aspect of effective leadership in this situation. To guarantee that change projects are effectively executed and welcomed by all stakeholders, this entails meticulous preparation, unambiguous communication, stakeholder involvement, and ongoing assessment. It is the leaders' responsibility to drive digital transformation in their organisations by reinventing business processes, encouraging an innovative culture, and coordinating technical projects with strategic goals (Leadership and Change Management_ Navigating Organizational Transitions - The Economic Times n.d.).

Modern leaders also need to place a high value on flexibility and agility, being able to quickly adjust to changes in the market, welcome experimentation, and provide people the freedom to develop. Leaders must handle matters like data privacy, cybersecurity, and proper use of developing technology, all of which are highly ethical. Making choices that respect honesty, openness, and social responsibility is necessary for this (Cultivating Leadership Skills in the Digital Age - The Economic Times n.d.).

In order to be a modern leader, one must invest in training programmes (Hill and Fenn III 2019), cultivate a culture of learning, and maintain a constant state of curiosity about best practices and new trends (Donaldson 2006). Leaders can effectively negotiate the dynamic difficulties of the digital era, promote growth, and lead their organisations through technology changes by combining these ideas (Cortellazzo, Bruni, and Zampieri 2019).

1.2. Significance of Adapting to the Megatrends for the Future Success of Organizations

Organisations must quickly adapt to megatrends if they hope to succeed in the fast-changing global economy (Retief et al. 2016). These megatrends, which include significant changes in economics, demography, technology, and the environment, have a significant impact on enterprises in a variety of sectors. Long-term growth and competitiveness are more likely for organisations that proactively accept and adjust to these megatrends (PWC 2018).

Technological innovation is a major megatrend that is revolutionising several industries and opening up new avenues for efficiency and growth (Jeflea et al. 2022). Organisations may achieve operational efficiency, improve customer satisfaction, and foster innovation-driven initiatives by adopting technologies like blockchain, automation, AI, and IoT (Javaid, Haleem, Singh, Suman, and Gonzalez 2022).

Changes in the workforce's demographics and in customer preferences are also significant factors. In order to spur innovation and maintain market relevance, organisations need to adjust to a varied workforce, meet the requirements and expectations of many generations, and take advantage of demographic changes (Germain 2021).

Globalisation, digitization of economies, and the realignment of economic power centres are examples of economic megatrends that bring opportunities as well as challenges. Businesses can enter new markets, establish strategic alliances, and profit from new business models if they comprehend and manage these economic changes (Samuel and Danso Evans Twum 2019).

Business strategies are being more and more shaped by environmental megatrends like resource shortages, climate change, and sustainability issues. In addition to helping to create a more sustainable future, businesses that emphasise sustainability, lessen their environmental impact, and innovate with eco-friendly methods also improve their brand recognition and draw in eco-aware customers (Kalia, Shailesh Tyagi, and Saha 2022).

2. THE EVOLUTION OF LEADERSHIP STYLES ACROSS ORGANIZATIONAL FUNCTIONS

In light of upcoming megatrends in leadership and technology across industries, predictive and prescriptive analytics are essential tools for businesses and organisations looking to make data-driven choices and optimise their operations for better results. These methods use data to predict future trends, spot possible dangers and opportunities, and suggest the best courses of action (Kini n.d.).

Organisations face complicated issues in the quickly changing leadership and technology landscape, which are driven by megatrends such technological innovation, demographic shifts, economic changes, and environmental concerns. Organisations may forecast consumer behaviour, market trends, and competitive dynamics with the use of predictive analytics. Predictive analytics is the application of algorithms and historical data analysis to forecast future situations with high accuracy. This capability enables leaders to take preemptive measures and seize new possibilities (D'Cruz et al. 2022).

Prescriptive analytics is a kind of predictive analytics that goes beyond outcome prediction to suggest the optimal course of action for achieving objectives. This method evaluates different options for decisions and identifies the best courses of action by combining simulation, machine learning, and optimisation algorithms. Prescriptive analytics offers actionable insights and decision assistance to help executives handle complexity, ambiguity, and rapid change in the context of future megatrends (Understanding 3 Types of Business Analytics to Improve Decision-Making _ Brightly n.d.).

Prescriptive and predictive analytics are becoming essential tools for strategy planning, resource allocation, risk management, and performance optimisation across a wide range of industries, including manufacturing, retail, healthcare, and finance. By utilising these analytical tools, leaders may boost competitiveness, stimulate innovation, and build long-term value for their companies (Bhatt Mishra et al. 2023).

Furthermore, the capacity to use data-driven insights becomes even more crucial as megatrends continue to reshape the business environment. Businesses that engage in prescriptive and predictive analytics skills are better able to handle demographic changes, take advantage of business opportunities, respond to technology disruptions, and successfully handle environmental concerns (Why is Data-Driven Analytics of Interest to Companies_ _ Institute of Data n.d.).

2.1. The Changing Role of the C-Suite Leadership

2.1.1. Transformation of Leadership at the Executive Level

One important factor in the dynamic and changing corporate landscape is the evolution of executive leadership, especially in the C-suite. The modern business climate has brought about a dramatic transformation in the position of executives in the C-suite, as they navigate through rapid technical breakthroughs, evolving market dynamics, and changing consumer tastes (The New Path to the C-Suite_ Leadership Skills and Business Fundamentals for Mid-Career Leaders - The Economic Times n.d.).

The transformation's emphasis on strategic agility and foresight is one of its main features. It is required of C-suite executives to be well-versed in the disruptive technologies, new trends, and market dynamics affecting their sector. They need to be able to see possibilities, foresee changes, and take the initiative to steer their organisations towards innovation and expansion (The impact of agility: How to shape your organization to compete | McKinsey 2023).

In the C-suite, inclusive and collaborative leadership is also receiving more attention. At every level of the company, executives are urged to promote a culture of empowerment, diversity, and teamwork. This entails utilising the combined knowledge and perceptions of varied groups to stimulate creativity, solve problems, and make decisions (Thompson et al. 2022).

The integration of digital skills is a critical component of the transformation of C-suite leadership. Executives are improving consumer experiences, operational efficiency, and strategic decision-making by utilising digital tools, data analytics, and artificial intelligence (McCarthy, Sammon, and Alhassan 2022). To do this, executives must adopt a new approach known as "data-driven leadership," in which they employ data analytics to obtain practical insights, streamline workflows, and enhance corporate results (Datnow and Park 2014).

2.1.2. Relevance of Concepts Like Empathetic Leadership, Purpose-Driven Leadership, and Collaborative Leadership

At the C-suite level, understanding ideas like collaborative leadership, purpose-driven leadership, and empathetic leadership is essential to establishing organisational culture, advancing strategic goals, and creating long-term success. C-suite executives should pay special attention to these leadership paradigms since they are crucial in establishing the tone for the values, vision, and behaviour of the company (Groysberg, Kevin Kelly, and MacDonald 2011).

Understanding and sympathising with the many viewpoints, needs, and concerns of stakeholders, including as workers, clients, shareholders, and communities, is a prerequisite for compassionate leadership at the C-suite level. Establishing a culture of psychological safety, encouraging open communication, and cultivating trustworthy connections are top priorities for C-suite executives that demonstrate empathic leadership skills. This gives them the ability to motivate employees, foster loyalty, and strengthen organisational resilience in the face of adversity (Berman 2019).

The C-suite level of purpose-driven leadership involves communicating an engaging vision, mission, and values that connect with stakeholders and direct strategic decision-making. Executives in the C-suite who lead with purpose balance corporate goals with a larger sense of sustainability, social responsibility, and purpose. Purpose-driven CEOs inspire dedication, spur innovation, and produce long-term value for the company and society by outlining a clear purpose and uniting stakeholders around it (Gyori and Kazakova 2020).

C-suite executives must practise collaborative leadership in order to take use of the combined knowledge, skill, and inventiveness of external partners and cross-functional teams. At the C-suite level, cooperation entails dismantling organisational silos, encouraging teamwork, and cultivating a collaborative and knowledge-sharing culture. Prioritising collaborative leadership among C-suite executives empowers teams, fosters diversity of thought, and promotes alignment towards shared objectives, all of which contribute to improved organisational performance, increased agility, and quicker decision-making (Sadun et al. 2022).

2.1.3. Alignment of the Newer Leadership Styles with Future Organizational Goals and Societal Expectations

A strategic approach that incorporates these leadership paradigms into fundamental business processes and decision-making frameworks is necessary to ensure that emerging leadership philosophies, such as purpose-driven, collaborative, and empathetic leadership, are in line with future organisational objectives and societal expectations (New leadership in an era of thriving organizations | McKinsey n.d.).

Emotionally intelligent and able to comprehend and relate to the viewpoints of stakeholders, empathetic leadership is in line with future organisational objectives through talent development, diversity and inclusion, and well-being of employees. Through the use of data-driven insights on employee engagement, the development of a psychological safety culture, and the encouragement of empathy-driven communication techniques, C-suite executives may put empathetic leadership tactics into reality (The et al. 2022).

Driven by purposeful innovation, stakeholder value creation, and sustainable practices, purpose-driven leadership is in line with future organisational goals. It prioritises a clear sense of purpose, values, and social responsibility. Through the integration of purpose-driven metrics into performance evaluations, the establishment of corporate social responsibility (CSR) initiatives that are in line with strategic objectives, and the dissemination of purpose-driven narratives to stakeholders, C-suite executives can effectively align business strategies with societal expectations (Jimenez, Franco, and Smith 2021).

The purpose of collaborative leadership is to enhance agility, creativity, and strategic alignment across multiple teams and stakeholders. It is centred on promoting teamwork, cross-functional collaboration, and collective problem-solving, all of which are in line with future organisational goals. Through the use of collaborative tools, cross-functional team workshops, and performance measures connected to common objectives and results, C-suite executives can encourage collaborative leadership (The Rise of Collaborative Leadership - CXO Mag n.d.).

2.2. Emerging Trends for Sales and Marketing Leaders

2.2.1. Intersection of Technology and Customer-Centric Leadership

In order to generate growth, improve customer experiences, and gain a competitive edge in the modern digital age, organisations in the sales and marketing area must investigate the convergence of technology and customer-centric leadership. This point of contact signifies a strategic convergence wherein leadership effectiveness guarantees that sales and marketing initiatives are in line with customer wants and expectations, and technology facilitates customer-centricity (Leah and Don 2023).

The way that sales and marketing teams interact with customers is changing dramatically as a result of technological innovations like marketing automation platforms, artificial intelligence, CRM (Customer relationship management) systems, and data analytics. In this context, customer-centric leadership entails using technology to obtain useful insights into the behaviour, preferences, and journey touchpoints of customers. Managers in charge of sales and marketing may promote the use of customer-centric technologies, set up data-driven plans, and cultivate a customer-centric culture within the company (Haleem, Javaid, Asim Qadri, et al. 2022).

Organisations can leverage real-time customer data and predictive analytics to personalise marketing campaigns, customise product offerings, and optimise sales processes by using the convergence of technology and customer-centric leadership. This makes it possible for marketing and sales teams to provide customers with relevant, tailored experiences that spark interest and, in turn, boost conversions and customer loyalty (Okorie et al. 2024).

In order to provide a smooth, integrated customer experience, sales and marketing departments must be in sync, according to customer-centric leadership. In order to ensure consistent messaging and brand positioning across all consumer touchpoints, leaders must assist in dismantling organisational barriers and promoting communication between the sales and marketing teams. Organisations can establish a cohesive strategy to customer interaction and promote sustainable success by coordinating technology investments with customer-centric objectives and cross-functional cooperation (Shields 2021).

2.2.2. Role of AI in Personalized Marketing and Sales Strategies

By using data analytics, machine learning algorithms, and predictive modelling to examine consumer behaviour, preferences, and purchasing patterns, artificial intelligence (AI) plays a critical role in personalised marketing (Haleem, Javaid, Asim Qadri, et al. 2022). This makes it possible for businesses to design experiences that are unique to each consumer and their requirements, interests, and purchasing paths. Leaders in marketing and sales may take the lead in integrating AI technology by investing in AI-powered tools and platforms, supporting data-driven decision-making, and encouraging an innovative and experimental culture (Davenport et al. 2020).

AI enables businesses to segment their client base based on data-driven insights, develop campaigns and communications that are specifically targeted at them, and distribute pertinent information through a variety of channels in personalised marketing. AI-driven personalisation gives the correct message to the right customer at the right moment, which improves customer engagement, boosts conversion rates, and fortifies brand loyalty (Verma et al. 2021).

Similar to this, AI is essential to customised sales strategies since it can automate tedious work, give sales teams useful insights, and enable lead grading and forecasting based on predictive data. Chatbots, virtual assistants, and sales analytics platforms are a few examples of AI-powered sales technologies that enable salespeople to concentrate on high-value tasks, forge closer bonds with clients, and increase sales effectiveness and efficiency (Haleem, Javaid, Asim Qadri, et al. 2022).

Guiding organisational goals, cultivating a data-driven culture, and guaranteeing the ethical use of AI technology are all aspects of leadership in the context of AI-driven personalised marketing and sales strategies. Leaders have the opportunity to set an exemplary example by showcasing how AI can enhance personalised customer experiences, boost sales, and propel corporate expansion. They can also create governance frameworks for AI implementation, give AI talent acquisition and development top priority, and encourage accountability and openness in AI-driven decision-making (Mittal and H. Davenport 2020).

2.3. Operations and Management: New Age Leadership

2.3.1. The Rise of Data-Driven Decision-Making in Operational Leadership

Operational leaders are essential in encouraging their organisations to implement data-driven decision-making procedures (Calzon 2022). They develop a culture that prioritises data-driven insights, support the use of data analytics tools, and make investments in data infrastructure and skills. Operational leaders may increase operational efficiency, better allocate resources, and more successfully manage risks by adopting data-driven techniques (David Waller 2020).

Operational leadership employs data-driven decision-making, which entails gathering and evaluating data from a variety of sources, including as external sources, IoT devices, and internal systems. Then, using sophisticated analytics methods like machine learning, predictive modelling, and data visualisation, this data is turned into insights that can be put to use. Operational leaders use these insights to drive performance and innovation through informed decision-making, process optimisation, and opportunity identification (Stedman 2023).

2.3.2. Exploration of Agile Leadership and Its Impact on Optimizing Processes and Responding to Market Demands

Operational leaders that follow the concepts of agile leadership place a high priority on adapting quickly to shifting client expectations, competitive environments, and market conditions (Embrace Agile Leadership _ Mailchimp n.d.). They assist teams in rapidly iterating, experimenting with new concepts, and making necessary course corrections by cultivating a culture of cooperation, creativity, and swift decision-making. Agile leaders foster accountability and openness in operations management, enable teams to take responsibility of their work, and support cross-functional cooperation (De Smet 2018).

Agile leadership has a significant effect on process optimisation. Agile executives use approaches like Lean, Six Sigma, and Agile to improve operational efficiency, reduce waste, and streamline workflows (Laureani and Antony 2021). Using data-driven decision-making, continuous feedback loops, and iterative development to bring value to consumers is their top priority. Faster time-to-market, shorter cycle times, and higher-quality goods and services are the outcomes of this (Korherr et al. 2022).

Additionally, by encouraging change, seizing opportunities, and quickly adjusting to market developments, agile leadership helps organisations to effectively respond to market demands. Agile leaders strategically allocate resources, prioritise activities, and make educated decisions by utilising data analytics, market insights, and customer feedback. In a dynamic and cutthroat business climate, this helps firms to stay ahead of the competition, innovate pro-actively, and satisfy customers (Korherr et al. 2022).

2.3.3. The Importance of Adaptability and Continuous Learning in Management Roles

The responsibilities of operations managers include managing vital procedures, maximising effectiveness, and fostering organisational success (The Backbone of Efficiency_ The Vital Responsibilities of Operations Managers - The Economic Times n.d.). Operations managers need to be able to adjust to changing market conditions, technical breakthroughs, regulatory constraints, and consumer preferences. Being flexible allows them to anticipate problems, proactively identify and solve them, modify plans and procedures as necessary, and guarantee seamless transitions throughout times of change (Whyte, Stasis, and Lindkvist 2016).

Operations managers also need continuous learning. It enables them to remain current with market trends, new technological developments, and industry best practices. (MOSKOWITZ and WARD 1998). Through process changes and new initiatives, this continuous learning process enables operations managers to spot possibilities for innovation, put new ideas into practice, and propel organisational growth. As operations managers use data analytics, benchmarking, and cross-functional cooperation to handle operational difficulties, optimise resource allocation, and improve decision-making processes, continuous learning also strengthens problem-solving skills (Helo and Hao 2022). AI-driven continuous learning is imperative for effective leaders to navigate the evolving landscape of technological advancements and lead their organizations towards innovation and sustainable growth (Pavitra and Agnihotri 2024).

2.4. The Future of Human Resources and Talent Management

2.4.1. The Role of Emotional Intelligence in Future HR Leadership

Future HR leaders will need to possess emotional intelligence (EI), which is becoming more and more acknowledged as a critical factor in determining both organisational performance and employee well-being. The ability to successfully recognise, regulate, and navigate one's own emotions as well as those of others is referred to as emotional intelligence. EI is essential to HR leadership in a number of important ways (Landry 2019).

First of all, a positive work culture and increased employee engagement are made possible by EI. Strong emotional intelligence enables HR directors to build rapport with staff members, comprehend their wants and worries, and foster a collaborative and encouraging work atmosphere. Higher levels of motivation, production, and employee satisfaction result from this (Ahsan 2023).

Second, EI is essential for resolving disputes inside the company. Strong emotional intelligence enables HR directors to resolve disputes and challenging circumstances with tact, understanding, and good communication (Papoutsi, Drigas, and Skianis 2019). They can preserve harmonious connections and positive working relationships by facilitating constructive communication, reducing conflicts, and identifying win-win solutions (Fadi Smiley n.d.).

Emotional intelligence is also essential for HR leadership development programmes. Effective coaching, mentoring, and emotional support can be given to other leaders in the organisation by leaders with emotional intelligence (EI) skills . In order to lead diverse teams, foster trust, and propel organisational success, this helps leaders enhance their self-awareness, empathy, and interpersonal abilities (Coronado-Maldonado and Benítez-Márquez 2023).

Emotional intelligence is also crucial for talent management procedures (Agnihotri et al. 2023). HR directors that possess emotional intelligence (EI) are able to comprehend the goals and motives of their staff, offer individualised career development programmes, and foster an inclusive, diverse workplace culture. This helps to build a favourable employer brand and draw in and keep top personnel (Hafidz 2022).

2.4.2. Inclusive Leadership and Its Impact on Fostering Diverse and Innovative Workplace Cultures

Promoting inclusive leadership techniques within their organisations is a vital responsibility of HR leaders. Their job is to develop ideas, programmes, and policies that support DEI (diversity, equity, and inclusion) at all organisational levels (Bourke and Espedido 2019). This entails putting diversity-focused recruitment tactics into practice, offering chances for training and development that promote cultural competency, and cultivating a culture of belonging where all staff members feel encouraged to offer their special insights and ideas (Coleman, Dossett, and Dimick 2021).

Inclusive leadership has a significant effect on creating innovative and varied work environments. Employees are more likely to work well together, communicate honestly, and contribute to creative solutions when they feel appreciated and included for who they are as individuals. Moreover, inclusive leadership helps to establish a psychologically secure workplace where workers are at ease taking chances, trying out novel strategies, and questioning the status quo. As a result, there is a culture of innovation and ongoing development where different perspectives and experiences stimulate creativity, critical thinking, and well-informed decision-making (Wu and Li 2023).

2.4.3. Addressing Challenges and Opportunities Posed by Remote Work and Hybrid Work Models

Sustaining employee engagement and connection in remote and hybrid work environments is one of the major problems facing HR leadership. HR directors are responsible for putting plans and programmes in place to help remote and hybrid teams feel connected, cooperative, and communicative. This entails utilising technology to facilitate online team-building exercises, offering chances for interpersonal engagement, and encouraging clear and honest lines of communication (Haque 2023).

Ensuring performance and efficiency in remote and hybrid work environments is another difficulty. HR directors are essential in setting clear performance standards, offering resources and training for remote work, and putting in place performance management systems that prioritise results over hours spent. In addition, they must address possible problems with burnout, mental health, and work-life balance among workers who are remote or in hybrid arrangements (Raj et al. 2023).

On the other hand, HR leadership can also benefit from remote and hybrid work arrangements. These models provide increased flexibility, access to a wide range of talent pools, and the capacity to support employees' work-life balance. HR directors may take advantage of these chances by putting in place flexible work schedules, providing technical infrastructure for remote work, and encouraging a climate of trust, autonomy, and accountability (Kossek, Gettings, and Misra 2021).

Moreover, HR directors can reinvent personnel management procedures including hiring, onboarding, and development with the use of remote and hybrid work models. To effectively attract, onboard, and develop people in a distributed work environment, they might make use of digital learning platforms, remote onboarding programmes, and virtual recruitment techniques (Sani et al. 2022).

2.5. Finance Professionals and Leadership Trends

2.5.1. Impact of Blockchain Technology on Financial Transactions and Security

It is the responsibility of finance leaders to comprehend and capitalise on the potential that blockchain technology offers, while simultaneously managing the obstacles and hazards that come with its implementation (Javaid, Haleem, Singh, Suman, and Khan 2022). The promise for improved processing efficiency, transparency, and trust is one of the main effects of blockchain on financial transactions. Blockchain improves confidence between parties by enabling near real-time settlement of transactions, cutting out middlemen, lowering transaction costs, and offering a transparent, tamper-proof record of transactions (Mhlanga 2023).

Additionally, blockchain technology provides improved security measures that guard against fraud, manipulation, and unauthorised access to financial data and transactions. The risk of data breaches and cyberattacks is decreased by the use of cryptographic techniques, decentralised consensus processes, and smart contracts, which guarantee the integrity and secrecy of financial transactions (Albshaier, Almarri, and Hafizur Rahman 2024).

Finance leaders must, however, also overcome obstacles related to blockchain adoption, scalability, interoperability, and regulatory compliance. To create interoperable solutions, industry standards, and regulatory frameworks that support the ethical and long-term use of blockchain in financial transactions, they must work in conjunction with regulators, industry players, and technological partners (Habib et al. 2022).

2.5.2. Integration of ESG (Environmental, Social, Governance) Factors in Investment Decision-Making

The incorporation of Environmental, Social, and Governance (ESG) considerations into investment decision-making is indicative of a wider acknowledgement of the significance of these elements in promoting long-term value generation and risk mitigation (Sultana, Zulkifli, and Zainal 2018). Finance leaders are essential in ensuring that investment plans meet ESG standards, assessing the benefits and risks associated with ESG, and interacting with stakeholders to encourage responsibility and openness (Boffo and Patalano 2020).

Among the main advantages of incorporating ESG considerations into investment decision-making is the possibility of generating financial rewards along with favourable social and environmental effects. Leaders in finance can evaluate an organization's and an investment opportunity's sustainability performance by using ESG data, metrics, and benchmarks (Henisz, Koller, and Nuttall 2019). This entails assessing elements like corporate governance frameworks, diversity and inclusion policies, supply chain ethics, and carbon emissions (Koller, Nuttall, and Henisz 2019).

Furthermore, by detecting and reducing major ESG risks that could have an influence on investment portfolios, the incorporation of ESG elements improves risk management methods. Financial executives can utilise ESG analysis to pinpoint possible risks related to ESG concerns that could affect operations, reputation, regulations, and finances (Ma 2023). Investors may safeguard the long-term value of their investments and make better judgements by integrating ESG factors into risk assessment models and due diligence procedures (OECD 2017).

Finance executives must, however, also overcome obstacles including data accessibility, standardisation, and ESG factor measurement techniques. To create uniform ESG disclosure guidelines, reporting structures, and performance measures that enable insightful ESG analysis and comparison across businesses and industries, they must engage with industry groups, authorities, and ESG rating agencies (Zahid, Saleem, and Maqsood 2023).

3. TECHNOLOGICAL ADVANCEMENTS ACROSS DIFFERENT SECTORS AND INDUSTRIES

Technological developments in various fields and industries constitute an important field of research with broad consequences for innovation, economic growth, and societal advancement. The following section highlights the effects of technology advancements in a variety of industries, including healthcare, manufacturing, education, IT, and communication, and FMCGs (Fast Moving Consumer Goods).

3.1. Fast-Moving Consumer Goods (FMCG) and Consumer Durables (CD)

Technological developments in the FMCG business, including automation, automation, data analytics, and Internet of Things (IoT) applications, have improved supply chain efficiency, streamlined production processes, and improved product quality. These developments have boosted customer happiness and raised FMCG firms' competitiveness by enabling them to customise products, react swiftly to market trends, and optimise inventory management (Nozari et al. 2021).

Similar to this, technological advancements have completely changed the CD industry's product design, production methods, distribution networks, and consumer experiences. The CDs industry landscape has changed as a result of innovations like digital platforms, energy-efficient technology, smart appliances, and Internet of Things enabled gadgets. These developments have changed how customers engage with and get value from CD goods, in addition to enhancing product performance, functionality, and longevity (F. Li 2020).

Furthermore, in the FMCG and CDs sectors, technological advancements have been a major force for innovation and sustainability. FMCG firms are using technology to create environmentally friendly packaging, cut waste, improve product traceability, and satisfy consumer demands for products that are sustainable and mindful of the environment. Innovations in digital services, recyclable materials, and energy-efficient technology have all helped to make CDs more user-friendly and sustainable (Why eco-friendly, sustainable packaging is the future of FMCG _ Science, Engineering & Life Science Recruitment, Jobs & Staffing _ SRG n.d.).

For FMCG organisations, supply chain visibility, accuracy, and efficiency have increased dramatically with the incorporation of IoT and RFID technology in inventory management. Businesses may trace product movements across the supply chain, minimise stockouts and overstocking, and improve inventory management procedures by utilising IoT sensors and RFID tags. They may also check inventory levels in real time (Y. Lee, Cheng, and Leung 2009), (Kumar Sagar, Garg, and Dutta 2018).

AI has also revolutionised the packaging and design of FMCG products. Businesses may now analyse customer preferences, trends, and feedback to build unique and customised products by using AI-powered algorithms and design tools. AI-driven packaging solutions can improve sustainability, appeal, and product safety, which raises consumer satisfaction and brand loyalty (Impact of AI on Packaging Design_ The Next Big Thing! n.d.).

Furthermore, demand forecasting for FMCG companies depends heavily on big data analytics and machine learning approaches. Through extensive data analysis of sales, weather, market trends, and customer behaviour, businesses are able to forecast demand precisely, manage inventory levels, and predict changes in the market. This improves supply chain performance overall, reduces stockouts and surplus inventory, and helps FMCG companies fulfil customer demand effectively (Seyedan and Mafakheri 2020).

The importance of innovation and digital transformation in fostering operational excellence, competitiveness, and customer-centricity is highlighted by these technological developments in the FMCG industry (Garcia-Perez and Simkin 2021). Businesses who adopt and use these technologies will have a strategic advantage in terms of process optimisation, customer value delivery, and market adaptation. As a result, researching these developments offers insightful information about how FMCG operations and strategies will develop in the future, opening the door for more innovation and sector expansion (Rathore 2019).

3.2. Pharma and Healthcare

An era of innovation and capabilities has been brought about by technological breakthroughs in the pharmaceutical and healthcare sectors, which have been fuelled by megatrends such ageing populations, digital transformation, personalised medicine, and rising healthcare costs. The use of artificial intelligence (AI), machine learning (ML), telemedicine, personalised medicine, 3D printing, augmented and virtual reality (AR and VR), remote monitoring, and other technologies are among these developments (Agnihotri 2024), (Stoumpos, Kitsios, and Talias 2023).

In the pharmaceutical and healthcare industries, AI and ML technologies are transforming patient care, clinical research, and drug development. In order to find trends, forecast results, and improve treatment plans, artificial intelligence (AI) systems examine enormous volumes of data, including genetic information, patient records, and medical literature (Vora et al. 2023). Improved patient outcomes and economical healthcare solutions are the results of using machine learning (ML) models to improve medication discovery, diagnostics, and treatment effectiveness (Javaid, Haleem, Pratap Singh, et al. 2022).

With the advent of digital platforms, telemedicine has revolutionised the way that healthcare is delivered by facilitating remote consultations, diagnosis, and treatment. In addition to improving access to healthcare services and improving patient convenience and satisfaction, telemedicine technologies enable healthcare providers to reach and serve patients in remote or underserved locations through the use of AI-powered diagnostic tools and remote monitoring equipment (Haleem et al. 2021).

Thanks to developments in genomics, molecular biology, and data analytics, personalised medicine adjusts medical interventions and therapies to each patient individually depending on their genetic composition, lifestyle choices, and health profiles. With the use of tailored treatments and AI-driven predictive models, precision medicine techniques improve treatment outcomes, lower side effects, and open the door to more individualised and efficient healthcare solutions (Johnson et al. 2021).

Because 3D printing technologies offer customisation, cost-effectiveness, and quick prototyping capabilities, they have revolutionised the manufacturing of medications, implants, prostheses, and medical equipment. By offering patients and healthcare professionals immersive and interactive experiences, augmented reality (AR) and virtual reality (VR) technologies improve patient education, surgery planning, medical training, and therapy outcomes (Zoabi et al. 2022).

Healthcare providers may now remotely monitor patients' vital signs, medication adherence, and illness development thanks to remote monitoring technologies made possible by wearable sensors, IoT devices, and AI analytics. This improves patient outcomes and lowers healthcare costs by enabling proactive healthcare treatments, early diagnosis of health concerns, and continuous patient monitoring in home and community settings (C. Li et al. 2024).

Megatrends and digital breakthroughs are driving these technological developments in the pharmaceutical and healthcare sectors, which are changing patient care, medical research, and healthcare delivery. They address issues including ageing populations, chronic diseases, and the shortage of healthcare resources while providing hitherto unseen prospects for enhancing healthcare access, quality, and efficiency. Future healthcare holds great promise for revolutionary breakthroughs and better health outcomes worldwide as long as research and development continue to spur innovation in these fields (Thimbleby 2013).

3.3. Manufacturing and Supply Chain

Automation, robotics, the Internet of Things (IoT), artificial intelligence (AI), and 3D printing are just a few of the technologies that have revolutionised manufacturing production processes and increased flexibility, quality, and productivity. By automating repetitive activities, lowering human error, and increasing operational efficiency, automation and robotics are essential for optimising manufacturing processes (Javaid, Haleem, et al. 2021). Manufacturers can watch inventory levels, keep an eye on equipment performance, and optimise production schedules in real time by integrating IoT devices for supply chain monitoring. This ensures smooth operations and on-time delivery of goods (Soori, Arezoo, and Dastres 2023).

Additionally, manufacturers may get data from a variety of sources in the production environment, including wearables, machines, and sensors, thanks to IoT devices. This data can be used to improve processes, control quality, and anticipate maintenance needs (Chauhan and Agnihotri 2024). Demand forecasting, production scheduling, and inventory management are all improved by AI-driven analytics, allowing for more flexible and quick manufacturing processes (Javaid, Abid Haleem, et al. 2021). Furthermore, 3D printing technologies promote innovation and flexibility in manufacturing processes by providing customised, quick prototyping, and affordable production of intricate parts and components (Ngo et al. 2018).

Technological innovations like blockchain, big data analytics, cloud computing, and self-driving vehicles are changing supply chain and logistics, changing how things are sourced, moved, and delivered. Blockchain technology ensures data integrity throughout supply chain networks and creates immutable records of transactions, which improves supply chain transparency, traceability, and security (Kamble et al. 2023). Big data analytics enable predictive and prescriptive analytics for inventory optimisation, supplier management, and risk reduction by offering insights into supply chain performance, demand patterns, and market trends. Cloud computing solutions improve agility and resilience by enabling real-time collaboration, data sharing, and supply chain operations scalability. Drones and self-driving trucks are examples of autonomous vehicles that provide economical and effective transportation, last-mile delivery, and warehouse automation, cutting lead times and increasing delivery accuracy (Nguyen et al. 2017).

3.4. IT, Communications, and Related Fields

Innovations in IT infrastructure, like software-defined networking (SDN), cloud computing, and edge computing, have made it possible for businesses to improve the security, scalability, and flexibility of their IT systems (Abbasi et al. 2019). Cloud computing platforms enable flexible development, cost optimisation, and on-demand access to apps, storage, and computing resources (What Is Cloud Computing_ _ IBM n.d.). By bringing computing power closer to the consumer, edge computing solutions lower latency and boost responsiveness for real-time apps and Internet of Things devices. SDN solutions improve network performance, security, and agility by enabling centralised management and automation of network infrastructure (Khan et al. 2019).

Technological developments in communications, like 5G networks, Internet of Things (IoT) connectivity, and Unified Communications as a Service (UCaaS), have revolutionised business communication, collaboration, and stakeholder connections (Unified Communications (UC) and IoT_ Opportunities Challenges n.d.). High-speed, low-latency connectivity is provided by 5G networks, facilitating IoT applications, video conferencing, and speedier data transfer. The seamless integration of wearables, sensors, and connected devices made possible by IoT connectivity offers significant data insights and boosts operational effectiveness. UCaaS systems allow remote work, virtual meetings, and effective communication amongst dispersed teams by combining audio, video, messaging, and collaboration technologies into a single platform (Dziembek and Turek 2018).

Furthermore, big data analytics, machine learning, and predictive modelling techniques are utilised by data analytics platforms to extract insights, trends, and patterns from massive amounts of data, which makes them indispensable for business intelligence and decision-making. By analysing consumer behaviour, industry trends, and operational performance, these platforms help businesses make data-driven decisions, streamline workflows, and improve customer experiences (Sarker 2021).

Algorithmic trading and AI-powered financial consulting services have completely changed the way financial organisations handle risk, investments, and trading tactics. In order to offer clients individualised financial advice, portfolio management, and investment suggestions, AI algorithms examine market data, trends, and signals. Trading efficiency, liquidity, and risk management in financial markets are all enhanced by algorithmic trading algorithms, which carry out deals in accordance with predetermined rules, market circumstances, and risk criteria (Addy et al. 2024).

Furthermore, data security, privacy, and trust in digital transactions and communications have improved because to developments in blockchain platforms, digital identity solutions, and cybersecurity technology (Yassine et al. 2020). Real-time threat detection, response, and mitigation are made possible by cybersecurity technologies including endpoint protection, security analytics, and next-generation firewalls. Users on many digital platforms can benefit from secure authentication, access management, and identity verification thanks to digital identity solutions. Blockchain solutions improve trust and integrity in digital ecosystems by providing decentralised, transparent, and unchangeable record-keeping for supply chain management, digital asset management, and financial transactions (Gad et al. 2022).

3.5. Education and EdTech

Personalised learning made possible by AI and machine learning technology are among the major developments in education. These technologies adjust learning content, pace, and assessments to meet the needs and learning styles of each individual student by analysing their data, preferences, and performance indicators (Das, Malaviya, and Singh 2023). Deeper learning and academic achievement are encouraged by AI-powered adaptive learning platforms, intelligent tutoring systems, and personalised learning pathways that improve motivation, engagement, and understanding of educational topics (Kabudi, Pappas, and Olsen 2021).

Furthermore, simulation-based training and experiential learning have been transformed in education by virtual reality (VR) and augmented reality (AR) applications. Students may explore virtual worlds, carry out virtual experiments, and participate in hands-on learning experiences thanks to the immersive and engaging learning environments that VR and AR technologies generate. Virtual reality (VR) simulations in disciplines like science, engineering, medicine, and the arts provide realistic and captivating learning experiences that improve understanding, memory, and critical thinking abilities (Zhao, Ren, and Cheah 2023).

Additionally, a wide range of cutting-edge tools and solutions that facilitate remote learning, teamwork, and digital literacy are included in EdTech developments. Learning management systems (LMS), interactive e-books, gamified learning applications, online learning platforms, and video conferencing tools allow students to access lectures, assignments, and educational materials at any time and from any location. These tools support inclusivity, adaptability, and flexibility in education by meeting the requirements and preferences of a wide range of learners (Haleem, Javaid, Qadri, et al. 2022).

Additionally, learning analytics tools and data analytics platforms offer insightful information about student performance, engagement, and learning outcomes, enabling administrators and educators to personalise interventions for struggling students, make data-driven decisions, and pinpoint areas that need improvement. In online learning environments, gamification components like leaderboards, prizes, and badges increase participation, motivation, and engagement (Bienkowski, Feng, and Means 2014).

Assessment technology innovations, like computer-based testing, adaptive assessments, and automated grading systems, simplify the evaluation process, give students prompt feedback, and lighten the administrative load on teachers. By helping educators gain new skills, exchange best practices, and work together with colleagues around the world via online learning communities and professional networks, EdTech solutions also support teachers' ongoing professional development (Zhai and Wiebe 2023).

4. CHALLENGES AND OPPORTUNITIES IN EMBRACING FUTURE LEADERSHIP STYLES AND EVOLVING TECHNOLOGY

The speed at which technology is changing and digital disruption is occurring is one of the main obstacles to adopting megatrends. To be competitive and relevant in a digital-first world, organisations need to upskill their staff, embrace emerging technologies, and manage complicated technology environments. Planning strategically, making investments in digital capabilities, and fostering an innovative and ever-learning culture are all necessary for this (Digital Upskilling_ Preparing everyone, everywhere_ PwC n.d.).

Integrating analytics and data-driven decision-making into leadership practices presents another difficulty. To derive useful insights, promote thoughtful decision-making, and streamline company procedures, leaders need to leverage the potential of data analytics, artificial intelligence, and machine learning. To ensure the proper use of data and algorithms, however, strong data governance, privacy safeguards, and ethical concerns are needed (Farayola et al. 2023).

Leaders must also address how environmental stewardship and sustainability are becoming more and more important in corporate operations. This entails putting sustainable practices into action, lowering carbon emissions, and coordinating corporate strategy with social and environmental objectives (Fallah Shayan et al. 2022). A comprehensive strategy that takes environmental, social, and governance (ESG) considerations into account during the decision-making process is necessary for sustainability-focused leadership (Craig 2023).

However, organisations and leaders stand to gain a great deal from embracing megatrends. Through the use of digital business models, process optimisation, and technology adoption, digital transformation helps organisations improve their agility, innovation, and customer experiences. In a digital landscape that is changing quickly, leaders that adopt digital leadership philosophies like agile leadership, digital literacy, and strategic foresight may spearhead digital transformation projects and add value (Pelser and Gaffley 2020).

Furthermore, data-driven decision-making gives businesses the chance to strengthen consumer insights, increase operational effectiveness, and obtain a competitive edge. Leaders are better able to identify development possibilities, make well-informed decisions, and reduce risks when they make use of predictive modelling, AI-driven technologies, and data analytics platforms (Awan et al. 2021).

Furthermore, companies that prioritise sustainability in their leadership have the chance to stand out from the competition, develop a positive brand image, and draw in investors and customers who share their social conscience. A leader may create long-term value, build stakeholder trust, and drive positive impact by prioritising sustainability, corporate social responsibility (CSR), and ethical practices (ETSpecial 2023).

Organisations face a variety of ethical concerns as they integrate increasingly advanced technologies, especially in fields like artificial intelligence (AI) and data analytics. These issues should be carefully considered and managed proactively. These difficulties include moral conundrums involving AI-driven decision-making, worries around data privacy, and the requirement for moral frameworks and norms to properly manage technological advancement (Pazzanese 2020).

A key ethical conundrum concerns the autonomous decision-making processes driven by artificial intelligence (AI), whereby algorithms and machine learning models determine things on their own that have the potential to have a big impact on people's rights, opportunities, and well-being (Charles, Rana, and Carter 2022). Concerns about algorithmic bias, accountability, transparency, fairness, and fairness bring up moral questions about the possibility of injustice, discrimination, and unforeseen consequences in AI-driven systems. It is imperative for organisations to guarantee that AI systems are created, implemented, and overseen with a strong ethical foundation, human supervision, and procedures in place to identify and rectify biases and mistakes (N. T. Lee, Resnick, and Barton 2019).

In an era where digital technologies permit significant data gathering, storage, and analysis, data privacy is a pressing ethical concern. There are good reasons to be concerned about consent, security, and privacy of data given its spread. To protect sensitive information and respect people's right to privacy, organisations must give priority to data protection, confidentiality, and user consent in their data practices. They must also abide by legal requirements like the General Data Protection Regulation (GDPR) and implement privacy-enhancing technologies (Quach et al. 2022).

To help organisations navigate moral conundrums and make wise decisions in the field of technological breakthroughs, ethical frameworks and guidelines are essential. A systematic method with guiding principles, values, and best practices for moral behaviour, risk assessment, and decision-making is offered by ethical frameworks. Organisations may responsibly handle technological breakthroughs, cultivate ethical practices that are consistent with societal values and expectations, and establish trust with stakeholders by proactively addressing ethical considerations (Deloitte 2020).

5. CONCLUSION

In conclusion, organisations face a dynamic environment of opportunities and challenges as a result of the convergence of future leadership styles and technological trends across many departments and industries. In order to foster innovation, resilience, and long-term success, leaders must adopt a forward-thinking strategy that combines technological know-how, ethical responsibility, and leadership agility.

It is anticipated that future leadership philosophies will incorporate traits like empathy, digital fluency, adaptability, and strategic vision. In an increasingly complex and competitive environment, leaders who can quickly adapt to changing market dynamics, promote an inclusive and collaborative culture, effectively use digital tools and data insights, and predict future trends and disruptions will be well-positioned to guide their organisations to success.

Technological developments in a variety of fields and sectors are changing how companies work together, operate, and provide value to their clients. Organisations are utilising these developments to streamline operations, improve consumer experiences, and spur innovation throughout the value chain. Examples of these innovations include AI-driven automation, data analytics, blockchain-enabled transactions, and immersive technologies like AR and VR.

Looking ahead, in order to take advantage of new technologies and successfully negotiate the moral and legal issues raised by digital transformation, executives need to place a high priority on talent development, ongoing education, and strategic alliances. Key factors influencing how leadership and technology will develop in many industries in the future include collaborative ecosystems, agile processes, and an emphasis on sustainability and social responsibility.

Organisations may unlock new opportunities, promote positive impact, and create value for stakeholders while navigating the difficulties of a quickly expanding digital landscape by adopting a holistic approach that integrates leadership qualities with technology breakthroughs. It is critical that leaders continue to be flexible, imaginative, and moral as we set out on this transformative journey to shape technology and leadership in the years to come.

REFERENCES

Abbasi. (2019). Software-Defined Cloud Computing: A Systematic Review on Latest Trends and Developments. *IEEE Access*.

Addy, W. (2024). Algorithmic Trading and AI: A Review of Strategies and Market Impact. *World Journal of Advanced Engineering Technology and Sciences*, *11*(1), 258–267. doi:10.30574/wjaets.2024.11.1.0054

Agnihotri. (2023). Artificial Intelligence Shaping Talent Intelligence and Talent Acquisition for Smart Employee Management. *EAI Endorsed Transactions on Internet of Things* 10.

Ahsan, M. J. (2023). The Role of Emotional Intelligence in Effective Corporate Social Responsibility Leadership. *The International Journal of Organizational Analysis*, *31*(8), 75–91. doi:10.1108/IJOA-02-2023-3615

Albshaier, L., Almarri, S., & Hafizur Rahman, M. M. (2024). A Review of Blockchain's Role in E-Commerce Transactions: Open Challenges, and Future Research Directions. *Computers*, *13*(1), 27. doi:10.3390/computers13010027

Awan, U., Shamim, S., Khan, Z., Zia, N. U., Shariq, S. M., & Khan, M. N. (2021). Big Data Analytics Capability and Decision-Making: The Role of Data-Driven Insight on Circular Economy Performance. *Technological Forecasting and Social Change*, *168*, 120766. doi:10.1016/j.techfore.2021.120766

Berman, W. H. (2019). Coaching C-Suite Executives and Business Founders. *Consulting Psychology Journal*, *71*(2), 72–85. doi:10.1037/cpb0000128

Bienkowski, Feng, & Means. (2014). Enhancing Teaching and Learning through Educational Data Mining and Learning Analytics. *An Issue Brief*.

Boffo & Patalano. (2020). ESG Investing Practices, Progress Challenges. *OECD Paris*.

Bourke, J., & Espedido, A. (2019). *Why Inclusive Leaders Are Good for Organizations, and How to Become One*. Academic Press.

Calzon, B. (2022). The Importance of Data Driven Decision Making for Business. *Business Intelligence*. https://www.datapine.com/blog/data-driven-decision-making-in-businesses/

Charles, Rana, & Carter. (2022). Artificial Intelligence for Data-Driven Decision-Making and Governance in Public Affairs. *Government Information Quarterly, 39*(4), 101742. https://www.sciencedirect.com/science/article/pii/S0740624X22000788

Chauhan & Agnihotri. (2024). Industry 4.0 and Indian Manufacturing Companies: Barriers towards Sustainability. *Journal of Informatics Education and Research, 4*.

Coleman, Dossett, & Dimick. (2021). Building High Performing Teams: Opportunities and Challenges of Inclusive Recruitment Practices. *Journal of Vascular Surgery, 74*(2), 86S-92S. https://www.sciencedirect.com/science/article/pii/S0741521421006510

Coronado-Maldonado, I., & Benítez-Márquez, M.-D. (2023). Emotional Intelligence, Leadership, and Work Teams: A Hybrid Literature Review. *Heliyon, 9*(10), e20356. doi:10.1016/j.heliyon.2023.e20356 PMID:37790975

Cortellazzo, L., Bruni, E., & Zampieri, R. (2019). The Role of Leadership in a Digitalized World: A Review. *Frontiers in Psychology, 10*, 1938. doi:10.3389/fpsyg.2019.01938 PMID:31507494

Craig, S. (2023). ESG Strategy and Management: Complete Guide for Businesses. *TechTarget*.

D'Cruz, P., Du, S., Noronha, E., Parboteeah, K. P., Trittin-Ulbrich, H., & Whelan, G. (2022). Technology, Megatrends and Work: Thoughts on the Future of Business Ethics. *Journal of Business Ethics, 180*(3), 879–902. doi:10.1007/s10551-022-05240-9 PMID:36212627

Das, A., Malaviya, S., & Singh, M. (2023). The Impact of AI-Driven Personalization on Learners' Performance. *International Journal on Computer Science and Engineering, 11*, 15–22.

Datnow, A., & Park, V. (2014). *Data-Driven Leadership*. Wiley. https://books.google.co.in/books?id=-xURAwAAQBAJ

Davenport, T., Guha, A., Grewal, D., & Bressgott, T. (2020). How Artificial Intelligence Will Change the Future of Marketing. *Journal of the Academy of Marketing Science, 48*(1), 24–42. doi:10.1007/s11747-019-00696-0

De Smet, A. (2018). The Agile Manager Who Manages in an Agile Organization? And What Exactly Do They Do? *The McKinsey Quarterly*, (June), 1–6.

Deloitte. (2020). *Making Ethical Tech a Priority*. https://www2.deloitte.com/us/en/insights/topics/digital-transformation/make-ethical-technology-a-priority.html

Donaldson, G. (2006). *Cultivating Leadership in Schools: Connecting People, Purpose, and Practice.* Teachers College Press. https://books.google.co.in/books?id=CDGRDQAAQBAJ

Dziembek, D., & Turek, T. (2018). Characteristics and Application of Unified Communications as a Service (UCaaS) in Enterprises. *Informatyka Ekonomiczna, 4*(50), 47–65. doi:10.15611/ie.2018.4.04

ETSpecial. (2023). *Ethical Leadership and Corporate Social Responsibility: Leading with Integrity and Impact.* Academic Press.

Farayola, O., Olatoye, F., Chinwe, N., & Daraojimba, C. (2023). Business intelligence transformation through AI and data analytics. *Engineering Science & Technology Journal, 4*(5), 285–307. doi:10.51594/estj.v4i5.616

Gad, Mosa, Abualigah, & Abohany. (2022). Emerging Trends in Blockchain Technology and Applications: A Review and Outlook. *Journal of King Saud University - Computer and Information Sciences, 34*(9), 6719–42. https://www.sciencedirect.com/science/article/pii/S1319157822000891

Garcia-Perez, A., & Simkin, P. L. (2021). *ECKM 2021 22nd European Conference on Knowledge Management.* Academic Conferences and Publishing Limited. https://books.google.co.in/books?id=mXxGEAAAQBAJ

Germain, M.-L. (2021). The Impact of Changing Workforce Demographics and Dependency on Technology on Employers' Need for Expert Skills BT - Expertise at Work: Current and Emerging Trends. Cham: Springer International Publishing. doi:10.1007/978-3-030-64371-3_9

Groysberg, B., Kelly, L. K., & MacDonald, B. (2011). The New Path to the C-Suite. *Harvard Business Review, 89*(3).

Gyori & Kazakova. (2020). *Purpose-Driven Leadership for the 21st Century: Transitioning to a Purpose-First Economy through the New Business Logic.* Academic Press.

Habib, G., Sharma, S., Ibrahim, S., Ahmad, I., Qureshi, S., & Ishfaq, M. (2022). Blockchain Technology: Benefits, Challenges, Applications, and Integration of Blockchain Technology with Cloud Computing. *Future Internet, 14*(11), 341. doi:10.3390/fi14110341

Hafidz, L. (2022). *People Matters - Interstitial Site — People Matters.* https://www.peoplematters.in/article/recruitment/beating-your-chatbot-interviewer-and-landing-your-dream-job-21266

Haleem, A. (2023). Management 4.0: Concept, Applications and Advancements. *Sustainable Operations and Computers, 4*, 10–21. https://www.sciencedirect.com/science/article/pii/S2666412722000277

Haleem, A., Javaid, M., & Qadri, M. A. (2022). Artificial Intelligence (AI) Applications for Marketing: A Literature-Based Study. *International Journal of Intelligent Networks, 3*, 119–132. doi:10.1016/j.ijin.2022.08.005

Haleem, A., Javaid, M., Qadri, M. A., & Suman, R. (2022). Understanding the Role of Digital Technologies in Education: A Review. *Sustainable Operations and Computers, 3*, 275–85. https://www.sciencedirect.com/science/article/pii/S2666412722000137

Haleem, A., Javaid, M., Singh, R. P., & Suman, R. (2021). Telemedicine for Healthcare: Capabilities, Features, Barriers, and Applications. *Sensors International*, *2*, 100117. doi:10.1016/j.sintl.2021.100117 PMID:34806053

Haque. (2023). The impact of remote work on HR practices: Navigating challenges, embracing opportunities. *European Journal of Human Resource Management Studies, 7*.

Helo, P., & Hao, Y. (2022). Artificial Intelligence in Operations Management and Supply Chain Management: An Exploratory Case Study. *Production Planning and Control*, *33*(16), 1573–1590. doi:10.1080/09537287.2021.1882690

Henisz, W., Koller, T., & Nuttall, R. (2019). Five Ways That ESG Creates Value. *The McKinsey Quarterly*, (November), 1–12.

Hill, J. D., & Fenn, N. E. III. (2019). The Future of Pharmacy Leadership: Investing in Students and New Practitioners. *American Journal of Health-System Pharmacy*, *76*(23), 1904–1906. doi:10.1093/ajhp/zxz224 PMID:31724040

Javaid, M., & Haleem, A. (2021). Upgrading the Manufacturing Sector via Applications of Industrial Internet of Things (IIoT). *Sensors International*, *2*, 100129. doi:10.1016/j.sintl.2021.100129

Javaid, M., Haleem, A., & Singh, R. P. (2022). Significance of Machine Learning in Healthcare: Features, Pillars and Applications. *International Journal of Intelligent Networks*, *3*, 58–73. doi:10.1016/j.ijin.2022.05.002

Javaid, M., Haleem, A., Singh, R. P., & Suman, R. (2021). Substantial Capabilities of Robotics in Enhancing Industry 4.0 Implementation. *Cognitive Robotics, 1*, 58–75. https://www.sciencedirect.com/science/article/pii/S2667241321000057

Javaid, M., Haleem, A., Singh, R. P., Suman, R., & Gonzalez, E. S. (2022). Understanding the Adoption of Industry 4.0 Technologies in Improving Environmental Sustainability. *Sustainable Operations and Computers, 3*, 203–17. https://www.sciencedirect.com/science/article/pii/S2666412722000071

Javaid, M., Haleem, A., Singh, R. P., Suman, R., & Khan, S. (2022). A Review of Blockchain Technology Applications for Financial Services. *BenchCouncil Transactions on Benchmarks, Standards and Evaluations, 2*(3), 100073. https://www.sciencedirect.com/science/article/pii/S2772485922000606

Jeflea, F. V., Danciulescu, D., Sitnikov, C. S., Filipeanu, D., Park, J. O., & Tugui, A. (2022). Societal Technological Megatrends: A Bibliometric Analysis from 1982 to 2021. *Sustainability (Basel)*, *14*(3), 1543. doi:10.3390/su14031543

Jimenez, Franco, & Smith. (2021). A Review of Corporate Purpose: An Approach to Actioning the Sustainable Development Goals (SDGs). *Sustainability, 13*(7). https://www.mdpi.com/2071-1050/13/7/3899

Johnson. (2021). Precision Medicine, AI, and the Future of Personalized Health Care. *Clinical and Translational Science, 14*(1), 86–93.

Kabudi, T., Pappas, I., & Olsen, D. H. (2021). AI-Enabled Adaptive Learning Systems: A Systematic Mapping of the Literature. *Computers and Education: Artificial Intelligence, 2*, 100017. https://www.sciencedirect.com/science/article/pii/S2666920X21000114

Kalia, C., Tyagi, S., & Saha, S. (2022). *How ESG Megatrends and Opportunities Are Shaping Our Future.* https://www.ey.com/en_in/climate-change-sustainability-services/how-esg-megatrends-and-opportunities-are-shaping-our-future

Kamble. (2023). Blockchain Technology's Impact on Supply Chain Integration and Sustainable Supply Chain Performance: Evidence from the Automotive Industry. *Annals of Operations Research, 327*(1), 575–600. . doi:10.1007/s10479-021-04129-6

Khan, W. (2019). Edge Computing: A Survey. *Future Generation Computer Systems*, 97.

Koller, T., Nuttall, R., & Henisz, W. (2019). ESG Framework. *McKinsey Quarterly.* https://www.mckinsey.com/capabilities/strategy-and-corporate-finance/our-insights/five-ways-that-esg-creates-value#/

Korherr, Kanbach, Kraus, & Mikalef. (2022). From Intuitive to Data-Driven Decision-Making in Digital Transformation: A Framework of Prevalent Managerial Archetypes. *Digital Business, 2*(2), 100045. https://www.sciencedirect.com/science/article/pii/S2666954422000254

Kossek, E. E., Gettings, P., & Misra, K. (2021). The Future of Flexibility at Work. *Harvard Business Review.* https://hbr.org/2021/09/the-future-of-flexibility-at-work

Landry, L. (2019). Emotional Intelligence in Leadership: Why It's Important. *Business Insights Blog, 79*(40), 45. https://online.hbs.edu/blog/post/emotional-intelligence-in-leadership

Laureani, A., & Antony, J. (2021). Integrating Innovation, Agile and Lean Six Sigma. In *Leading Lean Six Sigma* (pp. 83–92). Emerald Publishing Limited. doi:10.1108/978-1-80071-064-120211007

Leah, L., & Don, S. (2023). Using Technology to Create a Better Customer Experience. *Harvard Business Review.* https://hbr.org/2023/03/using-technology-to-create-a-better-customer-experience

Lee, N. T., Resnick, P., & Barton, G. (2019). Algorithmic Bias Detection and Mitigation: Best Practices and Policies to Reduce Consumer Harms. *Brookings Institute.* https://www.brookings.edu/research/algorithmic-bias-detection-and-mitigation-best-practices-and-policies-to-reduce-consumer-harms/

Lee, Cheng, & Leung. (2009). A Quantitative View on How RFID Can Improve Inventory Management in a Supply Chain. *International Journal of Logistics-research and Applications, 12*, 23–43.

Li, C., Wang, & Zhang. (2024). A Review of IoT Applications in Healthcare. *Neurocomputing, 565*, 127017. https://www.sciencedirect.com/science/article/pii/S0925231223011402

Li, F. (2020). The Digital Transformation of Business Models in the Creative Industries: A Holistic Framework and Emerging Trends. *Technovation, 92–93*, 102012. doi:10.1016/j.technovation.2017.12.004

Ma, N. (2023). Integration of ESG Factors in Portfolio Management: International Trends and Practices. *Frontiers in Business, Economics and Management, 12*(2), 149–152. doi:10.54097/fbem.v12i2.14778

McCarthy, P., Sammon, D., & Alhassan, I. (2022). Digital Transformation Leadership Characteristics: A Literature Analysis. *Journal of Decision Systems, 32*(1), 79–109. doi:10.1080/12460125.2021.1908934

Mhlanga, D. (2023). Block Chain Technology for Digital Financial Inclusion in the Industry 4.0, towards Sustainable Development? *Frontiers in Blockchain*, *6*(February), 1–13. doi:10.3389/fbloc.2023.1035405

Mishra, B., Deepa, S. N., Gunasekaran, A., & Dutta, V. (2023). Prescriptive Analytics Applications in Sustainable Operations Research: Conceptual Framework and Future Research Challenges. *Annals of Operations Research*. Advance online publication. doi:10.1007/s10479-023-05251-3 PMID:37361099

Mittal, N., & Davenport, T. H. (2020). How CEOs Can Lead a Data-Driven Culture. *Harvard Business Review*. https://hbr.org/2020/03/how-ceos-can-lead-a-data-driven-culture

Moskowitz, H., & Ward, J. (1998). A Three-phase Approach to Instilling a Continuous Learning Culture in Manufacturing Education and Training. *Production and Operations Management*, *7*(2), 201–209. doi:10.1111/j.1937-5956.1998.tb00452.x

New Leadership in an Era of Thriving Organizations. (n.d.). https://www.mckinsey.com/capabilities/people-and-organizational-performance/our-insights/new-leadership-for-a-new-era-of-thriving-organizations

Ngo. (2018). Additive Manufacturing (3D Printing): A Review of Materials, Methods, Applications and Challenges. *Composites Part B: Engineering*, *143*, 172–96. https://www.sciencedirect.com/science/article/pii/S1359836817342944

Nguyen, T. (2017). Big Data Analytics in Supply Chain Management: A State-of-the-Art Literature Review. *Computers & Operations Research*.

Nozari, Fallah, Kazemipoor, & Najafi. (2021). Big Data Analysis of IoT-Based Supply Chain Management Considering FMCG Industries. *Business Informatics, 15*.

OECD. (2017). Investment Governance and the Integration of Environmental, Social and Governance Factors. *OECD*.

Okorie, G. (2024). Leveraging big data for personalized marketing campaigns: A review. *International Journal of Management & Entrepreneurship Research*, *6*(1), 216–242. doi:10.51594/ijmer.v6i1.778

Papoutsi, C., Drigas, A., & Skianis, C. (2019). Emotional Intelligence as an Important Asset for HR in Organizations: Attitudes and Working Variables. *International Journal of Advanced Corporate Learning*, *12*(2), 21. doi:10.3991/ijac.v12i2.9620

Pavitra & Agnihotri. (2024). *Artificial Intelligence in Corporate Learning and Development: Current Trends and Future Possibilities*. Academic Press.

Pazzanese, C. (2020). Ethical Concerns Mount as AI Takes Bigger Decision-Making Role – Harvard Gazette. *Harvard Business Review*. https://news.harvard.edu/gazette/story/2020/10/ethical-concerns-mount-as-ai-takes-bigger-decision-making-role/

Pelser, T., & Gaffley, G. (2020). Implications of Digital Transformation on the Strategy Development Process for Business Leaders. doi:10.4018/978-1-7998-4882-0.ch001

PWC. (2018). *Megatrends*. PwC. https://www.pwc.co.uk/issues/megatrends.html

Quach, S., Thaichon, P., Martin, K. D., Weaven, S., & Palmatier, R. W. (2022). Digital Technologies: Tensions in Privacy and Data. *Journal of the Academy of Marketing Science*, *50*(6), 1299–1323. doi:10.1007/s11747-022-00845-y PMID:35281634

Raj, R., Kumar, V., Sharma, N. K., Singh, S., Mahlawat, S., & Verma, P. (2023). The Study of Remote Working Outcome and Its Influence on Firm Performance. *Social Sciences & Humanities Open*, *8*(1), 100528. doi:10.1016/j.ssaho.2023.100528

Rathore. (2019). Exploring the Impact of Digital Transformation on Marketing Management Strategies. *Eduzone : International Peer Reviewed/Refereed Academic Multidisciplinary Journal, 8*, 2319–5045.

Retief, F., Bond, A., Pope, J., Morrison-Saunders, A., & King, N. (2016). Global Megatrends and Their Implications for Environmental Assessment Practice. *Environmental Impact Assessment Review*, *61*, 52–60. doi:10.1016/j.eiar.2016.07.002

Sadun, R., Fuller, J., Hansen, S., & Neal, P. J. (2022). The C-Suite Skills That Matter Most. *Harvard Business Review*.

Sagar, K., Pramod, K. G., & Dutta, C. (2018). Application of Internet of Things in Fast Moving Consumer Goods Sector to Increase Business Efficiency. *2018 Second International Conference on Green Computing and Internet of Things (ICGCIoT)*, 629–36.

Samuel, B., & Twum, D. E. (2019). Leadership Style in the Global Economy: A Focus on Cross-Cultural and Transformational Leadership. *Journal of Marketing Management*, *9*(2), 25.

Sani, K., Adisa, T., Adekoya, O., & Oruh, E. (2022). Digital Onboarding and Employee Outcomes: Empirical Evidence from the UK. *Management Decision*, 61.

Sarker, I. H. (2021). Data Science and Analytics: An Overview from Data-Driven Smart Computing, Decision-Making and Applications Perspective. *SN Computer Science*, *2*(5), 377. doi:10.1007/s42979-021-00765-8 PMID:34278328

Seetharaman, T., Sharma, V., Balamurugan, B., Grover, V., & Agnihotri, A. (2023, August). An Efficient and Robust Explainable Artificial Intelligence for Securing Smart Healthcare System. In *2023 Second International Conference On Smart Technologies For Smart Nation (SmartTechCon)* (pp. 1066-1071). IEEE. 10.1109/SmartTechCon57526.2023.10391664

Seyedan, M., & Mafakheri, F. (2020). Predictive Big Data Analytics for Supply Chain Demand Forecasting: Methods, Applications, and Research Opportunities. *Journal of Big Data*, *7*(1), 53. doi:10.1186/s40537-020-00329-2

Shayan, F., Niloufar, N. M.-K., Alavi, S., & Zahed, M. A. (2022). Sustainable Development Goals (SDGs) as a Framework for Corporate Social Responsibility (CSR). *Sustainability*, *14*(3). https://www.mdpi.com/2071-1050/14/3/1222

Shields, K. (2021). Leading a Customer Centric Strategy. Academic Press.

Soori, M., Arezoo, B., & Dastres, R. (2023). Internet of Things for Smart Factories in Industry 4.0. *RE:view*.

Stedman, C. (2023). What Is Business Intelligence (BI)? *TechTarget*. https://www.techtarget.com/searchbusinessanalytics/definition/business-intelligence-BI

Stoumpos, A. I., Kitsios, F., & Talias, M. A. (2023). Digital Transformation in Healthcare: Technology Acceptance and Its Applications. *International Journal of Environmental Research and Public Health*, *20*(4), 3407. doi:10.3390/ijerph20043407 PMID:36834105

Sultana, S., Zulkifli, N., & Zainal, D. (2018). Environmental, Social and Governance (ESG) and Investment Decision in Bangladesh. *Sustainability (Basel)*, *10*(6), 1831. doi:10.3390/su10061831

Tagscherer, F., & Carbon, C.-C. (2023). Leadership for Successful Digitalization: A Literature Review on Companies' Internal and External Aspects of Digitalization. *Sustainable Technology and Entrepreneurship, 2*(2), 100039. https://www.sciencedirect.com/science/article/pii/S2773032823000032

The Impact of Agility: How to Shape Your Organization to Compete. (2023). https://www.mckinsey.com/capabilities/people-and-organizational-performance/our-insights/the-impact-of-agility-how-to-shape-your-organization-to-compete

Thimbleby, H. (2013). Technology and the Future of Healthcare. *Journal of Public Health Research*, *2*(3), e28. doi:10.4081/jphr.2013.e28 PMID:25170499

Verma, S., Sharma, R., Deb, S., & Maitra, D. (2021). Artificial Intelligence in Marketing: Systematic Review and Future Research Direction. *International Journal of Information Management Data Insights*, *1*(1), 100002. doi:10.1016/j.jjimei.2020.100002

Vora. (2023). Artificial Intelligence in Pharmaceutical Technology and Drug Delivery Design. *Pharmaceutics, 15*(7).

Waller, D. (2020). 10 Steps to Creating a Data-Driven Culture. *Harvard Business Review*. https://hbr.org/2020/02/10-steps-to-creating-a-data-driven-culture

Whyte, J., Stasis, A., & Lindkvist, C. (2016). Managing Change in the Delivery of Complex Projects: Configuration Management, Asset Information and 'Big Data.'. *International Journal of Project Management*, *34*(2), 339–351. doi:10.1016/j.ijproman.2015.02.006

Wu, G. F., & Li, M. (2023). Impact of Inclusive Leadership on Employees' Innovative Behavior: A Relational Silence Approach. *Frontiers in Psychology*, *14*(March), 1–10. doi:10.3389/fpsyg.2023.1144791 PMID:36949905

Yassine, M. (2020). *Blockchain for Cybersecurity and Privacy: Architectures*. Challenges, and Applications.

Zahid, R. M. A., Saleem, A., & Maqsood, U. S. (2023). ESG Performance, Capital Financing Decisions, and Audit Quality: Empirical Evidence from Chinese State-Owned Enterprises. *Environmental Science and Pollution Research International*, *30*(15), 44086–44099. doi:10.1007/s11356-023-25345-6 PMID:36681761

Zhao, X., Ren, Yu., & Cheah, K. S. L. (2023). Leading Virtual Reality (VR) and Augmented Reality (AR) in Education: Bibliometric and Content Analysis From the Web of Science (2018–2022). *SAGE Open*, *13*(3), 21582440231190820. doi:10.1177/21582440231190821

Zoabi, A., Redenski, I., Oren, D., Kasem, A., Zigron, A., Daoud, S., Moskovich, L., Kablan, F., & Srouji, S. (2022). 3D Printing and Virtual Surgical Planning in Oral and Maxillofacial Surgery. *Journal of Clinical Medicine*, *11*(9), 2385. doi:10.3390/jcm11092385 PMID:35566511

Chapter 14
Future Mega Trends in Leadership and Technology

Poornima Tyagi
Noida Institute of Engineering and Technology, India

Divya Sahu
https://orcid.org/0000-0002-8398-3879
Noida Institute of Engineering and Technology, India

Renuka Sharma
SGT University, India

ABSTRACT

In the past decade, leadership has evolved significantly due to the integration of machine learning and AI in the business environment. These advancements have enabled leaders to make well-informed decisions based on real-time data, enhancing their collaborative, innovative, and efficient capabilities. The strategic integration of these technologies has revolutionized leadership decision-making, enabling data-driven decisions, improved security, and transparency. Next-generation leadership, focusing on managing change and demonstrating resilience, is crucial for the 21st century leadership landscape. Agile leaders can quickly adapt to novel circumstances, while self-aware leaders can identify strengths and limitations.

1. INTRODUCTION

The landscape of leadership is changing rapidly because of economic, technical, and sociological upheavals. Leaders now find themselves at the center of both revolutionary possibilities and hitherto unseen difficulties, and these developments are reshaping their position. Leaders are required to adjust to a continually changing environment because of the metaphorical fabric that interweaves disruption and innovation. Leaders are in the front of a paradigm change that will see more flexible and cooperative models replace traditional hierarchies. This shift requires an agile and proactive response, with leaders

DOI: 10.4018/979-8-3693-1946-8.ch014

taking on the role of change agents. At the centre of this change is technology, which is altering decision-making procedures, teamwork skills, and the very nature of leadership. As more and more leadership roles are explored, the blending of personal and professional elements is emphasized. The landscape of leadership is changing dramatically because of economic, technical, and sociological events. Leaders are situated at the intersection of historically high stakes and revolutionary possibilities. Recognizing that leadership in the twenty-first century transcends traditional limits, the examination of redefining leadership positions emphasizes the fusion of personal and professional facets. It takes nimbleness and self-awareness for leaders to handle changing conditions and shifting markets. These days, leadership is a dynamic force that needs constant adjustment rather than a static concept.

1.1. Evolution of Leadership Concepts

Modern leadership requires a reassessment of established paradigms due to a confluence of circumstances that cause a significant change in the field. Leaders must negotiate this complex web of change, as they find themselves at the intersection of extremely challenging circumstances and game-changing opportunities. This introduction lays the groundwork for a careful investigation that will concentrate on the significance of technology developments, the complicated evolution of roles, and the necessity of redefining leadership concepts in a time of dynamic complexity and swift change. The way that leadership acts has been redefined in large part by technology. In the past, hierarchical systems were frequently linked to leadership, and decision-making and task delegation were expected of leaders. But as technology has advanced, attention has turned to a strategy that is more inclusive and collaborative. It is now required for leaders to use digital tools and platforms to empower and engage their workforce. This encourages candid dialogue, idea exchange, and creativity. Leaders may develop a more dynamic and successful leadership style by utilizing technology to achieve desired outcomes.

1.2. Leadership Transformation

The way that leadership is understood and practised has changed significantly over time. In the past, people believed that having specific qualities or talents made them good leaders. This view of leadership was based on personal attributes. But the job of a leader has changed as the globe has grown more linked and complex. Nowadays, being a leader means having the flexibility to adjust to changing circumstances, interact and communicate with others in constructive manners, and make sense of complex and unclear situations (Oreg & Berson, 2019). The speed at which firms, organizations, technology, politics, and society are changing are just a few of the reasons for this revolution in leadership. Technology's introduction has had a significant influence on the change of leadership.

As technology evolves, executives need to reassess their responsibilities and adjust to a transforming landscape. To successfully traverse the digital world, they require a strong digital vision, the ability to maximize the use of technology in organizational operations, and competencies in data analysis, business intelligence, and strategic decision-making. In addition to utilizing technology, effective leaders must provide a clear plan, encourage creativity, and support ongoing development among their teams. Because technology is developing so quickly, it has had a significant influence on how leaders' function and lead inside businesses (Heukamp, 2020). This is because leaders now have access to a variety of data and information that may help them make better decisions and develop strategic plans. But technology by itself cannot propel a company to success.

1.3. Role of Technology in Leadership Transformation

Modern businesses are completely dependent on technology, which shapes and influences many facets of leadership. Technological developments have given leaders new opportunities and given them the ability to lead more effectively and efficiently. For instance, the usage of digital tools and platforms has revolutionized communication, enabling executives to stay in touch with their employees no matter where they are in the world. Technology has also given leaders accessibility to a variety of data and information, allowing them to create strategic plans and make well-informed judgments. Additionally, via automation and digitalization, technology has helped executives enhance productivity and streamline procedures by (Galgali, 2017). A culture of creativity and ongoing learning has also been promoted using technology in leadership change. It is now an opportunity for leaders to adopt new technology and use them to boost the success and expansion of their organizations. Additionally, via automation and digitalization, technology has helped executives improve productivity and streamline procedures. A culture of creativity and ongoing learning has also been promoted using technology in leadership change. It is now the chance for leaders to adopt new technology and use it to speed up the success and expansion of their organizations.

2. LITERATURE REVIEW

Technology is largely responsible for the transformation of the leadership landscape. It has significantly altered the way in which leaders carry out their responsibilities and engage with their teams. Digital tools and platforms have made it possible for leaders to empower and engage their teams in ways that have never been possible before. The potential of technology to promote candid communication and teamwork is one of its main advantages for leaders. Leaders may now quickly and easily exchange information, ideas, and comments with their teams using a variety of digital platforms and tools. This makes it possible to adopt a more inclusive and participatory strategy in which team members are appreciated and given a voice in decision-making. Technology has also completely changed how executives obtain and handle information. Leaders today have constant, quick access to a variety of information and resources because to the development of digital technology. Their ability to make well-informed and data-driven judgments is enhanced, leading to increased efficacy and efficiency in their leadership capacities. According to Fernandes (2019), leaders may use data to pinpoint areas in need of development, track advancement, strategically distribute resources, promote instructional improvement, and involve stakeholders. Furthermore, technology has created new avenues for invention. Thanks to technology improvements, leaders may now encourage innovation and problem-solving among their staff. Greater creativity and success can result from the use of digital platforms and tools to support idea sharing, brainstorming sessions, and collaborative project management.

2.1. Technology as a Catalyst for Transformation

Technology has changed leadership by making it possible for leaders to engage with their teams more productively and encouraging creativity and teamwork. The primary conclusions indicate by authors that leaders play a crucial role in the formation of a digital culture (Cortellazzo, Bruni, & Zampieri, 2019). They must establish connections with many dispersed stakeholders and concentrate on facilitating cooperative processes in intricate environments, all the while addressing urgent ethical issues. Digital tools and platforms have allowed for this transition from a top-down to a more inclusive and collaborative manner of problem solving. This facilitates candid dialogue, idea exchange, and creativity. The blurring of lines between the personal and professional spheres is one of the problems that technology poses for leaders. Given that technology enables them to access work-related information from anywhere at any time, leaders need to strike a balance between their personal and professional lives. Because of technology, leaders now have more duties and responsibilities. They must manage data-driven decision making, use analytics to get insights, and spearhead digital transformation inside their companies. Leaders now must adjust to managing across geographic borders and make efficient use of virtual communication technologies due to the increase of remote work and virtual teams. Because of these developments, leaders now need to be flexible, tech-savvy, and able to lead in a digitally-driven setting.

2.2. Intersecting Personal and Professional Domains

The distinctions separating the personal and professional spheres have become hazier due to technological advancements. According to Veena Latha, K. (2019), work-life balance is an important aspect of leadership. Today's leaders must navigate these crossings and strike a balance between their personal and professional lives. Technology has the potential to enhance flexibility and productivity by providing leaders with access to work-related information at any time and location. It also makes it difficult to establish work-life balance because of the continual temptation to be online all the time. In the digital era, striking this balance has become essential to effective leadership.

Leadership and organizational paradigms are being revolutionized by digital transformation, which calls for new approaches and ways of thinking to succeed. Important components are: strategic vision, in which executives outline how technology will advance organizational objectives; change management, which requires skilful handling of shifts and resistance through benefits communication, employee empowerment, and support provision; innovation and agility, which necessitates a culture of ongoing innovation, experimentation, and adaptation; and customer orientation, which emphasizes customized experiences, improved engagement, and long-lasting customer relationships. To effectively promote digital transformation and ensure organizational competitiveness in changing marketplaces, leaders must skilfully traverse these intersections.

2.3. Changing Roles and Responsibilities

With technology infiltrating every part of companies, leaders are taking on new roles and responsibilities. Sonmez Cakir and Adiguzel (2020), discusses how the concept of leadership has evolved and how the job of a leader has changed as the world has become more connected and complex. They must now manage data-driven decision making, using analytics to get knowledge and make wise selections. Leaders must also spearhead the digital transformation of their companies and make sure that technology is seamlessly incorporated into operational procedures. As remote work and virtual teams become more common, executives must also learn to manage across geographic boundaries and use virtual communication technologies smoothly. The role of leadership has evolved due to technology, and today's leaders must be flexible, tech-savvy, and ready to lead in a world that is driven by the internet.

2.4. Enhancing Collaborative Capabilities

The emergence of technology has significantly improved leaders' capacities for collaboration. Digital technologies provide leaders the ability to create a more inclusive and cooperative work environment (Fernandes, 2019). Better communication is one of the main ways that technology fosters cooperation. Regardless of geographical limitations, executives and team members may connect and work together in real-time using digital platforms like email, instant messaging, and video conferencing. This makes it easier for distant teams to collaborate and share ideas and information. Technology also makes it possible for managers to set up online offices where staff members may exchange papers, work together on projects, and offer input. Because team members can collaborate easily regardless of where they are physically located, this promotes better co-creation and cooperation. Technology also encourages diversity and inclusion in leadership cultures. Leaders may quickly get opinions and comments from team members with different backgrounds and experiences by using digital platforms. This encourages a decision-making process that is more inclusive and raises the possibility of creative solutions and results.

3. REVOLUTIONARY METHODS IN LEADERSHIP DECISION-MAKING

Making decisions as a leader is a difficult process that calls for a variety of abilities, know-how, and experience. Leaders must move quickly and wisely in the fast-paced world of today, since their actions may have a big influence on their companies. According to Bachtiar, Guntoro, Riyantie, and Ridwan (2023), leadership decision-making is changing because of innovative techniques like augmented reality, blockchain, machine learning, and artificial intelligence. Despite the enormous promise of AI (artificial intelligence) and ML (machine learning), businesses frequently underutilize them. Determining the judgments made by robots and making the process of decision-making more visible are challenges. Digital twin, metaverse, and Internet of Things technologies might all be made possible by blockchain technology. AI, VR (Virtual Reality) and AR (Augmented reality) integration in leadership education has the potential to close the gap between theory and practice and represent a significant advance in leadership training. AI improves decision-making, creates predictive models, and increases efficiency in business operations.

3.1. Artificial Intelligence in Decision-Making

The dynamic area of AI has the potential to completely transform decision-making in a wide range of businesses. It includes computer programs that can learn, reason, and solve problems much like a person. According to Fleming (2020), that explains how AI is transforming the workplace and the need to adjust their workforces and reallocate capital while maintaining profitability. The promise of AI is found in its capacity to handle large amounts of data rapidly, which enables effective decision-making and notable efficiency gains. AI is excellent at seeing patterns and trends, which helps with forecasting and insight generation. In the end, it improves overall business performance by facilitating quicker, more consistent, and informed decision-making through anomaly detection, trend forecasting, and catastrophe response. These developments do, however, come with hazards and ethical issues. While the development of AI-powered autonomous weaponry presents ethical problems and the possibility of misuse, bias in AI decision-making raises challenges about accuracy and fairness. To ensure the benefits of AI and its safe application, it is imperative to address these concerns. While bias in AI decision-making raises concerns about accuracy and fairness, the development of AI-powered autonomous weapons poses ethical issues and the potential for misuse. These issues must be addressed if AI is to be used safely and to its full potential.

3.2. Blockchain's Influence on Decision-Making

Another ground-breaking technology that is changing the way decision-makers make decisions is blockchain. Information may be safely stored and shared via blockchain, a decentralized ledger. The authors demonstrates how putting a blockchain protocol into practice enhances people's decision-making processes and brings goals and results closer together (Cerf, Matz, & Berg, 2020). Blockchain gives decision-makers access to real-time data, which can assist them in making better judgments. Blockchain technology offers a transparent and secure transaction platform that can assist leaders in mitigating the danger of fraud and corruption.

Blockchain technology has become a transformational force that is upending established procedures and transforming several sectors. The influence of blockchain on decision-making is one of its major effects. Blockchain technology offers a decentralized, transparent, and unchangeable ledger that might revolutionize decision-making in businesses, governments, and even personal relationships. Blockchain technology has the potential to improve trustworthiness, cooperation, organization, identity, credibility, and transparency. The research carried out by different authors that demonstrates how this technology and its attributes can be advantageous to open science (Brookbanks & Parry, 2022).

- **Improving Openness and Trust**

Because blockchain is decentralized, it does not require middlemen to support transactions or decision-making, like banks or other third-party entities. Blockchain networks facilitate trust and transparency by means of consensus procedures, which provide all members equal access to the same information. This increased trust lowers the possibility of fraud or manipulation and promotes more informed decision-making.

- **Unchangeable and Verifiable Documents**

Because of the immutability of blockchain technology, decisions and transactions once recorded on the network cannot be changed without the network's participants' consent. This feature makes it simpler to look back and examine the reasoning behind specific decisions by offering an auditable and visible trail of decision-making processes. Additionally, this auditable record can help with accountability, compliance, and dispute resolution purposes.

- **Automating Decision-Making with Smart Contracts**

Smart contracts, or programmable agreements, are frequently supported by blockchain systems. Without the need for middlemen, these self-executing contracts automatically verify and uphold predetermined norms. Automating decision-making procedures according to preset criteria is made possible by smart contracts. This improves total company governance by decreasing human error, increasing efficiency, and guaranteeing that decisions are carried out in a clear and impenetrable manner.

- **Security and Integrity of Data**

High levels of data security and integrity are offered by distributed consensus processes and cryptographic methods found in blockchain technology. Because of its innate resistance to data manipulation and illegal access, decision-making processes are guaranteed to be founded on correct and trustworthy information. Blockchain gives decision-makers the confidence to trust the data-driven insights that come from blockchain systems by guaranteeing data confidentiality and integrity.

- **Making Decisions More Democratic**

Another benefit of blockchain's decentralized structure is that it democratizes decision-making. People can directly participate in decision-making processes using decentralized governance models or blockchain-based voting systems. By empowering stakeholders, decision-making processes may become more open and inclusive while depending less on centralized power structures.

3.3. Machine Learning and Augmented Reality in Leadership

Two other cutting-edge technologies that are revolutionizing the way leaders make choices are augmented reality and machine learning. Large-scale data analysis is possible using machine learning algorithms, which may also yield insights that support decision-making for decision-makers. The study emphasizes on how crucial it is to create AI-based systems with the capacity to learn from data and adjust to shifting surroundings (Alqadhi, Hamdan, & Nasseif, 2022; Duan, Edwards, & Dwivedi, 2019). It also covers the drawbacks of using AI-based systems, including ethical concerns, data privacy, and quality concerns. Leaders may make better decisions by using augmented reality to see data and information in new ways. Leadership techniques might undergo a radical transformation because of two fast developing technologies such as AR and ML. ML and AR provide executives with the ability to make well-informed choices, spur innovation, and maintain a competitive edge in today's fast-paced corporate environment by using the power of data-driven insights and augmenting human perception. This work examines how executives may use ML and AR to improve decision-making and advance organizational success.

4. DATA-DRIVEN DECISION-MAKING

ML gives decision-makers the ability to sift through enormous volumes of data and derive important insights that inform choices. Leaders may see patterns, trends, and correlations with ML algorithms that they would miss with traditional methods. By utilizing these insights, leaders may reduce risks and maximize possibilities by making more precise and knowledgeable decisions.

- **Forecasting and Predictive Analytics:** ML algorithms may use past data to forecast future events, giving decision-makers the ability to act proactively. Leaders can foresee consumer behaviour, market trends, and possible hazards by using predictive analytics. This kind of insight gives the ability to plan, spend money wisely, and foster creativity inside their companies.

- **Personalized Leadership Development:** Leaders may customize their programs for professional development and training by using machine learning algorithms to analyze individual performance data and discover areas of strength and improvement. This kind of individualized training equips leaders to handle their problems, improve their abilities, and lead more successfully.
- **Augmented Reality for Better Decision-Making:** By superimposing digital data on the actual environment, AR gives decision-makers access to real-time insights. Leaders can see their enterprises holistically because to AR's ability to present complicated data, key performance indicators (KPIs), and pertinent information in real-time through visualizations. Leaders who enhance their perception are better able to evaluate events fast, make data-driven choices, and adapt to changing surroundings.
- **Virtual Collaboration and Remote Leadership:** Thanks to ML and AR technologies, leaders may interact and work together with teams who are located far apart. Through the overlaying of virtual items, designs, or presentations onto real-world situations, AR-powered remote collaboration solutions can improve communication and promote creativity. This capacity enables executives to lead successfully from a distance, fostering an inclusive and flexible work atmosphere.
- **Continual Learning and Adaptability:** Machine learning algorithms can learn from and adjust to incoming data, giving leaders ongoing input. Leaders can pinpoint areas for development, make real-time strategy adjustments, and react quickly to shifting market situations by utilizing ML-powered insights. This never-ending cycle of learning helps leaders become more flexible and confident in their capacity to handle ambiguity.

Another cutting-edge technique that is revolutionizing the way leaders make decisions is data-driven decision-making. Making decisions based on data is known as data-driven decision-making. The research emphasizes on the value of data-driven decision-making in educational leadership and how it can be used to identify areas for improvement, generate positive change, strategically allocate resources, involve stakeholders, and promote a continuous improvement culture (Fernandes, 2019). Leaders may benefit from AI and machine learning by receiving insights that enable them to make well-informed choices by analysing large volumes of data. Technologies for real-time data analytics can support decision-making by leaders in a timely and accurate manner. Technology-enabled informed decision-making may assist in making wiser choices and raising the effectiveness of their companies. Today's corporate procedures are built around data-driven decision-making. Organizations may make more objective and well-informed decisions that result in enhanced performance, streamlined procedures, and strategic success by employing data analysis and insights.

4.1. Benefits of Data-Driven Decision Making

- **Objective Decision-Making:** Data-driven decision-making does not depend on gut feeling or personal judgment. Rather, it emphasizes quantitative analysis and empirical data. Organizations may lessen biases, make more objective judgments, and raise their chances of success by basing decisions on appropriate information. With the use of this strategy, executives may make judgments that are based on real evidence rather than their gut feelings.

- **Identifying Trends and Patterns:** Data analysis gives businesses the ability to find correlations, trends, and patterns in large datasets. Organizations may learn more about consumer behavior, market dynamics, operational inefficiencies, and other crucial issues by gaining these insights. Decision-makers are better equipped to capitalize on new possibilities, make strategic adjustments, and reduce potential risks using this knowledge.
- **Predictive Analytics:** Predictive analytics is a tool used in data-driven decision-making that makes predictions about the future based on past data. Through the utilization of statistical models and machine learning algorithms, firms may forecast market shifts, client preferences, and trends. Proactive decision-making is made possible by this foresight, which aids businesses in staying one step ahead of the competition and making timely adjustments.
- **Measuring Performance and KPIs:** Organizations may track KPIs and assess performance with integrity thanks to data-driven decision-making. Through the acquisition and examination of data pertaining to sales, customer happiness, production, and other pertinent domains, establishments may evaluate their advancement, detect any obstacles, and formulate informed selections to enhance efficiency and accomplish objectives.
- **Process and Resource Allocation Optimization:** Data analysis enables businesses to find inefficiencies and improve procedures. Organizations may find areas for improvement, cut expenses, and increase operational efficiency by examining data on resource allocation, workflow, and performance. Organizations may efficiently manage resources, optimize workflows, and promote continuous development by using data-driven decision-making.

4.2. Considerations for Embracing Data-Driven Decision-Making

- **Data Validity and Quality:** It is critical to make sure that the information utilized to make decisions is correct, dependable, and current. Maintaining the integrity of the insights drawn from the data requires appropriate quality control, validation procedures, and data collecting techniques.
- **Data Security and Privacy:** To safeguard sensitive information, organizations need to give data privacy and security top priority. Sustaining trust and protecting consumer and corporate data requires strict adherence to applicable data protection legislation and the deployment of strong security measures.
- **Data Literacy and Accessibility:** Equipping staff members with data literacy abilities and guaranteeing that pertinent data is accessible are essential to fostering a culture of data-driven decision-making. To successfully analyze and apply data in decision-making processes, personnel might benefit from training programs and easily navigable analytics tools.
- **Balancing Human Judgment with Data Insights:** Although data-driven decision-making has its advantages, it must be calibrated with human judgment and expertise. There may be circumstances in which subjective evaluations are necessary, and not all judgments can be made exclusively based on statistics. Making more thorough decisions is possible when intuition, experience, and data insights are combined.

5. INTEGRATION OF BLOCKCHAIN AND AUGMENTED REALITY IN LEADERSHIP

Another ground-breaking technique that is revolutionizing the way leaders make choices is the combination of augmented reality and blockchain. The use of blockchain technology to fundraising, organizational behaviour, and data integrity is examined in (Richard, Prabowo, Trisetyarso, & Soewito, 2022). It emphasizes how it can adhere to rules, reaches a worldwide user base, and alter organizational behaviour. The future effects on leadership techniques are also examined in this research. While augmented reality may assist leaders in seeing data and information in new ways, blockchain can be utilized to securely store and distribute information. This can assist in making wiser choices and raising the effectiveness of their companies. Augmented reality and blockchain technology integration have enormous potential to improve leadership techniques. By merging the immersive qualities of augmented reality with the transparency and immutability of blockchain, executives can promote trust inside their businesses, stimulate innovation, and make better decisions.

5.1. Blockchain's Role in Leadership

Blockchain technology presents a special chance to change leadership techniques by encouraging trust, traceability, and transparency. Because of its decentralized and unchangeable structure, it offers a safe environment for information capture and sharing, empowering decision-makers to act on information.

- **Secure and transparent decision-making:** Blockchain promotes a transparent and accountable culture by making sure that all decisions are recorded and available to all parties involved. Better decision-making procedures and a rise in mutual trust between team members and leaders may result from this.
- **Streamlined administrative processes:** Recordkeeping, payments, and approval processes are just a few of the administrative chores that may be automated with the help of smart agreements or self-executing contracts kept on the blockchain. Leaders can focus on strategic endeavours with more time to spare because of the substantial administrative burden being reduced.
- **Enhanced collaboration and communication:** By offering a common platform for document sharing, project updates, and task management, blockchain can enable safe and effective cooperation between team leaders and members.
- **Empowering employees**: Blockchain may empower workers by granting them more ownership and control over their work by decentralizing power structures. Increased motivation and staff engagement may result from this.

5.2. Ethical Considerations in Blockchain Integration

Blockchain may empower workers by granting them more ownership and control over their work by decentralizing power structures. The application of blockchain technology in people operations is examined in Sharif and Ghodoosi (2022) with an emphasis on exit, intra-organizational procedures, and entrance. It addresses the moral ramifications of contractarianism, deontology, utilitarianism, and virtue ethics. Increased motivation and staff engagement may result from this. The various challenges in adopting blockchain for any organization are:

- **Data privacy:** Since blockchain transactions are usually public, privacy and security issues are brought up. To guarantee that personal data is secure, leaders must put in place strong data governance systems.
- **Accessibility:** Not everyone can take part in blockchain-based systems since not everyone has access to the required infrastructure and technology. Digital marginalization and inequity may result from this. Leaders must figure out how to close the digital gap and guarantee that everyone can make use of blockchain's advantages.
- **Environmental impact:** One big worry is the amount of energy needed to run blockchain networks. Leaders must look for methods to lessen the environmental effects of blockchain technology and make it more sustainable. Leaders should take these ethical issues very seriously before putting blockchain ideas into practice. Leaders can make sure blockchain is utilized ethically and responsibly to improve their leadership practices by proactively addressing these issues.

5.3. Augmented Reality in Remote Collaboration

With the use of AR technology, one may create a hybrid experience that blends virtual and physical aspects by superimposing digital information over the actual environment. The assessment discussed in Bhanu, Sharma, Piratla, and Chalil Madathil (2022) delves into the application of AR in the construction, engineering, and architectural sectors for remote collaboration. It uncovers notable reductions in time and errors, enhanced risk communication capabilities, and prospects for further investigation. There is a lot of promise here for improving leadership situations' distant cooperation through technology. Here is some ways AR can benefit remote collaboration:

- **Transparent and Immutable Data Recording:** A decentralized, transparent, and impenetrable ledger is made possible by blockchain technology. Leaders may record and validate data, including financial transactions, supply chain details, and performance measures, by combining blockchain technology with augmented reality. Data-driven decision-making is made easier, confidence is increased, and stakeholders may obtain real-time information thanks to this transparent and unchangeable data recording.
- **Enhanced communication and engagement:** Geographically scattered team members can communicate more naturally and engagingly when using AR technologies. Leaders may utilize AR, for instance, to deliver presentations, carry out virtual tours, and offer remote help.
- **Improved spatial awareness and understanding:** Team members may see complicated facts and concepts more intuitively with the use of augmented reality. This is particularly useful when working together on projects involving real locations or tangible items.
- **Reduced travel and associated costs:** For meetings, training sessions, and other cooperative activities, AR can replace the necessity for actual travel. Organizations may save money, time, and resources by doing this.
- **Increased accessibility and inclusion:** AR technology offers other methods for people with impairments to engage with information and take part in meetings, which can increase accessibility for collaboration.

Regardless of the physical location of their teams, leaders may foster a more productive and collaborative work environment for remote teams by utilizing the special qualities of augmented reality.

5.4. Augmented Reality's Impact on Collaboration

Augmented reality is a new force in technology that can lead to revolutionary cooperation. AR transforms teamwork by enabling seamless engagement and removing geographical borders by superimposing virtual components onto the actual environment. AR has a significant influence because technology improves problem-solving through immersive experiences, stimulates creative thought, and enables real-time communication. In his discussion of the potential of AR and VR to advance fairness and inclusion, Dick (2021) addresses how these technologies may address latent prejudices, increase access to opportunities, and open new avenues for cooperation and communication. The presented work explores the disruptive impact of augmented reality on collaboration, showing how it enhances creativity, transforms teamwork, and establishes new benchmarks for dynamic, networked work spaces. Collaboration may be greatly impacted using AR into leadership practices in several ways:

- **Enhanced decision-making:** Leaders may make better decisions by using AR technologies to see data and information in 3D space.
- **Improved problem-solving:** Through the provision of a shared virtual environment where team members may visualize ideas and collaborate to discover answers, AR can support collaborative brainstorming and problem-solving.
- **Increased innovation:** Teams may explore and experiment with new ideas in a more immersive and engaging way with AR, which can stimulate innovation. AR may be used by designers to envision product or environment prototypes, and by engineers to model complicated systems. As a result, the workplace may become more inventive and creative.
- **Enhanced communication and engagement:** By offering a shared virtual arena where team members may interact with one another and their surroundings, AR can foster better team engagement and communication. For geographically scattered or distant teams, this may be quite helpful.
- **Reduced training costs:** With the use of AR, training simulations that are interactive and realistic may be created to aid employees in learning new processes and abilities more quickly and effectively. Employee productivity may increase as a result, and training expenses may decrease.
- **Improved customer service:** With augmented reality, you can provide your consumers a more participatory and interesting experience. Retailers may utilize AR to let customers visually try on furniture or clothing before they buy it. Sales growth and more customer satisfaction are possible outcomes of this.
- **Enhanced safety:** Augmented Reality has the potential to enhance workplace safety by giving employees access to up-to-date information about their surroundings and any threats. For instance, before starting work, manufacturing workers can use augmented reality to check where electrical cables and other risks are located.
- **Increased efficiency:** Teams may function more effectively when AR gives them the knowledge and resources, they need to finish jobs quickly and simply. When working on equipment, field service professionals, for instance, can utilize AR to consult schematics and instructions.
- **Accessibility:** AR can improve accessibility in the workplace for those with impairments. For instance, those who are hard of hearing can utilize augmented reality to view spoken conversation subtitles.

- **Auditable Decision-Making Processes:** When blockchain and augmented reality are combined, decision-making processes may be made auditable and traceable by leaders. AR enables leaders and stakeholders to see the reasoning behind decisions by superimposing pertinent decision-making information onto real-world situations. This auditable document promotes compliance, encourages responsibility, and facilitates educated dialogue about these choices.
- **New business models**: With AR, new business prospects and models may be developed. Businesses may employ AR to develop virtual goods or experiences that they can market to consumers.

5.5. Enhancing Virtual Environments for Decision-Making

In comparison to conventional approaches, the study assesses how immersive systems affect decision-making, highlighting successful examples and suggesting areas for more research to increase efficacy (Liberatore & Wagner, 2021). Virtual Leaders' perceptions of and interactions with virtual environments might be completely transformed by AR, which would eventually result in better informed and efficient decision-making.

- **Comprehensive Understanding:** AR gives executives a comprehensive understanding of complicated data and its spatial linkages by superimposing virtual information onto the actual world. Charts and graphs are examples of standard data representations; this visualization can be significantly more informative and intuitive.
- **Trend Identification:** Leaders may change data in real-time with AR's interactive components, which enables them to spot hidden patterns and trends that static representations could miss. A deeper comprehension of the context and consequences of the data is made possible by this proactive approach.
- **Scenario Exploration:** Leaders may design and experiment with different simulations and situations inside the virtual world thanks to augmented reality. This enables people to anticipate probable results of many choices and select the one that will have the most positive effects, minimizing risks and optimizing success.
- **Collaborative Decision-Making:** AR enables leaders to collaborate with their team members in real-time on virtual models and simulations. Richer conversations, a wider range of viewpoints, and ultimately, more informed judgments are the results of this participatory process.

5.6. Drawbacks and Ethical Dilemmas in Augmented Reality

The obstacles that come with integrating AR technology into daily life are numerous and include ethical concerns as well as drawbacks. Among the main issues are:

A. Privacy Issues

- **Data Security:** Since augmented reality apps often gather and handle user data, privacy concerns regarding data security and possible misuse are warranted.
- **Invasion of Privacy:** The usage of AR in public areas may result in unintentional monitoring, violating people's privacy without their knowledge or agreement.

B. Safety Concerns

- **Safety & Distraction:** AR apps have the potential to divert users' attention, which increases the risk of accidents or injuries, particularly when driving or strolling through crowded areas.
- **Addiction and reliance:** Extended usage of AR gadgets can lead to addiction and reliance on technology, which can have negative effects on users' mental and physical health.

C. Ethical Use of AR in Marketing and Advertising

- **Manipulative Advertising:** Personalized and targeted advertising using augmented reality can sway user decisions and perceptions without the express permission of the user.
- **False Realities**: Producing augmented material that obfuscates the distinction between virtual and real-world aspects presents moral questions regarding veracity and openness.

D. Social Impact

- **Isolation:** While AR seeks to improve experiences, overuse of the technology can result in social isolation as users immerse themselves in virtual worlds rather than interact with the outside world.
- **Inequality:** A digital divide may result from unequal access to augmented reality technology, which might widen already-existing social and economic divides.

E. Unintentional Repercussions

- **Unintentional Uses:** AR technology might be used for harmful purposes like disseminating false information or producing fake material.
- **Security Vulnerabilities:** Hacking or unauthorized access might potentially lead to the abuse of private data on AR devices and applications.

F. Design and Development

- **Bias in AR Algorithms:** If AR applications are not well thought out, biases may be reinforced, producing discriminating results in domains such as object or face recognition.
- **Informed Consent:** For AR apps to be used ethically, users must be sufficiently informed about the data collecting, storage, and sharing policies of the applications.

5.7. Benefits of AR-enhanced Virtual Environments

- **Improved decision quality:** Decisions are more intelligent and successful when there is a deeper comprehension of the evidence and possible consequences.

- **Reduced risk:** Using scenarios, leaders may recognize and reduce possible hazards before they arise.
- **Enhanced collaboration:** Team members who engage in real-time communication and consider a variety of viewpoints are better able to collaborate and make well-informed decisions.
- **Increased efficiency:** Because AR is visible and interactive, it may expedite the decision-making process and save time and costs.
- **Improved outcomes:** Leaders can eventually improve results for their companies by utilizing AR's advantages.

All things considered, AR is a potent instrument for improving virtual environments and enabling executives to take better, more informed decisions that propel corporate performance. Inventory and supply chain management might undergo radical change because of the combination of blockchain technology with augmented reality. AR superimposes real-time inventory data into actual places, while blockchain tracks items from point of origin to destination, ensuring security and transparency. Leaders are more equipped to decide on inventory levels, demand forecasts, and logistics optimization because to this synergy. Furthermore, blockchain and augmented reality enable remote collaboration by establishing virtual conference rooms where international teams may exchange and work with digital information. AR enhances this secure connection, which is not limited by location. In addition, augmented reality improves data visualization by superimposing digital data on the actual environment. This allows decision-makers to analyze large, complicated data sets in real time and make well-informed choices.

5.8. Challenges and limitations of AR-enhanced Virtual Environments

- **Cost:** The development and application of AR technology can be costly.
- **Privacy concerns:** Because augmented reality technology has the potential to gather and preserve personal data, privacy issues are raised.
- **Technical limitations:** Although it is still in its infancy, augmented reality technology has many technological drawbacks.
- **User experience:** The user experience must be considered while designing augmented reality apps, since badly designed programs may be annoying and challenging to use.

6. COGNITIVE COMPUTING FOR DECISION-MAKING IN THE DIGITAL ERA

Cognitive computing is a form of self-learning systems that interact effortlessly between humans and computers in complex scenarios. These systems can adjust to changes in language, meaning, and context. Unlike "artificial intelligence," which implies independent machine intelligence, cognitive computing focuses on replicating human cognitive capacities rather than creating sentient computers (Demirkan, Earley, & Harmon, 2017). Cognitive computing symbolizes a paradigm change in the way leaders approach problem-solving and decision-making. Cognitive computing could change the way people lead in the digital age because it works in ways that are like how humans think. From optimizing decision-making processes with data-driven insights to automating routine tasks and streamlining operations, cognitive computing offers leaders a powerful toolkit for driving organizational success (Mumford, Todd, Higgs, & McIntosh, 2017).

Cognitive systems and cognitive computing have a big effect on leadership in tech-driven environments (Dragoni & Rospocher, 2018). Using big data analysis, as discussed in leaders using these technologies can improve decision-making processes by utilizing computational learning systems (Appel, Candello, & Gandour, 2017). Additionally, executives can assign work to intelligent systems by using cognitive computing capacity to imitate human reasoning processes, freeing up time for creative and strategic thinking (Varadarajan, Kommers, Piuri, & Subramaniyaswamy, 2020). Based on the work of, the goal of cognitive computing models is to make computers with sufficient intelligence to think, feel, and know (Gutierrez-Garcia & López-Neri, 2015).

6.1. Applications of Cognitive Computing in Various Fields

With its human-like reasoning processes, cognitive computing helps with diagnosis and treatment planning, which is beneficial to the medical field (Sabarmathi & Leelavathi, 2019). It improves customer service and fraud detection in banking (Finch, Goehring, & Marshall, 2017). It maximizes customer experience, marketing, and inventory in retail. It can be used in education to enable tailored instruction. Cognitive computing impacts enterprises through improved decision-making and efficiency and spurring innovation through the analysis of large data sets (Megha, Madhura, & Sneha, 2017). According to Jacobs (2019) an efficient fusion of leadership and cognitive computing is a difficult and dynamic task. According to Timotheou et al. (2016), leaders should concentrate on developing and carrying out a unit's value proposition and delivery since it is crucial to create and deliver value to stakeholders. By utilizing instruments like personality assessments and cognitive applications, emphasizes how important it is for leaders to grasp the delicate balance between managing and leading IT businesses (Janz & Honken, 2013). To investigate collaborative leadership in multi-team systems executing digital literacy programs, suggests a research methodology (Phelps, 2016). This could yield important insights into successful leadership techniques in the context of cognitive computing.

6.2. Ethical Considerations

There are several ethical issues with using cognitive computing in leadership positions. According to Jacobs (2019) highlights that leaders must discuss the ramifications of emerging technologies for society and policy. In the context of artificial intelligence. Cawthorpe (2023), presents a model for evaluating leadership that emphasizes flexibility and striking a balance between human and AI capabilities. The ethical responsibilities of computing professionals are pointed out by Loui and Miller (2008), and they are particularly crucial when considering cognitive computing in leadership. These include the requirement for peer review, informed consent, and ethical code observance. Contemporary leaders face a diverse range of difficulties that often seem excessively complex. However, the key to finding solutions comes in understanding the essentials, such as establishing a mission-aligned organisation, collecting the required capital and competitive expertise, utilising knowledge to generate long-lasting outcomes, and improving decision-making processes (Hewlett, 2006). Navigate the challenges and opportunities inherent in integrating cognitive computing into leadership strategies. Address concerns such as ethical dilemmas, data privacy, and the potential displacement of human workers, while also highlighting the transformative potential of cognitive computing to drive innovation and growth.

7. NEXT-GENERATION LEADERSHIP IN THE 21ST CENTURY

A fresh method of leadership that is future-oriented is called "next-generation leadership." Leaders of the future must be able to navigate their way through the complicated and quickly evolving 21st-century environment. They must be able to show perseverance in the face of difficulty and adjust to new possibilities and difficulties.

- **Next-Generation Leadership**

Future-oriented leadership is what distinguishes next-generation leadership. Future-ready leaders must be able to see patterns in the market and adjust to changing conditions. They must possess the ability to think creatively and come up with original solutions to challenging issues.

- **Essential Qualities of Future Leaders**

Essential traits that future leaders must have been flexibility, innovation, and resilience. They must possess agility, self-awareness, and the capacity to handle change. They must also be able to establish trusting bonds with their teams and communicate clearly.

- **Managing Change and Demonstrating Resilience**

Resilience and change management are critical skills for future leaders. Effective leaders must possess the ability to adjust to novel situations and prospects and exhibit perseverance when confronted with hardship. They must be able to convince their teams of the advantages of change and manage it well.

7.1. Factors Shaping the 21st Century Leadership Landscape

Numerous elements influence the leadership landscape of the twenty-first century. Geopolitical instability and ongoing change are two complex aspects that affect leadership. Using a theoretical and historical lens, the study examines organizational leadership and highlights problems and challenges facing leaders in the twenty-first century (Stehlik, Short, & Piip, 2013). It covers modern organizational structures, shifting worker demographics, the global environment, and theories of leadership and management. Unpredictability and disruptive technological breakthroughs are also influencing the leadership landscape of the twenty-first century.

- **Multifaceted Factors Influencing Leadership**

Technology breakthroughs, demographic shifts, and globalization are some of the many variables affecting leadership. These are aspects that leaders must be able to negotiate and adjust to new opportunities and difficulties.

- **Persistent Change and Geopolitical Instability**

The leadership landscape of the twenty-first century is being shaped by global instability and persistent change. Effective change management and the ability to adjust to new possibilities and challenges are essential skills for leaders.

- **Disruptive Technical Advancements and Unpredictability**

Rapid and disruptive technical breakthroughs characterize the 21st century. To succeed in this setting, executives need to be flexible, creative, and at ease with uncertainty. They must develop critical abilities such as emotional intelligence, technical fluency, agility, and strategic vision. Leaders may steer their firms towards success in the dynamic landscape by adopting these competencies.

7.2. Navigating the Dynamic 21st Century Leadership Landscape

The environment of leadership in the twenty-first century is dynamic and ever-changing. This environment requires leaders to be able to adapt and adjust to new possibilities and difficulties. Success in the twenty-first century requires leadership from the next generation. Leaders of the future generation must possess fundamental attributes like creativity, flexibility, and resilience. They must also exhibit agility, self-awareness, and the ability to handle change. Technological improvements, increasing complexity, and fast change define the 21st-century leadership landscape. To prosper in this ever-changing setting, leaders need to modify their methods, pick up new abilities, and adopt creative tactics.

- **Embrace Adaptability and Agility:** To successfully navigate the changing terrain, leaders need to be flexible and agile. Adopt a growth attitude that promotes ongoing learning and is open to change. Leaders must gain the flexibility to change course, adapt tactics, and act quickly in the face of new possibilities and difficulties. Foster a culture of innovation that values change as a spur for development and promotes experimentation.
- **Foster a Culture of Collaboration:** The leadership style of the twenty-first century has changed from being top-down to being team-oriented, with an emphasis on varied perspectives and cross-functional cooperation. An inclusive environment with decision-making participation from all stakeholders is necessary for successful leadership. It takes a collaborative culture that prioritizes open communication, information exchange, and team problem-solving to build a cooperative and synergistic atmosphere in the workplace.
- **Embrace Technological Advancements:** Technological developments are changing how businesses function and changing whole sectors. Leaders must be up to date on new technologies that are pertinent to their sectors and make strategic use of them. Adopt technology to satisfy changing client requirements and spur innovation. Examples of these technologies include digital platforms, automation, cloud computing, data analytics, and artificial intelligence.
- **Develop Emotional Intelligence and Empathy:** The need for interpersonal skills grows along with the complexity of the leadership environment in the twenty-first century. To build enduring bonds with their teams and stakeholders, leaders need to cultivate emotional intelligence, empathy, and effective communication techniques. Develop a leadership style that emphasizes building connections based on trust, empathy, and active listening. Leaders with emotional

intelligence are better equipped to comprehend and inspire their colleagues, encouraging cooperation and group achievement.
- **Foster a Learning Culture:** Continuous learning and growth are essential in the changing leadership landscape of the twenty-first century. Establishing a pervasive learning culture inside the organization is important for leaders, who should prioritize skill development, knowledge-sharing, and continual improvement. They can guarantee that the team has access to many resources, mentorship programs, and learning opportunities to support their professional development. Keep up with the latest developments in your field, take part in conferences, attend seminars, and wholeheartedly support the idea of lifelong learning. The dedication to continuous learning is not only a tactic but also a basic tenet of successful leadership in this age of unending change.
- **Ethical Leadership and Corporate Social Responsibility:** Leadership in the twenty-first century encompasses social responsibility and moral behaviour in addition to financial success. To positively influence communities, stakeholders, and the environment, it entails honesty, openness, accountability, sustainable practices, and embracing corporate social responsibility programs.

8. POSSESSION OF AGILITY AND SELF-AWARENESS

Amidst the tremendous global problems and swift advancements in technology, leaders need to possess agility and self-awareness to effectively traverse the intricacies of the future. When leaders exhibit these attributes, they can quickly adjust to changing environments, embracing innovation, and navigating through uncertainty. A thorough awareness of one's assets and weaknesses are fostered by self-awareness, which facilitates wise decision-making. Agility and self-awareness work together to enable leaders to take bold risks, be resilient, and have a clear grasp of the shifting dynamics that will shape the future. These qualities turn become necessary instruments for successful leadership in the face of ongoing change.

8.1. Crucial Attributes for Future Leaders

The capacity to swiftly adjust and flourish in a setting that is continuously changing is referred to as agility. This comprises:

- **Adaptability:** Executives need to be able to swiftly adapt to new situations, developing technology, and altering consumer needs. This necessitates a readiness to pick up new abilities and adopt creative thinking.
- **Decision-making:** Leaders must make well-informed judgments under pressure and with little information in a fast-paced work environment. They need to be competent at balancing possibilities and hazards.
- **Problem-solving:** Creatively recognizing and resolving complicated issues is a talent of agile leaders. They can use critical thinking to solve problems even in the face of ambiguity.
- **Resilience:** Effective leadership requires the capacity to overcome obstacles and recover from failures. Agile leaders are aware that making mistakes is a necessary component of growing and learning.

- **Self-awareness:** A deep insight of one's own motives, feelings, capabilities, and shortcomings is known as self-awareness. It improves interpersonal connections, encourages personal development, and provides information for decision-making. It creates a potent combination with agility that enables leaders to handle difficulties in the face of fast change with sincerity and flexibility.
- **Emotional intelligence:** Leaders need to understand both their own and others' feelings. This enables people to forge solid bonds with one another, promote teamwork, and skilfully handle challenging circumstances.
- **Self-reflection:** A vital component of personal development is the capacity to assess one's own advantages and disadvantages. Leaders that are self-aware are receptive to criticism and want to grow from their errors.
- **Authenticity:** People admire and trust leaders who are sincere and loyal to themselves. This promotes open communication and a pleasant team atmosphere.
- **Empathy:** Creating a sense of community inside an organization and establishing solid connections depend on one's ability to comprehend and share the emotions of others.

8.2. Adjusting to Novel Circumstances and Market Fluctuations

A leader's ability to navigate uncertainty and market shifts is essential. Effective leaders must possess resilience, strategic vision, and adaptability to encourage an innovative culture and enable their staff to welcome change. They also need to be proactive in tracking market trends, communicate well, and make well-informed judgments. Leaders who model organizational agility enable their staff to successfully adjust to changing market conditions and unique situations. Leaders possessing both agility and self-awareness will be better equipped to:

- **Navigate uncertainty and volatility:** Unexpected difficulties and quick changes are probably going to be features of the future. The leaders who can adjust fast and gain knowledge from past mistakes will be the most successful in this kind of setting.
- **Embrace new technologies:** For leaders to stay competitive, they must be open to accepting new tools and procedures as technology advances at an exponential rate. Being self-aware enables people to evaluate their own advantages and disadvantages in this area and, if needed, seek assistance.
- **Lead through crises:** Self-aware, flexible leaders can help their teams' overcome obstacles and come out stronger on the other side, whether they are faced with natural catastrophes, economic downturns, or other disturbances.
- **Construct resilient organizations:** Leaders may cultivate a workforce that is inventive, flexible, and able to flourish in the face of change by fostering an environment of agility and self-awareness inside their institutions.

9. FUTURE DIRECTIONS: LEADING IN THE DIGITAL ERA

In the coming years, leadership development will change to meet the changing needs of businesses in the face of accelerating technological progress. Leaders need to adjust, concentrating on important areas like: digital fluency, remote Leadership Skills, agility and adaptability, emotional Intelligence, etc. To effectively use emerging technologies like AI, blockchain, and data analytics, leaders need to develop an extensive understanding of them. To effectively manage distributed teams, leaders must be competent in virtual collaboration and communication platforms, as remote work is becoming more and more common. Leaders must cultivate agility in the face of swift change so that they can react quickly to evolving market conditions and technology advancements. Emotional intelligence becomes more significant as technology becomes more integrated. Subsequent initiatives will prioritize communication and empathy in order to develop positive team dynamics. Furthermore, technical advancements like AI, blockchain, data analytics, AR, VR, and other technological advances are also changing leadership methods and enabling leaders to make well-informed decisions. However, to ensure responsible and sustainable innovation, leaders must be guided by ethical issues including privacy, bias, transparency, and social effect.

According to Gilli, Lettner, and Guettel (2024); Jacobs (2019), the future of cognitive computing and leadership will be marked by ethics, collaboration, flexibility, and a deeper integration of technology into various areas of work and decision-making. In this changing environment, leaders who can effectively utilize cognitive computing in conjunction with their strong leadership attributes will have an advantage (Noor, 2014). Effective leadership, capable change management, and conceptual digitalization abilities are all necessary for this (Gilli, Lettner, & Guettel, 2024). For cognitive computing to advance, it will be essential to create a cognitive innovation ecosystem that includes integrated knowledge search and exploitation tools, cognitive modeling and visual simulation tools, and cognitive multimodal interfaces (Noor, 2014).

10. CONCLUSION

A transformative journey highlighting the significant shifts in leadership paradigms is presented in this chapter on Future Mega Trends in Leadership and Technology. The necessity to rethink leadership considering a changing environment is highlighted by the rise of technology as a catalyst for change. The development of leadership principles has resulted in significant modifications to duties and responsibilities as well as a revised view of the intersection of the personal and professional worlds. Technology is a catalyst that improves teamwork and introduces cutting-edge techniques for making decisions, such as machine learning, blockchain, and artificial intelligence, which encourage the use of data to make decisions.

The combination of augmented reality and blockchain presents ethical questions in addition to transparency promises. Developing next-generation leadership skills, handling change with resiliency, and recognizing complex elements like ongoing change and geopolitical instability are all necessary for navigating the dynamic leadership landscape. The conclusion highlights the need for self-awareness and agility for aspiring leaders, highlighting flexibility in the face of changing conditions. As technology and leadership merge, this dynamic environment opens new creative possibilities, necessitating leaders with the correct mix of abilities to guide companies through uncertainty with resilience and vision. Success in this dynamic environment depends on your capacity to strike a balance between innovation and adaptability in a world where technology and leadership are merging.

REFERENCES

Alqadhi, B., Hamdan, A., & Nasseif, H. (2022). Artificial Intelligence for Decision Making in the Era of Big Data. In *International Conference on Business and Technology* (pp. 604–612). Springer.

Appel, A. P., Candello, H., & Gandour, F. L. (2017). Cognitive computing: Where big data is driving us. Handbook of Big Data Technologies, 807–850.

Bachtiar, A., Guntoro, G., Riyantie, M., & Ridwan, N. (2023). The Role of Leadership in Digital Transformation Management in Organisations. *Jurnal Minfo Polgan*, *12*(1), 1306–1314. doi:10.33395/jmp.v12i1.12731

Bhanu, A., Sharma, H., Piratla, K., & Chalil Madathil, K. (2022). Application of augmented reality for remote collaborative work in architecture, engineering, and construction–a systematic review. *Proceedings of the Human Factors and Ergonomics Society Annual Meeting*, *66*(1), 1829–1833. doi:10.1177/1071181322661167

Brookbanks, M., & Parry, G. (2022). The impact of a blockchain platform on trust in established relationships: A case study of wine supply chains. *Supply Chain Management*, *27*(7), 128–146. doi:10.1108/SCM-05-2021-0227

Cawthorpe, D. (2023). *Leadership constructs and artificial intelligence: Introducing a novel organizational assessment survey.* Qeios.

Cerf, M., Matz, S., & Berg, A. (2020). Using blockchain to improve decision making that benefits the public good. *Frontiers in Blockchain*, *3*, 13. doi:10.3389/fbloc.2020.00013

Cortellazzo, L., Bruni, E., & Zampieri, R. (2019). The role of leadership in a digitalized world: A review. *Frontiers in Psychology*, *10*, 1938. doi:10.3389/fpsyg.2019.01938 PMID:31507494

Demirkan, H., Earley, S., & Harmon, R. R. (2017). Cognitive computing. *IT Professional*, *19*(4), 16–20. doi:10.1109/MITP.2017.3051332

Dick, E. (2021). *Current and potential uses of AR/VR for equity and inclusion.* Information Technology and Innovation Foundation.

Dragoni, M., & Rospocher, M. (2018). Applied cognitive computing: Challenges, approaches, and real-world experiences. *Progress in Artificial Intelligence*, *7*(4), 249–250. doi:10.1007/s13748-018-0166-4

Duan, Y., Edwards, J. S., & Dwivedi, Y. K. (2019). Artificial intelligence for decision making in the era of Big Data–evolution, challenges and research agenda. *International Journal of Information Management*, *48*, 63–71. doi:10.1016/j.ijinfomgt.2019.01.021

Fernandes, V. (2019). Investigating the role of data-driven decision-making within school improvement processes. In *Evidence-based initiatives for organizational change and development* (pp. 201–219). IGI Global. doi:10.4018/978-1-5225-6155-2.ch010

Finch, G., Goehring, B., & Marshall, A. (2017). The enticing promise of cognitive computing: High-value functional efficiencies and innovative enterprise capabilities. *Strategy and Leadership*, *45*(6), 26–33. doi:10.1108/SL-07-2017-0074

Fleming, M. (2020). AI is changing work—And leaders need to adapt. *Harvard Business Review*.

Galgali, P. (2017). *Digital transformation and its impact on organization's Human Resource Management. IOR and Stakeholder Managment, MCM*. School of Communication and Information, Rutgers University.

Gilli, K., Lettner, N., & Guettel, W. (2024). The future of leadership: New digital skills or old analog virtues? *The Journal of Business Strategy*, *45*(1), 10–16. doi:10.1108/JBS-06-2022-0093

Gutierrez-Garcia, J. O., & López-Neri, E. (2015). Cognitive computing: a brief survey and open research challenges. In *2015 3rd international conference on applied computing and information technology/2nd international conference on computational science and intelligence* (pp. 328–333). IEEE. 10.1109/ACIT-CSI.2015.64

Heukamp, F. (2020). AI and the leadership development of the future. *The Future of Management in an AI World: Redefining Purpose and Strategy in the Fourth Industrial Revolution*, 137–148.

Hewlett, R. (2006). *The cognitive leader: Building winning organizations through knowledge leadership*. No Title.

Jacobs, G. (2019). A Perspective on Leadership in Cognitive Computing and its Social Consequences. In *2019 IEEE 18th International Conference on Cognitive Informatics & Cognitive Computing (ICCI*CC)* (pp. 28–33). IEEE. 10.1109/ICCICC46617.2019.9146051

Janz, K., & Honken, R. (2013). Personality inventories and cognitive frames: understanding the balance in managing and leading IT organizations. In *Proceedings of the 41st annual ACM SIGUCCS conference on User services* (pp. 143–150). 10.1145/2504776.2504798

Liberatore, M. J., & Wagner, W. P. (2021). Virtual, mixed, and augmented reality: A systematic review for immersive systems research. *Virtual Reality (Waltham Cross)*, *25*(3), 773–799. doi:10.1007/s10055-020-00492-0

Loui, M. C., & Miller, K. W. (2008). *Ethics and professional responsibility in computing*. Academic Press.

Megha, C. R., Madhura, A., & Sneha, Y. S. (2017). Cognitive computing and its applications. In *2017 International Conference on Energy, Communication, Data Analytics and Soft Computing (ICECDS)* (pp. 1168–1172). IEEE. 10.1109/ICECDS.2017.8389625

Mumford, M. D., Todd, E. M., Higgs, C., & McIntosh, T. (2017). Cognitive skills and leadership performance: The nine critical skills. *The Leadership Quarterly*, *28*(1), 24–39. doi:10.1016/j.leaqua.2016.10.012

Noor, A. K. (2014). Potential of cognitive computing and cognitive systems. *Open Engineering*, *5*(1). Advance online publication. doi:10.1515/eng-2015-0008

Oreg, S., & Berson, Y. (2019). Leaders' impact on organizational change: Bridging theoretical and methodological chasms. *The Academy of Management Annals*, *13*(1), 272–307. doi:10.5465/annals.2016.0138

Phelps, K. C. (2016). A proposed research design for exploring collective leadership (cl) within multi-team systems (mts) implementing digital literacy initiatives. *IConference 2016 Proceedings*.

Richard, R., Prabowo, H., Trisetyarso, A., & Soewito, B. (2022). How blockchain will change leadership strategies for effectively managing organizational change. *Frontiers in Psychology*, *13*, 907586. doi:10.3389/fpsyg.2022.907586 PMID:35719467

Sabarmathi, K. R., & Leelavathi, R. (2019). Application of Cognitive Computing in Healthcare. In *Cognitive Social Mining Applications in Data Analytics and Forensics* (pp. 265–272). IGI Global.

Sharif, M. M., & Ghodoosi, F. (2022). The ethics of blockchain in organizations. *Journal of Business Ethics*, *178*(4), 1009–1025. doi:10.1007/s10551-022-05058-5 PMID:35125568

Sonmez Cakir, F., & Adiguzel, Z. (2020). Analysis of leader effectiveness in organization and knowledge sharing behavior on employees and organization. *SAGE Open*, *10*(1). doi:10.1177/2158244020914634

Stehlik, T., Short, T., & Piip, J. (2013). The challenges of leadership in the twenty-first century. In Workforce Development: Perspectives and Issues (pp. 193–211). Springer.

Timotheou, N. M., Reumann, M., Milanovic, J. V., Kornegay, L. G., Stübner, R., Hernandez-Castro, J., . . . Riede, M. (2016). Plenary session 1: Engineering leadership & cognitive computing. In *2016 18th Mediterranean Electrotechnical Conference (MELECON)* (pp. 13–23). IEEE.

Varadarajan, V., Kommers, P., Piuri, V., & Subramaniyaswamy, V. (2020). Recent trends, challenges and applications in cognitive computing for intelligent systems. *Journal of Intelligent & Fuzzy Systems*, *39*(6), 8041–8042. doi:10.3233/JIFS-189309

Veena Latha, K. (2019). A study on work-life balance of the employees in the field of education: Strategic human resource management. *Journal of Emerging Technologies and Innovative Research*, *6*(2), 317. https://www.jetir.org

Compilation of References

. Canbek, M. (2020). Artificial Intelligence Leadership., 173-187. https://doi.org/. doi:10.4018/978-1-5225-9416-1.ch010

. Diwaker, C., Sharma, A., &Tomar, P. (2021). Artificial Intelligence in Higher Education and Learning., 62-72. https://doi.org/. doi:10.4018/978-1-7998-4763-2.ch004

Abbasi. (2019). Software-Defined Cloud Computing: A Systematic Review on Latest Trends and Developments. *IEEE Access*.

Abdul, A., & Zulkernine, M. (2018). Blockchain-based employee performance evaluation system. In *Proceedings of the 2018 IEEE/ACM International Conference on Advances in Social Networks Analysis and Mining* (pp. 890-897). IEEE.

Abdullah, A. (2010). Measuring TQM implementation: A case study of Malaysian SMEs. *Measuring Business Excellence*, *14*(3), 3–15. doi:10.1108/13683041011074173

Abdulwahid, A. H., Pattnaik, M., Palav, M. R., Babu, S. T., Manoharan, G., & Selvi, G. P. (2023, April). Library Management System Using Artificial Intelligence. In *2023 Eighth International Conference on Science Technology Engineering and Mathematics (ICONSTEM)* (pp. 1-7). IEEE.

Acciarini, C., Boccardelli, P., & Vitale, M. (2021). Resilient companies in the time of Covid-19 pandemic: A case study approach. *Journal of Entrepreneurship and Public Policy*, *10*(3), 336–351. doi:10.1108/JEPP-03-2021-0021

Addy, W. (2024). Algorithmic Trading and AI: A Review of Strategies and Market Impact. *World Journal of Advanced Engineering Technology and Sciences*, *11*(1), 258–267. doi:10.30574/wjaets.2024.11.1.0054

Agarwal, A., Gans, J., & Goldfrab, A. (2017, July 26). How AI Will Change the Way We Make Decisions. *Harward Business Review*.

Aggarwal, R., & Singhal, A. (2019). Augmented Reality and its effect on our life. *2019 9th International Conference on Cloud Computing, Data Science & Engineering (Confluence)*, 510-515. 10.1109/CONFLUENCE.2019.8776989

Agnihotri. (2021). Systemic- Processual Shared Leadership Model with reference to Team Variables in IT Industry in India. *Turkish Journal of Computer and Mathematics Education (TURCOMAT)*, *12*(7), 608–618.

Agnihotri. (2023). Artificial Intelligence Shaping Talent Intelligence and Talent Acquisition for Smart Employee Management. *EAI Endorsed Transactions on Internet of Things* 10.

Ahmad, A., Waseem, M., Liang, P., Fahmideh, M., Aktar, M., & Mikkonen, T. (2023). Towards Human-Bot Collaborative Software Architecting with ChatGPT. ArXiv, abs/2302.14600. https://doi.org//arXiv.2302.14600. doi:10.1145/3593434.3593468

Ahsan, M. J. (2023). The Role of Emotional Intelligence in Effective Corporate Social Responsibility Leadership. *The International Journal of Organizational Analysis*, *31*(8), 75–91. doi:10.1108/IJOA-02-2023-3615

Ahuja, J., Puppala, H., Sergio, R. P., & Hoffman, E. P. (2023). E-leadership is Un(usual): Multi-criteria Analysis of Critical Success Factors for the Transition from Leadership to E-leadership. *Sustainability (Basel)*, *15*(8), 6506. doi:10.3390/su15086506

Aksoy, C. (2024). İşletmelerin Dijital Dönüşümü ve Dijital Liderlik Yaklaşımı. *Trakya Üniversitesi Kalite ve Strateji Yönetimi Dergisi*, *4*(1), 1–28. doi:10.56682/ksydergi.1364569

Albshaier, L., Almarri, S., & Hafizur Rahman, M. M. (2024). A Review of Blockchain's Role in E-Commerce Transactions: Open Challenges, and Future Research Directions. *Computers*, *13*(1), 27. doi:10.3390/computers13010027

Alex Rajesh G., & Florence Sheeba J. (2022). A Study on Exploring Perceptions of Emotional Intelligence among Educators. *International Journal of Food and Nutritional Sciences*.

Allal-Chérif, O., Simón-Moya, V., & Ballester, A. (2021). Intelligent purchasing: How artificial intelligence can redefine the purchasing function. *Journal of Business Research*, *124*, 69–76. doi:10.1016/j.jbusres.2020.11.050

Alqadhi, B., Hamdan, A., & Nasseif, H. (2022). Artificial Intelligence for Decision Making in the Era of Big Data. In *International Conference on Business and Technology* (pp. 604–612). Springer.

Alsaeed, A., Adams, C., & Boakes, R. (2017). eService adoption during geopolitical instabilities: Case study of the Syrian refugees. *Proceedings of the European Conference on e-Government, ECEG Part F129463*, 20-28.

Altmeyer, K., Kapp, S., Thees, M., Malone, S., Kuhn, J., & Brünken, R. (2020). The use of augmented reality to foster conceptual knowledge acquisition in STEM laboratory courses—Theoretical background and empirical results. *British Journal of Educational Technology*, *51*(3), 611–628. doi:10.1111/bjet.12900

Altunışık, R., Coşkun, R., Bayraktaroğlu, S., & Yıldırım, E. (2007). *Sosyal Bilimlerde Araştırma Yöntemleri: SPSS Uygulamalı* (5. Baskı). Sakarya Yayıncılık.

Ameer, M. (2023). *The Impact Of Technology On Entrepreneurship - 5 Ways To Leverage It*. https://www.linkedin.com/pulse/impact-technology-entrepreneurship-5-ways-leverage-muslim-ameer/

Américas, E. (2016). *Sustainable Development Goals (SDGs): Our history and close relationship*. https://www.enel-americas.com/en/investors/a202107-sustainable-developmentgoals-sdgs-our-history-and-close-relationship.html

Antonopoulos, A. M. (2014). *Mastering Bitcoin: Unlocking Digital Cryptocurrencies*. Academic Press.

Antonopoulos, A. M. (2014). *Mastering Bitcoin: Unlocking Digital Cryptocurrencies*. O'Reilly Media.

Antonopoulou, H., Halkiopoulos, C., Barlou, O., & Beligiannis, G. N. (2021). Transformational Leadership and Digital Skills in Higher Education Institutes: During the Covid-19 Pandemic. *Emerging Science Journal*, *5*(1), 1–15. doi:10.28991/esj-2021-01252

Antony, J., & Kizgin, H. (2018). Blockchain technology in supply chain management: A proposed framework. In *International Conference on Industrial Engineering and Operations Management* (pp. 1174-1185). Springer.

Appel, A. P., Candello, H., & Gandour, F. L. (2017). Cognitive computing: Where big data is driving us. Handbook of Big Data Technologies, 807–850.

Arians, H. (2023). The impact of technology on leadership. *The People Development Magzine*. https://peopledevelopmentmagazine.com/2023/04/07/impact-of-technology/

Arif, T., Munaf, U., & Ul-Haque, I. (2023). The future of medical education and research: Is ChatGPT a blessing or blight in disguise? *Medical Education Online*, *28*(1), 2181052. Advance online publication. doi:10.1080/10872981.2023.2181052 PMID:36809073

Compilation of References

Asgary, N., & Thamhain, H. (2008). Effective leadership for culturally diverse technology projects. PICMET: Portland International Center for Management of Engineering and Technology, Proceedings, 1345-1350. doi:10.1109/PICMET.2008.4599746

Assibi, A. T. (2022). The Role of Enterprise Risk Management in Business Continuity and Resiliency in the Post-COVID-19 Period. *OAlib*, *9*(6), 1–19. doi:10.4236/oalib.1108642

Associated Chambers of Commerce and Industry of India. (2023). *India Leading the Global Digital Transformation Journey.* https://www.assocham.org/uploads/files/Digital%20Transformation.pdf

Avanzo, M., Trianni, A., Botta, F., Talamonti, C., Stasi, M., & Iori, M. (2021). Artificial Intelligence and the Medical Physicist: Welcome to the Machine. *Applied Sciences (Basel, Switzerland)*, *11*(4), 1691. Advance online publication. doi:10.3390/app11041691

Avurakoghene, O.P., & Oredein, A.O. (2023). Educational Leadership and Artificial Intelligence for Sustainable Development. *Shodh Sari-An International Multidisciplinary Journal.*

Awan, U., Shamim, S., Khan, Z., Zia, N. U., Shariq, S. M., & Khan, M. N. (2021). Big Data Analytics Capability and Decision-Making: The Role of Data-Driven Insight on Circular Economy Performance. *Technological Forecasting and Social Change*, *168*, 120766. doi:10.1016/j.techfore.2021.120766

Baboş, A. (2021). Artificial Intelligence as a Decision Making Tool for Military Leaders. *Land Forces Academy Review*, *26*(4), 269–273. doi:10.2478/raft-2021-0034

Bachtiar, A., Guntoro, G., Riyantie, M., & Ridwan, N. (2023). The Role of Leadership in Digital Transformation Management in Organisations. *Jurnal Minfo Polgan*, *12*(1), 1306–1314. doi:10.33395/jmp.v12i1.12731

Bang, Y., Cahyawijaya, S., Lee, N., Dai, W., Su, D., Wilie, B., Lovenia, H., Ji, Z., Yu, T., Chung, W., Do, Q., Xu, Y., & Fung, P. (2023). A Multitask, Multilingual, Multimodal Evaluation of ChatGPT on Reasoning, Hallucination, and Interactivity. ArXiv, abs/2302.04023. https://doi.org//arXiv.2302.04023. doi:10.18653/v1/2023.ijcnlp-main.45

Barker, T. T. (2021). Finding Pluto: An Analytics-Based Approach to Safety Data Ecosystems. *Safety and Health at Work*, *12*(1), 1–9. doi:10.1016/j.shaw.2020.09.010 PMID:33732523

Barney, J. (1991). Firm resources and sustained competitive advantage. *Journal of Management*, *17*(1), 99–120. doi:10.1177/014920639101700108

Baron, I., & Agustina, H. (2017). The Effectiveness of Leadership Management Training. *Polish Journal of Management Studies*, *16*(2), 7–15. doi:10.17512/pjms.2017.16.2.01

Barua, T., & Patranabis, I. C. (2023). Leadership Style in Times of Crisis: Traditional Mentoring to Remote Monitoring. In Agile Leadership for Industry 4.0: An Indispensable Approach for the Digital Era (s.155-173). Apple Academic Press Inc.

Bawono, M., Gautama, I., Bandur, A., & Alamsjah, F. (2022). The Influence of Ambidextrous Leadership Mediated by Organizational Agility and Digital Business Model Innovation on the Performance of Telecommunication Companies in Indonesia during the Covid-19 Pandemic. *WSEAS Transactions on Information Science and Applications*, *19*, 78–88. doi:10.37394/23209.2022.19.8

Beer, M., Finnstrom, M., & Schrader, D. (2016). Why leadership training fails - and what to do about it. *Harvard Business Review*, *94*(10), 50–57.

Behie, S. W., Pasman, H. J., Khan, F. I., Shell, K., Alarfaj, A., El-Kady, A. H., & Hernandez, M. (2023). Leadership 4.0: The changing landscape of industry management in the smart digital era. *Process Safety and Environmental Protection*, *172*, 317–328. doi:10.1016/j.psep.2023.02.014

Bennett, K., & Mayouf, M. (2021). Value management integration for whole life cycle: Post covid-19 strategy for the UK construction industry. *Sustainability (Basel)*, *13*(16), 9274. doi:10.3390/su13169274

Ben-Oni Ardelean. (2021). *Role of Technological Knowledge and Entrepreneurial Orientation on Entrepreneurial Success: A Mediating Role of Psychological Capital Front*. https://www.frontiersin.org/articles/10.3389/fpsyg.2021.814733/full doi:10.3389/fpsyg.2021.814733

Berman, W. H. (2019). Coaching C-Suite Executives and Business Founders. *Consulting Psychology Journal*, *71*(2), 72–85. doi:10.1037/cpb0000128

Bhanu, A., Sharma, H., Piratla, K., & Chalil Madathil, K. (2022). Application of augmented reality for remote collaborative work in architecture, engineering, and construction–a systematic review. *Proceedings of the Human Factors and Ergonomics Society Annual Meeting*, *66*(1), 1829–1833. doi:10.1177/1071181322661167

Bhatt, P., & Muduli, A. (2023). Artificial intelligence in learning and development: A systematic literature review. *European Journal of Training and Development*, *47*(7/8), 677–694. doi:10.1108/EJTD-09-2021-0143

Bienkowski, Feng, & Means. (2014). Enhancing Teaching and Learning through Educational Data Mining and Learning Analytics. *An Issue Brief*.

Boffo & Patalano. (2020). ESG Investing Practices, Progress Challenges. *OECD Paris*.

Bostrom, N. (2014). *Superintelligence - Paths, Dangers, Strategies*. Oxford University Press.

Bouchrika, I. (2024). 24 Leadership Training. https://research.com/careers/leadership-training-statistics

Bourke, J., & Espedido, A. (2019). *Why Inclusive Leaders Are Good for Organizations, and How to Become One*. Academic Press.

Boyce, L. A., LaVoie, N., Streeter, L. A., Lochbaum, K. E., & Psotka, J. (2008). Technology as a tool for leadership development: Effectiveness of automated web-based systems in facilitating tacit knowledge acquisition. *Military Psychology*, *20*(4), 271–288. doi:10.1080/08995600802345220

Brewer, G., Gajendran, T., & Runeson, G. (2013). ICT & innovation: A case of integration in a regional construction firm. *The Australasian Journal of Construction Economics and Building*, *13*(3), 24–36. doi:10.5130/AJCEB.v13i3.3484

Bringsjord, S., Bello, P., & Ferrucci, D. (2003). Creativity, the Turing test, and the (better) Lovelace test. *The Turing test: the elusive standard of artificial intelligence*, 215-239.

Brookbanks, M., & Parry, G. (2022). The impact of a blockchain platform on trust in established relationships: A case study of wine supply chains. *Supply Chain Management*, *27*(7), 128–146. doi:10.1108/SCM-05-2021-0227

Brown, B., & Anthony, S. D. (2011). *The New Leader's 100-Day Action Plan: How to Take Charge*. Build Your Team, and Get Immediate Results.

Brown, C. (2023). *ChatGPT prompts mastering: A guide to crafting clear and effective prompts—beginners to advanced guide*. Xtro Media.

Brown, M., Treviño, L., & Harrison, D. (2005). Ethical leadership: A social learning perspective for construct development and testing. *Organizational Behavior and Human Decision Processes*, *97*(2), 117–134. doi:10.1016/j.obhdp.2005.03.002

Brynjolfsson, E., & McAfee, A. (2017). The business of artificial intelligence. In *HBR at 100* (pp. 257–272). Harvard Business Review Press. (Original work published 2022)

Compilation of References

Bueno, F.B., Günther, W.M.R., & Philippi, A., Jr. (2017). Sustainable management for a contaminated area on campus. *World Sustainability Series*, 261-273. doi:10.1007/978-3-319-47877-7_18

Buterin, V. (2014). *Ethereum: A Next-Generation Smart Contract and Decentralized Application Platform*. Retrieved from: https://ethereum.org/en/whitepaper/

Büyükbeşe, T., Dikbaş, T., Klein, M., & Batuk Ünlü, S. (2022). A Study On Digital Leadership Scale (DLS) Development Dijital Liderlik Ölçeği (Djl) Geliştirme Çalışması. *Kahramanmaraş Sütçü İmam Üniversitesi Sosyal Bilimler Dergisi*, *19*(2), 740–760. doi:10.33437/ksusbd.1135540

Büyükbeşe, T., & Doğan, Ö. (2022). Dijital Liderliğin Yenilikçi İş Davranışı ve İş Performansı Üzerine Etkisi. *Akademik Araştırmalar ve Çalışmalar Dergisi*, *14*(26), 173–186. doi:10.20990/kilisiibfakademik.1072185

Byrd, T. A., Lewis, B. R., & Bradley, R. V. (2006). Is infrastructure: The influence of senior IT leadership and strategic information systems planning. *Journal of Computer Information Systems*, *47*(1), 101–113. doi:10.1080/08874417.2006.11645937

Calzon, B. (2022). The Importance of Data Driven Decision Making for Business. *Business Intelligence*. https://www.datapine.com/blog/data-driven-decision-making-in-businesses/

Cappel, J., & Windsor, J. (2000). Ethical Decision Making: A Comparison of Computer- Supported and Face-to-face Group. *Journal of Business Ethics*, *28*(2), 95–107. doi:10.1023/A:1006344825235

Casey, M. J., & Vigna, P. (2018). *The Truth Machine: The Blockchain and the Future of Everything*. Academic Press.

Cawthorpe, D. (2023). *Leadership constructs and artificial intelligence: Introducing a novel organizational assessment survey*. Qeios.

Çelik Şahin, Ç., Avcı, Y. E., & Anık, S. (2020). Dijital Liderlik Algısının Metaforlar Yoluyla İncelenmesi. *Elektronik Sosyal Bilimler Dergisi*, *19*(73), 271–286. doi:10.17755/esosder.535159

Cercone, K. (2008). Characteristics of adult learners with implications for online learning design. *AACE Journal*, *16*(2), 137–159.

Cerf, M., Matz, S., & Berg, A. (2020). Using blockchain to improve decision making that benefits the public good. *Frontiers in Blockchain*, *3*, 13. doi:10.3389/fbloc.2020.00013

Chandan, H. C. (2013). Knowledge management and its challenges in global business. Cultural and Technological Influences on Global Business, 290-315. doi:10.4018/978-1-4666-3966-9.ch016

Chandel, T. A. (2023). *Hybrid Energy Storage Systems for Renewable Energy Integration and Application*. doi:10.4018/978-1-6684-8816-4.ch011

Chandel, T. A. (2022). *Green and Sustainable Infrastructure in India, ebook Achieving the Sustainable Development Goals Through Infrastructure Development*. doi:10.4018/979-8-3693-0794-6.ch006

Charan, R., Barton, D., & Carey, D. (2015). *"People Before Strategy": A New Role for the CHRO*. Academic Press.

Charles, Rana, & Carter. (2022). Artificial Intelligence for Data-Driven Decision-Making and Governance in Public Affairs. *Government Information Quarterly, 39*(4), 101742. https://www.sciencedirect.com/science/article/pii/S0740624X22000788

Chatterjee, S., Chaudhuri, R., & Vrontis, D. (2022a). AI and digitalization in relationship management: Impact of adopting AI-embedded CRM system. *Journal of Business Research*, *150*, 437–450. doi:10.1016/j.jbusres.2022.06.033

303

Chatterjee, S., Chaudhuri, R., Vrontis, D., & Jabeen, F. (2022b). Digital transformation of organization using AI-CRM: From microfoundational perspective with leadership support. *Journal of Business Research*, *153*, 46–58. doi:10.1016/j.jbusres.2022.08.019

Chatterjee, S., Ghosh, S. K., & Chaudhuri, R. (2020a). Knowledge management in improving business process: An interpretative framework for successful implementation of AI–CRM–KM system in organizations. *Business Process Management Journal*, *26*(6), 1261–1281. doi:10.1108/BPMJ-05-2019-0183

Chatterjee, S., Nguyen, B., Ghosh, S. K., Bhattacharjee, K. K., & Chaudhuri, S. (2020b). Adoption of artificial intelligence integrated CRM system: An empirical study of Indian organizations. *The Bottom Line (New York, N.Y.)*, *33*(4), 359–375. doi:10.1108/BL-08-2020-0057

Chatterjee, S., Rana, N. P., Dwivedi, Y. K., & Baabdullah, A. M. (2021). Understanding AI adoption in manufacturing and production firms using an integrated TAM-TOE model. *Technological Forecasting and Social Change*, *170*, 120880. doi:10.1016/j.techfore.2021.120880

Chaudhary, V., Vemuri, V. P., Cavaliere, L. P. L., Verma, V., Manoharan, G., & Bharti, A. (2024, March). A comparative analysis of job satisfaction and motivational factors of employees in public versus private organizations. In AIP Conference Proceedings (Vol. 2816, No. 1). AIP Publishing.

Chaudhuri, R., Chatterjee, S., Vrontis, D., & Chaudhuri, S. (2022). Innovation in SMEs, AI dynamism, and sustainability: The current situation and way forward. *Sustainability (Basel)*, *14*(19), 12760. doi:10.3390/su141912760

Chauhan & Agnihotri. (2024). Industry 4.0 and Indian Manufacturing Companies: Barriers towards Sustainability. *Journal of Informatics Education and Research, 4*.

Chesbrough, H. W. (2003). *Open Innovation: The New Imperative for Creating and Profiting from Technology*. Academic Press.

Close, K., Grebe, M., Andersen, P., Khurana, V., Franke, M. R., & Kalthof, R. (2020). The digital path to business resilience. Boston Consulting Group Report.

Coleman, Dossett, & Dimick. (2021). Building High Performing Teams: Opportunities and Challenges of Inclusive Recruitment Practices. *Journal of Vascular Surgery, 74*(2), 86S-92S. https://www.sciencedirect.com/science/article/pii/S0741521421006510

Colfax, R. S., Santosa, A. T., & Diego, J. (2009). Virtual leadership A green possibility in critical times but can it really work. *Journal of International Business Research*, *8*(2), 133–139.

Contreras, F., Baykal, E., & Abid, G. (2020). E-Leadership and Teleworking in Times of Covid-19 and Beyond: What We Know and Where Do We Go. *Frontiers in Psychology*, *11*, 590271. doi:10.3389/fpsyg.2020.590271 PMID:33362656

Coronado-Maldonado, I., & Benítez-Márquez, M.-D. (2023). Emotional Intelligence, Leadership, and Work Teams: A Hybrid Literature Review. *Heliyon*, *9*(10), e20356. doi:10.1016/j.heliyon.2023.e20356 PMID:37790975

Corrales-Estrada, A. M., Gómez-Santos, L. L., Bernal-Torres, C. A., & Rodriguez-López, J. E. (2021). Sustainability and resilience organizational capabilities to enhance business continuity management: A literature review. *Sustainability (Basel)*, *13*(15), 8196. doi:10.3390/su13158196

Cortellazzo, L., Bruni, E., & Zampieri, R. (2019). The Role of Leadership in a Digitalized World: A Review. *Frontiers in Psychology*, *10*, 1938. doi:10.3389/fpsyg.2019.01938 PMID:31507494

Craig, S. (2023). ESG Strategy and Management: Complete Guide for Businesses. *TechTarget*.

Compilation of References

Crawford, J., Cowling, M., & Allen, K. (2023). Leadership is needed for ethical ChatGPT: Character, assessment, and learning using artificial intelligence (AI). *Journal of University Teaching & Learning Practice, 20*(3). Advance online publication. doi:10.53761/1.20.3.02

D'Cruz, P., Du, S., Noronha, E., Parboteeah, K. P., Trittin-Ulbrich, H., & Whelan, G. (2022). Technology, Megatrends and Work: Thoughts on the Future of Business Ethics. *Journal of Business Ethics, 180*(3), 879–902. doi:10.1007/s10551-022-05240-9 PMID:36212627

Das, A., Malaviya, S., & Singh, M. (2023). The Impact of AI-Driven Personalization on Learners' Performance. *International Journal on Computer Science and Engineering, 11*, 15–22.

Das, D. (2023). Understanding the choice of human resource and the artificial intelligence: "strategic behavior" and the existence of industry equilibrium. *Journal of Economic Studies (Glasgow, Scotland), 50*(2), 234–267. doi:10.1108/JES-06-2021-0305

Datnow, A., & Park, V. (2014). *Data-Driven Leadership*. Wiley. https://books.google.co.in/books?id=-xURAwAAQBAJ

Davenport, T. H. (2018). AI in HR: Artificial intelligence to augment human performance. *MIT Sloan Management Review, 59*(4), 1–14.

Davenport, T., Guha, A., Grewal, D., & Bressgott, T. (2020). How Artificial Intelligence Will Change the Future of Marketing. *Journal of the Academy of Marketing Science, 48*(1), 24–42. doi:10.1007/s11747-019-00696-0

Davis, M. C., Challenger, R., Jayewardene, D. N. W., & Clegg, C. W. (2014). Advancing socio-technical systems thinking: A call for bravery. *Applied Ergonomics, 45*(2, 2 Part A), 171–180. doi:10.1016/j.apergo.2013.02.009 PMID:23664481

De Cremer, D. (2019). Leading artificial intelligence at work: A matter of facilitating human-algorithm cocreation. *Journal of Leadership Studies, 13*(1), 81–83. doi:10.1002/jls.21637

De Smet, A. (2018). The Agile Manager Who Manages in an Agile Organization? And What Exactly Do They Do? *The McKinsey Quarterly*, (June), 1–6.

Deloitte. (2018). *Blockchain and the future of HR*. Deloitte University Press. Retrieved from https://www2.deloitte.com/content/dam/insights/us/articles/3849_The-blockchain-evolution-and-hr/DUP_Brookfield-Report_Final.pdf

Deloitte. (2019). *The Deloitte Global Millennial Survey 2019*. Retrieved from https://www2.deloitte.com/global/en/pages/about-deloitte/articles/millennialsurvey.html

Deloitte. (2020). *Making Ethical Tech a Priority*. https://www2.deloitte.com/us/en/insights/topics/digital-transformation/make-ethical-technology-a-priority.html

Demirkan, H., Earley, S., & Harmon, R. R. (2017). Cognitive computing. *IT Professional, 19*(4), 16–20. doi:10.1109/MITP.2017.3051332

Denny, C. A. (2023). The role of leadership in shaping the future of education. *Academy of Educational Leadership Journal, 27*(1), 1-2. www.bantamdell.com

Deviprasad, S., Madhumithaa, N., Vikas, I. W., Yadav, A., & Manoharan, G. (2023). The Machine Learning-Based Task Automation Framework for Human Resource Management in MNC Companies. *Engineering Proceedings, 59*(1), 63.

Di Napoli, G., & Lee, L. S. (2023). The brave new world of artificial intelligence: dawn of a new era. *iGIE, 2*(1), 62-69.

Dick, E. (2021). *Current and potential uses of AR/VR for equity and inclusion*. Information Technology and Innovation Foundation.

Dinçer, S. (2018). Content Analysis in Scientific Research: Meta-Analysis, Meta-Synthesis, and Descriptive Content Analysis. *Bartın Üniversitesi Eğitim Fakültesi Dergisi*, 176–190. doi:10.14686/buefad.363159

Dixit, S., & Maurya, M. (2021). Equilibrating Emotional Intelligence and AI Driven Leadership for Transnational Organizations. *2021 International Conference on Innovative Practices in Technology and Management (ICIPTM)*, 233-237. https://doi.org/10.1109/ICIPTM52218.2021.9388350

Donaldson, G. (2006). *Cultivating Leadership in Schools: Connecting People, Purpose, and Practice*. Teachers College Press. https://books.google.co.in/books?id=CDGRDQAAQBAJ

Dragoni, M., & Rospocher, M. (2018). Applied cognitive computing: Challenges, approaches, and real-world experiences. *Progress in Artificial Intelligence*, 7(4), 249–250. doi:10.1007/s13748-018-0166-4

Duan, Y., Edwards, J. S., & Dwivedi, Y. K. (2019). Artificial intelligence for decision making in the era of Big Data–evolution, challenges and research agenda. *International Journal of Information Management*, 48, 63–71. doi:10.1016/j.ijinfomgt.2019.01.021

Dubey, R., Bryde, D. J., Dwivedi, Y. K., Graham, G., Foropon, C., & Papadopoulos, T. (2023). Dynamic digital capabilities and supply chain resilience: The role of government effectiveness. *International Journal of Production Economics*, 258, 108790. doi:10.1016/j.ijpe.2023.108790

Dupont, B. (2019). The Cyber-Resilience of Financial Institutions: A preliminary working paper on significance and applicability of digital resilience. *Global Risk Institute*.

Dupont, B. (2019). The cyber-resilience of financial institutions: Significance and applicability. *Journal of Cybersecurity*, 5(1), tyz013. doi:10.1093/cybsec/tyz013

Durai, S., Manoharan, G., & Ashtikar, S. P. (2024). *Harnessing Artificial Intelligence: Pioneering Sustainable Solutions for a Greener Future. Social and Ethical Implications of AI in Finance for Sustainability*. 89-117. doi:10.4018/979-8-3693-2881-1.ch003

Duran, M., Simon, S., &Blasco, F. (2020). Science Education and Artificial Intelligence – A Chatbot on Magic and Quantum Computing as an Educational Tool. https://doi.org/. doi:10.38069/edenconf-2020-ac0011

Durga, S., Gupta, P., Kharb, L., Ranjit, P. S., Dornadula, V. H. R., Modak, K. C., & Manoharan, G. (2024). 9Leveraging Distributed Systems for Improved Educational Planning and Resource Allocation. *Meta Heuristic Algorithms for Advanced Distributed Systems*, 141-159.

Dziembek, D., & Turek, T. (2018). Characteristics and Application of Unified Communications as a Service (UCaaS) in Enterprises. *Informatyka Ekonomiczna*, 4(50), 47–65. doi:10.15611/ie.2018.4.04

Eberl, J. K., & Drews, P. (2021). Digital Leadership – Mountain or Molehill? A Literature Review. *Wirtschaftsinformatik 2021 Proceedings*, 48, 223–237. doi:10.1007/978-3-030-86800-0_17

Elgazzar, Y., El-Shahawy, R., & Senousy, Y. (2022). The role of digital transformation in enhancing business resilience with pandemic of COVID-19. *Digital transformation technology Proceedings of ITAF*, 2020, 323–333.

Elia, G., Margherita, A., & Passiante, G. (2020). Digital entrepreneurship ecosystem: How digital technologies and collective intelligence are reshaping the entrepreneurial process. *Technological Forecasting and Social Change*, 150, 119791. doi:10.1016/j.techfore.2019.119791

Elwood, T. (2023). Technological Impacts on the Sphere of Professional Journals. *Journal of allied health*, 52(1), 1.

Compilation of References

Ercan Önbıçak, A., & Akkoyun, B. (2022). Dijital Liderlik Çalışmalarının Yönetim Bilimleri Kapsamında İncelenmesi: Nitel Bir Araştırma. *Malatya Turgut Özal Üniversitesi İşletme ve Yönetim Bilimleri Dergisi*, *3*(2), 128–137.

Erer, B., Demirel, E., & Savaş, Y. (2023). Dijital Liderliğin Görsel Haritalama Tekniğine Göre Bibliyometrik Analizi. *Uluslararası Liderlik Çalışmaları Dergisi: Kuram ve Uygulama*, *6*(1), 1–22. doi:10.52848/ijls.1257255

ETSpecial. (2023). *Ethical Leadership and Corporate Social Responsibility: Leading with Integrity and Impact*. Academic Press.

European Smart Grids Technology Platform. (2006). *European Commission Directorate-General for Research Information and Communication Unit FutureLearn: How do organisations approach leadership development?* https://www.futurelearn.com/info/courses/designing-and-implementing-a-leadership-development-strategy/0/steps/380052#:~:text=Deliberate%20leadership%20development%20involves%20intentional,or%20standardised%20across%20the%20organisation

Farayola, O., Olatoye, F., Chinwe, N., & Daraojimba, C. (2023). Business intelligence transformation through AI and data analytics. *Engineering Science & Technology Journal*, *4*(5), 285–307. doi:10.51594/estj.v4i5.616

Fernandes, V. (2019). Investigating the role of data-driven decision-making within school improvement processes. In *Evidence-based initiatives for organizational change and development* (pp. 201–219). IGI Global. doi:10.4018/978-1-5225-6155-2.ch010

Finch, G., Goehring, B., & Marshall, A. (2017). The enticing promise of cognitive computing: High-value functional efficiencies and innovative enterprise capabilities. *Strategy and Leadership*, *45*(6), 26–33. doi:10.1108/SL-07-2017-0074

Fleming, M. (2020). AI is changing work—And leaders need to adapt. *Harvard Business Review*.

Flumian, M., Coe, A., & Kernaghan, K. (2007). Transforming service to Canadians: The Service Canada model. *International Review of Administrative Sciences*, *73*(4), 557–568. doi:10.1177/0020852307083458

Frost, M., & Sandrock, S. (2019, February). Leadership and self-learning software – hindering and beneficial factors for the motivation of employees in the world of work 4.0. *Analyze–evaluate–design in an interdisciplinary manner*.

Furr, N., Gerrick, D., Munro, P., & Vennix, P. (2019). *Blockchain for HR and Talent Management: Creating Digital Ecosystems*. Springer.

G7. (2023, April 30). *Ministerial Declaration: The G7 Digital and Tech Ministers' Meeting*. Retrieved November 1, 2023, from http://www.g7.utoronto.ca/ict/2023-declaration.html

Gad, Mosa, Abualigah, & Abohany. (2022). Emerging Trends in Blockchain Technology and Applications: A Review and Outlook. *Journal of King Saud University - Computer and Information Sciences, 34*(9), 6719–42. https://www.sciencedirect.com/science/article/pii/S1319157822000891

Galgali, P. (2017). *Digital transformation and its impact on organization's Human Resource Management. IOR and Stakeholder Managment, MCM*. School of Communication and Information, Rutgers University.

Gao, X., Kong, Y., & Cheng, L. (2023). Strategies and mechanisms for building digital resilience of container shipping platform in crisis situations: A network orchestration perspective. *Ocean and Coastal Management*, *246*, 106887. doi:10.1016/j.ocecoaman.2023.106887

GaoX.YudanK.LuC. (n.d.). Strategies and Mechanisms for Building Digital Resilience of Container Shipping Enterprises Under Crisis Situations: An Orchestration Role Perspective. *Available at* SSRN 4530751. doi:10.2139/ssrn.4530751

Garcia-Perez, A., & Simkin, P. L. (2021). *ECKM 2021 22nd European Conference on Knowledge Management*. Academic Conferences and Publishing Limited. https://books.google.co.in/books?id=mXxGEAAAQBAJ

Gawer, A., & Cusumano, M. A. (2008). How Companies Become Platform Leaders. *MIT Sloan Management Review*, *49*(2), 28–35.

Germain, M.-L. (2021). The Impact of Changing Workforce Demographics and Dependency on Technology on Employers' Need for Expert Skills BT - Expertise at Work: Current and Emerging Trends. Cham: Springer International Publishing. doi:10.1007/978-3-030-64371-3_9

Ghamrawi, N., Shal, T., & Ghamrawi, N. A. (2023). Exploring the impact of AI on teacher leadership: Regressing or expanding? *Education and Information Technologies*.

Gilbert, A. W., Davies, L., Doyle, J., Patel, S., Martin, L., Jagpal, D., Billany, J. C. T., & Bateson, J. (2021). Leadership reflections a year on from the rapid roll-out of virtual clinics due to COVID—Gioko, A. (2013). Creating an effective professional learning sessions model on technology integration for a Kenyan school district. *Education and Information Technologies*, *18*(2), 151–164. doi:10.1007/s10639-012-9236-6

Gilli, K., Lettner, N., & Guettel, W. (2024). The future of leadership: New digital skills or old analog virtues? *The Journal of Business Strategy*, *45*(1), 10–16. doi:10.1108/JBS-06-2022-0093

Glover, D., & Miller, D. (2002). The introduction of interactive whiteboards into schools in the United Kingdom: Leaders, led, and the management of pedagogic and technological change. *International Electronic Journal for Leadership in Learning*, *6*(1), 1–11.

Goleman, D. (1995). Emotional Intelligence. Bantam.

GPAI. (2023, September 7). *Generative AI, Jobs, and Policy Response*. Retrieved November 11, 2023, from https://gpai.ai/projects/future-of-work/policy-brief-generative-ai-jobs-and-policy-response-innovation-workshop-montreal-2023.pdf

Graham, P., Nikolova, N., & Sankaran, S. (2020). Tension between Leadership Archetypes: Systematic Review to Inform Construction Research and Practice. *Journal of Management Engineering*, *36*(1), 3119002. doi:10.1061/(ASCE)ME.1943-5479.0000722

Grant, D. (2023). *What is Data-Driven Decision Making? (And Why It's So Important)*. https://www.driveresearch.com/market-research-company-blog/data-driven-decision-making-ddm/

Greenwood, L. L., Hess, D., Abraham, Y., & Schneider, J. (2023). Capacity Building for Organizational Resilience: Integrating Standards on Risk, Disruption and Continuity in the Curriculum. *International Journal on Social and Education Sciences*, *5*(2), 327–340. doi:10.46328/ijonses.508

Groenfeldt, T. (2017). How Blockchain Technology Could Change The World. *Forbes*.

Groysberg, B., Kelly, L. K., & MacDonald, B. (2011). The New Path to the C-Suite. *Harvard Business Review*, *89*(3).

Guidi, C., & Traversa, C. (2021). Empathy in patient care: From 'Clinical Empathy' to 'Empathic Concern'. *Medicine, Health Care, and Philosophy*, *24*(4), 573–585. https://doi.org/10.1007/s11019-021-10033-4 doi:10.1007/s11019-021-10033-4 PMID:34196934

Guinness, H. (2023). *The 6 best eCommerce website building platforms for online stores in 2024*. https://zapier.com/blog/best-ecommerce-shopping-cart-software/

Compilation of References

Gutierrez-Garcia, J. O., & López-Neri, E. (2015). Cognitive computing: a brief survey and open research challenges. In *2015 3rd international conference on applied computing and information technology/2nd international conference on computational science and intelligence* (pp. 328–333). IEEE. 10.1109/ACIT-CSI.2015.64

Gyori & Kazakova. (2020). *Purpose-Driven Leadership for the 21st Century: Transitioning to a Purpose-First Economy through the New Business Logic*. Academic Press.

Habib, G., Sharma, S., Ibrahim, S., Ahmad, I., Qureshi, S., & Ishfaq, M. (2022). Blockchain Technology: Benefits, Challenges, Applications, and Integration of Blockchain Technology with Cloud Computing. *Future Internet*, *14*(11), 341. doi:10.3390/fi14110341

Hafidz, L. (2022). *People Matters - Interstitial Site — People Matters*. https://www.peoplematters.in/article/recruitment/beating-your-chatbot-interviewer-and-landing-your-dream-job-21266

Haleem, A. (2023). Management 4.0: Concept, Applications and Advancements. *Sustainable Operations and Computers*, *4*, 10–21. https://www.sciencedirect.com/science/article/pii/S2666412722000277

Haleem, A., Javaid, M., Qadri, M. A., & Suman, R. (2022). Understanding the Role of Digital Technologies in Education: A Review. *Sustainable Operations and Computers*, *3*, 275–85. https://www.sciencedirect.com/science/article/pii/S2666412722000137

Haleem, A., Javaid, M., & Qadri, M. A. (2022). Artificial Intelligence (AI) Applications for Marketing: A Literature-Based Study. *International Journal of Intelligent Networks*, *3*, 119–132. doi:10.1016/j.ijin.2022.08.005

Haleem, A., Javaid, M., Singh, R. P., & Suman, R. (2021). Telemedicine for Healthcare: Capabilities, Features, Barriers, and Applications. *Sensors International*, *2*, 100117. doi:10.1016/j.sintl.2021.100117 PMID:34806053

Hallo, L., & Gorod, A. (2020). Engineering management principles for improving quality and efficiency in patient-centred care. *ASEM 41st International Annual Conference Proceedings "Leading Organizations through Uncertain Times"*.

Halvorson, S. A. C., Tanski, M., Milligan, L., & Yackel, T. (2019). Transitioning from Volume to Value: Lessons Learned from the Dissolution of a Population Health Partnership. *Academic Medicine*, *94*(9), 1305–1309. doi:10.1097/ACM.0000000000002614 PMID:31460920

Hao, M., Lv, W., & Du, B. (2020). The Influence Mechanism of Authentic Leadership in Artificial Intelligence Team on Employees' Performance. *Journal of Physics: Conference Series*, *1438*(1), 012022. Advance online publication. doi:10.1088/1742-6596/1438/1/012022

Haque. (2023). The impact of remote work on HR practices: Navigating challenges, embracing opportunities. *European Journal of Human Resource Management Studies*, 7.

Harris, P. R. (2001). Ensuring European leadership in the global marketplace. *European Business Review*, *13*(6), 336–345. doi:10.1108/EUM0000000006196

Hatfield, A. J., & Brahmi, F. A. (2004). Angel: Post-implementation evaluation at the Indiana University School of Medicine. *Medical Reference Services Quarterly*, *23*(3), 1–15. doi:10.1300/J115v23n03_01 PMID:15364647

Hecht, B. (2017). Co-Creating More Livable Cities. Management for Professionals, Part F600, 157-174. doi:10.1007/978-3-319-46021-5_9

Helo, P., & Hao, Y. (2022). Artificial Intelligence in Operations Management and Supply Chain Management: An Exploratory Case Study. *Production Planning and Control*, *33*(16), 1573–1590. doi:10.1080/09537287.2021.1882690

Hemachandran, K., Verma, P., Pareek, P., Arora, N., Kumar, K., Ahanger, T., Pise, A., & Ratna, R. (2022). Artificial Intelligence: A Universal Virtual Tool to Augment Tutoring in Higher Education. *Computational Intelligence and Neuroscience, 2022*, 1–8. Advance online publication. doi:10.1155/2022/1410448 PMID:35586099

Henisz, W., Koller, T., & Nuttall, R. (2019). Five Ways That ESG Creates Value. *The McKinsey Quarterly*, (November), 1–12.

Hensellek, S. (2022). Digital Leadership. *Journal of Media Management and Entrepreneurship, 2*(1), 1–15. doi:10.4018/JMME.2020010104

Hettl, M. (2013). *Employee administration using the LEAD-Navigator*. Springer Professional Media Wiesbaden.

Heukamp, F. (2020). AI and the leadership development of the future. *The Future of Management in an AI World: Redefining Purpose and Strategy in the Fourth Industrial Revolution*, 137–148.

Hewlett, R. (2006). *The cognitive leader: Building winning organizations through knowledge leadership*. No Title.

He, Z., Huang, H., Choi, H., & Bilgihan, A. (2023). Building organizational resilience with digital transformation. *Journal of Service Management, 34*(1), 147–171. doi:10.1108/JOSM-06-2021-0216

Hill, J. D., & Fenn, N. E. III. (2019). The Future of Pharmacy Leadership: Investing in Students and New Practitioners. *American Journal of Health-System Pharmacy, 76*(23), 1904–1906. doi:10.1093/ajhp/zxz224 PMID:31724040

Hoenig, W., Milanes, C., Scaria, L., Phan, T., Bolas, M., & Ayanian, N. (2015). Mixed reality for robotics. *Proceedings of the IEEE/RSJ International Conference on Intelligent Robots and Systems (IROS)*.

Iansiti, M., & Lakhani, K. R. (2017). The truth about blockchain. *Harvard Business Review, 95*(1), 118–127.

IBM. (2019). *The Impact of Blockchain on HR and the Future of Work*. IBM Institute for Business Value. Retrieved from https://www.ibm.com/downloads/cas/X2KQAKO2

Jacobs, G. (2019). A Perspective on Leadership in Cognitive Computing and its Social Consequences. In *2019 IEEE 18th International Conference on Cognitive Informatics & Cognitive Computing (ICCI* CC)* (pp. 28–33). IEEE. 10.1109/ICCICC46617.2019.9146051

Jahn, M., Reber, J.-H., & Struck, R. (2022). What is the key to efficient airport facility management and high service quality? Learnings from Berlin Brandenburg Airport's Technical Control Centre transformation. *Journal of Airport Management, 16*(3), 256–267.

Jain, A., & Ranjan, S. (2020). Implications of emerging technologies on the future of work. *IIMB Management Review, 32*(4), 448–454. doi:10.1016/j.iimb.2020.11.004

Janz, K., & Honken, R. (2013). Personality inventories and cognitive frames: understanding the balance in managing and leading IT organizations. In *Proceedings of the 41st annual ACM SIGUCCS conference on User services* (pp. 143–150). 10.1145/2504776.2504798

Jaskaran Singh Saluja. (2021). *Indian infrastructure in sustainable development: Need of the hour*. The Daily Guardian. https://thedailyguardian.com/indian-infrastructure-in-sustainable-development-need-of-the-hour/

Javaid, M., Haleem, A., Singh, R. P., & Suman, R. (2021). Substantial Capabilities of Robotics in Enhancing Industry 4.0 Implementation. *Cognitive Robotics, 1*, 58–75. https://www.sciencedirect.com/science/article/pii/S2667241321000057

Javaid, M., Haleem, A., Singh, R. P., Suman, R., & Gonzalez, E. S. (2022). Understanding the Adoption of Industry 4.0 Technologies in Improving Environmental Sustainability. *Sustainable Operations and Computers, 3*, 203–17. https://www.sciencedirect.com/science/article/pii/S2666412722000071

Javaid, M., Haleem, A., Singh, R. P., Suman, R., & Khan, S. (2022). A Review of Blockchain Technology Applications for Financial Services. *BenchCouncil Transactions on Benchmarks, Standards and Evaluations, 2*(3), 100073. https://www.sciencedirect.com/science/article/pii/S2772485922000606

Javaid, M., & Haleem, A. (2021). Upgrading the Manufacturing Sector via Applications of Industrial Internet of Things (IIoT). *Sensors International, 2,* 100129. doi:10.1016/j.sintl.2021.100129

Javaid, M., Haleem, A., & Singh, R. P. (2022). Significance of Machine Learning in Healthcare: Features, Pillars and Applications. *International Journal of Intelligent Networks, 3,* 58–73. doi:10.1016/j.ijin.2022.05.002

Jeflea, F. V., Danciulescu, D., Sitnikov, C. S., Filipeanu, D., Park, J. O., & Tugui, A. (2022). Societal Technological Megatrends: A Bibliometric Analysis from 1982 to 2021. *Sustainability (Basel), 14*(3), 1543. doi:10.3390/su14031543

Jimenez, Franco, & Smith. (2021). A Review of Corporate Purpose: An Approach to Actioning the Sustainable Development Goals (SDGs). *Sustainability, 13*(7). https://www.mdpi.com/2071-1050/13/7/3899

Johnson. (2021). Precision Medicine, AI, and the Future of Personalized Health Care. *Clinical and Translational Science, 14*(1), 86–93.

Joyce, P. R., Selvaraj, F. J., Manoharan, G., Priya, C., Vijayalakshmi, R., Dwivedi, P. K., Gupta, S., & Veerakumar, K. (2024). To Study The Role Of Marketing In Human Resource Management. *Migration Letters : An International Journal of Migration Studies, 21*(S2), 1191–1196. doi:10.59670/ml.v21iS2.7072

Kabalisa, R., & Altmann, J. (2021). AI technologies and motives for AI adoption by countries and firms: a systematic literature review. In *Economics of Grids, Clouds, Systems, and Services: 18th International Conference, GECON 2021* (pp. 39-51). Springer International Publishing. 10.1007/978-3-030-92916-9_4

Kabudi, T., Pappas, I., & Olsen, D. H. (2021). AI-Enabled Adaptive Learning Systems: A Systematic Mapping of the Literature. *Computers and Education: Artificial Intelligence, 2,* 100017. https://www.sciencedirect.com/science/article/pii/S2666920X21000114

Kalia, C., Tyagi, S., & Saha, S. (2022). *How ESG Megatrends and Opportunities Are Shaping Our Future.* https://www.ey.com/en_in/climate-change-sustainability-services/how-esg-megatrends-and-opportunities-are-shaping-our-future

Kamble. (2023). Blockchain Technology's Impact on Supply Chain Integration and Sustainable Supply Chain Performance: Evidence from the Automotive Industry. *Annals of Operations Research, 327*(1), 575–600. . doi:10.1007/s10479-021-04129-6

Kander, R. G. (2003). A successful experiment in curriculum integration: Integrated Science and Technology at James Madison University. *Proceedings - Frontiers in Education Conference, 3,* S4A1-S4A5.

Kane, G. C., Palmer, D., Phillips, A. N., Kiron, D., & Buckley, N. (2016). Aligning the organization for its digital future. *MIT Sloan Management Review, 58*(1), 1–27.

Kar, S., Kar, A. K., & Gupta, M. P. (2021). Modeling drivers and barriers of artificial intelligence adoption: Insights from a strategic management perspective. *International Journal of Intelligent Systems in Accounting Finance & Management, 28*(4), 217–238. doi:10.1002/isaf.1503

Katyal, S. (2023, December 15). Exploring advances in AI-driven devices. AIding the future. *The Economic Times,* p.3.

Kauffeld, S., Tartler, D., Gräfe, H., Windmann, A.-K., & Sauer, N. C. (2022). What will mobile and virtual work look like in the future?—Results of a Delphi-based study [Wie sieht die mobile und virtuelle Arbeit der Zukunft aus? – Ergebnisse einer Delphi-basierten Studie]. *Zeitschrift fur Angewandte Organisationspsychologie, 53*(2), 189–214. doi:10.1007/s11612-022-00627-8

Kaushal, N., Kaurav, R. P. S., Sivathanu, B., & Kaushik, N. (2023). Artificial intelligence and HRM: Identifying future research Agenda using systematic literature review and bibliometric analysis. *Management Review Quarterly*, *73*(2), 455–493. doi:10.1007/s11301-021-00249-2

Kawtrakul, A., Ruengittinun, S., Rungrusamiwatanakul, N., & Khampachua, T. (2013). Thailand's transformation to c-government: Core challenges and roadmap. E-Government Implementation and Practice in Developing Countries, 349-366. doi:10.4018/978-1-4666-4090-0.ch016

Keefe, M., &Pesut, D. (2004). Appreciative inquiry and leadership transitions. *Journal of Professional Nursing*, *20*(2), 103-9. . doi:10.1016/j.profnurs.2004.02.006

Kerr, H. (2016). Organizational resilience. *Quality*, *55*(7), 40–43.

Keserwani, H., PT, R., PR, J., Manoharan, G., Mane, P., & Gupta, S. K. (2021). Effect Of Employee Empowerment On Job Satisfaction In Manufacturing Industry. *Turkish Online Journal of Qualitative Inquiry*, *12*(3).

Kesic, D. (2023). *Proactive vs. Reactive Leadership: Navigating the Path to Success.* https://www.linkedin.com/pulse/proactive-vs-reactive-leadership-navigating-path-success-dragan-kesic/

Khan, I. S., & Ahmed, M. (2019). Leveraging blockchain technology for HR and talent management: Current and prospects. *Proceedings of the 52nd Hawaii International Conference on System Sciences*.

Khan, W. (2019). Edge Computing: A Survey. *Future Generation Computer Systems*, 97.

Kiran, R. G. R., Manoharan, G., Durai, S., Ashtikar, S. P., & Kunchala. (2024). Higher Education in India and the Influence of Online Certification Programs. Evaluating Global Accreditation Standards for Higher Education, 149-163.

Kohn, V. (2023). *Operationalizing digital resilience–A systematic literature review on opportunities and challenges.* Academic Press.

Koller, T., Nuttall, R., & Henisz, W. (2019). ESG Framework. *McKinsey Quarterly*. https://www.mckinsey.com/capabilities/strategy-and-corporate-finance/our-insights/five-ways-that-esg-creates-value#/

Kopka, A., & Grashof, N. (2022). Artificial intelligence: Catalyst or barrier on the path to sustainability? *Technological Forecasting and Social Change*, *175*, 121318. doi:10.1016/j.techfore.2021.121318

Korherr, Kanbach, Kraus, & Mikalef. (2022). From Intuitive to Data-Driven Decision-Making in Digital Transformation: A Framework of Prevalent Managerial Archetypes. *Digital Business*, *2*(2), 100045. https://www.sciencedirect.com/science/article/pii/S2666954422000254

Kossek, E. E., Gettings, P., & Misra, K. (2021). The Future of Flexibility at Work. *Harvard Business Review*. https://hbr.org/2021/09/the-future-of-flexibility-at-work

Krithivasan, K. (2024). India will be the global nucleus of generative AI. *The Economic Times*, p.12.

Krzysztof, M. (2023). *Top 5 Digital Technologies Transforming the Energy Sector*. https://codete.com/blog/top-5-digital-technologies-transforming-the-energy-sector

Kumar, S. (2023). *Unleashing India's renewable energy potential: a global manufacturing hub.* https://www.ey.com/en_in/energy-resources/unleashing-india-s-renewable-energy-potential-a-global-manufacturing-hub#:~:text=India's%20renewable%20energy%20sector%20boasts,for%20its%20sustainable%20energy%20future

Kumar, C. S., Vani, D. D., Damodar, K., Manoharan, G., & Veerapaga, N. (2024). Climate Change Mitigation Through AI Solutions. In *Gastronomic Sustainability Solutions for Community and Tourism Resilience* (pp. 37–59). IGI Global. doi:10.4018/979-8-3693-4135-3.ch003

Compilation of References

Lacerenza, C., Reyes, D., Marlow, S., Joseph, D., & Salas, E. (2017). Leadership Training Design, Delivery, and Implementation: A Meta-Analysis. *The Journal of Applied Psychology, 102*(12), 1686–1707. doi:10.1037/apl0000241 PMID:28749153

Lacity, M., & Khan, S. (2019). *Blockchain as a Supply Chain Transparency Tool: A Comparative Case Study*. Academic Press.

Ladyshewsky, R., Geoghegan, I., Jones, S., & Oliver, B. (2008). A virtual academic leadership program using a blend of technologies. *International Journal of Learning, 14*(12), 53–62. doi:10.18848/1447-9494/CGP/v14i12/45535

Landry, L. (2019). Emotional Intelligence in Leadership: Why It's Important. *Business Insights Blog, 79*(40), 45. https://online.hbs.edu/blog/post/emotional-intelligence-in-leadership

Langa, M., & Marnewick, P. C. (2020). Adapting IT management for Effective IT strategy leadership. *26th International Association for Management of Technology Conference, IAMOT 2017*, 770-789.

Laureani, A., & Antony, J. (2021). Integrating Innovation, Agile and Lean Six Sigma. In *Leading Lean Six Sigma* (pp. 83–92). Emerald Publishing Limited. doi:10.1108/978-1-80071-064-120211007

Leah, L., & Don, S. (2023). Using Technology to Create a Better Customer Experience. *Harvard Business Review*. https://hbr.org/2023/03/using-technology-to-create-a-better-customer-experience

Lee, Cheng, & Leung. (2009). A Quantitative View on How RFID Can Improve Inventory Management in a Supply Chain. *International Journal of Logistics-research and Applications, 12*, 23–43.

Lee, N. T., Resnick, P., & Barton, G. (2019). Algorithmic Bias Detection and Mitigation: Best Practices and Policies to Reduce Consumer Harms. *Brookings Institute*. https://www.brookings.edu/research/algorithmic-bias-detection-and-mitigation-best-practices-and-policies-to-reduce-consumer-harms/

Lee, J. (2023). Can an artificial intelligence chatbot be the author of a scholarly article? *Journal of Educational Evaluation for Health Professions, 20*, 6. doi:10.3352/jeehp.2023.20.6 PMID:36842449

Lee, J., & Park, J. (2023). AI as "Another I": Journey map of working with artificial intelligence from AI-phobia to AI-preparedness. *Organizational Dynamics, 52*(3), 100994. doi:10.1016/j.orgdyn.2023.100994

Lee, M. C. M., Scheepers, H., Lui, A. K. H., & Ngai, E. W. T. (2023). The implementation of artificial intelligence in organizations: A systematic literature review. Information &amp. *Management, 60*(5), 103816.

Li, C., Wang, & Zhang. (2024). A Review of IoT Applications in Healthcare. *Neurocomputing, 565*, 127017. https://www.sciencedirect.com/science/article/pii/S0925231223011402

Liberatore, M. J., & Wagner, W. P. (2021). Virtual, mixed, and augmented reality: A systematic review for immersive systems research. *Virtual Reality (Waltham Cross), 25*(3), 773–799. doi:10.1007/s10055-020-00492-0

Li, F. (2020). The Digital Transformation of Business Models in the Creative Industries: A Holistic Framework and Emerging Trends. *Technovation, 92–93*, 102012. doi:10.1016/j.technovation.2017.12.004

Lin, C., Huang, A., & Yang, S. (2023). A Review of AI-Driven Conversational Chatbots Implementation Methodologies and Challenges (1999–2022). *Sustainability (Basel), 15*(5), 4012. Advance online publication. doi:10.3390/su15054012

Liu, L., Subbareddy, R., & Raghavendra, C. (2022). AI Intelligence Chatbot to Improve Students Learning in the Higher Education Platform. *J. Interconnect. Networks, 22*, 2143032:1-2143032:17. . doi:10.1142/S0219265921430325

Li, Z., & Li, D. (2018). Blockchain technology in the building materials supply chain: Potential strategic applications and challenges. *Journal of Industrial Information Integration, 12*, 34–42.

Lohchab, H. (2023, October 23). *GenAI claims lion's share of global AI startup funding*. Retrieved October 30, 2023, from https://economictimes.indiatimes.com/tech/funding/genai-claims-lions-share-of-global-ai-startup-funding/articleshow/104632269.cms

Loui, M. C., & Miller, K. W. (2008). *Ethics and professional responsibility in computing*. Academic Press.

Loureiro, S. M. C., Guerreiro, J., & Tussyadiah, I. (2021). Artificial intelligence in business: State of the art and future research agenda. *Journal of Business Research*, *129*, 911–926. doi:10.1016/j.jbusres.2020.11.001

Luan, L., Lin, X., & Li, W. (2023). Exploring the Cognitive Dynamics of Artificial Intelligence in the Post-COVID-19 and Learning 3.0 Era: A Case Study of ChatGPT. ArXiv, abs/2302.04818. https://doi.org//arXiv.2302.04818 doi:10.48550

Lund, B., & Ting, W. (2023). Chatting about ChatGPT: How May AI and GPT Impact Academia and Libraries? *SSRN Electronic Journal*. doi:10.2139/ssrn.4333415

Madiega, T. (2023, June 14). *EU Artificial intelligence act*. Retrieved Nov 17, 2023, from https://www.europarl.europa.eu/RegData/etudes/BRIE/2021/698792/EPRS_BRI(2021)698792_EN.pdf

Maity, S. (2019). Identifying opportunities for artificial intelligence in the evolution of training and development practices. *Journal of Management Development*, *38*(8), 651–663. doi:10.1108/JMD-03-2019-0069

Majumdar, R., & Agarwal, S. (2023). In AI, I is for India: Tech majors build cutting edge solutions for the world. *The Economic Times*. https://economictimes.indiatimes.com/tech/technology/in-ai-i-is-for-india-tech-majors-build-cutting-edge-ai-solutions-for-the-world/articleshow/103312655.cms?from=mdr

Makori, E. O., & Osebe, N. M. (2016). Koha enterprise resource planning system and its potential impact on information management organizations. *Library Hi Tech News*, *33*(4), 17–23. doi:10.1108/LHTN-01-2016-0005

Malakyan, P. G. (2020). Digital Leader-Followership for the Digital Age: A North American Perspective. In M. Franco (Ed.), *Digital Leadership - A New Leadership Style for the 21st Century*. doi:10.5772/intechopen.89820

Malik, A., Budhwar, P., Patel, C., & Srikanth, N. R. (2022). May the bots be with you! Delivering HR cost-effectiveness and individualised employee experiences in an MNE. *International Journal of Human Resource Management*, *33*(6), 1148–1178. doi:10.1080/09585192.2020.1859582

Mallick, M. A., Chandel, T. A., & Yasin, M. Y. (2021). *Performance Analysis of Rooftop Grid Connected Solar Photovoltaic System*. https://stm.bookpi.org/AAER-V13/article/view/1173 doi:10.9734/bpi/aaer/v13/9364D

Malyar, N., & Yazdani, A. (2019). Blockchain-based decentralized identity management for refugees. *IEEE Access : Practical Innovations, Open Solutions*, *7*, 18989–19000.

Ma, N. (2023). Integration of ESG Factors in Portfolio Management: International Trends and Practices. *Frontiers in Business, Economics and Management*, *12*(2), 149–152. doi:10.54097/fbem.v12i2.14778

Mandachian, M., Hussein, N., Noordin, F., & Taherdoost, H. (2016). Leadership Effectiveness Measurement and Its Effect on Organization Outcomes. *Procedia Engineering*, *181*, 1043–1047. doi:10.1016/j.proeng.2017.02.505

Mannuru, N. R., Shahriar, S., Teel, Z. A., Wang, T., Lund, B. D., Tijani, S., Pohboon, C. O., Agbaji, D., Alhassan, J., Galley, J. K. L., Kousari, R., Ogbadu-Oladapo, L., Saurav, S. K., Srivastava, A., Tummuru, S. P., Uppala, S., & Vaidya, P. (2023). Artificial intelligence in developing countries: The impact of generative artificial intelligence (AI) technologies for development. *Information Development*. doi:10.1177/02666669231200628

Manoharan, G., Ashtikar, S. P., & Nivedha, M. (2024). Integrating Artificial Intelligence in Library Management: An Emerging Trend. *AI-Assisted Library Reconstruction,* 144-157.

Compilation of References

Manoharan, G., Durai, S., & Rajesh, G. A. (2022, May). Emotional intelligence: A comparison of male and female doctors in the workplace. In AIP Conference Proceedings (Vol. 2418, No. 1). AIP Publishing.

Manoharan, G., Durai, S., Ashtikar, S. P., & Kumari, N. (2024). Artificial Intelligence in Marketing Applications. In Artificial Intelligence for Business (pp. 40-70). Productivity Press.

Manoharan, G., Durai, S., Rajesh, G. A., & Ashtikar, S. P. (2024). A Study on the Application of Expert Systems as a Support System for Business Decisions: A Literature Review. *Artificial Intelligence and Knowledge Processing*, 279-289.

Manoharan, G., & Ashtikar, S. P. (2024). A Theoretical Framework for Emotional Intelligence in Academic Leadership in Higher Education. In *Building Organizational Resilience With Neuroleadership* (pp. 96–112). IGI Global. doi:10.4018/979-8-3693-1785-3.ch007

Manoharan, G., Durai, S., Rajesh, G. A., Razak, A., Rao, C. B., & Ashtikar, S. P. (2023). A study on the perceptions of officials on their duties and responsibilities at various levels of the organizational structure in order to accomplish artificial intelligence-based smart city implementation. In *Artificial Intelligence and Machine Learning in Smart City Planning* (pp. 1–10). Elsevier. doi:10.1016/B978-0-323-99503-0.00007-7

Manoharan, G., Durai, S., Rajesh, G. A., Razak, A., Rao, C. B., & Ashtikar, S. P. (2023). An investigation into the effectiveness of smart city projects by identifying the framework for measuring performance. In *Artificial Intelligence and Machine Learning in Smart City Planning* (pp. 71–84). Elsevier. doi:10.1016/B978-0-323-99503-0.00004-1

Manoharan, G., Nithya, G., Rajchandar, K., Razak, A., Gupta, S., Durai, S., & Ashtikar, S. P. (2024). AI in Finance and Banking: The Act of Gyration. In *Revolutionizing Customer-Centric Banking Through ICT* (pp. 1–28). IGI Global. doi:10.4018/979-8-3693-2061-7.ch001

Manoharan, G., Razak, A., Rajchandar, K., Nithya, G., Durai, S., & Ashtikar, S. P. (2024). Digital Learning for Professional Development in Varied Fields of Service Sectors: Embracing Technological Advancements. In *Embracing Technological Advancements for Lifelong Learning* (pp. 111–137). IGI Global. doi:10.4018/979-8-3693-1410-4.ch006

Manoharan, G., Razak, A., Rao, C. G., Ashtikar, S. P., & Nivedha, M. (2024). Artificial Intelligence at the Helm: Steering the Modern Business Landscape Toward Progress. In *The Ethical Frontier of AI and Data Analysis* (pp. 72–99). IGI Global. doi:10.4018/979-8-3693-2964-1.ch005

Marr, B. (2020). How the Covid-19 Pandemic is Fast-tracking Digital Transformation in Companies. *Forbes*. https://www.forbes.com/sites/bernardmarr/2020/03/17/how-the-covid-19-pandemic-is-fast-tracking-digital-transformation-in-companies/#449f9158a8ee/

MaturityT. (2019, February). *The Transformation Journey*. Retrieved from https://emeraldworks.com/research-and-reports/strategy/the-transformation-journey#downloadReportForm

Mayfield, M., & Mayfield, J. (2016). The Effects of Leader Motivating Language Use on Employee Decision Making. *International Journal of Business Communication*, *53*(4), 465–484. doi:10.1177/2329488415572787

McCafferty, D. (2016, October 18). Delaying a digital transformation is bad business. *CIO Insight*, 1. Retrieved from http://eds.a.ebscohost.com.ezproxy.umuc.edu/eds/detail/detail?sid=9413cc58-0b27-406f-9d18-8cca931b71a6@sessionmgr4010&vid=1&hid=4203&bdata=JnNpdGU9ZWRzLWxpdmU mc2NvcGU9c2l0ZQ==#AN=118921693&db=heh

McCarthy, P., Sammon, D., & Alhassan, I. (2022). Digital Transformation Leadership Characteristics: A Literature Analysis. *Journal of Decision Systems*, *32*(1), 79–109. doi:10.1080/12460125.2021.1908934

McDougall, R. (2018). Computer knows best? The need for value-flexibility in medical AI. *Journal of Medical Ethics*, *45*(3), 156–160. doi:10.1136/medethics-2018-105118 PMID:30467198

McKinsey Global Institute (2023, June 1). *The economic potential of generative AI: The next productivity frontier.* McKinsey Global Institute.

Megha, C. R., Madhura, A., & Sneha, Y. S. (2017). Cognitive computing and its applications. In *2017 International Conference on Energy, Communication, Data Analytics and Soft Computing (ICECDS)* (pp. 1168–1172). IEEE. 10.1109/ICECDS.2017.8389625

Meijer, S. A., Følstad, A., & Brokking, D. (2018). Blockchain in Government: Benefits and Implications of Distributed Ledger Technology for Information Sharing. *Government Information Quarterly, 35*(3), 355–364.

Mer, A., & Virdi, A. S. (2023). Navigating the paradigm shift in HRM practices through the lens of artificial intelligence: a post-pandemic perspective. In P. Tyagi, N. Chilamkurti, S. Grima, K. Sood, & B. Balusamy (Eds.), *The Adoption and Effect of Artificial Intelligence on Human Resources Management* (pp. 123–154). Emerald Publishing Limited. doi:10.1108/978-1-80382-027-920231007

Mhlanga, D. (2023). Block Chain Technology for Digital Financial Inclusion in the Industry 4.0, towards Sustainable Development? *Frontiers in Blockchain, 6*(February), 1–13. doi:10.3389/fbloc.2023.1035405

Milton, J., & Al-Busaidi, A. (2023). New Role of Leadership in AI Era: Educational Sector. *SHS Web of Conferences.* 10.1051/shsconf/202315609005

Mishra, B., Deepa, S. N., Gunasekaran, A., & Dutta, V. (2023). Prescriptive Analytics Applications in Sustainable Operations Research: Conceptual Framework and Future Research Challenges. *Annals of Operations Research.* Advance online publication. doi:10.1007/s10479-023-05251-3 PMID:37361099

Mittal, N., & Davenport, T. H. (2020). How CEOs Can Lead a Data-Driven Culture. *Harvard Business Review.* https://hbr.org/2020/03/how-ceos-can-lead-a-data-driven-culture

Moffat, A., & McLean, A. (2010). Merger as conversation. *Leadership and Organization Development Journal, 31*(6), 534–550. doi:10.1108/01437731011070023

Mofijur, M., AlMaaruf, A., Reaz, M. B. I., & Noor, A. (2019). Blockchain in HR Recruitment Process. In *2019 IEEE/RSJ International Conference on Intelligent Robots and Systems (IROS)* (pp. 1-5). IEEE.

Mohannak, K., & Matthews, J. (2015). Knowledge integration within the innovation process: A technopreneurial perspective. *International Journal of Technoentrepreneurship, 3*(1), 17–36. doi:10.1504/IJTE.2015.067088

Möller, J., & Florea, A. (2017). Governance in blockchain technologies & social contract theories. *Ledger, 2*, 103–125.

Morris. (2017) *The Impact of Emerging Technology on Leadership Development.* doi:10.4018/978-1-5225-2399-4.ch034

Moskowitz, H., & Ward, J. (1998). A Three-phase Approach to Instilling a Continuous Learning Culture in Manufacturing Education and Training. *Production and Operations Management, 7*(2), 201–209. doi:10.1111/j.1937-5956.1998.tb00452.x

Mougayar, W. (2016). *The Business Blockchain: Promise, Practice, and Application of the Next Internet Technology.* Wiley.

Mukerji, D. (2019). *Sustainability in Project Management: Advancing the Synergy of Practice and Theory.* Palgrave Studies of Cross-Disciplinary Business Research, in Association with EuroMed Academy of Business. doi:10.1007/978-3-030-17523-8_13

Mumford, M. D., Todd, E. M., Higgs, C., & McIntosh, T. (2017). Cognitive skills and leadership performance: The nine critical skills. *The Leadership Quarterly, 28*(1), 24–39. doi:10.1016/j.leaqua.2016.10.012

Murcio, R., Scalzo, G., & Pinto, J. (2021). *Can AI Emulate Soft Skills?* . doi:10.4324/9781003094463-10-15

Compilation of References

Nakamoto, S. (2008). *Bitcoin: A Peer-to-Peer Electronic Cash System*. Retrieved from: https://bitcoin.org/bitcoin.pdf

Naqvi, A. (2017). *Responding to the will of the machine: Leadership in the age of artificial intelligence*. https://doi.org/. doi:10.1453/JEB.V4I3.1436

Naqvi, A. (2017). Responding to the will of the machine: Leadership in the age of artificial intelligence. *Journal of Economics Bibliography*, 4(3), 244–248.

Narayanan, A., Bonneau, J., Felten, E., Miller, A., & Goldfeder, S. (2016). *Bitcoin and Cryptocurrency Technologies: A Comprehensive Introduction*. Academic Press.

National Association of Software and Services Companies. (2021). *AI gamechangers: Accelerating India with innovation*. https://nasscom.in/ai-gamechangers2021/pdf/AI-Gamechangers0582021.pdf

National Association of Software and Services Companies. (2022). *AI adoption Index: Tracking India's Sectoral Progress on AI Adoption*. https://nasscom.in/knowledge-center/publications/nasscom-ai-adoption-index

New Leadership in an Era of Thriving Organizations. (n.d.). https://www.mckinsey.com/capabilities/people-and-organizational-performance/our-insights/new-leadership-for-a-new-era-of-thriving-organizations

Ngo. (2018). Additive Manufacturing (3D Printing): A Review of Materials, Methods, Applications and Challenges. *Composites Part B: Engineering, 143*, 172–96. https://www.sciencedirect.com/science/article/pii/S1359836817342944

Nguyen, T. (2017). Big Data Analytics in Supply Chain Management: A State-of-the-Art Literature Review. *Computers & Operations Research*.

Nilsson, N. (2009). *The Quest for Artificial Intelligence*. https://doi.org/. doi:10.1017/CBO9780511819346

Nkomo, L., & Kalisz, D. (2023). Establishing organisational resilience through developing a strategic framework for digital transformation. *Digital Transformation and Society*, 2(4), 403–426. doi:10.1108/DTS-11-2022-0059

Noe, R. A., Hollenbeck, J. R., Gerhart, B., & Wright, P. M. (2019). *Human Resource Management: Gaining a Competitive Advantage*. McGraw-Hill Education.

Noor, A. K. (2014). Potential of cognitive computing and cognitive systems. *Open Engineering*, 5(1). Advance online publication. doi:10.1515/eng-2015-0008

Noordin, M. F., & Othman, R. (2005). Challenges to an E-business model: Pre-and post-adoption. *Internet and Information Technology in Modern Organizations: Challenges and Answers - Proceedings of the 5th International Business Information Management Association Conference, IBIMA 2005.*

Nozari, Fallah, Kazemipoor, & Najafi. (2021). Big Data Analysis of IoT-Based Supply Chain Management Considering FMCG Industries. *Business Informatics,* 15.

Oberer, B., & Erkollar, A. (2018). Leadership 4.0: Digital Leaders in the Age of Industry 4.0. *International Journal of Organizational Leadership*, 7(4), 404–412. doi:10.33844/ijol.2018.60332

Ochieng, E. G., Ovbagbedia, O. O., Zuofa, T., Abdulai, R., Matipa, W., Ruan, X., & Oledinma, A. (2018). Utilizing a systematic knowledge management-based system to optimize project management operations in oil and gas organizations. *Information Technology & People*, 31(2), 527–556. doi:10.1108/ITP-08-2016-0198

OECD. (2017). Investment Governance and the Integration of Environmental, Social and Governance Factors. *OECD*.

Okorie, G. (2024). Leveraging big data for personalized marketing campaigns: A review. *International Journal of Management & Entrepreneurship Research*, 6(1), 216–242. doi:10.51594/ijmer.v6i1.778

Olin, S.-C. S., Hemmelgarn, A. L., Madenwald, K., & Hoagwood, K. E. (2016). An ARC-Informed Family Centered Care Intervention for Children's Community Based Mental Health Programs. *Journal of Child and Family Studies, 25*(1), 275–289. doi:10.1007/s10826-015-0220-9 PMID:28781510

Open, A. I. (2023, July 31). *Announcing Grok*. Retrieved October 30, 2023, from https://platform.openai.com/docs/models/gpt-3-5#GPT-3.5

Ordu, A., & Nayır, F. (2021). *Dijital Liderlik Nedir? Bir Tanım Önerisi*. E-International Journal of Educational Research. doi:10.19160/e-ijer.946094

Oreg, S., & Berson, Y. (2019). Leaders' impact on organizational change: Bridging theoretical and methodological chasms. *The Academy of Management Annals, 13*(1), 272–307. doi:10.5465/annals.2016.0138

Ozdemir, M., Sahin, C., Arcagok, S., & Demir, M.K. (2018). The effect of augmented reality applications in the learning process: A meta-analysis study. Eurasian. *The Journal of Educational Research, 18*, 165–186.

Ozorhon, B., & Karahan, U. (2017). Critical Success Factors of Building Information Modeling Implementation. *Journal of Management Engineering, 33*(3), 4016054. doi:10.1061/(ASCE)ME.1943-5479.0000505

Pahlevan-Sharif, S., Mura, P., & Wijesinghe, S. N. (2019). A systematic review of systematic reviews in tourism. *Journal of Hospitality and Tourism Management, 39*, 158–165. doi:10.1016/j.jhtm.2019.04.001

Pai, R. Y., Shetty, A., Shetty, A. D., Bhandary, R., Shetty, J., Nayak, S., Dinesh, T. K., & D'souza, K. J. (2022). Integrating artificial intelligence for knowledge management systems–synergy among people and technology: A systematic review of the evidence. *Economic Research-. Ekonomska Istrazivanja, 35*(1), 7043–7065. doi:10.1080/1331677X.2022.2058976

Panda, S. K. (2016). *A Leader's Role in Shaping People, Process & Technology, VP Global Service Operations*. https://www.linkedin.com/pulse/leaders-role-shaping-people-process-technology-sk-panda/

Pan, Y., & Froese, F. J. (2023). An interdisciplinary review of AI and HRM: Challenges and future directions. *Human Resource Management Review, 33*(1), 100924. doi:10.1016/j.hrmr.2022.100924

Papoutsi, C., Drigas, A., & Skianis, C. (2019). Emotional Intelligence as an Important Asset for HR in Organizations: Attitudes and Working Variables. *International Journal of Advanced Corporate Learning, 12*(2), 21. doi:10.3991/ijac.v12i2.9620

Park, J. (2020). A Program for University Student's IT Leadership Renovation. . doi:10.7236/IJIBC.2020.12.1.1

Park, K., King, D. R., Chaudhuri, S., Arikan, A. M., & Goulet, P. K. (2003). Integrating disciplinary perspectives on fifth-wave M&A research. *Proceedings of the IASTED International Conference on Alliances, Mergers and Acquisitions*, 45-49.

Parry, K., Cohen, M., & Bhattacharya, S. (2016). Rise of the machines: A critical consideration of automated leadership decision making in organizations. *Group & Organization Management, 41*(5), 571–594. doi:10.1177/1059601116643442

Pasek, Z. J. (2017). Helping engineers develop and exercise creative muscles. *Proceedings of the Canadian Engineering Education Association Conference (CEEA)*.

Patil, D. Y. (2023). *Understand the Impact of Technology on Entrepreneurship Development in 2023*. Jaro Education. https://www.jaroeducation.com/blog/understand-the-impact-of-technology-on-entrepreneurship-development-in-2023/

Paul, J., Lim, W. M., O'Cass, A., Hao, A. W., & Bresciani, S. (2021). Scientific procedures and rationales for systematic literature reviews (SPAR-4-SLR). *International Journal of Consumer Studies, 45*(4), 1–16. doi:10.1111/ijcs.12695

Pavitra & Agnihotri. (2024). *Artificial Intelligence in Corporate Learning and Development: Current Trends and Future Possibilities*. Academic Press.

Compilation of References

Pavitra, K. & Agnihotri, A. (2024). *Artificial Intelligence in Corporate Learning and Development: Current Trends and Future Possibilities*. Academic Press.

Pazzanese, C. (2020). Ethical Concerns Mount as AI Takes Bigger Decision-Making Role – Harvard Gazette. *Harvard Business Review*. https://news.harvard.edu/gazette/story/2020/10/ethical-concerns-mount-as-ai-takes-bigger-decision-making-role/

Peifer, Y., Jeske, T., & Hille, S. (2022). Artificial intelligence and its impact on leaders and leadership. *Procedia Computer Science*, *200*, 1024–1030. doi:10.1016/j.procs.2022.01.301

Pelser, T., & Gaffley, G. (2020). Implications of Digital Transformation on the Strategy Development Process for Business Leaders. doi:10.4018/978-1-7998-4882-0.ch001

Perkins, M. (2023). Academic integrity considerations of AI Large Language Models in the post-pandemic era: ChatGPT and beyond. *Journal of University Teaching & Learning Practice*, *20*(2). Advance online publication. doi:10.53761/1.20.02.07

Petry, T. (2018). Digital Leadership. In K. North, R. Maier, & O. Haas (Eds.), *Knowledge Management in Digital Change* (pp. 209–218). Springer. doi:10.1007/978-3-319-73546-7_12

Phelps, K. C. (2016). A proposed research design for exploring collective leadership (cl) within multi-team systems (mts) implementing digital literacy initiatives. *IConference 2016 Proceedings*.

Pratt, L. (2023). *What is Technological Leadership and What Does it Mean for Your Business?* https://future-business.org/what-is-technological-leadership-and-what-does-it-mean-for-your-business/

Priya, S. S., Jain, V., Priya, M. S., Dixit, S. K., & Joshi, G. (2023). Modelling the factors in the adoption of artificial intelligence in Indian management institutes. *Foresight*, *25*(1), 20–40. doi:10.1108/FS-09-2021-0181

Promsri, C. (2019). Developing Model of Digital Leadership for a Successful Digital Transformation. *Business Management Gph-International Journal, 2*(8).

PWC. (2018). *Megatrends*. PwC. https://www.pwc.co.uk/issues/megatrends.html

PWC. (2023, June 20). *Global Workforce Hopes and Fears Survey 2023*. Retrieved November 5, 2023, from https://www.pwc.com/gx/en/issues/workforce/hopes-and-fears.html

Quach, S., Thaichon, P., Martin, K. D., Weaven, S., & Palmatier, R. W. (2022). Digital Technologies: Tensions in Privacy and Data. *Journal of the Academy of Marketing Science*, *50*(6), 1299–1323. doi:10.1007/s11747-022-00845-y PMID:35281634

Quaquebeke, N. V., & Gerpott, F. H. (2023). The Now, New, and Next of Digital Leadership: How Artificial Intelligence (AI) Will Take Over and Change Leadership as We Know It. *Journal of Leadership & Organizational Studies*, *30*(3), 265–275. doi:10.1177/15480518231181731

Quigley, M., Conley, K., Gerkey, B., Faust, J., Foote, T., & Leibs, J. (2009). An open-source robot operating system. *Proceedings of the ICRA Workshop on Open-Source Software*.

Radanliev, P., Roure, D., Maple, C., & Santos, O. (2022). *Forecasts on future evolution of artificial intelligence and intelligent systems*. IEEE Access. doi:10.1109/ACCESS.2022.3169580

Rajchandar, K., Kothandaraman, D., Manoharan, G., & Kabanda, G. Robotics and its Navigation Techniques: The Present and Future Revelations. *Handbook of Artificial Intelligence and Wearables,* 189-204.

Rajpara, S. (2020). *6 Internet of Things Benefits in the Education Sector*. https://justtotaltech.com/internet-of-things-benefits/

Raj, R., Kumar, V., Sharma, N. K., Singh, S., Mahlawat, S., & Verma, P. (2023). The Study of Remote Working Outcome and Its Influence on Firm Performance. *Social Sciences & Humanities Open, 8*(1), 100528. doi:10.1016/j.ssaho.2023.100528

Ramamoorthy, R. (2023, December 15). Past, present, future. AIding the future. *The Economic Times*, 3.

Ramesh, N., & Ravi, A. (2017). Enhancing the performance of micro, small and medium-sized cluster organizations through lean implementation. *International Journal of Productivity and Quality Management, 21*(3), 325-342. https://doi.org/10.1504/IJPQM.2017.08445811

Ramesh, N., & Ravi, A. (2017). Enhancing the performance of micro, small and medium-sized cluster organizations through lean implementation. *International Journal of Productivity and Quality Management, 21*(3), 325–342. doi:10.1504/IJPQM.2017.084458

Ramirez, R. L. (2023). Managing the Remote Employee. In The New World of Work: People Leadership in the Digital Age (p.89-98), Routledge, Taylor & Francis Group.

Rathore. (2019). Exploring the Impact of Digital Transformation on Marketing Management Strategies. *Eduzone : International Peer Reviewed/Refereed Academic Multidisciplinary Journal, 8*, 2319–5045.

Razak, A., Nayak, M. P., Manoharan, G., Durai, S., Rajesh, G. A., Rao, C. B., & Ashtikar, S. P. (2023). Reigniting the power of artificial intelligence in the education sector for the educators' and students competence. In *Artificial Intelligence and Machine Learning in Smart City Planning* (pp. 103–116). Elsevier. doi:10.1016/B978-0-323-99503-0.00009-0

Retief, F., Bond, A., Pope, J., Morrison-Saunders, A., & King, N. (2016). Global Megatrends and Their Implications for Environmental Assessment Practice. *Environmental Impact Assessment Review, 61*, 52–60. doi:10.1016/j.eiar.2016.07.002

Reynolds, G., & Freshman, B. (2011). Technology integration and graduate health management education: A review of competency models and application to electronic medical records. Encyclopedia of E-Leadership, Counseling and Training, 1, 233-246. doi:10.4018/978-1-61350-068-2.ch017

Richard, R., Prabowo, H., Trisetyarso, A., & Soewito, B. (2022). How blockchain will change leadership strategies for effectively managing organizational change. *Frontiers in Psychology, 13*, 907586. doi:10.3389/fpsyg.2022.907586 PMID:35719467

Romine, J. D. (2012). *Business Continuity and Resilience Engineering: How Organizations Prepare to Survive Disruptions to Vital Digital Infrastructure* (Doctoral dissertation, The Ohio State University).

Roy & Lohchab. (2024, January 4). Indian GenAI Firms Raised $700m in 3 yrs, says Nasscom. *The Economic Times*, 7.

Roy, A. (2024, April 29). Firms rush to recruit chief AI officers amid AI tech frenzy. *The Economic Times*, 16.

Sabarmathi, K. R., & Leelavathi, R. (2019). Application of Cognitive Computing in Healthcare. In *Cognitive Social Mining Applications in Data Analytics and Forensics* (pp. 265–272). IGI Global.

Sadun, R., Fuller, J., Hansen, S., & Neal, P. J. (2022). The C-Suite Skills That Matter Most. *Harvard Business Review*.

Sagar, K., Pramod, K. G., & Dutta, C. (2018). Application of Internet of Things in Fast Moving Consumer Goods Sector to Increase Business Efficiency. *2018 Second International Conference on Green Computing and Internet of Things (ICGCIoT)*, 629–36.

Saita, S., Serradell-López, E., Jiménez-Ramírez, A., Martínez-Bazán, N., & Arciniegas, J. (2020). A blockchain approach for secure collaborative business process execution. *Information Systems, 92*, 101558.

Samuel, B., & Twum, D. E. (2019). Leadership Style in the Global Economy: A Focus on Cross-Cultural and Transformational Leadership. *Journal of Marketing Management, 9*(2), 25.

Compilation of References

Sani, K., Adisa, T., Adekoya, O., & Oruh, E. (2022). Digital Onboarding and Employee Outcomes: Empirical Evidence from the UK. *Management Decision*, 61.

Sarahrudge. (2023). *Technologies used in the energy sector.* https://energy-oil-gas.com/news/top-5-technologies-used-in-energy-sector/

Sarker, I. H. (2021). Data Science and Analytics: An Overview from Data-Driven Smart Computing, Decision-Making and Applications Perspective. *SN Computer Science*, 2(5), 377. doi:10.1007/s42979-021-00765-8 PMID:34278328

Sawhney, D. (2017). Technology integration in Indian schools using a value-stream-based framework. *IEEE Region 10 Humanitarian Technology Conference 2016, R10-HTC 2016 - Proceedings*, 7906787. doi:10.1109/R10-HTC.2016.7906787

Saxena, S. (2023). *Lead school.* https://leadschool.in/blog/what-technology-is-used-in-schools/

Schemmer, M., Heinz, D., Baier, L., Vössing, M., & Kühl, N. (2021, June). Conceptualizing Digital Resilience for AI-based Information Systems. In ECIS.

Schneider, P. (2018). Managerial challenges of Industry 4.0: An empirically backed research agenda for a nascent field. *Review of Managerial Science*, 12(3), 803–848. doi:10.1007/s11846-018-0283-2

Schneier, B. (2015). *Applied Cryptography: Protocols.* Algorithms, and Source Code in C.

School of Education. (2023). https://soeonline.american.edu/blog/educational-leadership/

Schrettenbrunnner, M. B. (2020). Artificial-intelligence-driven management. *IEEE Engineering Management Review*, 48(2), 15–19. doi:10.1109/EMR.2020.2990933

Schwuchow, K., & Gutmann, J. (Eds.). (2018). Künstliche Intelligenz und das Lernen der Zukunft. HR-Trends 2019 - Inklusive Arbeitshilfen Online, 197–208. https://doi.org/10.34157/9783648116128-197

Scribante, N., Pretorius, L., & Benade, S. (2017). Requirements engineering principles applicable to technology and innovation management. *PICMET 2017 - Portland International Conference on Management of Engineering and Technology: Technology Management for the Interconnected World, Proceedings 2017*, 1-8. 10.23919/PICMET.2017.8125350

Seetharaman, T., Sharma, V., Balamurugan, B., Grover, V., & Agnihotri, A. (2023, August). An Efficient and Robust Explainable Artificial Intelligence for Securing Smart Healthcare System. In *2023 Second International Conference On Smart Technologies For Smart Nation (SmartTechCon)* (pp. 1066-1071). IEEE. 10.1109/SmartTechCon57526.2023.10391664

Seyedan, M., & Mafakheri, F. (2020). Predictive Big Data Analytics for Supply Chain Demand Forecasting: Methods, Applications, and Research Opportunities. *Journal of Big Data*, 7(1), 53. doi:10.1186/s40537-020-00329-2

Shalender, K., & Yadav, R. K. (2019). Strategic flexibility, manager personality, and firm performance: The case of Indian Automobile Industry. *Global Journal of Flexible Systems Managment*, 20(1), 77–90. doi:10.1007/s40171-018-0204-x

Shameem, A., Ramachandran, K. K., Sharma, A., Singh, R., Selvaraj, F. J., & Manoharan, G. (2023, May). The rising importance of AI in boosting the efficiency of online advertising in developing countries. In *2023 3rd International Conference on Advance Computing and Innovative Technologies in Engineering (ICACITE)* (pp. 1762-1766). IEEE.

Shang, S. S. C., & Liao, L.-Y. (2008). An analysis of the management capabilities of ICT innovation for sustained competitiveness in SMEs. *14th Americas Conference on Information Systems, AMCIS 2008*, 1, 293-305.

Sharif, M. M., & Ghodoosi, F. (2022). The ethics of blockchain in organizations. *Journal of Business Ethics*, 178(4), 1009–1025. doi:10.1007/s10551-022-05058-5 PMID:35125568

Shayan, F., Niloufar, N. M.-K., Alavi, S., & Zahed, M. A. (2022). Sustainable Development Goals (SDGs) as a Framework for Corporate Social Responsibility (CSR). *Sustainability*, *14*(3). https://www.mdpi.com/2071-1050/14/3/1222

Sheehan, A. (2023). *11 Best Ecommerce Platforms for Your Business in 2024*. https://www.shopify.com/blog/best-ecommerce-platforms

Shields, K. (2021). Leading a Customer Centric Strategy. Academic Press.

Shipman, K., Burrell, D. N., & Huff Mac Pherson, A. (2023). An Organizational Analysis of How Managers must Understand the Mental Health Impact of Teleworking During Covid-19 on Employees. *The International Journal of Organizational Analysis*, *31*(4), 1081–1104. doi:10.1108/IJOA-03-2021-2685

Shukla, A., Mishra, L., & Agnihotri, A. (2023). A Comprehensive Review of the Effects of Digital Technology on Human Resource Management. In Technology, Management and Business. Emerald Publishing Limited. doi:10.1108/S1877-636120230000031002

Singh, C. R., & Manoharan, G. (2024). Strengthening Resilience: AI and Machine Learning in Emergency Decision-Making for Natural Disasters. In *Internet of Things and AI for Natural Disaster Management and Prediction* (pp. 249–278). IGI Global. doi:10.4018/979-8-3693-4284-8.ch012

Sinha, R., & Ola, A. (2021). Enhancing business community disaster resilience. A structured literature review of the role of dynamic capabilities. *Continuity & Resilience Review*, *3*(2), 132–148. doi:10.1108/CRR-03-2021-0009

Sipola, J., Saunila, M., & Ukko, J. (2023). Adopting artificial intelligence in sustainable business. *Journal of Cleaner Production*, *426*, 139197. doi:10.1016/j.jclepro.2023.139197

Smith, T. (1984). Artificial intelligence and its applicability to geographical problem solving. *The Professional Geographer*, *36*(2), 147–158. doi:10.1111/j.0033-0124.1984.00147.x

Solderits, T. (2022). The Impact of Artificial Intelligence on Leadership in the Corona Crisis. *Pandémia – fenntartható gazdálkodás – környezettudatosság.* doi:10.35511/978-963-334-411-8_s1_Solderits

Soltas. (2022). The Impact Of Artificial Intelligence On The Future Of Workforces. *The European Union And The United States Of America*.

Song, P., Yu, H., & Winkler, S. (2009). Vision-based 3D finger interactions for mixed reality games with physics simulation. *Proceedings of the ACM SIGGRAPH International Conference on Virtual Reality Continuum and Its Applications in Industry*. 10.20870/IJVR.2009.8.2.2717

Soni, B., Gautam, A., & Soni, D. (2023). *Exploring the Advancements and Implications of Artificial Intelligence*. International Journal of Scientific Research in Engineering and Management. doi:10.55041/IJSREM17358

Sonmez Cakir, F., & Adiguzel, Z. (2020). Analysis of leader effectiveness in organization and knowledge sharing behavior on employees and organization. *SAGE Open*, *10*(1). doi:10.1177/2158244020914634

Soori, M., Arezoo, B., & Dastres, R. (2023). Internet of Things for Smart Factories in Industry 4.0. *RE:view*.

Srivastava, P. (2023). Indian institutes are keen to participate in Worlds Rankings to have a global visibility. *Times of India*. https://timesofindia.indiatimes.com/education/news/indian-institutes-are-keen-to-participate-in-world-rankings-to-have-a-global-visibility/articleshow/98471868.cms

Stedman, C. (2023). What Is Business Intelligence (BI)? *TechTarget*. https://www.techtarget.com/searchbusinessanalytics/definition/business-intelligence-BI

Compilation of References

Stefan, R., & Căruțașu, G. (2019). How to Approach Ethics in Intelligent Decision Support Systems. . doi:10.1007/978-3-030-44711-3_3

Stefan, R., & Căruțașu, G. (2021). A Validation Model for Ethical Decisions in Artificial Intelligence Systems using Personal Data. *MATEC Web of Conferences*. 10.1051/matecconf/202134307016

Stehlik, T., Short, T., & Piip, J. (2013). The challenges of leadership in the twenty-first century. In Workforce Development: Perspectives and Issues (pp. 193–211). Springer.

Stelios, S. (2023). Artificial Intelligence or Artificial Morality. *Technology, Users and Uses: Ethics and Human Interaction through Technology and AI*.

Steuer, L., & Leicht-Scholten, C. (2017). Innovation and diversity: Integrating new perspectives into research associations. *Proceedings of the European Conference on Innovation and Entrepreneurship, ECIE 2017*, 767-776.

Stobierski, T. (2023). *The advantages of data-driven decision-making*. Harvard Business School. https://online.hbs.edu/blog/post/data-driven-decision-making

Stoumpos, A. I., Kitsios, F., & Talias, M. A. (2023). Digital Transformation in Healthcare: Technology Acceptance and Its Applications. *International Journal of Environmental Research and Public Health*, *20*(4), 3407. doi:10.3390/ijerph20043407 PMID:36834105

Strohmeier, S., & Piazza, F. (2018). Blockchain in HR. In *Human Resource Management* (pp. 151–164). Springer.

Subrahmanyam, S. (2023). Navigating global leadership strategies for e-enabling technology deployment. *Journal of Law and Sustainable Development*, *11*(6), e01220. doi:10.55908/sdgs.v11i6.1220

Sullivan, C. (2012). Remote Working and Work-life Balance. In Work and Quality of Life. (p. 275-290). Springer.

Sultana, S., Zulkifli, N., & Zainal, D. (2018). Environmental, Social and Governance (ESG) and Investment Decision in Bangladesh. *Sustainability (Basel)*, *10*(6), 1831. doi:10.3390/su10061831

Suryaningtyas, D., Sudiro, A., Eka, T. A., & Dodi, I. W. (2019). Organizational resilience and organizational performance: Examining the mediating roles of resilient leadership and organizational culture. *Academy of Strategic Management Journal*, *18*(2), 1–7.

Suryosumarto, H. (2023). *Absentee Leadership is The Silent Killer of Corporate Transformation Efforts*. https://www.linkedin.com/pulse/absentee-leadership-silent-killer-corporate-efforts-suryosumarto/

Swan, M. (2015). *Blockchain: Blueprint for a New Economy*. Academic Press.

Swan, M. (2015). *The Business Blockchain: Promise*. Practice, and Application of the Next Internet Technology.

Syed, H. A., Schorch, M., Hassan, S. S., Skudelny, S., Grinko, M., & Pipek, V. (2020). *From technology adoption to organizational resilience: A current research perspective*. Academic Press.

Tagscherer, F., & Carbon, C.-C. (2023). Leadership for Successful Digitalization: A Literature Review on Companies' Internal and External Aspects of Digitalization. *Sustainable Technology and Entrepreneurship, 2*(2), 100039. https://www.sciencedirect.com/science/article/pii/S2773032823000032

Tandon, A., Dhir, A., Almugren, I., AlNemer, G. N., & Mäntymäki, M. (2021). Fear of missing out (FoMO) among social media users: A systematic literature review, synthesis and framework for future research. *Internet Research*, *31*(3), 782–821. doi:10.1108/INTR-11-2019-0455

Tandon, U., Ertz, M., & Sakshi, K. (2021). POD mode of payment, return policies and virtual-try-on technology as predictors of trust: An emerging economy case. *Journal of Promotion Management*, *27*(6), 832–855. doi:10.1080/10496491.2021.1888174

Tapscott, D., & Tapscott, A. (2016). *Blockchain revolution: how the technology behind bitcoin is changing money, business, and the world*. Academic Press.

Tapscott, D., & Tapscott, A. (2016). *Blockchain Revolution: How the Technology Behind Bitcoin is Changing Money, Business, and the World*. Penguin.

Tarisayi, K. S. (2023). Strategic leadership for responsible artificial intelligence adoption in higher education. *CTE Workshop Proceedings*.

Tatum, C. B. (1989). Managing for increased design and construction innovation. *Journal of Management Engineering*, *5*(4), 385–399. doi:10.1061/(ASCE)9742-597X(1989)5:4(385)

Tester, J. T., Nicewicz, K., & Oswalt, J. (2021). Development of online engineering management masters at Tennessee Tech University. *2021 ASEM Virtual International Annual Conference "Engineering Management and The New Normal"*, 438-445.

Tetteh, E. N. (2023). Leadership and the fourth industrial revolution: A systematic literature review. *International Social Science Journal*, *73*(250), 939–957. doi:10.1111/issj.12380

Thamhain, H. J., & Asgary, N. (2015). Team collaboration in multinational R&D projects. *2013 International Conference on Engineering, Technology and Innovation, ICE 2013 and IEEE International Technology Management Conference, ITMC 2013*, 7352710. 10.1109/ITMC.2013.7352710

Thang, S. M., Hall, C., Murugaiah, P., & Azman, H. (2011). Creating and maintaining online communities of practice in Malaysian smart schools: Challenging realities. *Educational Action Research*, *19*(1), 87–105. doi:10.1080/09650792.2011.547724

The Economic Times Bureau. (2023). Gen AI could boost India's economy by $1.5t in 7 years. *The Economic Times*, 10.

The Economic Times. (2023a). Experts speak. AIding the future. *The Economic Times*, 3.

The Economic Times. (2023b). Why AI is not a job-stealing, creativity-killing monster and how to regulate it. *The Economic Times*. https://economictimes.indiatimes.com/opinion/et-commentary/why-ai-is-not-a-job-stealing-creativity-killing-monster-and-how-to-regulate-it/articleshow/104222327.cms?from=mdr

The Hindu Bureau. (2023). India's AI penetration factor at 3.09, highest among all G20, OECD countries: Nasscom. *The Hindu*. https://www.thehindu.com/business/Industry/indias-ai-penetration-factor-at-309-highest-among-all-g20-oecd-countries-nasscom/article66522647.ece

The Impact of Agility: How to Shape Your Organization to Compete. (2023). https://www.mckinsey.com/capabilities/people-and-organizational-performance/our-insights/the-impact-of-agility-how-to-shape-your-organization-to-compete

Thees, M., Kapp, S., Strzys, M. P., Beil, F., Lukowicz, P., & Kuhn, J. (2020). Effects of augmented reality on learning and cognitive load in university physics laboratory courses. *Computers in Human Behavior*, *108*, 106316. doi:10.1016/j.chb.2020.106316

Thimbleby, H. (2013). Technology and the Future of Healthcare. *Journal of Public Health Research*, *2*(3), e28. doi:10.4081/jphr.2013.e28 PMID:25170499

Tigre, F. B., Curado, C., & Henriques, P. L. (2023). Digital Leadership: A Bibliometric Analysis. *Journal of Leadership & Organizational Studies*, *30*(1), 40–70. doi:10.1177/15480518221123132

Timotheou, N. M., Reumann, M., Milanovic, J. V., Kornegay, L. G., Stübner, R., Hernandez-Castro, J., . . . Riede, M. (2016). Plenary session 1: Engineering leadership & cognitive computing. In *2016 18th Mediterranean Electrotechnical Conference (MELECON)* (pp. 13–23). IEEE.

Tîrnăcop, A.B. (2023). *Leadership in the digital era: exploring the AI-EI nexus*. CACTUS.

Titareva, T. (2021, February 5). *Leadership in an Artificial Intelligence Era* [Conference Presentation]. School of Strategic Leadership Studies, James Madison University.

Titareva, T. (2021). *Leadership in an Artificial Intelligence Era*. Presented at *Leading Change Conference*.

Tripathi, M. A., Tripathi, R., Effendy, F., Manoharan, G., Paul, M. J., & Aarif, M. (2023, January). An In-Depth Analysis of the Role That ML and Big Data Play in Driving Digital Marketing's Paradigm Shift. *In 2023 International Conference on Computer Communication and Informatics (ICCCI)* (pp. 1-6). IEEE. 10.1109/ICCCI56745.2023.10128357

Truby, J., & Truby, E. (2018). Trusting records: Is Blockchain technology the answer? *Records Management Journal*, *28*(2), 110–129.

Tsai, C.-Y., Marshall, J. D., Choudhury, A., Serban, A., Tsung-Yu Hou, Y., Jung, M. F., Dionne, S. D., & Yammarino, F. J. (2022). Human-robot collaboration: A multilevel and integrated leadership framework. *The Leadership Quarterly*, *33*(1), 101594. doi:10.1016/j.leaqua.2021.101594

Turing, A. M. (1950). I.—Computing Machinery and Intelligence. *Mind*, *59*(236), 433–460. h doi:10.1093/mind/LIX.236.433

Ulu, S., & Özgener, Ş. (2023). Covid-19 Pandemi Döneminde E-liderlik: Fırsatlar ve Sorunlar, Ö. Demirtaş & Ö. Üstün. In *Sağlık Yönetimi ve Güncel Yaklaşımlar*. Atlas.

Usakli, A. B., & Tokdemir, G. (2019). A blockchain-based supply chain risk management framework and its empirical validation. *International Journal of Production Research*, *57*(7), 2072–2093.

Usman. (2023). *Role of Technology in Modern Entrepreneurship*. https://www.linkedin.com/pulse/role-technology-modern-entrepreneurship-usman-zaheer/

Vaidya, D. R., Prasad, D. K., & Mangipudi, D. M. R. (2020). Mental and emotional competencies of leader's dealing with disruptive business environment-A conceptual review. *International Journal of Management*, *11*(5).

Valadas, S. T., Fernandes, P., Figueiredo, C., & Vilhena, C. (2022). Digital Platforms and Technologies in School Clusters in Portugal: The Perspective of School Leaders. *International Journal of Educational Organization and Leadership*, *17*(2), 59–72. doi:10.18848/2329-1656/CGP/v29i02/59-72

Varadarajan, V., Kommers, P., Piuri, V., & Subramaniyaswamy, V. (2020). Recent trends, challenges and applications in cognitive computing for intelligent systems. *Journal of Intelligent & Fuzzy Systems*, *39*(6), 8041–8042. doi:10.3233/JIFS-189309

Varma, A., Dawkins, C., & Chaudhuri, K. (2023). Artificial intelligence and people management: A critical assessment through the ethical lens. *Human Resource Management Review*, *33*(1), 100923. doi:10.1016/j.hrmr.2022.100923

Varsha, P. S. (2023). How can we manage biases in artificial intelligence systems–A systematic literature review. *International Journal of Information Management Data Insights*, *3*(1), 100165.

Veena Latha, K. (2019). A study on work-life balance of the employees in the field of education: Strategic human resource management. *Journal of Emerging Technologies and Innovative Research*, *6*(2), 317. https://www.jetir.org

Verma, S., Sharma, R., Deb, S., & Maitra, D. (2021). Artificial Intelligence in Marketing: Systematic Review and Future Research Direction. *International Journal of Information Management Data Insights*, *1*(1), 100002. doi:10.1016/j.jjimei.2020.100002

Verner, I., Cuperman, D., Gamer, S., & Polishuk, A. (2020). Exploring affordances of robot manipulators in an introductory engineering course. *International Journal of Engineering Education*, *36*, 1691–1707.

Verner, I., Cuperman, D., & Polishuk, A. (2022). Inservice teachers explore RACECAR MN in physical and augmented environments. *Proceedings of the 2022 17th Annual System of Systems Engineering Conference (SOSE)*, 228–230. 10.1109/SOSE55472.2022.9812639

Vora. (2023). Artificial Intelligence in Pharmaceutical Technology and Drug Delivery Design. *Pharmaceutics*, *15*(7).

Vrontis, D., Chaudhuri, R., & Chatterjee, S. (2023). Role of ChatGPT and Skilled Workers for Business Sustainability: Leadership Motivation as the Moderator. *Sustainability (Basel)*, *15*(16), 12196. doi:10.3390/su151612196

Waller, D. (2020). 10 Steps to Creating a Data-Driven Culture. *Harvard Business Review*. https://hbr.org/2020/02/10-steps-to-creating-a-data-driven-culture

Wang, B., Rau, P. L. P., & Yuan, T. (2022). Measuring user competence in using artificial intelligence: Validity and reliability of artificial intelligence literacy scale. *Behaviour & Information Technology*, 1–14. doi:10.1080/0144929X.2022.2072768

Wang, Y. (2021). Artificial intelligence in educational leadership: A symbiotic role of human-artificial intelligence decision-making. *Journal of Educational Administration*, *59*(3), 256–270. doi:10.1108/JEA-10-2020-0216

Watson, G. J., Desouza, K. C., Ribiere, V. M., & Lindič, J. (2021). Will AI ever sit at the C-suite table? The future of senior leadership. *Business Horizons*, *64*(4), 465–474. doi:10.1016/j.bushor.2021.02.011

Webber, C. F. (2003). Technology-mediated leadership development networks. *Journal of Educational Administration*, *41*(2), 201–218. doi:10.1108/09578230310464693

West, J., & Bogers, M. (2014). *Leveraging external sources of innovation: A review of research on open innovation*. Academic Press.

Westerman, G., Bonnet, D., & McAfee, A. (2014). *Leading Digital: Turning Technology into Business Transformation*. Academic Press.

Whitby, B. (2008). Computing machinery and morality. *AI & Society*, *22*(4), 551–563. doi:10.1007/s00146-007-0100-y

White House. W. (2023, October 30). *FACT SHEET: President Biden Issues Executive Order on Safe, Secure, and Trustworthy Artificial Intelligence*. Retrieved November 7, 2023, from https://www.whitehouse.gov/briefing-room/statements-releases/2023/10/30/fact-sheet-president-biden-issues-executive-order-on-safe-secure-and-trustworthy-artificial-intelligence/

Whyte, J., Stasis, A., & Lindkvist, C. (2016). Managing Change in the Delivery of Complex Projects: Configuration Management, Asset Information and 'Big Data.'. *International Journal of Project Management*, *34*(2), 339–351. doi:10.1016/j.ijproman.2015.02.006

Wijayati, D., Rahman, Z., Fahrullah, A., Rahman, M., Arifah, I., & Kautsar, A. (2022). A study of artificial intelligence on employee performance and work engagement: The moderating role of change leadership. *International Journal of Manpower*, *43*(2), 486–512. Advance online publication. doi:10.1108/IJM-07-2021-0423

Compilation of References

Willmer, M. A. P. (1986). Can artificial intelligence do better than humans at leadership? *IFAC Proceedings Volumes, 19*(17), 241-258.

Wilson Learning. (n.d.). https://global.wilsonlearning.com/resources/balance-essence-form/

Wisskirchen, G., Biacabe, B. T., Bormann, U., Muntz, A., Niehaus, G., Soler, G. J., & von Brauchitsch, B. (2017). Artificial intelligence and robotics and their impact on the workplace. *IBA Global Employment Institute, 11*(5), 49–67.

World Economic Forum. (2018). *Blockchain in Humanitarian Action*. World Economic Forum. http://www.weforum.org/dpcs/WEF_Blockchain_in_Humanitarian_Action_2018.pdf

Wu, G. F., & Li, M. (2023). Impact of Inclusive Leadership on Employees' Innovative Behavior: A Relational Silence Approach. *Frontiers in Psychology, 14*(March), 1–10. doi:10.3389/fpsyg.2023.1144791 PMID:36949905

Wu, M. (2008). Catalogers Explore a New Frontier: Establishing a NEASC Evidence Center. *Journal of Academic Librarianship, 34*(1), 67–71. doi:10.1016/j.acalib.2007.11.003

Wu, W. N. (2021, July). Organizational Resilience: Examining the Influence of Information Cost and Organizational Capacity on Business Continuity Management. In *International Conference on Human-Computer Interaction* (pp. 444-455). Cham: Springer International Publishing. 10.1007/978-3-030-77750-0_28

XAI. (2023, November 4). *Announcing Grok*. Retrieved November 5, 2023, from https://x.ai/

Xiong, W. (2022, December). AI and Leadership. In *2022 7th International Conference on Modern Management and Education Technology (MMET 2022)* (pp. 497-503). Atlantis Press. https://www.tivian.com/us/our-products/employee-experience/360-feedback/

Xu, S., Stienmetz, J., & Ashton, M. (2020). How will service robots redefine leadership in hotel management? A Delphi approach. *International Journal of Contemporary Hospitality Management, 32*(6), 2217–2237. doi:10.1108/IJCHM-05-2019-0505

Yasin, M. Y., Chande, T. A., & Mallick, M. A. (2020). Performance of Rooftop Grid Connected Solar Photovoltaic System. *International Journal of Recent Technology and Engineering, 9*(1).

Yasmeen, H., Wang, Y., Zameer, H., & Ahmad, Z. (2020). Environmental turbulence as a moderator on the impact of transformational leadership and IT business strategy alignment on EIS adaptation. *International Journal of Information Systems in the Service Sector, 12*(3), 74–92. doi:10.4018/IJISSS.2020070105

Yassine, M. (2020). *Blockchain for Cybersecurity and Privacy: Architectures*. Challenges, and Applications.

Yıldırım, A., & Şimşek, H. (2006). *Sosyal Bilimlerde Nitel Araştırma Yöntemleri* (5. baskı). Seçkin Yayıncılık.

Yukl, G. (2012). Effective Leadership Behavior: What We Know and What Questions Need More Attention. *The Academy of Management Perspectives, 26*(4), 66–85. doi:10.5465/amp.2012.0088

Zahari, A. I., Mohamed, N., Said, J., & Yusof, F. (2022). Assessing the mediating effect of leadership capabilities on the relationship between organisational resilience and organisational performance. *International Journal of Social Economics, 49*(2), 280–295. doi:10.1108/IJSE-06-2021-0358

Zahid, R. M. A., Saleem, A., & Maqsood, U. S. (2023). ESG Performance, Capital Financing Decisions, and Audit Quality: Empirical Evidence from Chinese State-Owned Enterprises. *Environmental Science and Pollution Research International, 30*(15), 44086–44099. doi:10.1007/s11356-023-25345-6 PMID:36681761

Zeeshan, K., Hämäläinen, T., & Neittaanmäki, P. (2022). *Internet of things for sustainable smart education: An overview. Sustainability, 14, 4293*. doi:10.3390/su14074293

Zeike, S., Bradbury, K., Lindert, L., & Pfaff, H. (2019). Digital leadership skills and associations with psychological well-being. *International Journal of Environmental Research and Public Health*, *16*(14), 2628. Advance online publication. doi:10.3390/ijerph16142628 PMID:31340579

Zhao, H., & Liu, Q. (2018). The practice and research on the promotion mode of MOOCs in higher education are based on the innovation diffusion theory. *Proceedings - 2018 7th International Conference of Educational Innovation through Technology, EITT 2018*, 198-203. 10.1109/EITT.2018.00047

Zhao, X., Ren, Yu., & Cheah, K. S. L. (2023). Leading Virtual Reality (VR) and Augmented Reality (AR) in Education: Bibliometric and Content Analysis From the Web of Science (2018–2022). *SAGE Open*, *13*(3), 21582440231190820. doi:10.1177/21582440231190821

Zheng, Z., Xie, S., Dai, H. N., Chen, X., & Wang, H. (2018). Blockchain challenges and opportunities: A survey. *International Journal of Web and Grid Services*, *14*(4), 352–375. doi:10.1504/IJWGS.2018.095647

Zoabi, A., Redenski, I., Oren, D., Kasem, A., Zigron, A., Daoud, S., Moskovich, L., Kablan, F., & Srouji, S. (2022). 3D Printing and Virtual Surgical Planning in Oral and Maxillofacial Surgery. *Journal of Clinical Medicine*, *11*(9), 2385. doi:10.3390/jcm11092385 PMID:35566511

About the Contributors

Balamurugan Balusamy completed his B.E. (Computer Science) from Bharathidasan University and M.E. (Computer Science) from Anna University. He completed his Ph.D. in cloud security domain specifically on access control techniques. He has published papers and chapters in several renowned journals and conferences.

* * *

Sunitha Ashtikar is pursuing her doctorate program at SR University.

Tarana Afrin Chandel is an Associate Professor in Integral University, had Ph.D. from Integral University. M. Tech degree from UPTU & B. Tech degree from Magadha University. She is Principal Investigator of the project "Performance Analysis of 1MW Grid Connected Solar Photovoltaic System using Image Analysis. She is honored as Indo Asian – Best Researcher Award 2022 in Renewable Energy & VLSI on 28.02.2022, International Teaching Excellence Award 2021 on 18.12.2021, Incredible Academician of INDIA-21 by Record Owner, 25.09.2021, Excellence in Research 30.06.2021, Recognition of Academic Excellence & Recognition of Research Excellence (Ph.D.) on 16.01.2021, Excellence in Reviewing in recognition of an outstanding contribution on 21.09.2020, Best Research Award 2020 NESIN 2020, on 18.11.2020, Pride of India on 12.09.2018, Excellent Teaching award in Higher Education for on 8.03.2018, Best Faculty award in Rural Institution on 25.11.2017, Best Paper Award: 19th - 20th Feb 2016, "Rashtriya Gaurav Award" on 24.05.2010.Life member of Solar Energy Society of India, The Institution of Engineers (India), President and Life member of Robotic Society.

Suendra Das is presently working as an Associate Professor at the School of Management Studies, GIET University, Gunupur, Odisha. He has more than 20 years of teaching, research, and industry experience. He has published more than 75 articles in national and international journals, conference proceedings, and book chapters. He also authored and edited 14 books. Dr Das have participated and presented many papers in seminars, conferences, and workshops in India and abroad. He has organized many FDPs and workshops in his career. He is an academician, author, and editor. He has also published three patents also. He is an active member of various professional bodies such as ICA, ISTE and RFI. In the year 2023, he has been awarded as the best teacher by Research Foundation India.

JaLl Koundal is a Doctoral Scholar at Department of Management, Suresh Gyan Vihar University, Jaipur. MBA from IMT Ghaziabad, Leadership certification from XLRI, bachelor's in technology from Hyderabad, Bachelor of Art from Vidyasagar University and schooling from Himachal Pradesh Board. Currently he is working as Group Head in the Trade Marketing Department at Panasonic. His research interest includes Sales Team Behavior in Customer Orientation and Omnichannel Marketing.

Dayananda L. N., Assistant Professor in the Department of Electronics and Communication Engineering, received his bachelor's degree in Electrical and Electronics Engineering from Channabasaveshwara Institute of Technology, Gubbi, M.Tech in Microelectronics and Control Systems from N.M.A.M Institute of technology, Nitte affiliated to Visvesvaraya Technological University, Karnataka in 2009 and 2011 respectively. He has 2 years of Industry experience and 10 years of academic experience. His research interests include Renewable Energy Systems, Battery management systems, Electric vehicles, Power Electronics and Embedded Systems.

Blamurugan M. is currently working as Assistant Professor in Department of EEE, Dayananda Sagar College of Engineering, Bangalore. He received his Ph.D. degree in (Power Electronics Application in Renewable Energy Systems) from VIT University, Vellore, Tamil Nadu in 2019. He has 5 years of teaching experience and 3 years of research experience as Junior Research Fellow for sponsored project funded by Department of Science and Technology (DST) in School of Electrical Engineering at VIT University, Vellore, India. He has been elevated to IEEE Senior Membership in 2023. He has also awarded as Best Researcher in the year 2016 by VIT University. He has published more than 30 papers in international journals, book chapters and conferences of high repute. He is the Guest Editor of MDPI Energies and Frontier Journals. His research interests are cascaded Multilevel Inverter, Electric Vehicle, Smart Grid, Power Electronics application in Renewable energy systems.

Sihar Manohar is currently working In Doctoral Research Center, Chitkara University, completed his doctorate in the area of Services Marketing from VIT Business School, VIT University. He has a Bachelor of Technology and Dual Masters in Business Administration and Organization Psychology. Dr. Sridhar further certified with FDP at IIM-A. He is expertise in Service Marketing, Innovation and Entrepreneurship, Scale Development Process and Multivariate Analytics and interests in teaching Business Analytics, Innovation and Entrepreneurship, Research Methodology and Marketing Management. He has published around 20 research papers that includes Scopus listed and ABDC ranked International Journals like – Society and Business Review, Benchmarking-An International Journal, Electronics Market, Corporate Reputation Review, International Journal of Services and Operations Management, International journal of Business Excellence and presented papers and ideas in numerous international conferences.

Geetha Manoharan is currently working in Telangana as an assistant professor at SR University. She is the university-level PhD program coordinator and has also been given the additional responsibility of In Charge Director of Publications and Patents under the Research Division at SR University. Under her tutelage, students are inspired to reach their full potential in all areas of their education and beyond through experiential learning. It creates an atmosphere conducive to the growth of students into independent thinkers and avid readers. She has more than ten years of experience across the board in the business world, academia, and the academy. She has a keen interest in the study of organizational

About the Contributors

behavior and management. More than forty articles and books have been published in scholarly venues such as UGC-refereed, SCOPUS, Web of Science, and Springer. Over the past six-plus years, she has participated in varied research and student exchange programs at both the national and international levels. A total of five of her collaborative innovations in this area have already been published and patented. Emotional intelligence, self-efficacy, and work-life balance are among her specialties. She organizes programs for academic organizations. She belongs to several professional organizations, including the CMA and the CPC. The TIPSGLOBAL Institute of Coimbatore has recognized her twice (in 2017 and 2018) for her outstanding academic performance.

Mariofanna Milanova is a professor in the Department of Computer Science at UA Little Rock and has been a faculty member since 2001. She received a M.Sc. in Expert Systems and Artificial Intelligence and Ph.D. in Engineering and Computer Science from the Technical University, Sofia, Bulgaria. Dr. Milanova conducted post-doctoral research in visual perception at the University of Paderborn, Germany. Dr. Milanova has extensive academic experience at various academic and research organizations worldwide. Dr. Milanova is an IEEE Senior Member, Fulbright U.S. Scholar, and NVIDIA Deep Learning Institute University Ambassador. Dr. Milanova's work is supported by NSF, NIH, DARPA, DoD, Homeland Security, NATO, Nokia Bell Lab, NJ, USA and NOKIA, Finland. She has published more than 120 publications, over 53 journal papers, 35 book chapters, and numerous conference papers. She also has two patents.

Nitish Kumar Minz is an exceptional Bachelor of Commerce student specializing in Business Administration and Management at K.R. Mangalam University. With an unwavering commitment to excellence and a remarkable work ethic, Mr. Minz has consistently demonstrated his dedication to academic and professional pursuits. His academic achievements extend beyond the classroom, as he has made significant contributions to several research papers and book chapters that are currently in the final stages of publication. His insightful contributions and research expertise have earned him recognition within his field of study. Nitish Kumar Minz, as the President of the Student Council at K.R. Mangalam University, holds a prestigious position. In this leadership role, he has demonstrated exceptional skills in managing various projects and strategic initiatives. His internship at KEIC (KRMU Entrepreneurship & Incubation Center) has allowed him to further refine his project management and strategic planning abilities, providing valuable hands-on experience in the field. Furthermore, he has been selected as NEP SAARTHI- Student Ambassador for Academic Reforms in Transforming Higher Education at K.R. Mangalam University. This esteemed role demonstrates his passion for educational reforms and his commitment to improving the quality of higher education. As a Student Ambassador, Mr. Minz actively engages with fellow students, faculty, and staff, promoting a culture of academic excellence and facilitating positive changes within the university. Recognizing his outstanding accomplishments and exceptional contributions, he has recently been honored with the prestigious CHANCELLOR'S EXCELLENCE AWARD. This esteemed award serves as a testament to his dedication, hard work, and exemplary performance throughout his academic journey. Mr. Nitish Kumar Minz's academic prowess, research contributions, leadership roles, and recognition through awards highlight his exceptional abilities and potential for future success. He continues to inspire and make a significant impact within the academic community, demonstrating his commitment to excellence in all his endeavors.

Raghu N. has 10 years of experience in Academic and Research. He received the Ph.D. (2020) in Electronics Engineering from Jain University, and B.E. in Electronics and Telecommunications Engineering from VTU University, Karnataka. His research interests were in RF Communication and Image Processing. He has published his research findings in various Scopus indexed Journals and International conferences. He is a member of various professional bodies.

Mohammad Faraz Naim is presently an Assistant Professor at the Department of Management, BITS Pilani India. He has completed PhD in Human Resources Management from Indian Institute of Technology, Roorkee India. Prior to that, he completed his MBA in Human Resource Management and holds a bachelor's in biotechnology. His research interests include GenY/Millennials, talent management, knowledge management, high performance work systems, social media in HR and employee branding.

Richa Nangia has more than fourteen years of teaching, research and professional assignments experience with reputed institutions. Currently she is working as Associate Professor at K. R. Mangalam University, Gurgaon, India. She has earned her doctorate from University of Rajasthan on the topic Human Resource Development in Automobile Industry (A Comparative study on Tata Motors and General Motors). She has done master's in business administration in HR & IT from Rajasthan Technical University. She has many publications in reputed refereed and peer-reviewed international journals and has presented many research papers in various International and National Conferences. She has authored a book, few articles and book reviews. She is the member of editorial board of various UGC approved journal. Currently Supervising six Ph.D students and three students have been awarded Ph.D under her supervision. Her areas of interest include Organization Behaviour, Training & Development and Human Resource Development.

Joianta Panda is presently working as an IT Professional at Tata Consultancy Services, Bhubaneswar, Odisha. He has more than 20 years of industry experience in delivery and project management in Cognitive Business Operations, cyber security, Internet Of Things and Cloud Computing. He has participated and presented many papers in seminars, conferences, and workshops in India and abroad. Has been certified as ITIL V3 Expert, CCNP, Ethical Hacker, PRINCE2 Practitioner, MCSE in MS Windows server and MS Azure.

Moushami Panda is presently working as an IT Professional at Tata Consultancy Services, Bhubaneswar, Odisha. She has more than 20 years of industry experience in Digital Transformation Services, cyber security practice and ELearning. She has participated and presented many papers in seminars, conferences, and workshops in India and abroad. Has been certified as ITIL V3 Expert, CCNP, Ethical Hacker, PRINCE2 Practitioner, MCSE in MS Windows server and MS Azure.

SrtKumar Sahoo is presently working as a Professor and Dean (Post Graduate Study & Research) in the Department of Electrical Engineering at Parala Maharaja Engineering College, Govt. of Odisha, Berhampur, Odisha, India. He has served as Professor and HOD, in the School of Electrical Engineering, VIT University, Vellore, Tamilnadu from 2008 to 2018. He has 22 years of teaching and research experiences. He has received his Master's degree in Computer Application to Industrial Drives, from Visvesvaraya Technological University, Belgaum, Karnataka and Ph.D. from JNTU, Hyderabad. He

About the Contributors

was Principal Investigator for the project funded by, Department of Science and Technology (DST), Govt. of India and Co-PI for a project granted by Department of Science & Technology (DST) Govt. of India and Ministry of Science, Technology & Research, Sri Lanka. He is CoPI for the project funded by NPIU under TEQIP Collaborative Research Scheme. He has guided 7 and guiding 3 Doctoral students. He has published 160 International peer-reviewed journals, conference publications, Magazine articles and has published 3 books. His research interests are Grid-Tie-Inverters for Solar Energy application, Distributed Generation; Rural Electrification, Electric Vehicle etc. He received travel grant from DST, Govt. of India, for attending Conference AUPEC-2017, hosted by Victoria University, Australia. He has been awarded Chartered Management Institute Level-5 certificate in Management and Leadership and selected for study tour to UK under AICTE-UKIERI leadership development program in October 2019. He has visited Australia, Singapore, Malaysia, Thailand, Srilanka and China for giving honoring lectures and to attend international conference as key note speaker. He is Guest Editor in MDPI Journal- Energies, Frontiers in Energy Research and Frontiers in Energy Efficiency. His name was listed as "Top 2% of Researchers in the World" published by Stanford University, USA on October 10, 2022 and on 4th October 2023. He is a Senior Member IEEE, Chattered Engineer, Fellow Institute of Engineer, Fellow IETE and served as expert for various competitive examinations in India.

Smruti Rekha Sahoo is currently serving as an Assistant Professor at the School of Management Studies, GIET University, Gunupur. She has a 10 years of rich experience in academics and research. Dr.Smruti Rekha Sahoo has published quality articles in journals and recognized conferences. She has also published 6 patents. She has also presented articles in seminars, conferences in India. She has also an editor of an international published book.

Sitha Ankanahalli Shankaregowda received her Ph.D. (2020) in electronics from University of Mysore, India. She received her Master of Technology degree in 2011. She was a visiting research scholar in the department of materials science and engineering of Southern University of Science and Technology, Shenzhen, P. R. China in 2018-2020. She worked as research assistant professor at Peking University, Beijing, P. R. China. Her research interest is low cost fabrication of energy harvesting devices, triboelectric nanogenerator and soft robotics. Currently she is working as assistant professor in the department of electronics and communication engineering, BGS institute of technology, Adichunchanagiri University, Karnataka, INDIA.

Renuka Sharma is a highly accomplished professional based in Noida, India, with a wealth of experience and expertise in government initiatives and technical business incubation. She currently serves as Deputy Dean Research in SGT University, Gurugram. Dr. Sharma holds a Ph.D. in Virology showcasing her dedication to advancing knowledge in her field. Dr. Sharma has been recognized for her outstanding achievements, receiving the Young Achiever Award in 2021 by InSc. Her core competencies include excellent communication and articulation skills, management, leadership, technology proficiency, problem-solving, team management, marketing, and the ability to handle high-pressure work situations. She is known for her adaptability and determination, which have been crucial in her dynamic professional journey. In her executive profile, Dr. Sharma is described as a passionate expert with experience in business incubation and entrepreneurship within government organizations. She specializes in project planning and management for innovation and strategy projects in the high-technology industry.

Saurabh Sugha is a Doctoral Scholar at Department of Management, Birla Institute of Technology and Science, Pilani (BITS Pilani). He holds Senior Management Certification from IIM Ahmedabad, master's in technology from BITS in A.I. and Machine Learning and bachelor's in biotechnology. Currently he is working as Head Digital Transformation in the Trade Marketing Department at Panasonic. His research interests include Digital Transformation, Data Driven Marketing Insights, Data Modelling, Machine Learning, A.I., Digital Psychology, Clinical Psychology and Organizational Neuroscience.

Ponma Tyagi is a seasoned professional with over 13 years of comprehensive experience in the field of Computer Science. Holding a Ph.D. in Distributed Systems, Dr. Tyagi has made significant contributions to the realms of Artificial Intelligence (AI), Machine Learning (ML), and Cybersecurity. Throughout her distinguished career, Dr. Tyagi has demonstrated a deep commitment to advancing knowledge in her chosen domains.

Index

A

Agility 3, 35, 43, 52, 58, 60, 62-63, 65, 84, 95-97, 103-104, 124, 129, 188, 203, 251, 253-254, 262, 264-265, 273, 278, 291-295

AI 7, 11-12, 20, 34, 41-45, 51, 54, 56, 61-63, 65, 68-69, 76-89, 107-133, 139-150, 153-155, 157-160, 168, 176-177, 219, 225-226, 228, 250-251, 255, 260-263, 265-266, 268-269, 271, 275, 279-280, 282, 290, 294-295, 297

Analytics 20, 24, 41, 43, 51, 53, 55, 61, 63, 65, 107-108, 110, 115-116, 147, 162, 170-173, 177, 209, 225, 227, 230, 232, 250-256, 260-268, 271-272, 275, 278, 281-283, 292, 294-295, 297-298

AR 162-164, 167-170, 172-177, 261, 263, 266, 274, 279, 281-282, 285-289, 295-296

Artificial General Intelligence 120-121

Artificial Intelligence 7, 11-13, 20, 34, 41-42, 46, 48, 53-55, 63, 65, 76, 78, 82, 86-89, 96, 105, 107-122, 125, 128-129, 131-133, 137, 139-148, 150-151, 155, 158-161, 166, 168, 176, 225, 228-229, 251, 253-255, 261-262, 264-269, 271-273, 275, 279, 289-290, 292, 295-296

Artificial Intelligence (AI) Tools 137, 139

Augmented Reality 30, 162-164, 168, 172, 174-178, 261, 263, 274, 279, 281-282, 284-289, 295-297

B

Bibliometric Analysis 87, 105, 230-231, 233, 240-241, 245, 269

Blockchain 12, 57-58, 62-63, 65, 68, 176, 179-199, 201-214, 216-229, 250-251, 258-259, 262-263, 266, 268-271, 273, 275, 279-281, 284-285, 287, 289, 294-296, 298

C

Challenges 2-3, 6, 8-12, 16, 31-32, 34, 37, 42, 51-56, 58-60, 62-64, 66-68, 70-74, 77-78, 88-89, 91-94, 97-98, 111-112, 124-125, 128, 144, 147, 159, 170-172, 174, 180, 187-188, 191-192, 197, 199-200, 204-207, 211-212, 214, 216, 220, 223-224, 226, 228, 230-233, 244-248, 250-251, 258, 262, 264-269, 271, 273, 279-280, 284, 289-292, 296-298

ChatGPT 80, 89, 114-116, 130, 137, 141-143, 148-160

Cloud Computing 12-13, 20-21, 45, 78, 80, 108, 147, 177, 251, 262, 266, 268, 292

Cobots 162

Competency 72, 89, 123, 248, 257

Content Analysis 91-92, 96, 99-100, 104, 274

Cost-Effective 64-65, 171, 206-207

D

Data 5, 11-12, 20-21, 23, 30-31, 33-34, 39, 41, 43-45, 47-50, 52-53, 55, 57, 63-68, 71, 78, 82, 89, 95, 100, 107-108, 110, 112-116, 118-119, 123-124, 126, 129-130, 140, 142-143, 145-149, 154, 160, 162-163, 166, 168, 170-177, 179-187, 189-191, 193-197, 199, 202, 207, 209-211, 214-223, 225-228, 230, 232, 241, 244-245, 250-256, 258-268, 271-273, 275-277, 279-290, 292, 294-298

Data Analytics 20, 43, 55, 147, 170, 172-173, 209, 251, 253-256, 260-266, 268, 271-272, 275, 282, 292, 294-295, 297-298

Decentralization 179-181, 185-186, 188, 206, 211

Decision Support System 30, 33, 41, 137, 155

Deepfakes 128

Digital 5, 10, 12-13, 16, 18-20, 22, 24-26, 29-39, 41-58, 60-67, 69-71, 73-74, 76, 78, 80, 86-87, 91-96, 98-100, 102-108, 113, 118-119, 124, 131, 143, 146-147, 165, 169, 172-177, 180-181, 187-190, 192, 199-200, 203-206, 222-223, 228, 231, 249-251, 253-254, 258, 260-261, 263-266, 268, 270-273, 276-279, 282, 285, 288-290, 292, 294, 296-297

Digital Command Center 29-30, 41-42

Digital Culture 29, 32, 34, 37, 39, 41-43, 46, 277
Digital Leadership 29, 47, 91-92, 96, 100, 104-106, 118, 264
Digital Resilience 51-56, 58, 62-67, 69-71, 74
Digital Transformation 5, 26, 29-39, 41-50, 62, 70, 74, 76, 78, 86-87, 91-92, 94-96, 99, 102-103, 105, 251, 260-261, 264, 266, 270-273, 278, 296-297

E

Education 1, 5-6, 8-10, 13-14, 18, 25, 27-28, 60, 66, 74, 81, 84, 96, 102, 104, 111-115, 117-119, 124, 129, 139-144, 146-147, 149, 154, 157-159, 163, 165, 177-178, 203, 218-219, 223, 229, 244, 246-249, 259, 261, 263-264, 266-269, 271, 274, 279, 290, 298
Effective Leadership 5, 23-24, 51-52, 55-56, 60, 62, 96-97, 109, 111, 133, 150, 232, 243, 245, 250-251, 278, 293, 295
Efficiency 5, 10-13, 21, 42-43, 66, 110, 113, 115, 118, 121, 171-172, 174-175, 177, 180, 184, 186, 188, 192-193, 195-196, 200, 203, 206-207, 210-211, 213-214, 216, 219, 224, 227-228, 246, 250-251, 253, 255-256, 258, 260-263, 272, 277, 279, 281, 283, 286, 289-290
Emotional Intelligence 25, 59, 61, 84, 86, 89, 111, 113, 115-117, 122, 126, 129, 146, 158, 257, 266-267, 270-271, 292, 294-295
Empathy 58-59, 84, 89, 111, 113, 124, 131, 257, 265, 292, 294-295
Energy 1, 10, 12-13, 25-27, 38, 121, 166, 180, 201, 285, 297
Enhanced Leadership 137
Entrepreneurship 1, 5, 13, 19-20, 24-25, 27, 31, 73, 105, 248, 271, 273
Ethical Learning 137
European Union Artificial Intelligence Act 128
Executive 3, 9, 20, 77, 128, 250, 252

G

G20 Summit 1, 22

H

Harness 198-199, 207, 209, 226-227

I

India 1, 9-10, 13, 22, 25-27, 29, 51, 76-78, 81, 85-89, 107, 117, 120, 137, 162, 179, 203, 206, 230, 250, 275

Innovation 1-3, 9-10, 29-30, 32-34, 36-40, 42-49, 53, 55-56, 61-62, 67, 69, 72, 80, 87-88, 93, 95-96, 99, 102, 104, 108, 120, 130, 168, 177, 180, 182, 185, 187, 193, 196-199, 203-205, 220, 226-227, 232-233, 243, 246-249, 251-254, 256-262, 264-266, 270, 275, 277-278, 281, 284, 286, 290-293, 295-296
IoT 7, 11, 30, 43, 61, 63, 77, 175, 250-251, 256, 260-263, 270

L

Leader 1-2, 4-5, 9-10, 22, 27, 31-32, 34, 36, 38-39, 41-43, 45, 78, 80-81, 84-85, 89, 91-94, 102-103, 108-109, 112, 114-115, 123-124, 141, 145-146, 159, 204, 210, 239, 250-251, 265, 276, 278-279, 294, 297-298
Leadership 1-6, 8-10, 12, 19, 23-27, 29-30, 34-35, 37-38, 43-49, 51-56, 58-62, 66-68, 70-73, 75-87, 89, 91-92, 95-100, 102-124, 127, 129-133, 137, 142-147, 150-151, 155, 157-162, 164, 166, 179, 182, 185, 189, 192, 196, 203, 206, 209-211, 213-216, 219, 222, 224-225, 227-228, 230-233, 243-247, 249-258, 264-273, 275-279, 281-282, 284-286, 290-298
Leadership and Decision-Making 35, 107
Leadership in Crisis 51-52, 58, 66, 68, 70
Leadership Support 76, 79, 81-83, 87, 89

M

Machine Learning 7, 11-12, 41, 43, 63, 65, 77, 84, 96, 107-108, 110, 118-120, 144, 147-148, 168, 171-172, 176, 252, 255-256, 260-261, 263-265, 269, 279, 281-283, 295
Management 2, 7-8, 12, 16, 25, 29, 31, 33-34, 38, 41-51, 53, 56-57, 59-62, 64, 66-68, 70-75, 78, 80-81, 84-89, 92, 95-96, 98-99, 101-102, 105, 108, 111, 113, 116-117, 119, 124, 129, 131-133, 141, 144-145, 158, 160, 166, 175, 179-180, 183, 185, 188-189, 192-196, 198-200, 203-219, 221, 223, 225, 227-233, 240, 244-252, 254-260, 262-263, 266-273, 277-278, 284, 289, 291-292, 295-298
Moderator 79-82, 89-90, 249

N

Natural Language Processing 86, 107-108, 114, 149, 176
Next-Generation Leadership 122, 275, 291, 295

Index

O

OpenAI 120, 125, 130, 132, 176
Organizational Continuity 51-52, 55-56, 58, 68

P

Present and Future Generation Leadership 1

R

Robotics 30, 44, 85, 105, 118, 123, 162, 166, 168-169, 173, 177, 262, 269

S

Scalable 64-65, 206-207, 210
Security 12, 18, 21, 46, 51-54, 57, 63-67, 69, 73, 81, 141, 176-177, 180-182, 185-187, 189-190, 195, 198, 200-201, 206-208, 210-212, 216-217, 225-228, 258, 262-263, 265, 275, 281, 283, 285, 287-289
Singularity 121, 127
SLR 76, 78, 85
Superintelligence 120, 131
Support 3-4, 10-11, 19, 30, 32-33, 38-39, 41, 44, 46, 53, 59, 61, 68, 71-72, 76, 79-84, 86-87, 89, 95, 98, 111, 114-115, 118, 120-121, 123-124, 129-130, 137, 142, 144, 146-149, 153-155, 160, 163, 168, 173-174, 196-199, 201, 207, 218, 255-259, 264, 276-278, 280-282, 286, 293
Sustainability 7, 10, 28, 34, 45, 49, 56, 67, 70, 74, 79-80, 85, 87, 89, 104, 115-117, 124, 131, 159, 174, 194, 201, 203, 230, 244, 246-247, 250-251, 253, 259-260, 264-267, 269, 272-273

Systematic Literature Review 74, 76, 78, 86-87, 89-90, 132

T

Technology 1-2, 5-13, 18-20, 23-25, 27-30, 32, 34, 36, 39, 43-44, 46, 48, 51, 53-58, 60-63, 65, 68-69, 71-72, 74-78, 80-81, 84, 86, 88, 93, 98, 102-103, 107-108, 110, 112-116, 119, 133, 137, 140-146, 151, 154, 158, 160, 162-167, 170, 172, 175-177, 179-187, 189-193, 195-199, 201-207, 209-214, 216, 218-222, 224-233, 244-252, 254-255, 258-260, 262-264, 266-271, 273, 275-281, 284-289, 291-297
Technology Integration 76, 230-233, 245-246, 248, 284
Transformation 2, 5, 8, 10-12, 22-24, 26-27, 29-39, 41-50, 62, 65, 69-70, 74, 76, 78, 86-87, 91-96, 99, 102-103, 105, 112, 116, 141, 175, 205, 245, 247, 251-253, 260-261, 264, 266, 268, 270-273, 275-278, 281, 296-297
Transformative 29, 34-37, 41-42, 51-52, 64-66, 73, 95, 116, 173, 180, 199, 203, 206, 212-214, 216, 226-228, 239, 244, 250, 266, 291, 295
Transparency 12, 30, 47, 53-55, 57, 59-61, 68, 71, 127-128, 130-131, 179-188, 190, 192-198, 202-204, 206-207, 209-211, 214-217, 219, 221-224, 227-228, 258, 262, 265, 275, 280, 284, 289, 295
Trolley Problem 122, 125-127
Turing test 120-121, 125-126, 129-131, 134

X

xAI 125, 133

337

Publishing Tomorrow's Research Today

Uncover Current Insights and Future Trends in
Business & Management
with IGI Global's Cutting-Edge Recommended Books

Print Only, E-Book Only, or Print + E-Book.
Order direct through IGI Global's Online Bookstore at **www.igi-global.com** or through your preferred provider.

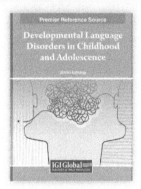

ISBN: 9798369306444
© 2023; 436 pp.
List Price: US$ **230**

ISBN: 9798369300084
© 2023; 358 pp.
List Price: US$ **250**

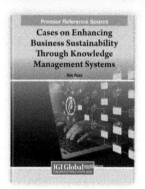

ISBN: 9781668458594
© 2023; 366 pp.
List Price: US$ **240**

ISBN: 9781668486344
© 2023; 256 pp.
List Price: US$ **280**

ISBN: 9781668493243
© 2024; 318 pp.
List Price: US$ **250**

ISBN: 9798369304181
© 2023; 415 pp.
List Price: US$ **250**

Do you want to stay current on the latest research trends, product announcements, news, and special offers?
Join IGI Global's mailing list to receive customized recommendations, exclusive discounts, and more.
Sign up at: **www.igi-global.com/newsletters**.

Scan the QR Code here to
view more related titles in Business & Management.

www.igi-global.com | Sign up at www.igi-global.com/newsletters | facebook.com/igiglobal | twitter.com/igiglobal | linkedin.com/igiglobal

Ensure Quality Research is Introduced to the Academic Community

Become a Reviewer for IGI Global Authored Book Projects

  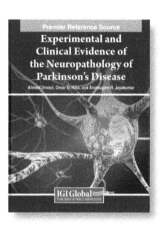 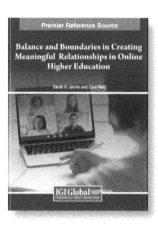

The overall success of an authored book project is dependent on quality and timely manuscript evaluations.

Applications and Inquiries may be sent to:
development@igi-global.com

Applicants must have a doctorate (or equivalent degree) as well as publishing, research, and reviewing experience. Authored Book Evaluators are appointed for one-year terms and are expected to complete at least three evaluations per term. Upon successful completion of this term, evaluators can be considered for an additional term.

If you have a colleague that may be interested in this opportunity, we encourage you to share this information with them.

Publishing Tomorrow's Research Today
IGI Global's Open Access Journal Program

Including Nearly 200 Peer-Reviewed, Gold (Full) Open Access Journals across IGI Global's Three Academic Subject Areas: Business & Management; Scientific, Technical, and Medical (STM); and Education

Consider Submitting Your Manuscript to One of These Nearly 200 Open Access Journals for to Increase Their Discoverability & Citation Impact

Web of Science Impact Factor 6.5	Web of Science Impact Factor 4.7	Web of Science Impact Factor 3.2	Web of Science Impact Factor 2.6
JOURNAL OF **Organizational and End User Computing**	JOURNAL OF **Global Information Management**	INTERNATIONAL JOURNAL ON **Semantic Web and Information Systems**	JOURNAL OF **Database Management**

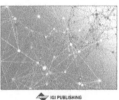   

Choosing IGI Global's Open Access Journal Program Can Greatly Increase the Reach of Your Research

Higher Usage
Open access papers are 2-3 times more likely to be read than non-open access papers.

Higher Download Rates
Open access papers benefit from 89% higher download rates than non-open access papers.

Higher Citation Rates
Open access papers are 47% more likely to be cited than non-open access papers.

Submitting an article to a journal offers an invaluable opportunity for you to share your work with the broader academic community, fostering knowledge dissemination and constructive feedback.

Submit an Article and Browse the IGI Global Call for Papers Pages

We can work with you to find the journal most well-suited for your next research manuscript.
For open access publishing support, contact: journaleditor@igi-global.com

Are You Ready to Publish Your Research

IGI Global offers book authorship and editorship opportunities across three major subject areas, including Business, STM, and Education.

Benefits of Publishing with IGI Global:

- Free one-on-one editorial and promotional support.
- Expedited publishing timelines that can take your book from start to finish in less than one (1) year.
- Choose from a variety of formats, including Edited and Authored References, Handbooks of Research, Encyclopedias, and Research Insights.
- Utilize IGI Global's eEditorial Discovery® submission system in support of conducting the submission and double-blind peer review process.
- IGI Global maintains a strict adherence to ethical practices due in part to our full membership with the Committee on Publication Ethics (COPE).
- Indexing potential in prestigious indices such as Scopus®, Web of Science™, PsycINFO®, and ERIC – Education Resources Information Center.
- Ability to connect your ORCID iD to your IGI Global publications.
- Earn honorariums and royalties on your full book publications as well as complimentary content and exclusive discounts.

Join Your Colleagues from Prestigious Institutions, Including:

 Australian National University

 Massachusetts Institute of Technology

 JOHNS HOPKINS UNIVERSITY

 HARVARD UNIVERSITY

 COLUMBIA UNIVERSITY IN THE CITY OF NEW YORK

Learn More at: www.igi-global.com/publish
or Contact IGI Global's Aquisitions Team at: acquisition@igi-global.com

Individual Article & Chapter Downloads
US$ 37.50/each

Easily Identify, Acquire, and Utilize Published Peer-Reviewed Findings in Support of Your Current Research

- Browse Over **170,000+ Articles & Chapters**
- **Accurate & Advanced** Search
- Affordably Acquire **International Research**
- **Instantly Access** Your Content
- Benefit from the **InfoSci® Platform Features**

It really provides an excellent entry into the research literature of the field. It presents a manageable number of highly relevant sources on topics of interest to a wide range of researchers. The sources are scholarly, but also accessible to 'practitioners'.

- Ms. Lisa Stimatz, MLS, University of North Carolina at Chapel Hill, USA

Milton Keynes UK
Ingram Content Group UK Ltd.
UKHW051601021224
3319UKWH00046B/1468